WRITING VIOLENCE ON THE NORTHERN FRONTIER

A BOOK IN THE SERIES

Latin America Otherwise: Languages, Empires, Nations

Series editors:

Walter D. Mignolo, Duke University

Irene Silverblatt, Duke University

Sonia Saldívar-Hull, University of

California at Los Angeles

Writing Violence on the Northern Frontier

THE

HISTORIOGRAPHY

OF SIXTEENTH-CENTURY

NEW MEXICO AND FLORIDA

AND THE LEGACY OF

CONQUEST

José Rabasa

DUKE UNIVERSITY PRESS

Durham & London

2000

© 2000 Duke University Press

Printed in the United States of America on acid-free paper ∞

Designed by C. H. Westmoreland

Typeset in Monotype Garamond by Tseng Information Systems, Inc.

Library of Congress Cataloging-in-Publication Data

appear on the last printed page of this book.

A CATHERINE

Contents

About the Series

Latin America Otherwise: Languages, Empires, Nations is a critical series. It aims to explore the emergence and consequences of concepts used to define "Latin America" while at the same time exploring the broad interplay of political, economic, and cultural practices that have shaped Latin American worlds. Latin America, at the crossroads of competing imperial designs and local responses, has been construed as a geocultural and geopolitical entity since the nineteenth century. This series provides a starting point to redefine Latin America as a configuration of political, linguistic, cultural, and economic intersections that demands a continuous reappraisal of the role of the Americas in history, and of the ongoing process of globalization and the relocation of people and cultures that have characterized Latin America's experience. *Latin America Otherwise: Languages, Empires, Nations* is a forum that confronts established geocultural constructions, that rethinks area studies and disciplinary boundaries, that assesses convictions of the academy and of public policy, and that, correspondingly, demands that the practices through which we produce knowledge and understanding about and from Latin America be subject to rigorous and critical scrutiny.

In *Writing Violence on the Northern Frontier,* José Rabasa develops the concept of writing violence, a practice that he places in the conflicting writing systems of the early modern/colonial world. Rabasa opens his reflection on writing violence with a discussion of two passages drawn from the anonymous Amerindian work *Historia de Tlatelolsco desde los tiempos más remotos* and Bartolomé de las Casas's *Brevísima relación de la destrucción de Indias,* which set the stage for a display of violence in narrative forms as well as in narration itself. These passages, representative of pre-Columbian and colonial periods, enable Rabasa to define the particular modes the conjunction between writing and violence assumed during the Spanish conquest of the Americas.

The epilogue to this volume is a tour-de-force in which history and subaltern studies are no longer conceived as representations of the subaltern but rather as producers of subalternity. Moreover, by underscoring characteristics of the early modern/colonial period, including the making of the Atlantic world and the emergence of modern forms of capital accumulation, Rabasa challenges the conception of history—expressed in South Asian Subaltern Studies—that attributes the beginnings of modernity to the age of Enlightenment. In sum, Rabasa has constructed a compelling dialogue between Subaltern Studies in the Americas and South Asia; between the colonial legacies of the European Renaissance in the Americas and of the European Enlightenment in Asia.

Figures

Color plates follow page 242

Acknowledgments

This project could not have been completed without the intellectual support of the Latin American Subaltern Studies Group. I am especially indebted to Patricia Seed, Sara Castro-Klarén, Abdul Karim Mustapha, Walter D. Mignolo, Ileana Rodríguez, John Beverley, and Javier Sanjinés, who made incisive readings of parts of this work. I presented versions of the chapters at a number of conferences and lectures where I received comments and critiques from which I benefited greatly. Because it is impossible to name all who contributed, I will limit myself to mentioning Maureen Ahern and Dan Reff, who commented on chapters pertaining to New Mexico and generously shared their work with me. Although it might surprise them to hear me admit it, my colleagues in the Department of Romance Languages at the University of Michigan provided an exciting intellectual climate that made the writing of this book a challenge. My special thanks go to Santiago Colás, William Paulson, and Catherine Brown. The comments of editors and anonymous readers of *Poetics Today* and *College Literature* and the editorial guidance of Patricia Galloway and William Taylor have all proven invaluable. I thank my students at the University of Maryland, the University of Michigan, and Berkeley, who challenged me in seminars I taught on sixteenth-century New World historiography. My wife and friend, Catherine Durand, read the manuscript and called my attention to passages that seemed unnecessarily dense, if not mystifying, for the nonacademic reader. I am also grateful to Tom Boggs and Monica Weinheimer for reading the introduction with "lay eyes." Anna More read the manuscript with an editorial eye that went beyond the mechanics of the English language by making suggestions where my thoughts needed further development and clarification. I am solely responsible for the final form. And Magali and Pablo reminded me of the joys of play.

I am also grateful to the following for their assistance and guidance in their archives and collections: Arlene Shy (William L. Clements Library, University of Michigan), Magdalena Canellas Anoz

(Archivo General de Indias), Florence Brouillard (Bibliothèque Nationale de France), Wayne Furman (New York Public Library), and Alessandra Corti (Alinari Archivi).

Chapters 1, 3, 4, and 5 are revisions of essays that first appeared as described as follows. Chapter 1 is an extensively revised version of "Allegory and Ethnography in Cabeza de Vaca's *Naufragios* and *Comentarios*," which appeared in *Violence, Resistance, and Survival in the Americas: Native Americans and the Legacy of Conquest,* ed. Franklin Pease and William Taylor (Washington, DC: Smithsonian Institution Press, 1994). Chapter 3, "Aesthetics of Colonial Violence: The Massacre of Acoma in Gaspar de Villagrá's *Historia de la Nueva Mexico,*" appeared in *College Literature* 20:3 (1993). Chapter 4 is adapted from an article appearing in *The Hernando de Soto Expedition: History, Historiography, and "Discovery" in the Southeast,* ed. Patricia Galloway, reprinted by permission of the University of Nebraska Press. © 1997 University of Nebraska Press. Chapter 5, "Porque soy Indio: Subjectivity in *La Florida del Inca,*" appeared in *Poetics Today* 16:1 (1995).

On Writing Violence:

An Introduction

Two brief passages offer points of entry for reflecting on the conjunction between writing and violence that grounded the Spanish conquest of the Americas in the sixteenth century and continues to haunt us all, even today. Before quoting the passages, I first provide frames of reference that lend the citations their epigrammatical quality.

The first passage comes from the anonymous *Historia de Tlatelolco desde los tiempos más remotos* (ca. 1528), arguably the first Nahuatl text using the Latin alphabet. Tlatelolco belonged to the same ethnic group as Tenochtitlan, the Mexica, but as a result of a civil war, Tlatelolco became a tributary of Tenochtitlan in 1473. Today an avenue in Mexico City separates these formerly independent cities. Although we do not have the original pictorial manuscript, the *Historia de Tlaltelolco* records an oral rendition of a pictographic history of this central Mexican city from its beginnings—*desde los tiempos más remotos* (from the most remote times)—in Aztlan (the mythical origin of the Nahua peoples located in the northern frontier of New Spain, the present-day U.S. states of New Mexico and Arizona) to the surrender of Tenochtitlan and Tlatelolco to the Spaniards in 1521. Tlatelolco, like many other cities and ethnic groups in central Mexico, provided warriors and settlers for the Spanish colonization of the north starting in the 1540s.

The second quotation is from the entry on Hispaniola in Bartolomé de Las Casas's *Brevíssima relación de la destruyción de Indias* (1552). As implied by the title, the *Brevíssima* is a short tract that covers all the areas in the Indies under Spanish rule up until 1552, when it was first published in Spanish. In reading the *Brevíssima* we have to keep in mind that it is a political pamphlet intended to bring to the attention of the Crown the atrocities its subjects were committing in the New World. Not once in the *Brevíssima* does Las Casas provide the name of a specific conquistador, thereby placing the blame for the destruction of the Indies on the institution of conquest itself and not on the abuses of particular conquistadores. This Dominican friar, however, also wrote a history that documented the specific atrocities, an anthropology that compared Amerindian and Old World societies, and theological tracts that theorized on the meaning and practice of evangelization. Let this broad outline of Las Casas suffice for now. Each of the chapters in this book addresses different aspects of Las Casas's work and his legacy.

The two passages share a nonconventional use of the term *writing*. As written expressions, these passages also convey the specific nature of speech as a bodily act, that is, a temporal present in which tone, gesture, dress, but also other accoutrements such as swords, horses, cannons, trumpets, conchs, war cries, and even mutilations are integral to verbal performances. Indeed, these passages suggest a historical continuum in which speech is both at the origin and at the end of writing. Note that the apparently arbitrary change of verb tense in the *Historia de Tlatelolco* makes sense once this text is understood as a primer for oral performance. The two passages also lend themselves to a clarification of the differences between the ways writing and power were articulated in the pre-Columbian period and under Spanish rule.

Here is the quotation from the *Historia de Tlatelolco:*

> Then the Mexica, whose wives were Colhuaque, examined each other: the women had brought their writings on *amate* paper. And the women, who had taken husbands there, brought their husbands' writings on *amate*.
>
> Then they consult each other and they say: "Where should we go? What should we project? Since we are not dead, we can still let you know what we will do. Gather together, collect all the writings of the Colhuaque that we have brought with us."
>
> When they had collected all the writings on *amate* paper, they filled [the statue made of sticks] with pigweed paste, they covered it with *amate* paper, they placed a head on it and they displayed it there for the first time. Then they made music and composed there the following chant:
>
> *By Iztacaltzinco was renewed our mountain made of* amate, *after [the statue] had been fabricated anew by hand in one night. On a plain was our mountain*

made of amate *paper fabricated by hand. Return again Nanociuatzin, he who bears the name of people. Allalleuaye! On a plain was our mountain made of* amate *paper fabricated by hand.*

The Coyouacatl, the Coyolhuacatl hear the song, whose sound reaches far. And they immediately call to arms: "Oh, Tepaneca! Let us reprehend them. Are there still too many Mexica? They are wrong in calling to arms."[1]

Now the quotation from Las Casas:

Otros y todos los que querían tomar a vida cortávanles ambas manos y dellas llevavan colgando, y dezíanles andad con cartas (conviene a saber) lleva las nuevas a las gentes que estaban huydas por los montes. (Las Casas 1991 [1552]: 11)
[To others, and all those they wanted to capture alive, they would cut both hands and would hang them round their necks, and would say "Go with the letters" (meaning) take the news to the people hiding in the mountains.]

From a narrow Western understanding of writing as the recording of phonemes by means of an alphabet, the glyphs and paintings on bark paper called *amatl*, the *amoxtli* (book of writing) mentioned in the *Historia de Tlatelolco* are not writing.[2] We can nevertheless recognize in this founding story of the Mexica a connection between *amoxtli* and power. By recording dialogue, the *Historia de Tlatelolco* evokes an oral performance only to erase it, yet in citing the song, in reproducing sound (*Allalleuaye!*), the *Historia de Tlatelolco* constitutes *speech* not only as its historical origin but also as the only way of keeping language alive, of curtailing the violence of alphabetical writing that fixes orality.

In the second quotation, Las Casas speaks of the Indians' mutilated hands as if they were letters to be taken to other Indians hiding in the mountains. This understanding of writing is not only unconventional, but also identifies writing with violence. Mutilation as a letter identifies a form of writing that effects violence in the process of its inscription as well as of its reception. In sending Indians with severed hands hanging from their necks, the Christians devised a heinous form of *speech as bodily act* in that the "letter" at once summons the Indians to recognize the new regime of law and conveys the force that will make the "news" effective. In the *Brevíssima* we learn from Las Casas that such uses of terror only led Indians to become maroons, and thus choose freedom over life itself.

According to the *Historia de Tlatelolco,* a history in Nahuatl apparently written in 1528, the Mexica built a statue of Nanociuatzin (a god who immolated himself to give rise to the fifth sun, the last era in Nahua cosmogony) using the *amoxtli* that the Colhua women had brought along with them when they intermarried with the Mexica. It is mind-boggling to imagine sixteenth-century Nahuas using alphabetical writing to tell this founding story of Mexico-Tenochtitlan in the midst of the fury of the missionaries who wished to destroy their culture by burning their precious books and breaking revered sculptures representing their gods.[3] One can imagine the Nahuas wondering why the missionaries would burn the *amoxtli* when they could be used to make crucifixes and statues of the Virgin. Nothing, perhaps, was more shocking to the Nahuas writing the *Historia de Tlatelolco* than the Spanish will to totally destroy their culture following Hernán Cortés's military defeat of Tenochtitlan in 1521. Yes, the so-called Aztecs are known for burning the archives of the places they colonized, but my point is not to oppose nor to equate destruction in Spanish and Amerindian ideologies of war and conquest. The use of the *amoxtli* to make the statue of Nanociuatzin testifies to the power of writing among the Nahuas. Was the making of the statue another modality of writing for the Nahuas? If so, then, what is writing? More specifically, what do we mean by writing violence in early modern colonialist discourses? Clearly, Spanish rule in the Americas involved more than military victory and sheer destruction.

In the course of the sixteenth century, Spanish colonial law legislated against using violent means to convert Indians to Christianity. Legislation prescribed forms of converting and subjecting Indians to Christianity and Spanish rule known today in academic circles by the term "peaceful conquest" (see, e.g., R. Adorno 1991, 1992, 1994; Poole 1965, 1987; Powell 1952, 1971; Hanke 1949). Recent scholars have used this term not only to paraphrase the Spanish rhetoric of empire, but also to endorse practices prescribed by the colonial laws. This oxymoron functions as an ironic trope that turns the act of conquest into a "good thing" as long as the conquistadores follow the rules of peaceful colonization. Thus, this story line opposes "good" and "bad" *conquistadores*. When taken to its final consequences, the oxymoron peaceful conquest entails the contradictory notion that because there were *colonial laws* intended to curtail the abuse of Indians, one cannot speak of *colonialism* in the sixteenth- and seventeenth-century Spanish Americas. The oxymoronic nature of peaceful conquest prompts an oppositional mode of inquiry based on an understanding of violence not limited to acts of war, but also including symbolism, interpretation, legislation, and other speech acts that scholars in different academic quarters refer to as *the force of law*.[4] In chapter 1, I examine how literary critics, filmmakers, and fiction writers have construed Alvar Núñez Cabeza de Vaca as a proponent of peaceful conquest. These readings ignore how the *Naufragios* and the *Comentarios* embody a *culture of conquest* insofar as Cabeza de Vaca portrays himself as a benevolent and law-abiding conquistador. Cabeza de Vaca's discourses on peaceful approaches to conquest lose their originality and uniqueness once we realize that he repeats the Ordenanzas of 1526, a body of laws prescribing the fair treatment of Indians to the letter. Let us recall that these Ordenanzas did not bar exerting violence against Indians, but rather prescribed the protocols for waging just wars.

Las Casas's *Brevíssima* is arguably the most influential text on the development of Spanish colonial laws. There is more to the passage linking mutilation with writing than a denunciation and indictment of Spain's atrocities in the Americas.[5] However hideous this act might seem to our sensibility, in the context of Las Casas, and sixteenth-century readers in general, mutilation amounts to an atrocity only if it is deemed unjust. The "letter" forces us to revise Louis Althusser's classic formulation of interpellation, in which by merely responding to a policeman who shouts "Hey, you there!" one subordinates oneself to dominant ideology. In Las Casas's example of colonial interpellation, the utterance must be revised to say, "Hey, you there, subordinate yourself to the Crown or I'll kill you."[6] But even before the "letter" conveyed the "news," the new regime of law had already interpellated Indians by constituting them as inferior humans destined to serve the Spaniards. The main contentious issue of the *Brevíssima* is the right of the conquistadores to demand that Indians subject themselves to the Spanish Crown and the further right to wage war against Indians if they refused to subordinate themselves. It was not the act of mutilation itself that was central to Las Casas's argument (as we will see later, torture, mutilation, and massacre remain viable modes of interpellation under laws prescribing peaceful colonization), but the validity of summoning Indians to surrender their political sovereignty and recognize a new regime of law. Although papal bulls granted Spain sovereignty over the Indies for the purpose of evangelizing Amerindians, it did not follow for Las Casas that Indians were to be politically subjected to the Crown or forced to accept Christianity. The Crown, in turn, co-opted Las Casas's denunciation and call for love and peaceful approaches to evangelization in the Nuevas Leyes (New Laws) of 1542 and the Ordenanzas of 1573 (see chapter 2). Let these statements on Las Casas stand as provocations for further thought on the significance of this great thinker.

WRITING VIOLENCE

Hate speech is pervasive, indeed, constitutive of colonial situations, but the implantation of colonial rule and the subordination of colonial subjects cannot be reduced to a modality of hate speech. "Love speech" is as central to colonization as spurting offensive yet injurious stereotypes. The challenge is to understand love speech as a powerful mode of subjection and effective violence. The most evident example is the declaration of love "We bring you the gift of Christ's blood," which is bound by the implicit obligation to accept the offering. This interpellation constitutes a form of love speech in which threat on the Indians' life and freedom (even when not explicit) always remains a possibility within the historical horizon if the summoning is not heeded. Whereas Las Casas's marooned insurgents attest that the initial call missed its mark, the mutilated Indians not only reiterate the interpellation but also illustrate the kinds of *compelling* force the Spaniards will use to establish their authority. Violence, force, or power is integral to the law and not simply an external instrument for its enforcement. The interpellated subjects have no option but to accept the terms of their subordination, the categories that define them as inferior, and the institutions that reorganize their life. We can furthermore define *symbolic violence* as *writing* that has the performative power to establish laws. The colonial order, however, never quite succeeded in effecting the magical act whereby colonial subjects forget that colonial rule of law has been imposed on them, as would be the case in the Althusserian understanding of interpellation (cf. Bourdieu 1987: 838). If the language of violence was increasingly rarefied in the Spanish Crown's evolving codes of laws, the task then is to understand how, in new legal codes that prescribed peaceful colonization, violence was effected on a symbolic level. Thus, chapter 4 argues that Gonzalo Fernández de Oviedo's condemnation of de Soto has less to do with a "change of heart" toward the Indians than with the new legal framework introduced by the Nuevas Leyes of 1542. Three contextual frames tend to accompany Oviedo's allusions and references to the Nuevas Leyes: (1) a condemnation of the behavior of Spaniards (specifically those he does not hold in high regard to begin with); (2) an implicit questioning of the reformist program in the Nuevas Leyes by laying the blame for the Indians' deaths on their idolatry, sodomy, and weak intellects; and (3) a direct critique of the power of the Dominican order (concretely, Bartolomé de las Casas). Consequently, the Nuevas Leyes function as a code Oviedo grudgingly accepted but used to advance his own policies. In the final analysis, Oviedo's denunciation of de Soto reproduced on a symbolic level the same violence he condemned.

Even if laws generated by the amorphous bureaucratic machinery known as "the Crown" bear the signature of the king, we cannot identify the king as the sovereign origin of power. Law introduces structures that seek to guarantee the objectivity of its officers, to define the kinds of discourses explorers will produce, to regulate the terms for subjugating Indians; this list exemplifies the many ways of exercising power that exceed the individuals who utter interpellatory statements, review juridical cases, and write accounts. The *Brevíssima* also manifests this diffusion of sovereign power in its refusal to identify the individuals responsible for the atrocities. Here it is not an issue of "good" versus "bad" conquistadores, but of denouncing the institution of conquest itself. Furthermore, Las Casas interpellates Prince Philip, who would become king of

Spain in 1557, by demanding that the Crown take responsibility for the atrocities committed in the Indies—for allowing them to continue after the king had been informed of their occurrence—and by declaring that no argument could be made to justify waging war against Indians. Las Casas tells us that he decided to publish the *Brevíssima* ten years after he had written the original account and orally presented it at the court, so that Philip II would be able to read it without difficulties: "Delibere . . . poner en molde . . . para que con más facilidad vuestra alteza las pueda leer" [I decided . . . to print them . . . so that your majesty can read them with greater ease] (1991 [1552]: 6).

Let me briefly return to the foundational story in the *Historia de Tlatelolco* to illustrate three working concepts that clarify what I mean by *writing violence* and the *violence of writing*.

Beyond the Alphabet

This story of the Mexica paper statue warns us against identifying the concept of writing violence with the use or the adoption of the Latin alphabet. The passage illustrates how writing violence is exercized by other forms of writing and exemplifies how the Latin alphabet is only a tool. As do all tools, alphabetical writing affects the mind and body of its users, and yet the expansion of the power of communication that comes with its adoption does not automatically exclude earlier forms of communication and understanding the world. The use of the alphabet to narrate the *Historia de Tlatelolco* suggests that the colonizing force of alphabetical writing resides in the ideologies that inform its dissemination and the rules that implement scriptural projects, rather than in the technology itself.[7] In this context, it is worth citing Michel de Certeau's definition of the modern scriptural enterprise in which the alphabet and the page are incidental, actually metaphors for a capitalist mode of production: "The island of the page is a transitional place in which an industrial inversion is made: what comes in is something 'received,' what comes out is a 'product.' . . . Combining the power of accumulating the past and that of making the alterity of the universe *conform* to its models, [the scriptural enterprise] is capitalist and conquering" (Certeau 1984: 135). The task, then, for understanding how

Writing Violence on the Northern Frontier

the modern scriptural economy effects violence is to identify rules for the production of knowledge and the articulation of the world, rules intended to discipline the bodies and selves of a new class of writers known in the Spanish world as *letrados* (literally, the lettered ones). One could further argue along with Certeau that the alphabet is not only a technology used for writing laws that inscribe bodies with precepts and prohibitions, but is also a tool that marks the user by developing postures, muscles, and sensorimotor functions. Moreover, I do not see why these undeniable physical transformations should be considered more significant than the changes brought about by horses, diet, dress, architecture, and other practices of everyday life—let alone punishment, mutilation, torture, and massacre (see Certeau 1984: 139–50). Certeau goes on to develop the metaphor of reading as poaching in which "every reader invents in texts something different from what they [the authors] 'intended'" (169), a suggestion that is contextualized by Johannes Fabian's statement that "imperial designs have been served, inadvertently or not, by thinking literacy mainly as the capacity to write while neglecting that any literacy can of course only have the insidious effect we ascribe to it when what is written is also read. When literacy ceases to be understood as the one-way activity of inscribing this must have consequences for the global assessment of literacy as an instrument of domination" (1993: 84–85). Both Certeau and Fabian underscore the need to reflect on the different practices of reading, which obviously cannot be limited to the disembodied modalities of reading that have prevailed in the West since the eighteenth century.[8] I would add that the transformation of the body that results from the adoption of Western practices need not *necessarily* annul previous habits and forms of viewing the world, or foreclose the development of new styles of riding, cooking, dressing, dwelling, and, of course, also of writing and reading.

Let us recall that although the missionaries burned native writings in the early years of the conquest, by the early 1540s Spanish administrators were encouraging and even sponsoring the production of texts using glyphs. It is worth keeping in mind that the alphabet does not stand for or take the place of glyphs, but reproduces speech. The eventual decay of pictographic writing has less to do with the adoption of the alphabet than with the disappearance of institutions that trained painters and interpreters who preserved a hermeneutic tradition (see Gruzinski 1993: 66–69). The art of reading, of giving an oral performance following paintings, went well beyond the identification of glyphs. From a contemporary perspective, the identification of glyphs is a relatively simple task when compared with the elucidation of the kinds of oral performances that interpreted the pictorial texts. Even when we have such performances, their meaning often remains inaccessible, especially when no effort was made to translate the spoken text to Western categories. The *Historia de Tlatelolco* is an instance where the interpretation of verbal language recorded by means of the alphabet presents more difficulties for a twentieth-century Western reader than the identification of units of meaning in the kinds of pictographic texts alphabetically literate Nahuas followed in writing an oral performance.

In the case of acts of war, the machinery of terror—the inscriptional power of whipping, hanging, mutilation, torture, or massacre—entails a series of legal instruments that found as well as conserve colonial rule. The best known is the *Requerimiento,* that infamous interpellation whereby conquistadores and missionaries, via their makeshift interpreters—that is, in the best of scenarios—explained to Indians that (to paraphrase) God created the world, that all men were descendants of Adam and Eve, that God had chosen Saint Peter to represent him on earth and rule over all men, and finally that Saint Peter's authority had been passed down a line of popes until a recent one who granted the kings of Spain sovereignty over their lands. The *Requerimiento* goes on to give Indians the choice of recognizing the Spanish Crown as their legitimate ruler or facing war and slavery. The voice of the conquistador signals a chain of *sovereign* subjects from which he derives his power—a regress that goes back to king to pope to Saint Peter to God. As in Las Casas's "letter," the *convincing* element of this voice resides in the display of the military force integral to the speech act—the bodily act—that performs the interpellation. Whether read in earnest or not, the logic of the *Requerimiento* exerts symbolic violence on Indians by giving them no option but to surrender or be cast as hostile in Spain's imperial historical telos. The *Requerimiento* mentions documents, the papal bulls, that the conquistador uttering the speech act would be willing to share with the addressed Indians, but we would be hard pressed to argue that the illocutionary force of the *Requerimiento,* its violence as a performative speech act, resides in its alphabetical nature rather than in the theatricality of its reading, in its oralization. Once Indians gave their obedience to the Crown, they were distributed among the conquistadores in *encomiendas,* a system of tribute in which Christian benefactors had the responsibility of looking after the Indians' spiritual health. Although the force of arms is inseparable from the founding as well as the conservation of Spanish sovereignty, the ideal subject would understand the truth of the *Requerimiento* and the benefits of the *encomienda* out of his or her own volition.

Under domination, subaltern subjects are bound—in their communications and exchanges with colonial authorities—to the instruments of colonial law without being forced to abandon social spaces informed by non-Spanish legal institutions encapsulated, if not reified, under the concept of *usos y costumbres* (uses and customs). The Spanish Crown recognized this form of plural-world dwelling when it prescribed that lay officers and missionaries investigate Indian *usos y costumbres* and apply them in cases involving disputes among Indians. *Usos y costumbres* also provided information on precontact indigenous patterns of tribute, systems of slavery, delineations of boundaries, sexual alliances, and so on that established antecedents that would naturalize and legitimize, if not legalize, colonial institutions replicating these structures of power. Up to the present, for instance in the context of the debates between the Zapatistas and the Mexican government, the definition of *usos y costumbres* remains a source of dispute (both within the indigenous communities and in negotiations with the state) because it retains the traces of its colonial origins. There is, nevertheless, a radical difference between discussing the validity of *usos y costumbres* in terms of Western legal and anthropological apparatuses, and discussing that validity within the indigenous communities in Indian languages and conceptual frameworks. By necessity, subaltern subjects dwell in at least two worlds; that is, they live the *usos y costumbres,* they do not just discuss them.

Savage Literacy, Domesticated Glyphs

Alphabetical writing does not belong to the rulers; it also circulates in the mode of a *savage literacy*. Bearing no trace of Spanish intervention in its production, the *Historia de Tlatelolco* exemplifies a form of grassroots literacy in which indigenous writers operated outside the circuits controlled by missionaries, *encomenderos,* Indian judges and governors, or lay officers of the Crown.[9] By all appearances, the *Historia de Tlatelolco* was written to perpetuate the history and identity of the Tlatelolcans. It depicts the Spanish conquest as motivated exclusively by greed, and makes no reference to the importation of Christianity—pure violence, as it were, without ideology. On the other hand, it represents the Tenochcas, who had subjected the Tlatelolcans in the previous century, murdering each other in a total state of social anomie. In the best of the pre-Columbian traditions, it is local history.[10] As for those groups of painters and writers operating under the supervision of missionaries or lay Spaniards, their interests were more often than not in conflict. Within these power struggles, glyphs could both lend legitimacy to colonial institutions as well as rhetorically enhance the information glyphs contained regarding patterns of tribute and forms of slavery and other *usos y costumbres* purportedly dating back to the pre-Columbian past. What could more powerfully constitute a link between the *encomienda* and tribute patterns before the conquest than an indigenous pictographic record (see Rabasa 1994b)? If it is true that glyphs were glossed, I must insist again that writing records speech about the image, not the image itself; it does not substitute for the force of paintings, especially in those cases where the use of glyphs fulfilled the rhetorical function of certifying the validity of the information. At any rate, the end product of glyph and alphabet is their oralization in reading and interpretation; otherwise, both systems remain mute. The oralization of writing cannot be isolated from the cultures of reading specific to historical moments, social groups, professions, and fields.[11]

The story of the Mexica founding moment can be read as a metaphor of how alphabetical writing reifies history by reducing to one oral performance the endless possible stories that could be told following glyph-scripted narratives. But the *Historia de Tlatelolco* also

Writing Violence on the Northern Frontier

mimics the making of the statue as it produces a new whole by aggregating stories representative of different genres of Nahua historical writing, which most likely were derived from independent *amoxtli:* an itinerary history that traced Nahuas' origins to the northern region of Chicomostoc or Aztlan, a dynastic account of Tlatelolco, an annal of the rise of Mexica hegemony under the Triple Alliance of Tenochtitlan, Texcoco, and Tlacopan (which included the subjection of Tlatelolco), and the new historical genre designed to tell of the destruction brought about by the Spanish invasion (see Boone 1994; Quiñones Keber 1995). As the record of an oral performance, the *Historia de Tlatelolco* included songs and dialogues as well as the historical narration of events. We may assume that the Nahuas read the *Historia de Tlatelolco* as they did their *pinturas,* that is, as an oral performance of a narrative that could lead to further interpretation and production of texts both oral and written. This would entail the kind of collective author as well as reader that Bruce Mannheim and Krista Van Vleet (1998) have identified in contemporary Southern Quechua narrative. We can further trace this mode of collectively authored and read Nahua *histories* in other Nahua texts such as *Leyenda de los soles* (a cosmogony) and Fernando Alvarado Tezozómoc's *Crónica mexicáyotl.* By contrast, dialogical production plays no part in the work of other authors, such as Fernando de Alva's *Historia de la nación Chichimeca* or Fray Diego de Duran's *Historia de la Nueva España e Islas de Tierra Firme,* which, although they follow pictorial histories, incorporate the information into a historical narrative in the guise of Western Romance both in their plot structure and their representations of speech; furthermore, they are written from the point of view of an individual author. As we will see in chapter 5, Garcilaso deconstructs his rendition of an Indian monologue by indicating that Indians speak collectively, not individually, thereby exposing the violence the conventions of Romance exert on indigenous narrative styles. Because Garcilaso was never in Florida, we can surmise that in thus prefacing Indian speech he was invoking the Quechua speeches he had listened to as a young man in Cuzco. In acknowledging the dialogical nature of indigenous oral performances in Garcilaso's hybrid Quechua-like Appalachian Indians or in the Nahua tradition, we should not ignore the power dynamics involved in the production of narratives such as the founding story of Mexico-Tenochtitlan in the *Historia de Tlate-lolco*. After all, the song is a war cry that marks the beginning of the Mexica military ascendancy in the Valley of Mexico. We must also keep in mind that sixteenth-century Nahuas wrote glyphs to promote and express Spanish ideology. This is because the Nahuas in the colonial period, just as before the Spanish conquest, understood all too well the power of glyph-scripted narratives. Thus, the pictographic history known as the *Codex of Tlatelolco* (ca. 1565) exalts the participation of the Tlatelolcans in the suppression of a rebellion on the northern frontier, during the Mixton War in 1541, by representing Tlatelolcan warriors in proportions that dwarf the Spaniards riding horses.[12]

Scriptural Economy

These two Tlatelolcan texts testify to the violence of writing in general but also to the subaltern subjects' heterogeneity that all forms of colonial rule must foment, create, indeed depend on, to impose and perpetuate dominance. Writing entails power structures: writing as the memory of subordination, as the record of theft, as the erasure of culture, as the process of territorialization, and as the imposition of regimes of law, regardless of the type of script or form of representation. In writing we are circumscribed by these power structures though not ineluctably co-opted or blocked from doing other things than those intended by discourses of domination. I would not be writing what I am writing now if I considered the exercise futile.

Although the two Tlatelolcan texts manifest instances of how writing performs violence, we need to differentiate between the different regimes of violence under which these writing performances operate. Whereas the *Historia de Tlatelolco* uses alphabet to elude colonial authorities, the *Codex of Tlatelolco* uses glyphs to secure a privileged position for Tlatelolco within the colonial order. The *Historia de Tlatelolco* exemplifies the centrality of local history in Mesoamerica, the assumption that even under the subordination of Tenochtitlan, the Tlatelolcans retain their identity and particular modalities of dwelling in the world. Tenochtitlan could not have its own identity, as it were, without a particular history that singled out

Writing Violence on the Northern Frontier

Mexico-Tenochtitlan from other ethnic groups. The same principle informs the prominence of the *Codex of Tlatelolco* gives to the Tlatelolcan warriors. In this regard we can note the anomaly between alphabetically written history for the internal consumption of the Tlatelolcan community in the years immediately after the conquest and a pictographic record of the participation of the Tlatelolcans in the conquest of the northern frontier primarily intended for the consumption of the colonial authorities. Likewise, the class of *letrados* cannot be limited to those using *letras* (letters), but must be expanded to include disciplined individuals embodying as well as implementing regimes of law and knowledge regardless of whether they can write letters on a page, that is, regardless of the writing tools and systems of representation or the traditions on which they claim expertise. Spanish sources often speak of Indians knowledgeable of their traditions as *letrados,* a term that we should, perhaps, simply translate as literate rather than putting too much weight on the use of letters. Take, for instance, the following passage from the Dominican friar Diego de Durán's *Historia de la Nueva España e Islas de Tierra Firme* (ca. 1581): "Queriéndome confirmar en si esto era verdad, pregunté a un indio viejo que me le vendieron por letrado en su ley natural . . . que me dijese si aquello era así, que allí tenía escrito y pintado" [Seeking to verify if this was true, I asked an old Indian who was presented to me as literate in his natural law . . . to tell me if things were thus, as I had there in written and painted text] (1984 [ca. 1581], 1:13). Note that in one breath, Durán refers to glyphs as both *pintados* (painted) and *escritos* (written). Indian, mestizo, and Spanish *letrados* participated in the power structure by drawing maps, painting glyphs, writing history, and interpreting Indian languages (see Leibsohn 1995).

Spanish colonialists knew that the colonized hardly constituted a homogeneous group. Indeed, they were very successful in using one group against the other and, perhaps even more important, in working with a native elite that looked after its own interests and sought to perpetuate its privileges within the colonial order. These subaltern elites facilitated the administration of the empire by fulfilling the role of judges and governors of Indians. Consequently, the Franciscan college of Santa Cruz of Tlatelolco and the Augustinian college of Tiripetio were established to form elite cadres of native scholars (see Gruzinski 1994: 59–62; Kobayashi 1974: 207–24; Sahagún 1950–82, 13:76–81). By the end of the sixteenth century this intellectual elite thought in terms of an epistemology that no longer bore a connection to the magicoreligious world of the everyday life of the common Nahuas. Thus, the fact that dominated Nahua elites were aware of their domination did not rule out "consent," the willing adoption of instruments, rationalities, narratives, and aesthetics imported by the rulers. On the other hand, members of this same elite might have known themselves to be dominated but were ignorant of how domination "worked" and in what ways they contributed to domination while "resisting" (cf. Scott 1990; Joseph and Nugent 1994a; Roseberry 1994; Sayer 1994). One could also argue that these questions could not have been formulated before the dissolution of the colonial world after World War II and the postcolonial condition of thought we associate with Frantz Fanon (1967, 1968) and, in general, with the emergence of a native intellectual elite that contests the historical and epistemological privileges of the metropolis.

AFTER POSTCOLONIALISM

If in this study I draw from and build on postcolonial theory and subaltern studies, it is not merely to apply this scholarship to the Spanish colonization of the Americas in the sixteenth and seventeenth centuries. We must keep in mind that the theoretical work in these fields has been conceived for the most part with other areas of the world and historical moments in mind. In reading the work of postcolonial scholars such as Ranajit Guha, Gayatri Spivak, Homi Bhabha, Dipesh Chakrabarty, Johannes Fabian, and Edward Said, I have come to realize that in the colonization of the Americas, Spain rehearsed, three centuries earlier, the imperialist categories that Britain and other Northern European powers came to deploy in India, Africa, and the Middle East at the end of the eighteenth century.[13] The *after* in the subheading for this section is intended to highlight that by *postcolonialism* I understand a series of intellectual projects in literary studies, cultural studies, and critiques of anthropology, history, and sociology that have common structures of

Writing Violence on the Northern Frontier

feeling and ethicopolitical positions enabling us to draw not only a critique of the colonialisms that once were, but also of neocolonial forms of exerting dominance and internal colonialisms that emerge in the wake of the dissolution of formal political ties to a metropolis. Moreover, the *after* points to the condition of thought that enables us to read in a new light collaboration, complicity, and resistance as well as opacity in the cultural artifacts that different sectors, groups, and representatives of subalterns and elites have produced under colonial rule. To dialogue with postcolonial scholars, we must elicit the categories and concepts from sixteenth- and seventeenth-century Spanish texts that articulate tutelage, civilizing mission, native collaboration, and colonial law and that are still influential today. Hence, postcolonialism, understood as a new condition of thought, cannot be equated with the end of a colonial period, nor should the questions postcolonial scholars raise be limited to the specific experiences of nineteenth- and twentieth-century colonialisms. For now, let me point out that this genealogy has had two detrimental consequences for the study of earlier periods in the Americas. At best, Enlightenment forms of producing otherness—for example, the opposition between peoples with and without history, or between peoples in a state of nature and those living under a state—assume a transhistorical applicability that erases historical specificity. At worst, postcolonial theorists reduce the colonial enterprises before the Enlightenment to crude modes of raping the land—for example, Portuguese trading posts and Spanish conquest—with no coherent civilizing mission worth mentioning. This book argues the exception of the Spanish imperial project, but a similar argument could be made for Portuguese modes of colonization in the early modern period.

But even more detrimental than the erasure of the Spanish colonial past is the loss of a possible history of the present that could result from an uncritical adoption of postcolonial theories that better apply to the Asian and African histories that gave rise to them. Historical differences between the Americas and Asia and Africa distinguish the relationship between elite and subaltern cultures in the Americas from the relationship between these two groups in Asia or Africa.[14] It is therefore as urgent to underscore the differences between the colonial pasts as between the presents—the historical nows—of subalterns and elites in India, Africa, and the Americas. I will return to this question in the epilogue, where I elaborate a critique of Dipesh Chakrabarty's understanding of the "time of history" and the "times of the gods" as mutually excluding the possibility of dwelling in both worlds. One crucial historical difference between these regions of the world is the long history of independence in the Americas. Another, as we have seen, is the development of the term *usos y costumbres,* which underlines the distinct trajectory colonial categories have had in the Americas (see Stavenhagen 1988; Zavala 1971, 1973; cf. Schwarz 1997). The texts from Tlatelolco that I examined above exemplify how, from the beginning of the conquest of Mexico, Nahuas dwelled in at least the two worlds of the *usos y costumbres* and the juridic and religious fields of the Spanish authorities. To the extent that Spanish authorities solicited and collected verbal and pictorial expressions of Nahua culture, they too were committing themselves to dwell in both worlds, at least from a hermeneutic necessity, though not necessarily from an affective affinity. The importance of the imposition of categories such as *usos y costumbres* may be seen in the fact that the meanings of *usos y costumbres,* cultural and linguistic rights, and the autonomy of Indian peoples have been central issues in recent debates between the Zapatistas and the representatives of the Mexican government. Whereas the government has displayed an incapacity to understand the demands of the Zapatistas and other indigenous groups, Indian leaders have once more shown their ability to dwell in modern and nonmodern worlds without incurring a contradiction (see Rabasa 1997; see also Gossen 1999; Le Bot 1997; Rojas 1995; cf. Chakrabarty 1997). Even if *usos y costumbres* is a colonial invention, there are ontological as well as epistemological differences in indigenous and modern discourses that articulate understandings of native laws. Unfortunately, the Mexican government today appears unwilling to listen to the Indians, regardless of whether they articulate their discourses in terms of indigenous languages and understandings of the world or in anthropological Western categories.

Given these concerns about the uncritical adoption of postcolonial theories, I welcome J. Jorge Klor de Alva's reminder of the different meanings the term colonialism has had in Western history and the fact that we should avoid projecting nineteenth-century British understandings of colonialism and its specific economic structures onto the sixteenth- and seventeenth-century Spanish possession in the New World (see Klor de Alva 1995; see also R. Adorno 1993). My proposed method of drawing what is particular to Spain in the sixteenth century would not only avoid a mechanical application of a "paradigm," but indeed would *identify* the ways in which sixteenth-century colonial enterprises, which clearly encompass nations other than Spain, constitute prototypes and inaugurate structures of power relations that remain in force during the so-called second wave of European expansionism. As for the issue of the applicability of the term colonial to the sixteenth-century Spanish enterprise, we face similar constraints in using other recent terms such as race and racism. Yet, because *race* did not exist before the eighteenth century does not mean that the categories and arguments that justified establishing hierarchies, subjugation, and the extermination of people based on physical (and not exclusively cultural) traits did not constitute forms of racism (see Delacampagne 1983). In parallel, our definition of the term colonial was not part of the Spanish lexicon of conquest and empire. Nevertheless, Spain articulated theories of empire and just war against the Indians, elaborated discourses on the inferiority of Amerindians, and demanded their subordination to the Spanish Crown. Rather than denying the existence of racism and colonialism in the sixteenth century, we ought to benefit from understanding the specific forms racism and colonialism assumed in early modern colonial discourses.[15] For instance, Spanish theories and colonial programs that use terms such as *poblar* (to settle) and *pacificar* (to pacify) cannot be equated with the establishment of Roman garrisons, even if this was the meaning given to the term *colony* by early modern Spanish authors (see Klor de Alva 1995: 264). Although garrisons were indeed a component of the Spanish invasion, they served to create an infrastructure for the religious conversion and political subjection of native populations. Indeed, the garrison was an important part of the "frontier" conquest in California, New Mexico, and Texas, and, unlike garrisons on the U.S.

frontier, there was a church centrally located in each. Colonialism, at least in the version practiced by Spaniards in the Americas, was not just about dominating people by the force of arms but about transforming Indians into able bodies and obedient subjects. Furthermore, as Patricia Seed (1995) has shown, the fact that English, French, Dutch, Portuguese, and Spaniards already in the sixteenth century had different imperial styles of claiming possession should warn us against making categorical statements that deny the existence of colonialism in the sixteenth century (see chapter 6).

THE FRONTIER

Writing Violence on the Northern Frontier consists of six essays on sixteenth-century texts pertaining to the colonization of Nuevo México (a territory ranging from the Pacific Coast to the present-day U.S. state of Kansas) and La Florida (which ranged from the Peninsula to the states of Tennessee and Arkansas). These essays examine visual and verbal representations, colonialist programs, and the theories of colonization that informed the writing of the territories on the northern frontier of New Spain. The frontier is a discursive category that ultimately refers back to the borderlands of the *reconquista* of Moslem territories in Spain and to heathen lands in general. In the Americas, the frontier held promises of wealth and, after Tenochtitlan and Cuzco, the specific expectation of finding rich kingdoms—hence the pursuit of Cibola, Quivira, Totonteac, Chicora, Appalachee, and so on in the texts we will examine. Thus, the frontier implies not solely the end of civilization, as in wilderness or terra incognita, but also the beginning of other civilized cultures, though qualified as barbarian for not being Christian. It must be underscored that the North and the frontier are colonial constructs that erase Indian organizations and experiences of space. From the Indians' perspective, the encroachment of the frontier is an invasion of their territories. In the course of history, the northern frontier emerges as a space populated by a plurality of ethnic groups often in conflict with each other and having different experiences and perspectives on the evolving structures of power through which the colonizers eventually become the colonized, in the transitions from the Spanish empire to the Mexican republic and to the American annexation.

Writing in the present as Indians, Hispanics, Mexicans, or Anglos, we ought to keep in mind the violence one exerts in privileging one's point of view. The northern frontier was and is a highly contested space that is best understood as the result of material, cultural, and ideological exchanges among evolving groups, rather than as an embodiment of a uniquely American culture, as Frederick Jackson Turner argued in his 1893 seminal address, "The Significance of the Frontier in American History" (1983). Semiotically, the frontier is an *empty signifier* that I use here for lack of a better term (cf. Laclau 1996: 36–46). Though Mary Louise Pratt's (1992) concept of a contact zone provides a conceptual framework to understand the culture of colonialism, it strikes me as a euphemism when speaking of slavery or wars of extermination. The term frontier in sixteenth-century usage refers to regions not yet under Spanish control and certainly lacked the meanings associated with the spirit of the Anglo-American frontier or the particular nature of the Mexican Norte.[16] This frontier is a geographic space that has been defined and culturally contested as "the West," "el Norte," "the Spanish borderlands," and, since 1848, "the U.S.-Mexico border." Like all these other terms, *the northern frontier of New Spain* exerts conceptual violence on the Indian peoples who inhabited and inhabit these lands. My use here seeks to foreground a geographic area that was written about, imagined, and mapped from a colonizing perspective, rather than a natural entity that was discovered, known, and charted. It would be erroneous, however, to think that the people involved in colonial enterprises lacked the resolve to verify what a philosophical realist would call the *brute physical facts* and were content with ideological, willful claims to the territories.[17] In reading colonial documents, we must learn to distinguish verbal and visual statements intended to accurately record factual information from those designed to symbolically lay claim to territories, and still others that develop theories of colonialism and violence. This methodological observation obviously does not exclude the possibility that statements of fact may also entail figurative meanings or establish symbols.

The concept of writing violence comprises both the representation of massacres, tortures, rapes, and other forms of material terror, as well as categories and concepts informing the representation of territories for conquest, the definition of Indian cultures as inferior, and the constitution of colonized subjectivities. Whereas the first meaning of writing violence is self-evident, the second might provoke readers to resist seeing the force of writing itself as violence. But the two meanings are also related, for writing codifies legal categories such as criminals, insurgents, deviants, and insubordinates, and legitimizes violence against these groups. Let us not forget the even more insidious forms of symbolic violence that underlie shared assumptions and self-evident concepts such as the frontier, savagery, cannibalism, social evolution, development, progress, and others that structure our relation to the objective world up to the present.

The difference, then, does not reside in *literal* versus *metaphorical* uses of the term violence, nor in the semantic difference in *writing as violence* versus *writing is violence*. Violence can be both literal and metaphorical, with no qualifications as to whether it is exercised on a material or a conceptual plane. Take, for instance, the quotation from Las Casas at the beginning of this introduction. His description of mutilation points at once to a literal act of violence and to a metaphorical function of sending the hands as letters. Here we have an instance where violence *is* a form of writing. What the message was that the mutilated Indians would convey remains unsaid in Las Casas. Furthermore, other descriptions of torture and terror in the *Brevísima* convey arbitrary forms of violence lacking any reason beyond the pleasure Spaniards derived from inflicting pain; they thus manifest a pragmatic use of violence for subordination.

Descriptions of torture and terror lend themselves to a clarification of the materiality of writing violence. I can anticipate someone observing that there is an ontological difference between terrorizing someone and describing the torture in writing. But description can fulfill at least two functions: to instruct in techniques and to set an example. These modes of writing pertain to a culture of violence, but they also exercise *material* violence inasmuch as they have psychological impacts; the first forms the subjectivity of torturers (I assume a numbing of sensibilities), and the second aims to terrorize a population (as in the mutilated hands in Las Casas). In addition to the numbness of future torturers, descriptions of terror committed against an enemy may also generate impulsions of violence on the readers and thereby solidify a war community. Description ensures the continuity of violence by shaping the sensibilities of those who will either endorse or commit future acts of terror. As I pointed out at the beginning of this introduction, the mutilated hands as "letter" metaphor exemplifies the force embedded in the act of interpellating Indians into subordinating themselves to the Spanish Crown. The performance of the *Requerimiento* replicates the mutilation-as-letter inasmuch as it is a threat of war and slavery that can only be effective, that is, terrorize the addressee into submission, if the bodily act of reading the interpellation displays the military power that will enforce it. Thus, the *Requerimiento* constitutes an instance of love speech, conveying the benefits to be derived from the gift of Christianity and Spanish forms of life, that in fact exerts violence in describing the consequences of not recognizing Spanish sovereignty as self-evident "news." This distinction defines writing in terms of production (description as a means to torture) and action (description as torture).

To understand these terms, we may turn to Aristotle. In the *Ethics* (bk. 6, chaps. 4 and 5) and the *Politics* (bk. 1, chap. 4), Aristotle suggests an identification of art and violence inasmuch as art belongs to production (*poiesis*) in contradistinction to action (*praxis*): "For while making [production] has an end other than itself, action cannot; for the good action itself is its end" (*Ethics* 1140b6–7).[18] In the *Politics* (bk. 1, chap. 2), Aristotle speaks of the weapons man is born with (language would be one) and places the legitimacy of *language as violence* in terms of means to achieve a just end: "For man, when perfected, is the best of animals, but, when separated from law and justice, he is the worst of all; since armed injustice is the more dangerous, and he is equiped at birth with arms [e.g., language], meant to be used by intelligence and virtue, which he may use for the worst ends" (*Politics* 1253a31–34). Torture as a form of writing implies that language can be viewed both as a means to achieve an end as well as constituting an end in itself. On the one hand, the terror and torture described by Las Casas could very well be inscribed in terms that validate any means necessary to a justified end—that is, the public display of mutilation as message that warns potential rebels of the consequences of insurrection. On the other hand, the law would derive its *symbolic force* from the categories and logical arguments that establish the truth and justness of demanding that Indians surrender their sovereignty to the Crown. Language, then, no longer functions as a weapon to achieve just or unjust ends, but as symbolic violence. The critical force of Las Casas, in turn, requires that we disassociate mutilation as letter from a discussion of justified means and view the regime of terror as an end in itself. Other missionaries and lay historians, however, interpreted this same violence as divinely ordained punishment of Indians.

Walter Benjamin's essay "Critique of Violence" identifies three forms of violence that correspond to those outlined above: "means to just end," "means as end in itself," and "pure violence with no consideration of ends or means." Benjamin shows that means and ends are inextricably bound to each other: "Natural law attempts, by the justness of the ends, to 'justify' the means, positive law to 'guarantee' the justness of the ends through the justification of the means" (Benjamin 1986: 278). Benjamin adds to his discussion of violence as means and ends what he calls unalloyed, pure violence. The emphasis on ends and means apparently sets up an opposition between violence as law making (establishing an end) and law preserving (conserving an order). Benjamin has in mind the manner in which the modern police's violence arbitrarily elides the distinction between founding and preserving the law. I wonder, however, if this arbitrary elision—the scandal of police violence—is not characteristic of the exercise of dominance without hegemony in colonial power relations. Las Casas's argument in part hinges on demonstrating that the conquistadores abrogated the right to make laws in making war against Indians. I say "in part" because either the conquistadores act illegally by making the unjust laws or they embody the king's unjust laws. At any rate, Benjamin also indicates that the founding of law is inseparable from the conserving of order, and there is no conservation of law that does not partake of a founding moment. Paraphrasing Derrida, we can say that in the founding of colonial law, the Spanish Crown carried the power

Writing Violence on the Northern Frontier

to determine as outlaw anyone who did not recognize its right to demand obedience (*obediencia*) (Derrida 1990: 987). In this light, we can read Las Casas's example as a founding moment inasmuch as sending mutilated Indians to convey the news corresponds to the establishment of a regime of law. In exposing this display of mutilated bodies as an arbitrary exercise of violence, Las Casas invokes a sense of justice that destroys the grounds on which wars of conquest could legitimize themselves. Even if Las Casas seeks to found a new law to ensure nonviolent evangelization, his call for justice goes beyond the calculability of the law (establishing an equivalence between injury and restitution) to the extent that the Indians' losses and suffering could never be adequately compensated. This call for justice, which goes beyond the calculable, leaves his critics with no option other than to accuse Las Casas of propagating the *leyenda negra* (black legend).

These examples of the *force of law* suggest that the culture of violence ultimately circumscribes the critic's practice of writing. To what extent can one write about violence without perpetuating it? What are the dangers of speaking and thereby generalizing writing as a form of violence? Would this equation necessarily imply losing perspective on material forms of violence? Should (writing) violence be a means to end violence? The essays in this book address these questions, which obviously lack straightforward answers. They examine issues pertaining to the culture of conquest, the mediation of the law, the aesthetics of colonial violence, the moralization of terror, the politics of authorship, and the symbolization of hatred. To the extent that the elucidation of the "culture of conquest" maps out conceptual complicities that haunt today's writing on colonial discourses, we begin to understand that laws determine texts that organize the world for colonization. The "mediation of the law" enables us to avoid assessing degrees of justice (or, for that matter, comparing nations in terms of more or less benevolent colonial models) and attend to how the evolving bodies of law define styles of recording information, enable aesthetic representations of violence, and delimit the moralization of gratuitous acts of terror. In viewing colonialism from within the "culture of conquest," we also begin to understand the limits Las Casas and Garcilaso de la Vega faced as they were forced to elaborate their cri-

On Writing Violence

tiques of colonialism from within the universal parameters of Roman Catholicism.

In the case of Garcilaso's *La Florida del Inca,* we find a brilliant instance of a subject who, in embodying the language of universality, exposed the contradictions of Roman Catholicism, at least in the Spanish version, inherent in the category of the *converso* (the recent convert) and the Estatutos de Limpieza de Sangre (Statutes of Blood Purity). The universal call of all peoples into the Church entails a hierarchization that institutes inequality by means of the category of the *converso,* which defined new converts as less Christian than the *cristianos viejos* (Old Christians), and the statutes of *limpieza de sangre,* which limited the social and intellectual world of all those who could not trace a line of clean Visigoth blood for seven generations (cf. Balibar 1994: 191–204). Even such a subject as Garcilaso, who mastered Spanish forms of life and personally overcame the deprecatory effects of interiorized stereotypes about Amerindians, could not carve out a cultural space unconstrained by the double bind of Spanish Catholicism. In *La Florida,* Garcilaso explores the *force of law* in its most insidious form of exerting symbolic violence: the constitution of subjectivities at fault (see chapter 5).

In developing theories of violence, writing, and colonialism that emphasize stable oppositions between the colonizers and the colonized, one runs the risk of undermining the theoretical sophistication of the programs and policies as well as the aesthetics of violence that articulate and mediate imperialistic enterprises. Texts such as Juan Ginés de Sepúlveda's *Democrates Alter,* known in Spanish as the *Tratado de las justas causas de la guerra contra los Indios,* the laws the Spanish Crown designed to regulate exploration, or the Huguenot corpus on Florida elaborate complex theories of violence and strategies of colonization, not just ideological or moral justifications of conquest. Take, for instance, the statement of possession that Juan de Oñate read to the Pueblo Indians in which he outlines a colonizing program that envisions Indians trading with Spaniards, learning trades and technologies, adopting new cattle, seeds, and vegetables, learning forms of ordering the economic affairs of their families, houses, and persons, in short, the designs for developing a mestizo culture: "vistiéndose los desnudos y los ia bestidos mejorándose" [the naked clothed and the now-clothed bettering themselves]. This version of the statement Oñate read comes from Gaspar de Villagrá's *Historia de la Nueva México* (1992 [1610]: 136).[19] Chapter 3 traces a twofold purpose in Villagrá's *Historia*. The most obvious was to legitimize the war against Acoma. But on a second plane, a colonization of the body and subjectivity of the Acomans in the representation of their "barbarism" further complemented the ideological validation of the massacre. By means of an aesthetic of colonial violence, an epic treatment "civilizes" the "barbarity" of the Spaniards, that is, of the massacre of Acoma. Clearly, Villagrá's account of the ceremony of possession in terms of peaceful colonization in the *Historia,* which reflects the Crown's regulations on *poblar* (to settle) and *pacificar* (to pacify), is intended to justify the massacre, but we should not write off Acoma's refusal to accept Spanish "development." Inasmuch as the Acomans, and Indians in general, had their own ideas about the kinds of relations they wanted to have with the Spaniards, they should be seen as contesting Spanish rule, not as the passive subjects manipulated in Spanish accounts.

We must recall that the invasion of the northern frontier was carried out mainly by criollos (Spaniards born in America), mestizos, and such friendly Indians as the Tlaxcaltecas, who were taken to the North not only as a labor force, but also as examples of acculturation for Indians on the frontier (see chapter 2). Earlier in this introduction we saw that as early as the 1560s the *Codex of Tlatelolco* highlighted the protagonism of the Tlatelolcans in the Mixton War.[20] Furthermore, the culture of conquest that informed the push north beginning in the 1540s was as much the invention of Indians and mestizos from central Mexico as of Spaniards. "Invention" here refers to developing strategies and concepts of colonization as well as to the mental maps that fabricated the fabulous kingdoms of Cibola, Quivira, Totonteac, Chicora, and Apalache. We must also add to the mix the informants and interpreters who were forced or willingly offered themselves to lead the way and to interpret for the invading armies.

In explaining how empire works, we must keep in mind that colonialist texts *speak* colonialism in explicit, unambiguous terms. Colonial programs, representations, and theories *do things:* they formulate speech acts that structure (among other things) patterns of settlement and modes of subjecting Indians. In unmasking or de-mystifying "representations," one runs the risk of developing tau-tological descriptions of colonizing processes that reproduce the same categories that enable domination. To what extent does an assumed privileged perspective entail a historical hubris that uni-versalizes a particular version of Western culture? Do tautological reproductions of colonialism contribute to a regime of power by signaling what makes it effective? Do present-day truths perpetuate categories that further exercise colonial violence, paradoxically, by being blind to how these forms of thought were key to earlier theo-ries of colonization? My end is to move beyond these impasses that burden critiques of colonialism by foregrounding *writing violence* as a slippery terrain that inevitably haunts the project of *writing about vio-lence*. Therefore, this book not only seeks to explain what colonial-ist texts do but, in reflecting on what they do, to change our ways of thinking about colonial discourse. In denouncing colonialism we should also explore new ways of feeling that will make readers sensitive to how colonialisms past and present affect not only our intellectual work but also our daily lives.

Leyenda Negra

Outlining a critique of Spanish colonialism may contribute to the *leyenda negra* (black legend). It should be evident from the above that my concerns with the *leyenda negra* have nothing to do with a rehabilitation of the Spanish imperial enterprise—that is, of cre-ating a *leyenda blanca* (white legend) to correct the distortions of the Spanish characters by Protestant Northern Europeans. Indeed, there runs an equally pernicious Anglo-American version of the *leyenda blanca,* which became part of Nuevomexicana culture, per-haps nowhere better captured than in Nina Otero de Warren's evo-cation of an ideal Hispanic legacy in the title of her book *Old Spain in Our Southwest* (see Calderón and Saldívar 1991: 5; Padilla 1991: 46). One must underscore that the destruction of cultures, the enslave-ment and exploitation and, in some cases, wholesale extermination of peoples pertain to colonialism in general, whether of the Span-ish, French, English, Dutch, Portuguese, or U.S. variety. *Leyenda negra* ideologies are not content with mere denunciations of Spanish atrocities in the New World but constitute platforms for projecting and legitimating new colonial enterprises with a rhetoric of anti-conquest (see Pratt 1992). In one breath, sixteenth-century Protestant French or English anticonquest ideologues condemn Spanish colonialism, delegitimate Spain's exclusive rights to America, and establish territorial claims (see chapter 6). Indeed, the exponents of the *leyenda negra,* from Las Casas's reformist policies (which corresponds to one moment in the life of this great anticolonial writer) to the English and French anti-Spanish pamphleteers, simply propose better forms of colonization.

There always remains, however, the uncertainty that the modern critic of colonialism—in disbelieving Spanish "representations," in formulating more credible ethical stances, and in developing more powerful epistemologies—is not repeating the same pattern, the let-me-do-it-instead position. One need not be an apologist of conquest nor condone colonial atrocities to recognize the vitality and sophistication of Hernán Cortés's letters to Charles V, the debates between Las Casas and Sepúlveda, the complexity of Indian and mestizo historians such as Alva Ixtlilxóchitl, Alvarado Tezozómoc, and Garcilaso de la Vega, the statistical (in the sense of collecting information for the state) quality of the *Relaciones geográficas,* and, in general, the body of texts pertaining to sixteenth-century New Mexico and Florida.

It is particularly pertinent to the history of the northern frontier of New Spain that we complicate the writing and reading of colonial texts by showing their complexities and complicities, as well as recognize the repercussions reductive readings may have in the present, regardless of our good intentions. This early Spanish period of U.S. history is quickly glossed over in survey courses and textbooks even though, at least in that northern Mexican territory that became the Southwest, the descendants of the original settlers as well as recent immigrants constitute a significantly large Hispanic population, in some areas a majority. As for the Southeast, and in general for the United States, Hernando de Soto figures as the favorite son of the *Conquistadores* (note the caps and the Spanish), perhaps because there are no descendants of sixteenth-century settlers in the Southeast to lay strong cultural claims for a

Hispanic past. Coronado is also a darling *Conquistador,* but mainly due to the wacky, romantic legend that surrounded his pursuit of the legendary Seven Cities of Cibola. In the case of Cabeza de Vaca, he is taught in all standard Texas history courses, which are required to cover everything having to do with the state of Texas.[21] Otherwise, the tendency has been to cast the conquistadores as pure evil: objects of hatred that get transposed to an amorphous population of Latinos living in the United States and Latin America. And here is where the colonialist impulse of the *leyenda negra* gets tricky. For the *leyenda negra*'s definition of a corrupt, lazy, evil Spanish character fulfills the function, to paraphrase Frantz Fanon, of distorting, disfiguring, and destroying the past of an oppressed people (Fanon 1968: 211). In addressing issues concerning the *leyenda negra,* the essays in this book explore the implications of critiquing Spanish colonialism rather than elaborate a systematic study of anti-Spanish prejudice.

CHAPTER I

Reading Cabeza de Vaca, or How We
Perpetuate the Culture of Conquest

Alvar Núñez Cabeza de Vaca's *Naufragios* (literally, the Shipwrecks) is among those chronicles of the Indies that literary critics have traditionally singled out for their literary value. Insufficient attention, however, has been paid to the ideological implication of reading colonial texts for their artistic worth. Recent trends in scholarship in literary studies have critiqued the concept of the *literary* as an elitist category that serves to undermine the cultural contributions of non-Western cultures and thus perpetuate a closed canon.[1] But the preference for anthropological or historical readings that accentuate the uniqueness of the *Naufragios* as a founding text of Latin American heterogeneity or of Cabeza de Vaca as an exception to the colonial ethos of the conquistadores, paradoxically, would seem to confirm the seductive power of the *literary* at work in the *Naufragios*. We have come to understand the literary as a construct, but we have left it at that, rather than taking this insight further to analyze the force of the aesthetic — its violence.

It seems to me that the seductive powers of the *Naufragios,* that is, what makes it a brilliant literary piece, have led historians and critics alike (including recent literary and cinematic renditions) to argue that Cabeza de Vaca underwent a personal transformation that enabled him to formulate and exemplify a "peaceful conquest" (see R. Adorno 1991, 1992, 1994; Sheridan 1994; Echevarría 1989; Molloy 1987; Pastor 1988 [1983]). Take, for instance, Rolena Adorno's assessment of the differences between Nuño de Guzman and Cabeza de Vaca: "In contrast [to Guzmán], Cabeza de Vaca provided what was, to date, the most successful and the most peaceful of conquests. It was the prototype of expeditions that were to be called, according to Phillip II's 1573 laws, not conquests but 'acts of pacification'" (1991: 191). By reading the *Naufragios* in the legal context of the 1526 Ordenanzas regulating exploration and conquest, we come to question the purported originality of Cabeza de Vaca's advocacy of peaceful colonization. We need, moreover, to attend to the ways in which the oxymoron "peaceful conquest" manages to negotiate colonial dominance with hegemonic consent: the right kind of treatment will ensure that potentially "hostile" Indians will turn out "servile." The oxymoron also remains blind to, hence complicitous with, the rhetorical slippages in Cabeza de Vaca's texts where ideology (hegemonic will) gives way to violence (dominance) (cf. Guha 1997). Although toward the end of the *Naufragios* Cabeza de Vaca outlines an ideal form of imperialism and casts himself as an equally ideal servant of the Crown, it is the *Comentarios,* an account of Cabeza de Vaca's political fiasco in the Río de la Plata written by his amanuensis Pero Hernández, that dwells at length on his efforts to enforce colonial law in a colonial outpost ruled by terror. The power of the *Naufragios,* on the other hand, resides in the story of shipwreck, of complete loss of material civilization, of becoming a shaman, and of immersion in an Indian world. Colonial laws, nevertheless, constitute a subtext of the *Naufragios.*

Why privilege the *Naufragios* over the *Comentarios,* which, in spite of Cabeza de Vaca's pathetic return to Spain in chains, presents his account of the Río de la Plata as an exemplary history with moral and political lessons? What cultural forms and reading patterns inform literary appraisals of colonial texts, in particular the *Naufragios,* to the point of ignoring their colonialist impulse and their reduction of Native Americans to either servile or hostile characters in the Spanish imperial plot in the Americas? What deeply embedded historiographical prejudices keep these readings today from making allowances for indigenous rights to violently oppose Spanish invasions? Obviously, historians and anthropologists also tend to partake of these ethnocentric constructs in their use of colonial documents. I highlight literary criticism because this discipline purports to do the kind of textual and discursive analyses that ought to make manifest the rhetorical strategies that authorize representations of colonial encounters. It would turn out to be somewhat paradoxical, if not ironic, that the "literary turn" (beyond the so-called linguistic turn, I am thinking of the aesthetic mediations and literary tropes that lend force to representations of reality), which has had an important role in redefining work in anthropology and history, had bypassed literary and cultural critics in their urge to deconstruct the *literary* (see, e.g., White 1973, 1978, 1987a; Clifford 1988, 1997; Clifford and Marcus 1986).

THE CULTURE OF CONQUEST

I shall begin by quoting from a letter by Joseph Conrad to R. B. Cunninghame Graham, dated 26 December 1903, congratulating him on the publication of a book on Hernando de Soto, conqueror and explorer of Florida and the southeastern United States. The tone of the praise and the general colonial context in which it is inscribed exemplify the ubiquitous recurrence of what I define in this chapter as the culture of conquest:

> H. de Soto is most exquisitely excellent: your very mark and spirit upon a subject that only you can do justice to—with your wonderful English and your sympathetic insight into the souls of the Conquistadores. The glamour, the pathos and the romance of that time and of those men are only adequately, truthfully, conveyed to us by your pen; the sadness, the glory and the romance of the endeavour together with the vanity of vanities of the monstrous achievement are reflected in your unique style as though you had been writing of men with whom you had slept by the camp fire after tethering your horses on the threshold of the unknown. (Quoted in Watts 1969: 148)

Cabeza de Vaca is without a doubt one of the most romantic of the conquistadores. His writings inaugurate some of the most vivid and familiar topoi in representations of colonial encounters. (By topoi I mean those discursive spaces and places of memory—barbarism, cannibalism, superstition, evolutionary stages, as well as shipwreck and its travails, saintliness, going native—that written accounts reelaborate in the construction of a Western self and a colonial subject as its Other.)[2] The *Naufragios,* however, also stands out for its reversals of the stock images used in representing the Spanish versus Indian binary: it is the Spaniards who eat each other, undergo a complete loss of material civilization, suffer a political and ethical breakdown, and depend on Indian knowledge for sur-

Reading Cabeza de Vaca

vival. In this story shipwreck becomes a metaphor—quite in the literal sense of transport in Greek—that marks the movement from order to chaos. It is this metaphor that underlies both the fascination this text has produced for modern critics, leading them to raise it to the status of literature, as well as the anxiety it provoked among some of Cabeza de Vaca's contemporaries, leading them to censor passages in official chronicles.[3] If there is in Cabeza de Vaca's narrative a self-conscious hesitation to spell out figurative meanings, other "autobiographical" gestures and "novelesque" episodes interrupt the straightforward chronicle of events and thus call our attention to an expected tropological reading, one attentive to the vehicles that carry the imagination from the concrete to the abstract, from the particular to the universal (see Tyler 1986: 132; White 1978: 1–25). For a sixteenth-century European audience avid for adventure stories in exotic places, the wanderings through oceans, rivers, deserts, and jungles were not just traces on the face of the earth, to be reproduced in maps and written accounts, but historical figures, events with a transcendental significance. Indeed, explorers and conquerors wrote and designed their narratives anticipating that allegorical meanings would be drawn from the events. The conquistadores knew that their feats would be read as if they were inscriptions in golden letters on the pages of history. Therein lies the power and seduction of their self-consciously elaborate narratives and their contribution to the culture of conquest of colonial myths and anthropological categories that still haunt much of Western ethnography, literary criticism, and fiction.

Recent studies of the literary character of the so-called *crónicas* (a generic term that encompasses texts ranging from letters to multivolume histories) and in particular of Cabeza de Vaca's *Naufragios* have broadened our understanding and appreciation of their rhetorical and aesthetic sophistication (e.g., Maura 1995; Pupo-Walker 1987, 1992; Pastor 1988 [1983]; Carreño 1987; Invernizzi 1987; Molloy 1987; Barrera 1985; Dowling 1984; Barrera and Mora 1983; Lewis 1982; Lagmanovich 1978; Hart 1974). It is my belief, however, that we ought to step back and consider wherein lies the literary quality and charm of conquest narratives before defining a literary canon that would tend to perpetuate a whole array of ethnocentric terms, for example, the uncritical use of evolutionary categories, the reduction of the corpus of Spanish-American literature to texts written in Spanish, and the definition of literary value exclusively according to Western conventions.[4] Furthermore, we should note that even though Cabeza de Vaca portrays himself as a benevolent colonial official, he nonetheless reproduces on a symbolic level the colonial myths that structure and articulate the same violence he condemns. His denunciations, for instance, retain and reiterate the belief in the natural subordination of Native Americans to Spanish rule, the definition of cannibalism as a culinary aberration that warrants the destruction of a culture, and the reduction of native knowledge to sham and superstition inspired by the devil. Even when one can read ambivalence and playful reversals in Cabeza de Vaca's stock images of Indians in the *Naufragios*, we need to understand how the *Comentarios'* denunciation of Spanish terror uses these same images to accentuate the illegality and rampant abuse of Indians in the Río de la Plata. Current preferences for a Cabeza de Vaca who undergoes a conversion from what can only be a stereotype of a greedy conquistador to a panoply of "good" traits—critic of empire (Pastor 1988 [1983]), advocate of peaceful conquest (Howard 1997; R. Adorno 1991, 1992, 1994), first Chicano (Bruce Novoa 1993; Valdez and Steiner 1972), first Spanish transculturator of Indian culture (Spitta 1995)—suggest a need for a homey *Madre Patria*, for a counterdiscourse to the *leyenda negra*, for a founding moment of Latin America and modernity where imperialism was not always "bad." Thus, these readings manage to critique imperialism while retaining a redeemable view of Spanish colonialism in exceptional individuals. Have we been seduced by Cabeza de Vaca into an uncritical participation in and reproduction of the culture of conquest?

Joseph Conrad's letter to R. B. Cunninghame Graham, also known as Don Roberto, supports the notion that we always write from a specific time and place and that ultimately we should be responsible for our participation within the colonial legacy that determines our discourse. In an essay on *Nostromo*, Conrad's novel of exploitation and revolution in South America, Edward Said has pointed out that to the extent that we can see Conrad both "criticizing and reproducing the imperial ideology of his time," we have today the alternative between "the projection, or the refusal, of the

wish to dominate, the capacity to damn or the energy to comprehend and engage other societies, traditions, histories" (1988: 72). Indeed, we can further define the culture of conquest, what Said calls
our "Gringo eyes," through Conrad's letter. Conrad's praise of Don
Roberto's book on Hernando de Soto for its splendid, realistic capturing of the spirit of the conquistadores is followed by an indictment of the Belgian enterprise in the Congo and its recruits from
"the souteneurs, sous-offs, maquereaux, fruits-sec of all sorts on
the pavements of Brussels and Antwerp" (in Watts 1969: 149). Don
Roberto's book, adds Conrad, "gives me a furious desire to learn
Spanish and bury myself in the pages of the incomparable Garcilaso—if only to forget all about our modern Conquistadores" (148).
There is a nostalgia for the conquistadores, even an escapist yearn-
ing for the delightful prose of Inca Garcilaso de la Vega.

And yet, in Conrad's letter the Belgian enterprise in the Congo
still retains an aura of romance and adventure in the figure of Roger
Casement, who has, as Conrad puts it, "a touch of the Conquistador in him too." Conrad explains: "For I've seen him start off into
an incomparable wilderness swinging a crookhandled stick for all
weapons, with two bull dogs: Paddy (white) and Biddy (brindle) at
his heels and a Loanda boy carrying a bundle for all company"; he
adds that "some particle of Las Casas's soul had found refuge in
his indefatigable body" (in Watts 1969: 149). This image of Casement emerging from the wilderness "a little leaner, a little browner,
with his stick, dogs, and Loanda boy" reiterates the commonplace
in colonial literature of intrepid adventurers enduring the wilderness, but it also underlies much of the nostalgia in contemporary
films—*Passage to India, Out of Africa, The Mission*—for the colonial
period in the face of the absolutely unromantic Third World of the
postcolonial world order (see Rosaldo 1989). As I will point out later
on, Nicolás Echevarría's film *Cabeza de Vaca* (1990) mingles the portrayal of a nostalgic Cabeza de Vaca brooding for home with a celebration of a conquistador who deep down is really the origin of *us,*
the late-twentieth-century Mexicans: "Ellos, como Cabeza de Vaca,
comenzaron siendo unos pocos, ahora somos casi todo un país; una
cadena que se ha convertido en columna vertebral de nuestra cultura" [They, like Cabeza de Vaca, began being a few, now we are
almost a whole country; a chain that has become the vertebrate col-

umn of our culture] (Sheridan 1994: 15). One cannot but wonder who remains outside of the *somos casi todo un país,* "the vertebrate column of our culture." We will return to this question.

Those familiar with Michael Taussig's study in terror and healing, as he subtitles his *Shamanism, Colonialism and the Wild Man,* will recall his discussion of Conrad's letter to Don Roberto, the allusion to "a man called Casement," the importance of the latter's critical report in the early 1910s documenting the atrocities committed by the Peruvian Amazon Company during the rubber boom along the Putumayo River, and, more important for the purposes of this chapter, the topoi of nostalgia and its recurrence in the culture of conquest (Taussig 1987: 11–15).

Taussig reminds us that in both the defense and condemnation of the rubber industry in the Putumayo, truth hinged on the semantics of Spanish terms such as *conquistar, reducir, rescatar,* and *correrías,* which were first coined in the sixteenth century. Thus, Julio César Arana, the "soul" of the Peruvian side of the Peruvian and British rubber consortium in the Putumayo, explains in a report to the British House of Commons committee in charge of investigating the abuses: "Esa palabra 'Conquistar,' que según me han dicho en inglés suena muy fuerte, nosotros la usamos en español para atraer a una persona, conquistar sus simpatias" [This word "Conquistar," from what I have been told in English, sounds very strong. We use it in Spanish to attract a person, to conquer their sympathies] (quoted in Taussig 1987: 28). Arana's definition echoes volumes of Spanish colonial legislation that formulated peaceful approaches to conquest or, as it came to be called, *pacificación* (see chapter 2). For our purposes it makes no difference whether Arana was deceiving the committee or simply reflecting a way of speaking among the Whites in the Putumayo. What is central to our discussion is that the uncritical acceptance of "peaceful colonization," as a process of gaining the sympathies of Indians, remains a commonplace in studies of Cabeza de Vaca. From the committee's discussions on the semantics of Spanish colonial lingo, we learn that little is to be gained from squabbling over the correct meaning or even from documenting what really happened. From Taussig we learn that "when we put the two languages together it is not the blending of force with what Rocha called the art of persuasion that results, but a quite different conception [that] dissolves those domains so that violence and ideology, power and knowledge, become one—as with terror" (29). By dissolving the separation of the domains of violence and ideology we may call into question the difference between Cabeza de Vaca's colonial approach and that of slave raiders such as Nuño de Guzmán, between "good" and "bad" conquistadores, between the law and its criminals.

ADMONISHING SUBJECTS

In fact, if we based our perception on the language of the colonial laws regulating conquests in *Las ordenanzas sobre el buen tratatamiento de los indios* (The ordinances regarding the good treatment of Indians) of 1526, which were physically included in the *capitulaciones* (contracts) between Pánfilo de Narváez, the governor of the expedition, and the Crown (as in every other contract drafted between 1526 and 1540, including those of Francisco Vázquez de Coronado, Francisco Pizarro, Hernando de Soto, as well as Cabeza de Vaca's for the Río de la Plata), we would have to rule in favor of Arana's definition of *conquista* (Morales Padrón 1979: 374–79; *CDI,* 16: 67–87). But the passage from the language of love into a regime of (legal or criminal) terror seems to have escaped the good conscience of the critics of the rubber boom and the current celebrators of Cabeza de Vaca alike. As the title of the Ordenanzas underscores, it is the Crown that defines the proper behavior toward Indians. I summarize below the main points of the Ordenanzas to provide a background for reading Cabeza de Vaca as well as to further clarify the culture of conquest.[5] It would be more appropriate to speak of the laws as background in the sense that they are constitutive rules of truth and rightfulness in Cabeza de Vaca's accounts. The laws also structure the questionnaires in the *probanzas* (proofs) taken on his return in chains from the Río de la Plata. If in writing the *Naufragios* Cabeza de Vaca assumes familiarity with the Ordenanzas (though they are never explicitly mentioned), what are we to say about the privilege we grant to the *Crown's language of love* in current readings of the *Naufragios* as a "model for peaceful colonization," a "transcultural text," or a "critique of empire"? What in our postcolonial sensibilities keeps us from seeing the flip side of law and right, a menacing regime of terror, in Cabeza de Vaca's language?

Las ordenanzas sobre el buen tratatamiento de los Indios (1526) contains twelve chapters:

1. If, on the expeditions, any of the Crown's subjects committed "muertes y robos, y excesos y desaguizados" [deaths and thefts and excesses and damages] or "herraron índios *contra razón y justicia*" [enslaved Indians *contrary to reason and justice*], governors and officers of the Crown were under the obligation to investigate these acts and to write a *relación* (an account) on the expedition (Morales Padrón 1979: 375).

2. This chapter lists a series of abuses that should be avoided and corrected (e.g., "Indios [tenidos] por esclavos sacados e traídos de sus tierras y naturaleza *injusta e indebidamente,* los saquen de su poder" [Enslaved Indians who have been removed and taken from their lands and nature *unjustly and illegally* must be removed from their power] [376]), and specifies that "si los dichos indios fueren cristianos no se han de volver á sus tierras, *aunque ellos lo quieran* si no estuvieren [los de sus tierras] convertidos a nuestra santa fe catolica por el peligro que a sus ánimas se les puede seguir" [if such were Christian they must not be sent back to their lands *even if they might want to go* if those (in their lands) had not converted to our holy Christian faith because of the danger to their souls that could follow them] (376).

3. All enterprises must include at least two friars or clerics "para la instrucción y enseñamiento de los dichos indios y pedricación y conversión dellos conforme a la *bula de la concesión* de las dichas Indias a la corona Real destos Reynos" [for the instruction and teaching of the said Indians and preaching and conversion in conformity to *the bull of the concession* of the said Indies to the Royal crown of these kingdoms] (376; my emphasis).

4. Friars and clerics have the responsibility of making sure Indians are treated well ("sean bien tratados") and of immediately reporting any abuses ("de nos avisar luego") (376).

5. Captains and all others with a licence to make "descubrimien-

tos o poblaciones o rescates . . . lo hayan de hacer y hagan *con acuerdo y parecer* de nuestros oficiales . . . y de los clerigos" [discoveries and settlements or tradings . . . must *act in agreement and in consultation* with our officials . . . and the clerics] (376–77; my emphasis).

6. All captains and officials must seek to acquire a *lengua* (literally, a tongue, i.e., interpreter) to declare to the Indians how they were sent to teach them good mores, to correct the vice of eating human flesh, instruct them in the Faith, and to subject them to the sovereignty of the Crown so that they can be better treated than they are now, with the stipulation that if they do not comply, war and enslavement would be the consequences—in short, to convey the substance of the *Requerimiento:* "Mandamos que lleve el dicho requerimiento . . . y que se lo notifique y hagan entender particularmente por los dichos intérpretes una y dos y más veces cuantas pareciere . . . y fueren necesarias para que lo entiendan" [We order that the said requirement be carried . . . and that it be made public and made understood individually by the said interpreter one and two and more times as many as are considered . . . and are necessary for them to understand it] (377).

7. Once having read the *Requerimiento,* fortresses must be built in suitable places but without harming Indians: "Antes mandamos que les haga buen tratamiento y buenas obras . . . de manera que por ello y por ejemplo de sus vidas . . . vengan en conocimiento de nuestra fe y *en amor y gana de ser nuestros vasallos*" [Rather, we order that they are treated well and with good deeds . . . so that by those means and by the good example of their lives . . . they come to know our faith, and *to love and desire being our vassals*] (377; my emphasis).

8. Indians must always be treated fairly and never forced into transactions (*rescates*) (377).

9. No one must take slaves, unless, after having been admonished by clerics, Indians refuse to give their obedience to the Crown ("salvo en caso *que no quisier darnos la obediencia*"). This chapter also makes allowances for slavery in cases where Indians resist not only the summons of the *Requerimiento* but the rights Spaniards have to exploit natural resources: "O no consintieren, resistiendo o defendiendo con mano armada; que no se busquen minas . . . permitimos . . . *hacer guerra en ella* aquello que los derechos de nuestra santa fe y religión cris-

tiana permiten y mandan que se haga" [Or if they do not consent, and resist or defend themselves with arms; and do not allow the search for mines . . . *we permit war and in it allow* all that the right of our faith and Christian religion allow and order to be done] (378; my emphasis).

10. The said captains cannot compel Indians to go to work in the mines, but if they freely choose to go, the Crown allows for their employment as free persons; however, the captains are under the obligation to dissuade them from eating human flesh, making sacrifices, and practicing sodomy; to instruct them in Christianity; and to pay them for their work and service "lo que merecieren y fuera razonable, *considerada la calidad* de sus personas y la condición de la tierra" [what they deserve and is reasonable, *according to the quality* of their persons and condition of the land] (378; my emphasis).

11. If the quality and condition and "habilidad de dichos indios" (ability of the said Indians) to stop eating human flesh, practicing sodomy, and so on would benefit from their being subjects of an *encomienda* (tribute paid to Spaniards in exchange for instruction in the faith), the said clerics and friars can give them an *encomienda;* the *ordenanza* adds that the clerics and friars must provide "*información verdadera de la calidad y habilidad* de los dichos Indios y relación de lo que cerca dello hubieren ordenado [en a las encomiendas]" [*true information regarding the quality and ability* of the said Indians, and an account of the order they had followed] in establishing the *encomiendas* (378; my emphasis).

12. *Pobladores* (settlers) and conquistadores who have a license to *rescatar y poblar é descubrir* (trade and settle and discover) can staff their enterprises only with people from the kingdoms of Castille and other people not forbidden.

These laws form an outstandingly tight mesh capable both of regulating violence as well as providing mechanisms to control information. I have italicized terms that mark the slippage from the language of love, consent, and peaceful colonization to a regime of right and reason that justifies war, slavery, and even atrocities. The terms *calidad* (quality) and *habilidad* (ability) establish the criteria for an anthropological assessment of the most appropriate modes of *subjecting* Indians to the Crown, or, if necessary, of exterminating them.[6] *Razón* (reason) and *derecho* (right, law) constitute both a language to justify war as well as the justification of the consequences, that is, slavery, massacres, extermination.

The inclusion of the *Requerimiento* in the *capitulaciones* signals the priority of political subjection to religious conversion. The most primitive version of the *Requerimiento* played the role of a remedy, as it were, for establishing peace by explaining the Indians' obligation to recognize Spain's sovereignty over their lands as the condition for ending war. The formal version included in the Ordenanzas was first read by Pedrarias Dāvila in the Darien in 1514 and by such other conquistadores as Cortés in Mexico, but was not a legal stipulation in *capitulaciones* until 1526.[7] Cortés, given the need to justify mutiny, mentions its reading extensively to highlight the legality of his enterprise as well as to assuage the conscience of the Crown. In the *capitulaciones* with Pánfilo de Narváez (who held the title of governor in the disastrous expedition to Florida told in the *Naufragios*), the Crown's response to Narvaéz's request (*CDI*, 10:45) to enslave warlike Indians makes enslavement conditional on reading the *Requerimiento:* "Doy licencia y facultad a vos . . . para que a los indios que fueren rebeldes, siendo amonestados y requeridos, los podais tomar por esclavos" [I grant you the license and faculty . . . to enslave Indian rebels, after they have been admonished and required to recognize Spanish sovereignty] (*CDI*, 16: 72). Lest we want to idealize Cabeza de Vaca's emphasis on love as a unique formulation of peaceful colonization, we should trace this legal subtext in his writings. The force of the *Naufragios* and the *Comentarios* resides as much in Cabeza de Vaca's circumscription of the events and his acts according to the law as in the colonial topoi of shipwreck, going native, and becoming a shaman. From Cabeza de Vaca to Arana and beyond, the colonial world conveys fascination for as well as repulsion from the intertwinings of law, aesthetics, and violence.

Even the rubber boom has its myths, picturesque characters, and nostalgia for past adventure. Rivera's *La vorágine,* as Taussig reminds us, inspired more than one person to migrate "to the Putumayo on account of the mysterious excitement it conveyed about the jungle" (1987: 111); as critical as *La vorágine* might be of the rubber industry, "it is always the colonial view of the jungle that provides the means of representing and trying to make sense of the colonial situation"

Writing Violence on the Northern Frontier

(77). This colonial view of the jungle recurs in anecdotes about such historical characters, savvy in native ways, as Don Crisóstomo, who "would spend nights orating with Indian men around the tobacco pot, seducing them into doing his bidding with the power of *his* story telling" (108). According to Joaquín Rocha, who traveled the region at the turn of the century, Don Crisóstomo became "not only for the Indians the seductive orator and the invincible man of arms but also by these means something greater—because for the Huitotos he was their king and God" (108). And we all know that stories of men who would be kings and gods abound in the European repertoire of colonial myths. But let me round off the question of nostalgia with one more quotation drawn by Taussig from the epigraph to París Lozano's *Guerrilleros de Tolima,* a study of the War of One Thousand Days (1899–1901), that implicitly comments on the picturesqueness of Don Crisóstomo: "Aquellos eran otros hombres, más hombres que los de tiempos presentes, más bravos en la acción y más sazonados en la palabra" [Those were other men, more men than those of today, wilder in action and more seasoned in the word] (quoted in Taussig 1987: 109). These twentieth-century people and events in the Putumayo strike us as repetitions of legendary characters and atrocities already described in Cabeza de Vaca's accounts. Indeed, many pages in Taussig's study illustrate terror, exploitation, and seduction that could have been drawn from documents of Cabeza de Vaca's failed governorship in the Río de la Plata. Moreover, Casement, like Cabeza de Vaca, is a critic-ethnographer who reiterates on a symbolic level the mythology that structures and articulates the violence he denounces. We may accordingly define the culture of conquest as a set of beliefs, images, and categories that tends to determine the ideology not only of those who perpetrate atrocities but also of those who condemn them. With these preliminaries in mind, let us now examine Cabeza de Vaca's writings.

MISPLACING THE FICTIONAL

Born in Jerez de la Frontera sometime between 1490 and 1507 (little is known of his early life), Cabeza de Vaca participated as treasurer and *alguacil mayor* (provost marshal) in Pánfilo de Narváez's expedition to Florida. (This is the same Narváez who tried to topple Cortés at the beginning of the conquest of Mexico.) The expedition sailed from San Lúcar on 17 June 1527, stopped in Santo Domingo and Santiago de Cuba, and tried to get from Trinidad to Havana when a wind blew them toward Florida, where they landed on 12 April 1528. Thus began a disastrous expedition in which "four hundred men and eighty horses in four ships and a brigantine" were reduced to four survivors who stumbled into Culiacan, Sinaloa, in March 1537 after crossing Texas, New Mexico, Arizona, and the Mexican states of Chihuahua and Sonora.[8] Those that encounter them there are left speechless and amazed, as Cabeza de Vaca explains: "Y otro dia de mañana alcance quatro christianos de cauallo que recibieron gran alteracion de verme tan extrañamente vestido y en compañia de indios. Estuuieronme mirando mucho espacio de tiempo, tan atonitos que ni me hablauan ni acertauan a preguntarme nada" [And the next morning I overtook four mounted Christians, who were thunderstruck to see me so strangely dressed and in the company of Indians. They went on staring at me for a long space of time, so astonished that they could neither speak to me nor manage to ask me anything] (*CLD*, 5: 126; Núñez Cabeza de Vaca 1993: 110).[9]

Images of this kind convey the "mythic stuff" of Cabeza de Vaca's story and its attractiveness to both a sixteenth- and a late-twentieth-century audience. In Todorov's typology of attitudes toward Otherness in *The Conquest of America,* the *Naufragios* exemplifies, for instance, an evolved ethnographic viewpoint: "Cabeza de Vaca also reached a neutral point, not because he was indifferent to the two cultures but because he had experienced them both from within— thereby, he no longer had anything but 'the others' around him; without becoming an Indian, Cabeza de Vaca was no longer quite a Spaniard. His experience symbolizes and heralds that of the modern exile" (1987: 249). Todorov's narrative of an evolving ethnographic consciousness manifests a Western need to believe in its privileged capacity to understand other cultures. It is far from obvious whether Cabeza de Vaca would have recognized the value of not being the Other and yet not quite the same, in Todorov's characterization, but in his accounts there is certainly a self-representation as a benevolent, enlightened colonial official dutifully pursuing the interests of the Crown. Cabeza de Vaca sought the governorship of Florida, but by the time he returned to Spain in 1538, it had already been assigned to Hernando de Soto. Nevertheless, Cabeza de Vaca did gain the title of *adelantado* and governor of the Province of Río de la Plata, where he sailed on 2 November 1540. Five years later, Cabeza de Vaca returned to Spain in chains, accused of crimes ranging from such minor offenses as robbing the inhabitants of the Canary Islands of three cows on his outward journey to murdering friendly Indians, confiscating the property of Spaniards, and, the ultimate crime of sedition, calling himself king of the land; he was first jailed and then held under house arrest in a Madrid inn for a total of eight years (see Bishop 1933: 276–78; Graham 1968 [1924]: 157–60; Howard 1997: 187–91). The *Comentarios,* written by his secretary and amanuensis, Pero Hernández, tell us about these political failures.

Although the *Naufragios* and the *Comentarios* are generally published together, at least in the original Spanish versions, only the *Naufragios* has been singled out as one of the most accomplished narratives of the Conquest from a literary point of view. With the exception of Juan Francisco Maura (1989, 1995), who reads the *Naufragios* as a series of trumped-up extraordinary events intended to gain political favors, literary critics generally agree in finding a tension between the historical account of events and novelesque episodes, between an exceptional objective capacity to relate simply what was seen and a notable autobiographical projection (e.g., Pupo Walker 1987, 1992; Pastor 1988 [1983]; Dowling 1984; Lewis 1982; Lagmanovich 1978). Scholars generally find these separations clear-cut and insist that the *Naufragios* can be studied as literature as well as chronicle. Accordingly, critics identify a series of short stories seen as intercalated in an account of real events. Drawing mainly from the work of Mircea Eliade, however, Silvia Spitta (1995) has argued that those passages read by critics as novelesque actually contain anthropological information on shamanism, which testify to the deep immersion of Cabeza de Vaca in native culture. I will return to the anthropological reading of the *Naufragios.*

For now, let us look at how Lee Dowling has defined the distinction between story and discourse as the terms that enable literary claims (1984: 94). Story (the chronicle of events) is presumed separate from discourse (the commentary on the events). Dowling argues that such a distinction entails the priority of story to discourse, a concept that not only is suspect in fiction but reintroduces a false opposition because "it is debatable whether a story exists at all apart from the discourse" (97). The separation of story from discourse keeps us from seeing how both elements contribute to the formation and development of a plot in the *Naufragios*. The separation of story and discourse, then, does not make sense if we want to read the *Naufragios* as fiction. Only when we read the text as history is the distinction apt; then, as Dowling puts it, "the ferreting out of the true nature of the 'story' through historical investigation assumes real importance" (97). This line of reasoning suggests that the opposition of story and discourse is not inherent in the text but a product of our reading. The tension between fiction and history would, in the end, be the tension between seeing the *Naufragios* as similar either to adventure stories or to autobiography and historical account.[10]

Despite the problems with reading the *Naufragios* as fiction, it seems to me that displacing the tension to a historical reading creates, in turn, a false opposition: it is precisely the narrative form that creates similarities between history and fiction and makes each of them meaningful and truthful accounts (see White 1989a). The priority of story over discourse is false in fiction, but it is perhaps accurate to postulate the priority of meaning over facts, that is, of discourse over story in history (see Barthes 1981b: 16–17). The *Naufragios* is not simply an account of what happened because the significance of its facts depends on the instructions from the Crown, the required numerous readings of the *Requerimiento,* and in general an ideology of conquest that defines not only a legal framework but also general parameters of prudence and chivalry. In a *relación,* the failure to recite the *Requerimiento* would hardly constitute an inconsequential "factual" detail, for the Ordenanzas of 1526 required conquistadores and clerics to read it to Indians to legalize their political subjection to the Crown. Dowling's reduction of history to "what really happened" presumes that events can be constituted independently of ideological constraints and legal frameworks. Furthermore, Dowling's observation would imply that a *relación* could limit itself to providing a truthful account. In fact, the opposition between fiction and history that literary critics have found in the *Naufragios* could be explained as the result of a coexistence of different modes of writing about the past which would correspond to the different degrees of narrativity in *relaciones,* chronicles, and histories in the proper sense of the term (White 1989b; see also Lewis 1982: 686). There is indeed a self-conscious suspension of narrative resolution in the *Naufragios,* which hardly keeps the story of particular events from having universal significance.

Let us further observe how meaning and ideology define facts and how facts, in turn, provide lessons in some passages from Gonzalo Fernández de Oviedo's *Historia general y natural de las Indias,* in which he included a version of the *Informe Conjunto* (*Joint Report*) from Cabeza de Vaca, Alonso de Castillo, and Andrés Dorantes, the three surviving Spaniards. (Note that the fourth is a Black named Esteban, who does not have a last name, never counts as a full member of the expedition, and is mentioned only incidentally in Oviedo's version of the *Joint Report.*) After giving a summary of how the party's pursuit of Apalache ended up in disaster according to the *Joint Report,* which Oviedo finds more trustworthy than the *Naufragios,* he provides a parenthetical comment on the folly of Narváez and the Spaniards who followed him: "Querría yo que me dijesen qué les predicaron esos frailes e Pánfilo de Narváez a aquellos españoles que tan ciegos se fueron, dejando sus patrias tras falsas palabras" [I wanted them to tell me what those friars and Pánfilo de Narváez preached to those Spaniards that led them to venture so blindly, leaving their fatherland behind in pursuit of false words] (*HGN,* 4: 290).[11] His preference for the *Joint Report* has to do with how the narrative structure of the *Naufragios* invests events with meanings, not with disputing their occurrence. It is beside the point that Oviedo implicitly accepts Cabeza de Vaca's account of how he required Narváez not to continue the inland exploration without placing the ships in a safe haven. For Oviedo also draws from Cabeza de Vaca as he identifies him as a source in the *Joint Report,* "que es el que esto cuenta" [who is the one who tells this], how the governor refused to assist their boat, abdicating his responsibility as governor, "que hiciese lo que pudiese, que no era tiempo de aguardar a nadie" [that he must do what he could, that it was not time to wait for anybody] (291–92).

Indeed, a ferreting out of the true story of who said what and when would ultimately be a minor detail if not an irrelevant point from a sixteenth-century understanding of history (cf. Dowling 1984: 95–97). What matters is that the disaster holds a moral lesson for future explorations: "Es cosa que aunque no tiene remedio ni enmienda, tiene alguna parte aviso, o le causará esta relación" [Although this does not have a remedy nor correction, it does hold some kind of lesson, or this account will bring it forth] (*HGN,* 4: 291). There is a lesson in the disaster, and Oviedo adds that it will be brought forth by his own version of the events. History is allegorical beyond the intent of the participants; it is precisely the task of the historian to draw moral meanings and practical lessons from the events. Narváez and the friars were wrong in choosing to abandon the ships but also in seducing the others into proceeding without having a description of the territories made by previous explorers: "En este tractado hallarán de qué temer e de qué se deban recelar los que nuevas empresas de aquestas toman, pues cada día veo que las procuran e traen hombres al carnero, sin saber dónde los llevan, ni ellos adónde se van ni a quién siguen" [Those who are about to embark on this kind of new enterprise will find in this treatise what to watch out for and avoid, because every day I see how some begin new ones and lead men to the charnel house, without knowing where they are taking them, nor the others where they are going nor whom they are following] (*HGN,* 4: 291). There is a moral lesson to be derived from the events: for events to be meaningful, they must follow rules of procedure such as reading the *Requerimiento* several times, retaining a balance of power among the clergy, the officials of the Crown, and the governor, and keeping a written account of all transactions among Spaniards and with Indians. The dependence of relevant facts on instructions coupled with the possibility of transforming these facts into a moral history suggest that not only are facts the product of interpretation, but that ideology itself is also constitutive of action and sensibility. Oviedo spells out a moral reading that Cabeza de Vaca suggests but never brings to completion.

In fact, Oviedo sought to control the meaning of the *Naufragios:* "En alguna manera yo tengo por buena la relación de los tres, e por más clara que estrota que el uno sólo hace e hizo imprimir" [In a way, I take the account of the three as the good one, and clearer than this other one that he (Cabeza de Vaca) alone gives and has published] (*HGN*, 4: 315). Oviedo's ascription to the text of a lack of clarity manifests an ethnocentric view that has blocked an ethnographic reading of the *Naufragios*. By ethnographic reading I do not mean one that would elicit information on the peoples Cabeza de Vaca encountered or would identify the healing practices he describes, but rather one attentive to the narrative of a first encounter, the questioning of one's culture that results from empathetic descriptions of difference, the experience of magical phenomena that could only be read as miracles according to the criteria of the epoch, in short, one attentive to the historiographical difficulties Cabeza de Vaca encountered in telling the story of his experience of customs contrary to Western values. How does Cabeza de Vaca communicate a whole series of cultural phenomena usually associated with heresy, witchcraft, and superstition?[12]

We must insist that Cabeza de Vaca's task is not simply to convey New World phenomena to a European audience—his reversals of stock images manifest a mastery of the code—but to convey a sense of the uncanny that underlies his experience of the magical. In his classic study, "The Uncanny," Freud provides a way to read the *Naufragios* as a text that brings to light what should have remained secret: "According to [Schelling] everything is *unheimlich* that ought to have remained secret and hidden but has come to light." Freud complicates Schelling's definition by emphasizing an inherent ambiguity in the term *heimlich:* "On the one hand, it means what is familiar and agreeable, and on the other, what is concealed and kept out." Furthering this train of thought, Freud arrives at: "Thus *heimlich* is a word the meaning of which develops in the direction of ambivalence, until it finally coincides with its opposite, *unheimlich*" (1955, 17: 225–26). Eventually Freud reconciles these contradictory definitions that emphasize ambiguity by means of the concept of repression, in which the uncanny "is in reality nothing new or alien, but something which is familiar and old—established in the mind and which has become alienated from it only through the process of repression" (17:241). This chain of terms in the end generates the sense of the "canny" as homely, as origin, as womb, as the mother's genitals—what becomes uncanny by being brought to light. Shipwreck in Cabeza de Vaca's narrative marks the transition to a primordial time signified by physical nakedness and the revelation that European civilization is a very thin veneer, easily forgotten. This return to a first time entails not only a complete loss of material civilization, but also a complete dependence on Amerindian knowledge—including a plurality of possible worlds in which magic makes sense, works. Does Oviedo's concern with lack of clarity in the *Naufragios* actually betray his anxiety with respect to Cabeza de Vaca's revelations of "home"? Do contemporary critics domesticate the uncanny by classifying passages as novelesque, as made up, fictional stories (see, e.g., Maura 1995; Pupo-Walker 1987, 1992; Pastor 1988 [1983]; Barrera 1985; Barrera and Mora 1983; Lagmanovich 1978)? I would add that *irony* in the *Naufragios* is not accidental. Indeed, Oviedo seeks to control the significance of the events narrated in the *Naufragios* not only by spelling out the meaning of events, but also by limiting his version to the "clearer" account of the *Joint Report*.

In attributing a tension between fiction and history, critics have obviated the discussion of what they have assumed to be an antithetical relation between these terms. The concept of allegoresis, as defined by Hayden White, enables us to surpass this binary opposition: "Precisely insofar as the historical narrative endows sets of real events with the kinds of meaning found otherwise only in myth and literature, we were justified in regarding it as a product of *allegoresis*. Therefore rather than regard every historical narrative as mythic or ideological in nature, we should regard it as allegorical, that is, as saying one thing and meaning another" (1989a: 45). According to White, myth, fiction, and history share the systems of meaning production that have been produced by a given culture, group, or people. If "the contents of myth are tested by fiction," historical narratives test the capacity the typifications of fiction have "to endow 'real' events with meaning" (45). White follows Quintilian's definition of ironic allegory, in which "meaning is contrary to that

suggested by the words" (*Institutio Oratoria,* bk. 8, chap. 6, line 54).
What is crucial to allegory is the simultaneity of at least two equally
valid readings. We can further complement the meaning of allegory in ethnographic work with James Clifford's observation that
allegory (from the Greek *allos,* "other," and *agorevein,* "speak") is "a
representation that 'interprets' itself" (1986: 99). The allegorical as
defined by White and Clifford open the *Naufragios* to at least two
double registers: whereas for White passages "say one thing and
mean another," for Clifford "representations interpret themselves."

In praising or condemning the "novelesque" (purported made up
stories), commentators (at least since Oviedo) have negated Cabeza
de Vaca's testimony of experiences that are alien to the common
sense of Western rationality. Beyond being simply an aesthetic, the
real maravilloso (magic realism) in the *Naufragios* betrays just how ridden with contradictions is the representation (the magic of realism)
of another culture (the reality of magic) when one takes into consideration the fact that in the contact zone there is an encounter
of at least two sociolects (practices that define reality for a given
social group) whose conceptions of the world are often radically incommensurable.[13] Radical incommensurability, however, does not
preclude the existence of two (incommensurable) worlds in one
consciousness without incurring a contradiction. Rather, contradiction results from the attempt to translate one world into the
other. Depending on the register, Cabeza de Vaca at once conveys
the notion that magic exists and that magic does not exist. Critics
have consistently repressed this uncanny coexistence of two worlds
in the *Naufragios.*

The force of the ethnographic texts, according to Clifford
Geertz, "has less to do with either a factual look or an air of conceptual elegance than it has with their capacity to convince us that
what they say is a result of their having actually penetrated (or, if
you prefer, been penetrated by) another form of life, of having,
one way or another, truly 'been there.' And that, persuading us that
this offstage miracle has occurred, is where the writing comes in"
(1988: 4–5).[14] If an ethnographic text is a testimony of an experience
of "being there," its writing necessarily happens in a "being here,"
in a world of libraries, seminars, lecterns, blackboards, and, above
all, disciplinary expectations. Cabeza de Vaca also writes "being

here." In his case, the audience consists of the secular and ecclesiastical authorities of Charles V's Spain. The language of the real consists of the accepted images, concepts, and categories that had become sedimented in *relaciones* and chronicles of the New World. The preferred story line tells of the triumphs of empire. Thus, the "capacity to convince" depends on a balance between the two understandings of allegory that I outlined above: narrative endowing meaning to events (White) and self-interpretations in representations (Clifford). The *Naufragios* is at once a story that transforms failure into success and a series of narrative loops whereby Cabeza de Vaca corrodes stock New World images. The ambivalence of the uncanny as defined by Freud would seem to be at work in these transformations, where *heimlich* "finally coincides with its opposite, *unheimlich*." Nothing has been more repressed in readings of Cabeza de Vaca than his immersion in an Amerindian worldview embedded in magic. In this process, interpreters of the *Naufragios* (such as Oviedo, R. Adorno, and Echeverría, just to mention the most prominent) identify "magic" with Cabeza de Vaca, that is, with the European individual who alternately performs miracles, negotiates fear, and possesses healing powers. The shuttling back and forth of the canny and the uncanny must be seen as integral to what makes the *Naufragios* an allegorical text.

READING CABEZA DE VACA

Several drafts anticipated the version of the *Naufragios* we know today. These reflect the transformation of what would have been one more account of events by one more functionary of the Indies into a self-consciously labored text with literary pretensions. Two early versions, written in collaboration with the other survivors, were submitted to the viceregal authorities of New Spain and the Crown upon the author's arrival. There is a fragment with the title "Relacion de Cabeza de Vaca, tesorero que fué en la conquista," which also includes the instructions to Cabeza de Vaca as factor of the expedition (*CDI*, 14: 265–79), and we have Oviedo's summary of and commentaries on the *Informe conjunto* by Cabeza de Vaca, Castillo, and Dorantes quoted earlier. The *Naufragios* was first published in 1542 with neither *privilegio* nor chapter headings (as *La rela-cion que dio Alvar nu-/ñez Cabeça de vaca de lo acaescido en las Indias / en la armada donde yua por gouernador Pª. philo de narbaez / Desde el año de veinte / y siete hasta el año d' treinta y seis / que bolvio a Sevilla con tres / de su compania*) and, with further revisions, together with the *Comen-tarios* again in 1555 (as *La relacion y comentarios del gouerna / dor Aluar nuñez cabeça, de lo acaescido en las / dos jornadas que hizo a las Indias*). Al-though the term *Naufragios* appears in the table of contents of the 1555 edition, it was not used as a title until 1749, when the book was published as *Naufragios de Alvar Núñez Cabeza de Vaca, y Relación de la jornada, que hizo a la Florida con el adelantado Pánfilo de Narváez.*[15]

If this ongoing rewriting of a *relación* is particularly obsessive in Cabeza de Vaca, its impulse to draw a universal message does have illustrious antecedents among the narratives of successful enter-prises, for example, Columbus's *Diario* of the first voyage and Cor-tés's *Letters to Charles V,* which relate their particular feats as unique events that would affect the meaning of world history. Thus, Co-lumbus wrote his daily entries in the *Diario* as if every detail were an inscription bespeaking the coming of a new age, and Cortés in-sistently highlighted the Otherness of New Spain so that he could legitimize mutiny and claim political authority. Both Columbus and Cortés knew that their enterprises would be read as key parts of an emerging historical plot. Passages in their accounts underscore the uniqueness of their enterprises, but for the most part narrative is subordinated to an inconclusive chronological account. Cabeza de Vaca faced another task in the *Naufragios:* while retaining a truth-ful, open-ended account characteristic of the *relación,* he projects into the sequence of events the plot structure of romance. Emplot-ment, the constitution and organization of facts by means of a nar-rative structure, endows otherwise univocal statements with figura-tive meanings; nakedness, hunger, shipwreck, and healing become something more as they are given political, religious, and moral interpretations (see Pastor 1988 [1983]: 294–337; 1989: 136–46). To prevent the account from being filed away as one more report of a failed expedition, Cabeza de Vaca must underscore the unique-ness of his story by means of a narrative. By retaining the *rela-ción*like, inconclusive representation of events in time, as well as the narration's apparent autonomy, Cabeza de Vaca allows for several readings. His ethnographic register names and geographically situates the peoples within a narrative of evangelization and conquest whose meanings, in turn, exceed the adventures of Cabeza de Vaca and the other survivors.

From the point of view of reception, the adoption of the title *Naufragios* over the previous *La relación* illustrates the tropological field in the text. We may wonder why the editor of the 1749 edition chose *Naufragios* and not *Milagros* (miracles), *Peregrinajes* (pilgrimages), or even *Las aventuras de Cabeza de Vaca,* which would perhaps have been the closest to the title of the premier example of the novelesque genre, Daniel Defoe's *The Life and Strange Surprising Adventures of Robinson Crusoe* (1719), already published when the title *Naufragios* first appeared. Although the nature of the so-called *milagros* and Cabeza de Vaca's capacity to effect them have been subject to speculation and polemic, the metaphor of the shipwreck is the strongest motif; it dates to antiquity and recurs in the works of such prominent figures as Homer, Dante, and Defoe. Indeed, shipwrecks have a long tradition as vehicles for conveying the spiritual travails of saints and their miracles. Because Cabeza de Vaca undergoes a shipwreck, his account immediately lends itself to a religious reading, among others. Shipwreck entails a loss of material civilization, a transition to chaos and social anomie, but also a transition to a world where Western reason faces its limits and founders. As mentioned, Cabeza de Vaca's experience of magic is that which most resists interpretation. Readers of the *Naufragios* have repressed magic, turning magic into miracles effected by God and Cabeza de Vaca, in turn, into a saint of the conquest, and celebrated Cabeza de Vaca as a manipulator of fear or gullibility, turning him into an astute as well as benevolent, savvy, colonial frontier-type, when not a picaro.[16] Spitta's (1995) careful comparison of those passages purported to be fictions with shamanic practices described by Eliade and others spares us the need to analyze these practices in detail. Let us simply say that it is equally valid to speak of divine miracles, of an opportunistic conquistador, or of a Spaniard transculturating shamanism. These interpretations share a common need to impose order on *magic,* hence to kill, as it were, the spirit of the *Naufragios.* Is this what Andrés Serrano seeks to convey in his photograph *Cabeza de Vaca* (fig. 1)?

Writing Violence on the Northern Frontier

Figure 1. Andrés Serrano, *Cabeza de Vaca,* 1984, Cibachrome, 40 × 60 inches. Courtesy of Paula Cooper Gallery.

"This is not a cow's head"

Dead it is, the cow's head sitting on a pedestal, or is it a platter? The eye is particularly disturbing to me — the *punctum* of the photograph, Roland Barthes would say (1981a). It gives the sensation that the head is still warm, not quite dead. Is this uncanny image actually telling the story of how criticism has domesticated Cabeza de Vaca? Of how critics regurgitate a testimony of spirituality, giving it back to us on a platter for our safe consumption, putting it on a pedestal for our patriotic memorializing? Is Serrano bringing it back *home* with a Magritte-like gesture that says *This is not a cow's head* (cf. Foucault 1982; Mitchell 1994: 67)? Alternatively, the photograph says "This is Cabeza de Vaca, and only if you speak Spanish will you know that this is not a cow's head, but also that it is." As in ironic allegory, Serrano allows for multiple readings. It evokes legend, echoing the origin of the name given to the ancestor who in 1212 aided Christians during the *reconquista* by using a cow's skull to point out a passage through the mountains that would be undetected by the Muslim army, and creates a myth — the fleshed cow's head now can point a passage to elude English-only initiatives (see

Reading Cabeza de Vaca

Lippard 1990). It is at once a commentary on and a critique of Luis Valdez and Stan Steiner's *Aztlan* (1972), an anthology that included two passages from Haniel Long's literary adaptation of the *Naufragios* but made no reference to Cabeza de Vaca's text. It is a critique because Long (more accurately, the absent reference to the *Naufragios* in Valdez and Steiner) after all erases Spanish as the language in which to read Cabeza de Vaca, and a commentary because Long's text is the most passionate reading available on the spiritual significance of Cabeza de Vaca's healings. As Henry Miller puts it in his preface: "The important thing to bear in mind is precisely what the Interlinear [Long's dwelling in Cabeza de Vaca's narrative] brings out, namely that the civilized European of four centuries ago had lost something that the Indians still possessed" (in Long 1973 [1939]: xvi).

There is an interpretative moment in the *Naufragios* that Long's "interlinear" missed, but that lends support to Miller's contention that Indians still possessed a link to spirituality no longer available to the West. I am thinking of that place where Cabeza de Vaca has an Indian (using indirect speech, as Maureen Ahern [1993] has put it in her brilliant reading) explain why magic works.[17] The passage is long, but worth citing in its entirety:

> En aquella ysla que he contado nos quisieron hazer fisicos, sin examinarnos ni pedirnos los titulos, porque ellos curan las enfermedades soplando al enfermo y con aquel soplo y las manos echan dél la enfermedad, y mandaronnos que hiziessemos lo mismo y siruiessemos en algo; nosotros nos reyamos dello, diziendo que era burla y que no sabiamos curar, y por esto nos quitauan la comida hasta que hiziessemos lo que nos dezian. Y viendo nuestra porfia, vn indio me dixo a mi que yo no sabia lo que dezia en dezir que no aprouecharia nada aquello que el sabia, ca las piedras y otras cosas que se crian por los campos tienen virtud, y que el con vna piedra caliente, trayendola por el estomago, sanaua y quitaua el dolor, y que nosotros que eramos hombres, cierto era que teniamos mayor virtud y poder. En fin nos vimos en tanta necessidad que lo ouimos de hacer sin temer que nadie nos lleuasse por ello la pena. (*CLD,* 5: 56)
>
> [On that island that I have described they tried to make us into medicine men, without examining us or asking for credentials, for they

cure illnesses by blowing on the sick person, and by blowing and using their hands they cast the illness out of him; and they ordered us to do the same and to be of some use. We laughed at it, saying that it was a joke and that we did not know how to heal, and because of this they withdrew the food from us. And seeing our resistance, an Indian told me that I did not know what I was talking about when I said that what he knew would be of no use to me, for stones and other things that grow in the fields have virtue, and by using a hot stone and passing it over the stomach he could cure and take away pain; and we, who were men, surely had even greater virtue and power. At last we were under such pressure that we had to do it, without fear that we would be scorned for it. (Núñez Cabeza de Vaca 1993: 49)

Cabeza de Vaca goes on to describe how they cure by means of incisions, sucking, laying on of the hands, and cauterization; he adds that he tried these methods and they worked for him. He then goes on to explain that they cured by making the sign of the cross (*santiguándolos*) and blowing (*soplando*), praying an Our Father and a Hail Mary, and begging God to heal them. Even Spitta, who insists on Cabeza de Vaca's initiation into learning about medicinal herbs, rocks, and healing practices, feels pressed to emphasize the Christian component: "He does not manage to relinquish his Christian upbringing altogether" (1995: 37). Yet why should he relinquish Christianity? Why couldn't he be both a Christian and a shaman? Dwell in two worlds without incurring contradiction? Does it affect the healing practices that Cabeza de Vaca introduces Christian prayer? Isn't there room for innovation in shamanism? The Indian's explanation of magic, not Cabeza de Vaca's, seems to anticipate some of the ideas in Claude Lévi-Strauss's essays "The Effectiveness of Symbols" (1967) and "The Sorcerer and His Magic" (1967), as well as throw others into question. The first of these essays explains that shamanistic cures are effective when the ill person incorporates the structure of the narrative recited by the shaman. Thus, the "shaman provides the sick woman with a *language*," that is, with a structure bearing a connection between psychic and physical phenomena (193; emphasis in original). The second essay explains that the efficacy of magical practices depends on three complementary aspects: "First, the sorcerer's belief in the effectiveness of his techniques; second, the patient's or victim's belief in the sorcerer's power; and, finally, the faith and expectations of the group, which constantly act as a sort of gravitational field within which the relationship between sorcerer and bewitched is located and defined" (162). Sylvia Molloy has written that Lévi-Strauss's three complementary aspects would be pertinent to the *Naufragios* only when we consider that the belief of the shaman (i.e., Cabeza de Vaca's) would be last (1987: 439–40). For Rolena Adorno, on the other hand, already in Lévi-Strauss's essay the belief of the shaman is always last. We can readily interchange the name Quesalin with Cabeza de Vaca: "Quesalin did not become a great shaman because he cured his patients; he cured his patients because he had become a great shaman" (Lévi-Strauss 1967: 174; cf. R. Adorno 1991: 173). We are thus fully prepared to rationalize Cabeza de Vaca's healings as psychosomatic cures resulting from the patient's belief in his power. Lévi-Strauss furthermore enables us to understand both the sincerity as well as the cynicism of healers. In any case, the shaman must learn the practices of the community, though he can also experiment, as in Cabeza de Vaca's introduction of Christian prayers. Cabeza de Vaca also testifies to the power of shamanism to heal and damage, and clearly separates the curing methods from a rationalist medicine, "sin examinarnos ni pedirnos los titulos, porque ellos curan las enfermedades soplando" [without examining us or asking us for credentials, for they cure illnesses by blowing] (*CLD,* 5: 56; Cabeza de Vaca 1993: 49).

The Indian in the *Naufragios* explains the field of magic and healing as including humans alongside plants and rocks, but does not rationalize the effectiveness in terms of community belief in the shaman. The Christian prayers seem to confirm an observation Taussig has made regarding the obsession among structuralists such as Victor Turner with understanding healing as bringing order into chaos, and, more particularly, apropos of Lévi-Strauss's formulation, "the shaman provides a *language.*" "The point, in Cuna theory, is that the chant is addressed not to the patient but to the spirits and therefore has to be sung in their language, not that of colloquial Cuna" (Taussig 1992: 177). As in the case of the Cuna chants described by Holmer and Wassen (the source of the chant analyzed by Lévi-Strauss), where "the song of Mu-Igala cannot be rightly understood except by the medicine man himself or by those initiated by him," the Indians did not understand Cabeza de Vaca's prayers (quoted in Taussig 1992: 177). With this in mind, let us now return to the mysteries of Haniel Long and this insight on how shamans themselves theorize healing.

Murk and Luminosity

Haniel Long's little book was also an inspiration for Guillermo Sheridan, who wrote the screenplay of Nicolás Echevarría's *Cabeza de Vaca*: "Opté por no tener en las manos ningún otro material bibliográfico aparte de *Naufragios* escritos por el mismo Cabeza de Vaca y ver en ello, a la vez, un reto y una bendición. Recuerdo, sin embargo, que a la mitad de la redacción Echevarría me mandó el precioso librito que sobre Cabeza de Vaca escribió el texano Haniel Long" [I chose to have no other bibliographical materials than *Naufragios* written by Cabeza de Vaca himself and to see in that both a challenge and a blessing. I remember, however, that halfway through my writing Echevarría sent me that precious little book that the Texan Haniel Long wrote on Cabeza de Vaca] (Sheridan 1994: 23). If Long follows the *Naufragios* closely, anchoring Cabeza de Vaca's meditations on key passages, Sheridan shrugs off bibliographical materials, seeing in their lack "a challenge and a blessing" that gives him the license to invent. Sheridan's screenplay and Echevarría's film are not fictions but fantasies. If we can hold fiction accountable—especially historical fiction that aims for verisimilitude—for the accuracy of its representations, a historical fantasy would seem to operate according to rules that allow one to produce images and situations at one's will.

In Echevarría's film, images with a symbolic aura, with murky or luminous surfaces, are carefully crafted to affect our sensibilities. They say much while blinding us to their significance. Does Echevarría know what these images mean? As an example of epistemic murk, take the scene that first depicts the Indian world, where slime and guck invest bizarre objects with witchcraft. Personally, I was perplexed into asking Why? What's the point? His purpose might have been to reproduce the culture shock of the Spaniards, but why do it at the expense of Amerindian cultures? After all, that

Reading Cabeza de Vaca   59

is what the slime and guck stand for. As for examples of the luminous, those takes of Cabeza de Vaca wandering in the desert against a huge blue sky with dramatic cloud formations are obvious instances. They tell of his vulnerability and spiritual grandeur, but what are we to make of them? That Cabeza de Vaca holds a unique place in the Field of the Lord, only to be verified by a tree that suddenly bursts into flames at the end of the sequel? But also bearing luminosity is that image of Mala Cosa (Evil Thing), weeping after having grasped the uniqueness of Cabeza de Vaca, as it were, sensitized by being mysteriously touched by Western values (see Stone 1996: 317). It is never clear what this legless and armless evil dwarf was supposed to stand for to begin with. A symbol for Indian culture before Christian redemption, or the intuition of the Christian God? One also wonders what is gained by this arbitrary transformation of the Mala Cosa of the *Naufragios,* whose practice of slashing bodies and lifting houses into the air is reminiscent of other Native American texts such as the *Popol Vuh,* where the twins Ixbalanque and Hunapuh, after acquiring fame for performing parallel *collective illusions,* defeat the lords of Xibalba by cutting up their bodies *for real.*[18]

In his prologue to Sheridan's screenplay, the Colombian novelist Alvaro Mutis gives us a clue as to how to read these images: "Lo que hace de esta historia una hermosa parábola de todo destino humano, es el saber que, al final, los españoles parten convertidos de nuevo en lo que eran antes y los nativos se quedan en medio de sus precarias condiciones de una supervivencia al borde de la inanición y las tinieblas de un caos primario y sin salida" [What makes this film a beautiful parable of all human destiny is that we learn, at the end, that the Spanish depart converted again to what they were before and the natives remain in the midst of their precarious condition of a survival bordering inanition and the darkness of primitive chaos, without escape] (in Sheridan 1994: 8). We have here a violent response to *murk* that reduces Indian life to inanition, darkness, and primitive chaos, *without escape.* One is further baffled when Mutis states that reading the screenplay and then watching the film, "tenemos esa inquietante certeza de que, por primera vez, nos han contado las cosas como fueron" [we have that disquieting certainty that, for the first time, we have been told how things were] (8).

Nothing less than the *real thing!* What do the images say about Indians who have survived the past five hundred years of oppression? Are we now in a position to answer the question I posed earlier regarding what Echevarría meant by *somos casi todo un país,* "the vertebrate column of our culture"? The task, then, is to identify how images act—and on what social reality or form of life.

Does the Indian world as presented by Sheridan and Echevarría provide a visual text that would pretend to illustrate the *Naufragios*? Obviously, the film and the screenplay build on passages from Cabeza de Vaca (and borrow freely from Long), so they are not completely arbitrary, but for the most part the film (elaborating and modifying the verbal descriptions of the screenplay) fabricates images with no connection to the *Naufragios*. Again, if we read it as a fantasy, it does not really matter whether it is faithful to the original. Sheridan and Echevarría produce a visual text drawing from a wide variety of sources that include depictions of healing practices common among shamans as well as acts of witchcraft, next to which Frazer's examples in the *Golden Bough* and his rationalistic account of what he termed Sympathetic Magic would pale (see Frazer 1911).

The series of scenes that conclude with Cabeza de Vaca's conversion into a shaman and Mala Cosa's intuition of Western values occurs in the following sequence:

1. The witch that travels with Mala Cosa draws the silhouette of a man and then pierces its eye with a stick.
2. A shrieking giant emerges from a pond with a bruised eye.
3. Weeping Indian women tend to the giant.
4. A shaman blows into the giant and Cabeza de Vaca observes.
5. Cabeza de Vaca goes into a frenzy as he realizes that the powers that heal are within him.
6. The "deep" look of the Indian shaman tells us that something important is happening.
7. Cabeza de Vaca heals the giant with his touch.
8. Cabeza de Vaca is given an Indian cross like the one worn by the witch that cast the spell on the giant and that certifies him as a shaman.
9. The village celebrates the giant.

10. A glassy-eyed Mala Cosa looks at Cabeza de Vaca walking into the desert.

From the start, the cross mediates the capacity of humanizing the evil witch and becomes more visible after this series of scenes as it marks the passages from murk to luminosity. With the exception of healing by touching and blowing, these scenes have no relation to the *Naufragios*. Nowhere in the *Naufragios* is there a mechanical depiction of shamanism or magic, and, as we have seen above, he provides us with a theory of healing that anticipates and questions structuralist explanations.

We must now ask what Echevarría and Sheridan are doing to and with Cabeza de Vaca? I would say that, on the eve of the Columbian Quincentennial in 1992 when this film was produced, its ideological effect (at least on Mutis) was to counter, if not undermine and silence, the urgency that Indians felt throughout the Americas to condemn the invasion and subsequent colonization of the New World that began with Columbus's voyage in 1492. The portrayal of Native American Indians as Stone Age peoples ridden by sorcery, arbitrarily aggressive, loud and uttering incomprehensible grunts, and so on, hardly provides a just representation of Indian culture. If Echevarría's film, as Gustavo Verdesio (1997) has pointed out, is a parody of sixteenth-century chronicles, it reproduces—if not exacerbates—the *culture of conquest* that existed then and still plagues our discourse today. Let us now examine some of the preferred metaphors among literary critics.

Hostile Paleolithic Indians

The motif of the shipwreck calls to mind the notion of an unexpected mishap and its interpretation as a fall into chaos. As I pointed out above, according to Pranzetti (1993), the shipwreck actually functions as a metaphor that marks a transition (quite literally, functions as a vehicle) leading from order to chaos. The tendency among critics, however, has been to read chaos as an original or primitive state of the world attributed to Indian culture (by the way, very much along the same lines as Mutis's Indians living in conditions "bordering inanition and the darkness of primitive chaos and without escape"), and not simply as a complete loss of material culture on the part of the Spaniards. Pupo-Walker and Lagmanovich have respectively defined what they perceive as a historicotemporal voyage in the *Naufragios:* primitive chaos is but one step further from the characterization of Cabeza de Vaca's journey into North America as "un alucinante itinerario que lo llevó de la cultura renacentista a la barbarie indócil del paleolítico americano" [a hallucinatory itinerary that took him from the culture of the Renaissance to the hostile barbarism of the American Paleolithic Age] (Pupo-Walker 1987: 539) or "un viaje en el tiempo, de la civilización europea del siglo xvi a la edad de piedra" [a journey in time, from European civilization of the sixteenth century to the Stone Age] (Lagmanovich 1978: 32).[19]

If there is a lack of refinement in Cabeza de Vaca's narrative, it is among the Spaniards; for instance, when they are faced with the task of building ships, not one of them has the knowledge or the skills: "Nosotros no lo sabiamos hacer" [We did not know how to make them] (*CLD,* 5:32; Núñez Cabeza de Vaca 1993: 28). Moreover, if the Indians are hostile, one need not wonder why; the Spaniards raid villages for food, procuring "hasta cuatrocientas hanegas de maíz, aunque no sin contiendas y pendencias con los indios" [as many as four hundred *fanegas* of maize, though not without struggles and disputes with the Indians] (5:33; 28). Cabeza de Vaca does not mention any form of peaceful request or even any of the numerous legalistic readings of the *Requerimiento* that the instructions to Pánfilo de Narváez had demanded. And to the scandalized astonishment of the Indians, the Spaniards resort to cannibalism out of hunger: "Se comieron los vnos a los otros hasta que quedo uno solo, que por ser solo no huuo quien lo comiesse. . . . Deste caso se alteraron tanto los indios y ouo entre ellos tan gran escandalo, que sin dubda si al principio ellos lo vieran, los mataran y todos nos vieramos en grande trabajo" [They ate one another until there was only one left, who survived because there was no one left to eat him. . . . The Indians were so indignant about this, and there was so much outrage among them, that undoubtedly if they had seen this when it began to happen they would have killed them, and all of us would have been in dire peril] (5:52; 46). There is a certain irony in his insistence on the fact that there was no one left to eat the last Spaniard. In their abhorrence of Spanish cannibalism, the Indians embody European values, for Cabeza de Vaca imagines them inflicting death as a punishment.

Thus, the Indian's character is one more component of the plot that depends on the Spaniard's attitude. Yes, the peoples of Florida were hostile to Pánfilo de Narváez's invading army. It is also true that Cabeza de Vaca eventually comes into contact with nomadic peoples, but there is no justification, even if the term Stone Age were applicable, for the qualifier "indocile barbarism" (Pupo-Walker 1987: 539). Clearly, one can make reference to indocility only from an imperialist perspective. Indocility would read as resistance in a nonethnocentric reading of Indian responses to the Spanish rape of their lands. As literary critics we should not contribute to the culture of conquest by turning the right to make war against the invaders into hostile barbarism.

In late-twentieth-century studies of colonial texts we can do without such touches of color as Pupo-Walker and Lagmanovich propose in their texts: the time travels from European civilization to a Stone Age. On the other hand, it is interesting to note that immediately after introducing his time travel metaphor, Lagmanovich asserts that the *Naufragios* is the account of "una progresiva identificación del autor con el mundo que había partido para sojuzgar" [a progressive identification with the indigenous world that he had come to conquer] (1978: 32). In this sense, the *Naufragios* suggests a transition and conversion to an overarching critique of the Spanish conquest of the New World. Following these indications by Lagmanovich, Pastor has elaborated a detailed close reading of the *Naufragios* as an inversion of the Spanish imperial project (see Pastor 1988 [1983]: 294–337; 1989: 136–46). Before discussing the question of an ideological and political conversion, let us examine some other inversions of the code of conquest.

In *Cueros*

Cultural inversions define Cabeza de Vaca's ethnographic style and require him to endow his *relación* with a narrative. Thus in his preface, he anticipates the reception of his account, which has nothing to offer but a chronicle of disaster and survival:

Mas como ni mi consejo, ni diligencia, aprovecharon para que aquello a que eramos ydos fuesse ganado conforme al servicio de Vuestra Magestad, y por nuestros peccados permitiesse Dios que de quantas armadas a aquellas tierras han ydo ninguna se viesse en tan grandes peligros, ni tuuiesse tan miserable y desastrado fin, no me quedo lugar para hazer mas servicio deste, que es traer a vuestra Magestad relacion de lo que en diez años que por muchas y muy extrañas tierras que anduve en cueros, pudiesse saber y ver. (*CLD,* 5: 4) [But since neither my advice nor my best efforts sufficed to win what we had gone to accomplish in Your Majesty's service, and because God permitted, for our sins, that of all the fleets that have gone to these lands, none found themselves in such dangers or had such a miserable and disastrous end, no opportunity was afforded to me to perform more service than this, which is to bring an account of what I learned and saw in ten years during which I wandered naked through many and very strange lands. (Núñez Cabeza de Vaca 1993: 3–4)

In one breath Cabeza de Vaca first insists on his loyalty and that his prudence and advice were to no avail in preventing the catastrophe that kept the armada from winning the lands, and then goes on to highlight collective guilt ("por nuestros pecados" [for our sins]) and the uniqueness of the failure ("ninguna se viesse en tantos peligros" [none found themselves in such dangers]). Having thus exculpated himself, he can move on to single out the magnitude of the failed expedition and the mysterious designs of God. He concludes by saying that all he has to offer is the account of ten years spent in strange lands among barbarous nations, specifying that he was *en cueros* (naked). Cabeza de Vaca insists again on nakedness in the concluding lines of the preface where he states that the only service he can provide the king is the knowledge contained in the *relación,* "pues este solo es el que un hombre que salio desnudo pudo sacar consigo" [for this is the only thing that a man who left those lands naked could bring out with him] (*CLD,* 5: 5; Núñez Cabeza de Vaca 1993: 4). It contains information, certainly of value, for those who "fueren a conquistar aquellas tierras y juntamente traerlos a conoscimiento de la verdadera fee y verdadero señor y servicio de vuestra majestad" [in your name will go to conquer those lands and bring them to the knowledge of the true Faith and the true lordship and service of Your Majesty] (5:5; 4). His account thus proposes to contribute to the stock of knowledge about the Indies, while his insistence on his nakedness in the closing remark places the emphasis on autobiography and "cosas muy nuevas y para algunos muy difíciles de creer" [things very new and for some, very difficult to believe] (5:5; 4). Ultimately, all credibility depends on his claim to be truthful: "Pueden sin duda creerlas . . . y bastará para esto auerlo yo ofrecido a Vuestra Magestad por tal" [They may believe them without any doubt . . . and it should suffice that I have offered the account to Your Majesty as truth] (5:5; 4).

Nudity assumes a metaphorical dimension: all Cabeza de Vaca has to offer is the naked truth. Moreover, the term *en cueros,* literally "in skins," at once signals the kind of clothing he was wearing—Indian dress—and the complete loss of European material culture. Margo Glantz has taken the *en cueros*-as-nudity topoi beyond the rhetorical figure of *praeteritio* to document how *en cueros* is a term for nudity that slides into forms of Indian culture characterized as barbarian (1993a: 408 and passim). Yet in the passage cited above, where Cabeza de Vaca first runs into Spaniards, they marvel at his strange dress and *not* at his nakedness: "tan extrañamente vestido y en compañia de indios" [so strangely dressed and in the company of Indians] (*CLD,* 5: 126; Núñez Cabeza de Vaca 1993: 110). Underneath this semantic play lies the fact that the Spaniards end up really *naked* and depend on *real* Indian dress to survive.

Thus, the preface calls our attention to the allegorical nature of his text and ensures a reading in which Cabeza de Vaca emerges as an exemplary subject of Charles V. Knowledge of the territories as well as the specifics of the disaster and survival are subordinated to the production of this subject, the first person who surfaces in the narrative. It is not, however, an individual self, but an ideal, law-abiding, faithful servant of the Crown. Cabeza de Vaca's narrative produces a subject that, in the exemplariness of his travails, embodies an allegory of the Spanish enterprise in the Indies—that is, of what it sought to be.

Cabeza de Vaca's narrative inverts the prototypical chronicle of conquest: where in other accounts the successful conquistadores justify violence as necessary for material gains, his lack of material gains creates the need to idealize his performance as an officer of the Crown. In fact, Cabeza de Vaca embodies the possibility of peaceful conquest and evangelization. But these ideals not only literally follow the Crown's instruction and the Ordenanzas of 1526, but also morally absolve the king's conscience. We cannot ascertain from such inversions whether Las Casas underwent a conversion from an initially violent conquistador to an advocate of peaceful conquest. It is not even clear to me that Cabeza de Vaca presents himself anywhere in the *Naufragios* as an advocate of military conquest. What we can point out is that Cabeza de Vaca's position from the start is not extraneous to the discourse of the Crown. It seems to me that the lack of any mention of Narváez reading the *Requerimiento* before ordering raids of Indian villages entails a denunciation of Narváez's breach of the law. In Narváez's instructions (*CDI,* 16: 68–83) we find next to the *Requerimiento* a condemnation of violence that Bishop describes as follows in his biography of Cabeza de Vaca: "The voice is that of Charles V, but the words are those of Bartolomé de las Casas" (Bishop 1933: 24). Cabeza de Vaca's instructions, likewise, specifically obligate him to report any form of injustice toward the Indians (*CDI,* 14: 265–79). And so, toward the end of the *Naufragios,* precisely in the chapter before Cabeza de Vaca encounters the Spaniards in Culiacan and denounces their cruelties and abuses, he elaborates a statement on colonial policy that echoes or at least parallels the title of a book by Las Casas (1988 [ca. 1534]): "claramente se vee que estas gentes todas para ser atraydos a ser cristianos y a obediencia de la Imperial majestad han de ser lleuados con buen tratamiento, y que este es camino muy cierto, y otro no" [clearly shows that to attract all these peoples to be Christians and into obedience of Your Imperial Majesty, must be led by good treatment, and that this is a very sure way, and no other will suffice] (*CLD,* 5: 124; Núñez Cabeza de Vaca 1993: 108). Note that Cabeza de Vaca speaks in one breath of peaceful evangelization, *atraydos a ser cristianos,* and of political subjection to the Crown, *obediencia de la Imperial majestad.*

The full title in Latin of Las Casas's book is *De unico vocationis modo omnium gentium ad veram religionem* (1988 [ca. 1534]), better known by the shorter title *De unico modo* (translated into English by Helen Rand Parish as *The Only Way;* Las Casas 1992b).[20] As is well-known, the policies of this book inspired an experiment in peaceful evangelization in Vera Paz, Guatemala, from 1537 to 1550, but it is beyond the scope of this chapter to examine in any detail the results.[21] It suffices to note that in 1540 there was a surge of official support of Las Casas's position in a series of decrees destined to encourage peaceful colonizations; on 17 October alone, just before Cabeza de Vaca's departure for the Río de la Plata on 2 November, there were twelve such decrees (see Hanke 1942: 50). The passage from the *Naufragios* quoted earlier suggests at least the title of Las Casas's *De unico modo,* although in the narrative's temporal framework Cabeza de Vaca had not been in contact with Spaniards for eight years. Cabeza de Vaca's seemingly independent advancement of Las Casas's policies would certainly have been well received in the ideological climate of the late 1530s and very likely contributed to his gaining the governorship of the Río de la Plata. Whether Cabeza de Vaca arrived at the notion of peaceful conquest independently of Las Casas or just acted as if he had after becoming acquainted with his ideas upon arriving in New Spain, a comparison of *De unico modo* and the *Naufragios* reveals that if on the surface Cabeza de Vaca appears to be a *lascasista* (a follower of Las Casas), a close reading of key passages manifests major ideological differences.

As Rolena Adorno (1991, 1992, 1994) has pointed out, in chapter 124 of the *Apologética historia sumaria* (ca. 1555), Las Casas draws from the *Naufragios* to document the absence of idolatries and sacrifices among Indians in Florida as well as an example of peaceful evangelization (Las Casas 1967: 651–52). But to what extent did Cabeza de Vaca's information of idolatry and sacrifice merely respond to Ordenanza 11 of the 1526 Ordenanzas, which called for an investigation of the *habilidad* (ability) of the Indians and to evaluate if they would benefit from being placed under *encomiendas?* Las Casas does not mention the passage where Cabeza de Vaca uses language close to that of *De unico modo,* but instead underscores the events that follow Melchior Díaz's reading of the *Requerimiento* in chapter 38 of the *Naufragios:* the identification of God with Aguar and the Indians' willingness to resettle. This event supports Las Casas's contention that all Amerindians, regardless of cultural complexity, embody the best possible human traits. In an argument that seemingly espouses an evolutionary social model, people of the "lowest" rung are not only free of the idolatry and sacrifices common among the "higher" stages, but also have a clear intuition of the Christian God and willingness to listen to the gospel. Elsewhere, I have characterized this sort of rhetorical move as a form of utopian discourse in Las Casas's *Apologética* (Rabasa 1989b). For the purposes of the current discussion it is important to note that in this passage as well as in others in which Las Casas discusses Cabeza de Vaca, he does not mention the reading of the *Requerimiento* that prefaces the Indians' acceptance of resettlement. One also wonders whether, if Cabeza de Vaca had "found" idolaters, cannibals, and sacrificers, he would have advanced the same policies. Probably not, given that his discovery of these practices or, better said, these ideological phantoms informed and justified his repressive actions in the Río de la Plata. Maura has questioned Adorno's reading of Cabeza de Vaca as *lascasista* precisely on his record as *adelantado* (Maura 1995: 183).

Cabeza de Vaca's record in the Río de la Plata leads us either to question the sincerity of his conversion to a "peaceful conquistador" in the *Naufragios* or to speculate that he returned to his old conquistador ways — in either case, a very superficial conversion to peaceful colonization, if there was any. The *Requerimiento* is again key to the distinction between Las Casas and Cabeza de Vaca, and a way out of this apparent dilemma. Although Las Casas does not address the *Requerimiento* directly nor the Ordenanzas of 1526 in *De unico modo,* his position on demanding political subjection to the Crown could not be clearer: "Modus contrarius huic nimirum esset, si aliquibus forte, quibus predicare aut facere Evangelium infidelibus incumberet, magis congruum et facilius factu videretur prius ipsos infideles populi Christiani ditioni temporali velint nolint subici debere, quibus subiectis, praedicatio deinde ordinata subsequeretur" [The opposite way would certainly be this: If a group whose duty it was to preach the gospel to pagans, or to send them preachers, decided it would be quicker and better done if they first subjected pagans, willingly or not, to Christian temporal power. Once the pagans were subjected, they would be preached to in a methodical fashion] (Las Casas 1988: 378; 1992b: 117). Las Casas adds as a corollary, "Et quia nemo infidelium sua sponte velit se Christiani populi vel alicuius principis eius ditioni submittere, potissime infidelium reges, esset profecto necesse devenire ad bellum" [And since no infidels would willingly subject themselves to the dominion of a Christian people, or a Christian prince, especially the kings of infidels, there would inevitably have to be war] (378; 117).[22] Las Casas could not be more lucid in his assessment of how colonial rule necessarily moves from hegemonic will to military dominance. These statements by Las Casas are far more critical than Cabeza de Vaca's position on reading the *Requerimiento* in the *Naufragios* and the *Comentarios*.

The Ordenanzas of 1526 advocate a peaceful conquest, and Cabeza de Vaca's ideal imperial policies and legitimation of his procedures follow these laws to the letter. Peace was prefaced with multiple readings of the *Requerimiento:* "una y dos y más veces cuantas pareciere . . . y fueren necesarias para que lo entiendan" [one, and two and more times as many as are . . . necessary for them to understand it] (Morales Padrón 1979: 377). Supposedly, only after Indians fully understand the Crown's right to demand obedience and submission could war against Indians be legitimate. *De unico modo* denounces the *Requerimiento* only implicitly, but denounces its ends —the political submission of all Native Americans to the Crown— quite explicitly. In this explicit denunciation resides the radicalness of Las Casas. Needless to say, *De unico modo* was not well received by colonizers and *encomenderos* (recipients of grants of villages and even city-states who benefited from tribute in kind and in labor). Let us also recall that only three chapters of *De unico modo* have survived. For if chapter 5 establishes the ideal character and disposition of Amerindians to receive the faith, and love as the only way to attract them to Christianity, chapter 6 exposes the lack of precedents that would lend support to a method where Indians would first be politically subjected and then converted. The statement to

Writing Violence on the Northern Frontier

this effect cited above opened this discussion in chapter 6. But Las Casas went on in chapter 7 to denounce the illegality of all the wars against Indians and then ponders how to go about compensating for damages and restituting sovereignty to wronged Amerindians. Indeed, during the same years he was working on *De unico modo,* Las Casas published a manual for the confession of Spaniards in which he made the restitution and compensation of Indians a precondition to absolution (see Parish and Weidman 1992: 62–64). As we will see in chapter 2, *De unico modo* forced the Crown to revise the 1526 Ordenanzas in the Nuevas Leyes of 1542, where the Crown outlaws all forms of slavery as well as calling for the dismantling of the *encomiendas.* Las Casas was bitterly opposed not only by *encomenderos* but also by members of other religious orders such as the Franciscan Motolinía, just to mention the most prominent figure.[23] We should not assume, then, that Cabeza de Vaca was a *lascasista* in his compliance with the law, for Las Casas's arguments in *De unico modo* go well beyond advocating peaceful conquest and entails a critique of the 1526 Ordenanzas.

Of course, the *Requerimiento* could be manipulated despite the supervision of the clergy and the officers of the Crown; nothing could guarantee honesty. And this is precisely the ideological context of Cabeza de Vaca's political catastrophe in the Río de la Plata, where the virtuous governor encountered lascivious friars, murderous captains, and, in general, a colonial outpost ruled by terror. Cabeza de Vaca's actions appear to follow to the letter the *Requerimiento* and other instructions on fairness and peaceful colonization. Furthermore, there is no reason to question his sincerity, which obviously does not exclude the violence one would exercise in following imperial law. As I have argued in this chapter, rather than making a clear distinction between law and criminality, we should carefully consider the fine line separating legal from abusive violence in the exercise of colonial dominance. In the *Comentarios* and other accounts of the Río de la Plata, Cabeza de Vaca emerges as a law-abiding colonizer, especially when we compare him with the sordid world of Domingo de Irala and his followers, including the two Franciscan friars who traveled with a party of up to fifty Indian women. Irala, who had assumed the leadership after the death of the first *adelantado* Pedro de Mendoza, became a bitter enemy of

Cabeza de Vaca since his arrival in Asunción. However, the *probanza* (investigation) of eight years, to which Cabeza de Vaca was subjected after his forced return from the Río de la Plata, should warn us against taking his version of the events at their face value.

In what follows, I am less interested in clearing the legal case surrounding Cabeza de Vaca's activities in this colonial outpost than in furthering the argument that his supposed originality as an advocate of peaceful conquest amounts to an exemplary narrative that rhetorically exploits the ideals of empire expressed in the Ordenanzas of 1526. Recourse to the law to exonerate one's own or another's actions obviously was not unique to Cabeza de Vaca. One only has to read Oviedo's positive account of Nuño de Guzmán's exploits in Nueva Galicia, which immediately preceded the *Joint Report* in the *Historia general,* to realize the extent to which the appearance of criminality depended on the narrative one produced. Oviedo's Nuño de Guzmán is an exemplary colonizer in comparison to Narváez, de Soto, and Cabeza de Vaca—especially in the chapter he dedicates to the events in the Río de la Plata (see *HGN,* chap. 4 of bk. 5). In Oviedo's narrative, Cabeza de Vaca's failings in Río de la Plata range from political ineptness (his choice of Joan Pavón for *alcalde mayor* [chief magistrate] alienates him from the other Spaniards when this man "comenzó a hacer algunas extorsiones e agravios" [began to engage in extortions and other injuries]) to giving an Agace chief and his sons to friendly Caribs "para que los matasen y comiesen" [so that they would kill them and eat them] (*HGN,* 3: 283–84). According to Oviedo, these, among other crimes, led the officers of the Crown to judge that his behavior "era en ofensa del servicio de Dios y del Rey, y no para sustentar ni conquistar la tierra" [was an offense to the service of God and the King, and was not in the service of sustaining or conquering the land] (3:385). These chapters in Oviedo further manifest how in colonial narratives an adjective, an apparently minor detail, a breach of protocol, or a narrative inflection may mark the passage from exemplary to criminal act. And it is precisely in adjectives and technicalities where we can observe how the oxymoron peaceful conquest and the language of the benevolent critic of colonialism constitute modes of writing violence—that is, negotiating, articulating, and justifying *certain* regimes of terror.

Aside from the *Comentarios,* there are two other important accounts of Cabeza de Vaca's political shortcomings in the Río de la Plata. The first, his *Relación general,* contains a shorter chronological account of the events; the other, *Relación de las cosas sucedidas en el Río de la Plata* (1545), by Pero Hernández (the amanuensis of Cabeza de Vaca in the *Comentarios*), provides detailed descriptions of cruelty to and sexual abuse of Guarani women (see *CLD* 6). I cannot discuss these texts here in any detail; my reading will necessarily be impressionistic as I am mainly concerned with isolating the legalistic trappings in these otherwise stylistically distinct accounts. Serrano y Sanz (*CLD,* 5: n.p.) has compared description in the *Comentarios* to the lifting of roofs in the picaresque novel *El diablo cojuelo.* The following examples suggest Hernández's affinity for gory details and a voyeuristic sense of history:

> Una Yndia les avia hurtado cierto bastimento e les dixo [Domingo de Yrala]: *pues tomá esa yndia y cavalgalda tantas veces hasta que seays pagados.*
> [An Indian woman had stolen some supplies and (Domingo de Yrala) told them: *so take that Indian woman and ride her until you feel compensated.*]

> El dicho Domingo de Yrala por celos que tuvo de Diego Portugues lo colgó de su natura, de lo cual quedó muy malo e lastimado.
> [The aforementioned Domingo de Yrala out of jealousy he felt for Diego Portugal had him hung from his genitals, which resulted in great injury.]

> Un Francisco Palomyno rronpio a muchacha que tenia en su casa, de edad de seys o siete años, hija de su manceba . . . e la madre la truxo al pueblo corriendo sangre e llorando.
> [A Francisco Palomyno deflowered a girl six or seven years old, the daughter of his mistress . . . and the mother brought her to town bleeding and crying.] (*CLD,* 6: 318; emphasis in original)

From Hernández we also learn of the accusation his enemies had made "quel governador avia dicho que era rrey" [that the governor had said he was the king] (*CLD,* 6: 347). Although my intent is not to shed light on the historical record, given the potential to present a rosy account of the events and an idealization of the origins of

Paraguay as a mestizo nation, it is important to note that this outpost in the Río de la Plata was ruled by terror (see Salas 1960: 193 and passim). Beyond the immediate conflict with Cabeza de Vaca, other letters seem to confirm Domingo de Irala's tactics and the reigning regime of terror, such as using "friendly" Indians, the Axcas, to terrorize the land: "echando sus axcas y corredores por la tierra, robando y destruyendo los indios, tomandoles sus mugeres paridas y preñadas, y quitando a las paridas las criaturas de los pechos" [sending his Axcas and runners through the land, stealing and destroying the Indians, taking their wives who had recently given birth or were pregnant, and removing the infants from the breast of those who had recently given birth] (letter from Juan Muñoz de Carvajal to the emperor, Asunción, 15 June 1556, *CI,* 598). Another letter tells us: "A sucedido vender Yndias libres naturales desta tierra por caballos, perros y otras cosas, y ansi se usa dellas, como en esos reynos la moneda" [It has happened that they sell free Indian women native from this land for horses, dogs and other things, and so they use them, as money is used in those kingdoms] (letter from Martín González, cleric, to the emperor, Asunción, 25 June 1556, *CI,* 609). These passages are comparable to atrocities detailed in Las Casas's *Brevíssima relación de la destruyción de las Indias* (1552) and more recently to the events in the rubber boom on the Putumayo River and the ongoing practice of torture and terror in Latin America and elsewhere. Terror existed and exists.

Though the *Comentarios* avoids descriptions of specific instances of abuse, it does denounce the general climate of terror and the exchange of women. However, what interests us here about the *Comentarios* is not the specific atrocities Cabeza de Vaca condemns but the fact that through Hernández he represents himself as an exemplary *adelantado*. In the preface to the *Comentarios,* dedicated to the young Prince Don Carlos, Cabeza de Vaca implies — and all but states outright — that his account contains lessons, "preceptos de christiandad, caualleria y philosophia" [Christian, chivalric and philosophical precepts], for the education of the young prince (*CLD,* 5: 154). Thus, the *Comentarios* takes special care to underscore how he abided by the law in his proceedings with the Indians. Every time Cabeza de Vaca obtains food from the Indians, for instance, he insists that it was the result of a fair exchange, with such repetitive assurances as:

Y demas de pagarles el precio que valian, a los indios principales de los pueblos les dio graciosamente e hizo mercedes de muchas camisas.
[And besides paying them the fair price, he graciously and freely gave them many shirts.] (*CLD,* 5:170)

Demas de pagarles los mantenimientos . . . les hazia muchas mercedes . . . en tal manera que corria la fama por la tierra . . . y todos los naturales perdian el temor y venian a ver y a traer todo lo que tenian y se lo pagauan.
[Besides paying them for their provisions . . . he would give them many gifts . . . and so his fame extended throughout the land . . . and all the natives lost their fear and came to see them and brought all they had and they paid for it.] (5: 171–72)

Los salieron a rescebir, mostrando grande plazer con la venida del gouernador y gente, y les truxeron al camino muchos bastimentos, los quales se los pagaron segun lo acostumbrauan.
[They came out to receive them, showing great pleasure at the arrival of the governor and his people, and bringing out to the road many provisions, which they paid for, as was their custom.] (5: 174)

Los salieron a rescebir como hombres que tenian noticia de su venida y del buen tratamiento que les hazian, y le truxeron muchos bastimentos, porque los tienen.
[They came out to receive them as men who had news of their arrival and the fair treatment they gave them, and they brought many provisions, because they have them.] (5: 182)

And again, one sentence later, "En toda esta tierra los indios les seruian porque siempre el gouernador les hazia buen tratamiento" [Throughout the land the Indians would serve them because the governor treated them well], which closes his triumphant march from the coast to the falls of Iguazu. Cabeza de Vaca makes the gesture of a humble but seasoned explorer by removing his shoes and leading the march barefoot at the start of the expedition; as he explains in the colorful language of his *Relación general,* "Yo camyné sienpre a pie y descalço por animar la gente que no desmayase" [I always walked barefooted to encourage the people so they would not lose heart] (*CLD,* 6: 15). Likewise, he emphasizes how peaceful the penetration was "por . . . tienpo de cinco meses syn que diese alteración, ni rompimiento con los Yndios" [for . . . approximately five months without causing disturbance nor quarrel with the Indians] (6: 15). One can hear the Ordenanzas of 1526 in these exemplary passages. In both the *Relación general* and the *Comentarios,* the falls of Iguazu mark the first natural obstacle and the first conflict with the Indians. Here too, the Ordenanzas define the legality of his actions.

Conflict with the Indians increases and becomes commonplace after Cabeza de Vaca's meeting with Irala in Asunción, and is implicitly blamed on Irala's policies. The dancing and celebrating of his triumphant entrances to villages on his way from the coast now give way to the equally reductive and emblematic war cries, to "grande grita y toque de tambores . . . tan grande la bozeria y alaridos . . . que parescia que se juntaua el cielo con la tierra" [great shouting and beating of drums . . . that it seemed as if the sky and the earth were coming together] (*CLD,* 5: 194), and to the formulaic and repetitive insistence on reading the *Requerimiento* as a preface and justification of war: "Mando juntar todos los indios naturales vassallos de Su Magestad, y assi juntos delante y en presencia de los religiosos y clerigos les hizo su parlamento diziendoles como . . . avian de venir en conocimiento de Dios . . . debaxo de la obediencia de Su Magestad y fuessen sus vassallos, y que desta manera serian mejor tratados y fauorescidos que hasta alli auian sido" [He asked all the Indian natural vassals of Your Majesty to gather, and so together in front of the friars and clerics he addressed them, telling them how . . . they had to come to the knowledge of God . . . and under the jurisdiction of Your Majesty and be your vassals, and that thus they would be better treated and favored than they had been up to then] (5: 198). But Cabeza de Vaca does not insist merely on the repetition of the *Requerimiento* and how he solicited the opinion of the friars and clergy, but also over and over again on how he took care to "hazer los apercebimientos vna e dos e tres vezes con toda templança" [give the warnings soberly, one, two and three times] (5: 207). These repetitive readings of the *Requerimiento* throughout

Writing Violence on the Northern Frontier

the text—"una y dos y tres vezes y quantas mas deuiessen" [one and two and three, and as many times as needed] (5: 254)—are expressed in the same formulaic terms of the *Ordenanzas* and thus emphasize the legality of his procedures.

We should note that in the *Comentarios,* the *Requerimiento* is first read after the initial conflict with the Indians on Cabeza de Vaca's arrival in Asunción and that it is followed by a long description of cannibalism among the Guarani. Although it is most likely that Cabeza de Vaca did not observe ritual anthropophagy, the *Comentarios* provides an elaborate description of the captive's preparation: "Lo ponen a engordar y le dan todo quanto quiere a comer, y a sus mugeres e hijas para que aya con ellas sus plazeres" [They fatten him and they give him all he wants to eat, and his wives and daughters to have pleasure with them] (*CLD,* 5: 198). From the start of his march, Cabeza de Vaca had mentioned cannibalism as one more cultural trait alongside the enumeration of foodstuffs, houses, dances, and so on. All along, he had also taken care to write how he had taken possession of the territories and to comment on the Guarani's natural inclination to Christianity. His long statement on cannibalism precisely when conflict arises clearly suggests that cannibalism is a sufficient reason to declare war and enslave those who refuse to abandon its practice; this refusal, of course, amounts to not heeding the summons of the *Requerimiento.* Such passages justify Cabeza de Vaca's recourse to violence and war and substantiate a distinction between friendly and enemy Indians—a shifting ground, indeed. These passages also emphasize the gravity of Cabeza de Vaca's ultimate accusation against Irala: "Para valerse los oficiales y Domingo de Yrala con los indios naturales de la tierra les dieron licencia que matassen y comiessen a los indios enemigos dellos, y a muchos destos a quien dieron licencia eran christianos nueuamente conuertidos . . . cosa tan contra el seruicio de Dios y de Su Magestad" [In order to be favored by the native Indians of the land the officers and Domingo de Yrala gave them permission to kill and eat their Indian enemies, and many of those to whom they gave license to eat human flesh were recently converted Christians . . . a thing so against the service of God and Your Majesty] (5: 357). This permission to practice cannibalism, condemnable especially among those who had been Christianized, closes a long list of accusations of Irala's unjust treatment of the Indians and the descriptions of the rebellion against Cabeza de Vaca's rule in the Río de la Plata. As we have seen in Oviedo, Cabeza de Vaca was also subject to the same charges, further proving that cannibalism and its taboos, far from being a cultural practice empirically observed, functioned as a topoi—a panoply of stock images—that *cronistas* deployed to vilify an individual or a group of people.

We should recall here that in the *Naufragios,* after the collapse of authority, it is the Spaniards who eat each other and scandalize the Indians. In the *Apologética historia sumaria,* Las Casas cites these passages from Cabeza de Vaca's *Naufragios* to counter all usages of cannibalism as reason to justify conquest (Las Casas 1967, 2: 354). Indeed, Las Casas derives a certain satisfaction in recounting these examples of cannibalism among Christians, especially because the Indians who condemn the Spaniards are, according to Cabeza de Vaca, so poor and hungry "que si en aquella tierra ouiesse piedras, las comerian" [that if there were stones in that land, they would eat them] (*CLD,* 5: 70). Such passages in the *Naufragios* cause Las Casas to defend ritualistic anthropophagy and to dismiss cannibalism as a source of nutrition.

Cabeza de Vaca, however, never arrives at this corollary because these passages in the *Naufragios* are ultimately self-serving: he does not eat horse meat, much less human flesh. Margo Glantz has pointed out that even though shamans had several wives, Cabeza de Vaca—due to his *honestidad* (chastity), of course—had no intercourse with women, thus producing "un discurso erótico hábilmente soslayado" [an erotic discourse skillfully evaded] (Glantz 1993a: 421). Cristina Iglesia has also juxtaposed eroticism and cannibalism to single out an *honesto* Cabeza de Vaca who gazes at the body of an Indian woman, but only to praise her political fidelity: "Buscaron quatro mancebos . . . que se enboluiessen con la india, en lo qual no tuuieron mucho que hazer, porque de costumbre no son escasas de sus personas . . . y dandole muchas cosas, no pudieron saber ningún secreto" [They looked for four youths . . . so that they would get involved with the Indian woman, which was not difficult to do because Indian women are very generous with their persons . . . and giving her many things, they were not able to know any secret] (*CLD,* 5: 350). This Cabeza de Vaca, according to Iglesia, differs from Irala, who invents Indian women as commodities in lieu of gold: "El texto de Irala ofrece al conquistador un bien que ya equivale al oro: la mujer guaraní que abastece de alimento mediante su trabajo agrícola y de placer mediante su servicio sexual" [Irala's text offers the conquistador a good that is equivalent to gold: Guarani women who provide food through their agricultural labor and pleasure through their sexual service] (Iglesia and Schvartzman 1987: 23). Cabeza de Vaca's faithful Guarani woman constitutes a fine conclusion to a chapter that, in Iglesia's words, "posee un ritmo narrativo y vigoroso" [possesses a narrative and vigorous rhythm] (24). But what to say about the anecdotal certification of the "generous" sexual mores of the Guarani women, mores that Cabeza de Vaca further corroborates by citing them, wondering why they had been given a body if not for sex: "¿Para que se lo dieron sino para aquello?" [Why was it given to them if not for that?] (*CLD*, 5: 350)? Though Cabeza de Vaca goes on in the next chapter to denounce Irala's raids, his naturalization of Indian desire suppresses the culture of rape and sexual exploitation by seeing Guarani women as willing sexual commodities. Thus, the exemplary *adelantado* deftly reconciles an aesthetic of colonial desire, while condemning Irala with strategically placed formulaic repetitions of legal terms drawn from the Ordenanzas. Iglesia nevertheless validates Cabeza de Vaca's condemnation of Irala for allowing Indians to eat their enemies and singles out his critique of abuse: "Ninguna otra crónica rioplatense alcanza estos niveles críticos" [No other chronicle from the Río de la Plata reaches these levels of criticism] (1987: 26). We must address the question as to how the benevolent critic of empire symbolically reproduces the same violence he condemns. And we must emphasize again how his critique is scripted by imperial laws.

Let us note, then, that in the same chapter in the *Naufragios* where he tells of Spaniards eating each other, Cabeza de Vaca includes the description of a funerary practice of burning the remains of shamans, whose ashes are diluted in water and consumed a year later by the immediate members of the family: "a los parientes dan esos polvos a beber, de los huesos, en agua" (*CLD*, 5:54). Thus, Cabeza de Vaca suggests that if anthropophagy does occur among Native Americans, it assumes a highly symbolic form. One does not need to emphasize the irony implied in this description of ritual anthropophagy right after the anomie that led Spaniards to kill and devour each other. The Indians, however, embody Cabeza de Vaca's violent impulses as he imagines them murdering the Spaniards if they had known that they would eat human flesh. Thus, Cabeza de Vaca at once reverses the stereotype of the Indian cannibal and universalizes intolerance against any form of anthropophagy.

If at the end of the *Naufragios* we could trace parallels to Las Casas's *De unico modo,* Cabeza de Vaca never explicitly denounces the absurdity of the *Requerimiento* or the illegality of all wars of conquest in the New World. Even when in the *Naufragios* he alludes to peaceful measures as the only acceptable form of evangelization and subjection to the Crown, he abides by the logic of the *Requerimiento:* Recognize the Spanish sovereignty or face war and slavery. Peaceful conquest retains the *Requerimiento* as a last recourse to persuade Indians to subject themselves to the Crown. Thus, in the *Naufragios* he portrays Melchior Díaz threatening the Indians after offering goodwill if they resettle peacefully: "Mas que si esto no quisiessen hazer, los christianos les tratarian muy mal y se los llevarian por esclavos á otras tierras" [But if they did not wish to do this, the Christians would treat them very badly and would carry them off to other lands as slaves] (*CLD,* 5: 134; Núñez Cabeza de Vaca 1993: 117). This dutiful compliance with the *Requerimiento* is ultimately what differentiates Cabeza de Vaca's position from the slave raiders in Culiacan (even though Oviedo's Nuño de Guzmán follows the law) and Pánfilo de Narváez, who apparently never bothered reading the document after the landfall in Florida. Cabeza de Vaca could never have assumed the position Las Casas takes in the 1550s (a unique one indeed) of a total condemnation of the Spanish enterprise in the New World (see chapter 2; Rabasa 1989b). Cabeza de Vaca certainly strikes us as a conscientious and law-abiding servant of the Crown. We should not, however, project an anti-imperialist position or be seduced by his heroic, colorful narratives of colonial adventures, and especially not by his similarly vivid and colorful ethnographic sketches of servile or hostile Indians. Because of the self-serving nature of his narratives, resistance has no place in his representation and interpretation of the Indians. If Cabeza de Vaca reprehends Irala or, for that matter, the slave raiders in Culiacan for forcing Indians to abandon their villages and for hiding their women and children, he never justifies rebellion (another major difference between him and Las Casas).

Through the *Naufragios,* Cabeza de Vaca first sought to gain the governorship of Florida; as compensation, he was eventually granted governorship of the Río de la Plata. He emerges in the *Comentarios* and other documents as an exemplary *adelantado,* with worthy lessons for the young Don Carlos. Irala was appointed to the governorship in 1555, which perhaps explains the absence of all claims to the Río de la Plata in the preface to the *Comentarios* and his settling for fame as a writer: "Que cierto no hay cosa que mas deleyte a los lectores que las variedades de las cosas y tiempos y las bueltas de la fortuna, las quales, aunque al tiempo que se experimentan no son gustosas, quando las traemos a la memoria y leemos, son agradables" [There is certainly nothing that delights readers more than the variety of things and times and turns of fortune, which, although they are not delightful when experienced, are pleasurable when we recall them and read them] (*CLD,* 5:148). We do not know the exact date of Cabeza de Vaca's death, but most likely he did not learn of Irala's in 1557, probably from "peritonitis following on appendicitis" (Bishop 1933: 289). Nonetheless, Cabeza de Vaca knows the lessons to be derived from the whims of fortune and, perhaps, how the *relaciones* of his misfortunes would in the end redeem him.

Whether his accusations of Irala and followers are reliable representations of the events need not concern us, and perhaps the Paraguayan historian Enrique de Gandía is justified when he defines the two parties as follows: "Los españoles del Paraguay, sin frenos capaces de liberarlos de las tentaciones de las bellas guaraní, se condenaban el alma con aquellas infieles de las cuales cada uno poseía treinta, cuarenta y aún más, según las indignadas relaciones de los contados puritanos de aquel entonces, que sólo disfrutaban de media docena de indias" [The Spaniards from Paraguay, without the restraints that could free them from the temptations of the beautiful Guarani, would condemn their souls by living with those infidels of which each possessed thirty, forty and even more, according to the outraged relations of the few puritans of those times, who only enjoyed having half a dozen Indian women] (Gandía 1932: 119). Nevertheless, we may question Gandía's ironic detachment that allows him to blame not "los sentimientos de los españoles, que se pervertían al llegar a estas tierras, sino al medio ambiente en que ellos vivían y que, hasta un cierto punto los hacía irresponsables de sus actos" [the feelings of the Spaniards, that were perverted upon arrival, but the natural milieu in which they lived and that, up to a point, exempted them from responsibility for their acts] (127). In support of this statement Gandía quotes Francisco de Andrada, a cleric, who asks how the Spaniards could avoid taking Indian women when the Guarani had the "maldita costumbre" (damned custom) of being responsible for sowing and reaping. Gandía further substantiates the natural milieu with "las delicias de aquellas tierras paradisíacas, como la dulzura del clima, la facilidad de la vida y, sobre todo, la extraordinaria abundancia de mujeres" [the delights of those paradisiacal lands, the sweetness of the climate, the ease of life and, above all, the extraordinary abundance of women] (127). This "unimaginable Paraíso de Mahoma," as Gandía defines it, which leads Spaniards to abuse and exploit Guarani women, could easily be replaced by another explanatory commonplace in the colonial representation of the tropics: the infernal jungle, which also leads Europeans to commit the worst atrocities. As Alberto Salas has pointed out, if the traffic of women in the Río de la Plata led to the proliferation of mestizo offspring that defined the hybrid and bilingual culture of Paraguay, we should abstain from suppressing the fact that this was the forced subjection of Guarani women (1960: 193 and passim). Without eliding the culture of rape, we can now recognize with Salas the originality of the mestizo men who will rebel against the "fathers" and invent unique cultural forms. According to Salas, by 1580, "son numerosos, capaces, bien adaptados a la tierra, baqueanos, hombres que usan garrotes en lugar de espadas, porque no las hay para ceñir, lindos jinetes en ambas sillas" [they are numerous, capable, well adapted to the land, scouts, men who use clubs instead of swords, because there are none to carry, exquisite riders on both saddles] (197). With these closing remarks on Gandía and Salas, we come full circle to Conrad, Cunninghame Graham, and Casement. They provide two more examples of what I have attempted to define as the culture of conquest in which we historians, literary critics, and anthropologists are still implicated today.

In treating the discursive violence that the culture of conquest perpetuates through its reading and interpreting of colonial texts, this chapter has reiterated the lack of attention literary readings pay to indigenous resistance. The vulnerability of the four survivors in the *Naufragios* does not lend itself to a documentation of resistance, nor does the almost exclusive concern with the political conflicts with Irala in the *Comentarios*. But forms of resistance can be reconstructed from descriptions of military encounters in the so-called *entradas* (raids) without recurring to that all too imperialistic topoi of the hostile Indian. We should also resist the impulse to define Cabeza de Vaca's function as a shaman in the *Naufragios* with the topoi of the Western hero whose perspicacity enables him to play the role of a quack doctor and manipulate the *hijo del sol* (son of the sun) attribute.[24]

It is precisely because the topoi of ignorant and warlike Indians have played an integral function in colonialist literature that they lend artistic and literary value to the *Naufragios*. But in following Cabeza de Vaca's conception of Indians, literary critics not only perpetuate the culture of conquest but also lose track of the rhetorical devices that enabled him to convey knowledge of Native American cultures and personal experiences that questioned European taboos. The self-representation of a law-abiding colonial official and conquistador that I have traced in the *Naufragios* and the *Comentarios* may coexist with a colonizer whose writing *being here* has an exceptional story to tell about *being there*. It seems to me that only after we make room for this paradoxical coexistence of an imperial and an empathetic perspective will we be able to trace voices of resistance in Cabeza de Vaca. Identifying the use of formulaic phrases drawn from the Ordenanzas of 1526 has enabled us to deconstruct the purported originality of Cabeza de Vaca's critique of empire and advocacy for peaceful conquest. Those passages that critics tend to read as novelesque may thus in fact turn out to be allegorical.

CHAPTER 2

The Mediation of the Law in the New Mexico

Corpus, 1539–1610

The critique of the oxymoron "peaceful conquest" suggests that to speak of the mediation of the law in studies of colonial historiography has become a truism. Calling something a truism is a rhetorical gesture that, while accepting the veracity, if not the force, of an accepted idea, seeks to controvert it, to complicate it. It has become second nature to critics of colonialism to read laws as ideological maskings and rhetorical constructs.[1] Understandably, we distrust histories of colonialism that trace the evolution of juridic institutions. But when we critique the ideological underpinnings of studies that single out a particular sense of justice in Spanish legal institutions and sixteenth-century debates over the legality of Spanish sovereignty in the New World, we tend to disregard how emergent bodies of law articulated theories of empire and colonial programs that, in turn, shaped texts. Let me preface my discussion of the mediation of the law with synopses of the work of a historian and a literary critic who, in my opinion, constitute exemplary modes of theorizing Spanish law and colonialism.

For historian Patricia Seed, the *Requerimiento* defines the style of Spanish ceremonies of possession in the New World (Seed 1992, 1995). The *Requerimiento* is ubiquitous, according to Seed, manifest both in documents making explicit reference to it as well as in those where it is suspiciously absent. In Seed's analysis, its absence is symptomatic of a growing awareness of the origins of the *Requerimiento* in Islamic jihad, a holy war ordained by God. This point is thoroughly documented by Seed, but at the expense of understanding how the "masking" of Islamic roots in Spain's ideology of conquest became part of debates that were not limited to concerns about similarities with Islam but also involved questions posed from within a Judeo-Christian tradition with respect to the pope's authority to grant Spain sovereignty over the New World or, indeed, whether war against Indians was just. Seed (1993) views these debates and transformations of Spanish laws primarily as ideological forms of both legitimating conquest and the exercise of power in the New World. As Seed has reminded us, in *De unico modo,* Bartolomé de las Casas (without naming the *Requerimiento*) characterized as Muslim the premise that infidels should first be politically subjected to a Christian people and then converted peacefully to Christianity (Las Casas 1988 [ca. 1534]: 438–55; Seed 1995: 76). Las Casas knew the rhetorical force of naming and identifying the *Requerimiento* with Islam, but his argument addresses a more fundamental issue.

As we saw in chapter 1, Las Casas objected to the practice of the *Requerimiento* on the grounds that no infidel people, let alone an infidel king, would willingly accept Christian dominance; consequently, war would be inevitable if one followed this method of attracting people to the Christian faith (1988 [ca. 1534]: 378). Thus, Las Casas makes manifest a contradiction in the Crown's ideology of peaceful conquest. Clearly, the Crown did not abandon its claims to political sovereignty (which should be differentiated from the responsibility to preach Christianity, as Las Casas argued) based on the papal donations made through a series of bulls that divided the non-Christian world between Spain and Portugal (see Parry and Keith 1984). But to respond to Las Casas's irrefutable arguments the Crown devised laws and *ordenanzas* that rarefied the language of violence and dominance. Without idealizing Spain's colonial program, it must be credited with devising modes of colonization beyond military force. In making the *Requerimiento,* hence military-religious conquest, central to Spanish policy, Seed ignores that Spanish *ordenanzas* also entailed pragmatically minded laws designed to collect information, transform Indians into laborers, and above all, to police and control colonial initiatives. In the course of the sixteenth century, laws certainly refined the parameters of acceptable use of force. These amendments were made not only because the *Requerimiento* invoked Islamic jihad, but because it blatantly entailed a contradiction—that is, the oxymoronic nature of Spain's ideology of peaceful conquest.

Literary critic Roberto González Echevarría traces the origins of the picaresque novel and colonial historiography, in particular the *relación,* in notarial rhetoric (1990: 55 and passim). In his analysis the *relación* functions as the opposite of what he calls official historiography. Thus, González Echevarría characterizes Las Casas's *Historia de las Indias* (1527–1563), because of its contentious tone, as a prototype of the *relación.* According to this view, individuals writing *relaciones* faced the task of literally writing their "selves" into the dominant discourse. Even though there is a convincing element in tracing the origins of the picaresque—as a parody—to *relaciones* or *vidas* (and ultimately to confession and torture as the locus where the self produces its truth), it seems to me redundant, if not disingenuous, to speak of an influence of notarial rhetoric on the *relación.* The *relación* is both a form of historiography with its own generic constraints and a legal document whose style and contents were increasingly defined by laws and *ordenanzas* during the course of the sixteenth century. Whereas the *relación* would provide a truthful testimony on a set of particular events, a history, in the strict sense of the term, would draw out the universal significance of the events. In legal terms, the field of the *relación* pertains to law and the field of history to justice. And it is precisely in the dialectic between the particular (law and *relación*) and the universal (justice and history) that hegemony is contested. In this dialectic, laws are written and amended as particular cases modulate changes in concepts of justice. Both Seed's and González Echevarría's conceptions of law as ideological masking and rhetorical formula ignore this dialectic between the particular and the universal, between *relaciones* and histories. Let us clarify further these generic differences through Las Casas.

Las Casas's *Brevíssima relación de la destruyción de las Indias* (1552) and his *Historia de las Indias* (1527–1563) are emblematic of these generic distinctions. On the one hand, in the *argumento* of the *Brevíssima* Las Casas denounces what he ironically calls the marvel of the discovery by identifying it with unheard-of atrocities that have been committed in the New World (1991 [1552]: 3). On the other hand, in the *prólogo* to the *Historia,* he situates his work in terms of historiographical traditions and types of history that he traces back to antiquity (1965 [1527–1563]: 3–22). The task of the *Historia* consists not only of denouncing the errors and abuses but also of interpreting

Writing Violence on the Northern Frontier

Divine Providence to define the meaning as well as the ends of the discovery. Whereas the *Brevíssima* exemplifies propagandistic pamphleteering at its best, the *Historia* adopts critical history to expose philosophical errors and document their consequences.

In the *Brevíssima,* Las Casas's denunciation of an arbitrary code of law (in particular, the Ordenanzas of 1526) that at once prescribed peaceful colonization and made war inevitable debunks the idea that violence in the New World could be narrated other than as atrocity. There is nothing illegal, or atrocious per se, in the massacres and mutilations described in the *Brevíssima,* at least according to sixteenth-century legal treatises. The sense that these acts of violence are atrocities depends on the premise of their illegality, which, in turn, is meaningful only if one accepts that it is just that there be laws forbidding *all* violence against Indians, the central postulate in both the *Brevíssima*'s record of particulars and the *Historia*'s interpretation of Divine Providence. The same violence could very well be seen by other historians as *honesta fuerza* (honest force), to borrow Joseph de Acosta's (1590) phrase with which he sought to establish the legality of using violence to compel and subjugate Indians to church and empire. Whereas the *Brevíssima*'s opinionated tone seeks to intervene in the present, the *Historia*'s grounding in Divine Providence seeks to keep a memory for posterity beyond the immediate debates. It is indicative, perhaps ironic, of this intended long-term impact of the *Historia* that Las Casas specified in his testament that this work should not be published until forty years after his death, so that its truth would not be undermined by polemics.[2]

Las Casas wrote these texts with different ends in mind and against specific historians such as Gonzalo Fernández de Oviedo and theoreticians such as Juan Ginés de Sepúlveda.[3] In the middle of the sixteenth century, however, there was no official history, regardless of how much Oviedo aspired to be the Crown's official chronicler. The post of *cronista mayor,* as we will see later, was not constituted until 1569. As for Oviedo, parts 2 and 3 of his *Historia general y natural de las Indias* (1535–1549) were never published, mainly because of Las Casas's objections to Oviedo's representations of Amerindians. Las Casas's major works, the *Historia de las Indias* and *Apologética historia sumaria* (ca. 1555), were also never published during the colonial period.[4] The writing of history in the mid–sixteenth century was a highly contested practice on all flanks. Law provides the language and the space of contention where historians and theoreticians articulated their views of empire and where individuals narrated the particulars of their involvement in specific colonial enterprises. In this regard, laws do much more than create ideological subterfuges or provide rhetorical models for writing history. By official history we may also speak of all those *relaciones,* histories, maps, and any other documents whose publication the Crown chose to authorize. Texts were kept from the public eye because their contents included knowledge to be kept from other nations, narratives of events that would tarnish the image of Spain abroad, or ethnographic histories with questionable utility for the evangelization of Indians. Thus, the kinds of texts that could be "official," that is, made public, depended on the different policies of censorship developed over the course of the sixteenth century.

We should differentiate *relaciones* in which the writing of truth followed the dictates of the law and thus might include sensitive materials, from publishable *relaciones* or histories — or at least those written with the intention of publishing — that not only did not include sensitive material but, even better, articulated a legitimate and just, in some cases aesthetically pleasing, version of the colonial order. As we will see below, laws sought to regulate the behavior of explorers and settlers, but also the substance and style of *relaciones.*

A NEW ETHOS OF VIOLENCE

It is not by chance that I have selected Oviedo, Las Casas, and Sepúlveda to open my discussion of the mediation of the law in the New Mexico corpus. Debates among these three either prepared the ground for the Nuevas Leyes of 1542 or provided commentaries and critiques of these laws that set the tone for the new legislation and regulation of conquest and exploration of the Ordenanzas of 1573. The relatively short twelve chapters of the Ordenanzas of 1526 grew into these two complex legal tracts: where the Nuevas Leyes address Las Casas's critiques by outlawing slavery (law 22) and by dismantling *encomiendas* given in perpetuity (law 29), the Ordenanzas of 1573 ordain the Crown's monopoly over all expeditions and formulate models for the *pacificación* and settlement of new territories. These Ordenanzas number 148 and are organized according to the following rubrics: 31 under "El orden que se ha de tener en descubrir y poblar (On the order one must keep in discovering and settling); 105 under "Nuevas poblaciones" (New settlements); and 10 under "Pacificaçiones" (Pacifications) (Morales Padrón 1979: 489–518). The *Requerimiento* is not mentioned in the Ordenanzas of 1573; however, *ordenanza* 136 provides language for legitimizing violence:

Si los naturales se quisieren poner en defender la poblaçion se les de a entender como se quiere poblar alli no para hazerles algun mal ni tomarles sus haziendas sino por tomar amistad con ellos y enseñarlos a biuir politicamente y mostrarles a conocer a dios y enseñarles su ley por la cual se salbaran dandoseles a entender por medio de los religiosos y clerigos y personas que para ello diputare el gouernador y por buenas lenguas procurando por todos los medios posibles que la poblacion se haga con su paz y consentimiento y si todavia no lo consintieren hauiendoles requerido por los dichos medios diuersas vezes los pobladores hagan su poblacion sin tomar de lo que fuere particular de los indios y sin hazerles mas daño del que fuere menester para defensa de los pobladores y para que la poblaçion no se estorue. (515) [If the natives try to impede the settlement, one must explain to them that one wants to settle there not to cause them any harm nor to take their goods, but to gain their friendship and teach them how to live politically and show them how to know God and teach them His law by means of which they will save themselves; this will be made understood by means of friars and clerics and any person designated by the governor and entrusted by a good interpreter, making sure by all possible means that the settlement is built peacefully and with their consent, and, if they still do not consent, having required them several times by the above-mentioned means, the settlers will build their settlements without taking what belongs to the Indians and without doing more harm than that necessary for the defense of the settlers and so that the settlement is not hindered.]

A great deal of violence could be justified under "sin hazerles mas daño que el que fuere menester" [without doing more harm than

that necessary]. And certainly the assumed universality of Western understandings of private property ("sin tomar de los que fuere particular a los indios" [without taking what belongs to the Indians]), a cornerstone of the same principle informing the presumed right to settle in Indian territories, underlies the thinking that has led over the centuries to massacre and genocide under the pretense of self-defense, of defending settlers' claims to ownership and territoriality. The new *ordenanzas* might not explicitly require the acceptance of the Spanish sovereignty as did the *Requerimiento,* but the political subjection of Indians now plays a part in the historical telos of the settlements. Furthermore, once settlements have been established, *ordenanza* 138, which begins the section on *Pacificaçiones,* outlines the process by which they will be brought into the Church and give their obedience to the Crown. The process whereby Spaniards gain the *obediencia* (obedience) of Indians involved conveying the purpose of the Spanish settlements and the benefits of subjecting themselves to Spanish rule of law. The *ordenanzas* go on to outline the means and methods of gaining consensus from the Indians. Pledging *obediencia* entailed having Indians fully understand how they would become bound to Spanish rule, which entailed paying tribute to Spanish *encomenderos,* settling in Spanish-like towns (no more nomads or mountainous strongholds like the Peñol of Acoma), and welcoming missionaries to preach the gospel. Needless to say, defying any of these consequences of pledging *obediencia* would amount to rebellion in Spanish eyes.

In conveying the meaning of *obediencia,* interpreters such as Tomás, who translated for Juan de Oñate in New Mexico, inevitably faced the kinds of miscommunications endemic to reading the *Requerimiento.* The difference now is that they would not be threatened with violence if they did not accept the summons, but once seduced or misled into obedience they would be subject to legitimate Spanish violence. *Ordenanza* 144 prescribes that after the *adelantado* has pacified the land, he should distribute the Indians in *encomiendas* among the settlers: "Estando la tierra paçifica y los señores della reducidos a nuestra obediençia el gobernador trate de repartir entre los pobladores" (Morales Padrón 1979: 517). The *Proceso que se hiço contra los yndios del pueblo de Acoma por haber muerto alebosamente a don juan de çaldivar oñate maese de canpo general y a dos capitanes y dos moços y otros*

delitos [Trial of the Indians of the town of Acoma for treacherously killing the general field marshal don Juan de Çaldívar and two captains and two grooms and other crimes] exemplifies how the act of *obediencia* carried with it the foundation of a rule of law and its conservation by force (AGI, Patronato 22, ramo 13, fols. 1036r–1085r).[5] The Acomans rebelled and killed Juan de Zaldívar when he tried to force them into providing the Spanish with food, either not fully understanding at first the obligations entailed in rendering obedience or, perhaps, simply changing their minds. But to make the refusal a legal case, the heading of the *Proceso* underscores the fact that the murders were committed *alebosamente* (treacherously). War was declared against Acoma, the subject of Gaspar de Villagrá's *Historia de la Nueva Mexico* (see chapter 3).

Let's not forget that what the Spaniards called settlements (a right never questioned) in fact amounted to invasions. Indeed, the detailed instructions in the order to explore, settle, and pacify territories read as prescriptions for the kinds of exchanges and communications that should have gone on over the course of the prescribed multiple readings, "una é dos é mas vezes" [one and two and more times], that was supposed to ensure the understanding of the *Requerimiento*. Under the new law (*ordenanza* 136), war would be waged after "hauiendoles requerido por los dichos medios diuersas vezes" [having required them several times by the above-mentioned means] to recognize the Spaniards' right to build settlements. At any rate, the new policies proposed modes of establishing contact, securing obedience, and seducing Indians that actually can be read as providing substance to unimaginative clerics and officers who under the *Requerimiento* would have been content with merely stating it *una é dos é mas vezes*.

The multiple summons to pledge obedience could include tricking unreceptive Indians into a situation in which they would be forced to listen to friars, clerics, and officers rant about the virtues of Christianity and Western civilization; the proposed methods also include examples of theatricality for seducing Indians. The formula for entrapment states that friendly Indians would invite hostile Indians under false pretenses to their village; once there, "quando sea tiempo se descubran [los frailes] a los que estan llamados y . . . comienzen a enseñar la doctrina xpiana y para que los oyan con mas veneraçion y admiraçion esten rebestidos a lo menos con albas o sobrepelliçes y estolas y con la cruz en la mano" [when the time comes (the friars) shall reveal themselves to those whom they have summoned and . . . begin teaching the Christian doctrine and so that they listen to them with greater veneration and admiration they must wear at least albs or surplices and stoles and with a cross in hand] (Morales Padrón 1979: 517). *Ordenanza* 143 also recommends playing music "para amanssar y pacificar a los indios" [to tame and pacify the Indians] and holding Indian children hostage "so color de los enseñar" [under the pretense of instruction] (517). Here, as in the case of the Ordenanzas of 1526, the language of peaceful colonization masks violence in the use of such terms as *amanssar* and *pacificar* and in the right to remove children from the care of their parents and communities for the purpose of converting them.

Juan de Ovando was responsible for these *ordenanzas* as well as for the post of *cronista mayor.* We must note that if the Crown used Las Casas's denunciations of violence against the Indians to curtail the power of the *encomenderos,* laws and *ordenanzas* also sought to control the exploration and settlement of territories as well as to systematize the collection of information. Gangsters such as Pánfilo de Narváez and Hernando de Soto, and no less violent and destructive dreamers such as Francisco Vázquez de Coronado, led whole armies into disaster, but little knowledge was gained from their expeditions. We have seen in chapter 1 that in the wake of Narváez's failed attempt to conquer Florida in 1526, Cabeza de Vaca's *Naufragios* presents itself as an ideal model of a *relación* that would render a service to the Crown. Regulations and instructions in the Nuevas Leyes and the Ordenanzas of 1573 seek to modify not only the everyday practice of the colonies but the style as well as the content of *relaciones* and histories.

Law 36 of the Nuevas Leyes, for instance, for the first time required that after every voyage of discovery (the new preferred term for invasions and wars of conquest), the "discoverers" (or explorers, a more appropriate term in English) would report to the corresponding *audiencia,* which, in turn, would forward a *relación* to the Council of the Indies: "Yten que el tal descubridor buelva a dar cuenta a la Audiençia de lo que oviere hecho y descubierto, y, con entera rrelación que tome dello, la Audiençia lo embíe al nuestro

Consejo de las Yndias" [Item, that upon his return the said discoverer report to the *Audiencia* what he has done and discovered, and the resulting complete account be sent by the *Audiencia* to the Council of the Indies] (Morales Padrón 1979: 438). Although the language of the law suggests that explorers would give oral reports, it obviously does not exclude the possibility that this account be written. Its language would seem to anticipate illiterate conquistadores like the Pizarros, who (as so vividly represented in Werner Herzog's film, *Aguirre, the Wrath of God*) signed their names using molds. The Nuevas Leyes, however, did not establish specific modes of collecting and recording geographic, anthropological, mineralogical, or botanical data in the *relaciones*. Nevertheless, the centralizing impulse of the requirement to submit a *relación* obviously called for compliance with the other sections of the laws that sought to regulate behavior. It is also important to note that the first eighteen laws of the Nuevas Leyes focus on the rationalization of procedures and the definition of a body of professional experts in the law to safeguard objectivity and neutrality in juridical cases. As for the Ordenanzas of 1573, *ordenanza* 22 specifically requires that "los descubridores por mar o por tierra hagan comentario e memoria por dias de todo lo que vieren y hallaren . . . e todo lo vayan asentando en un libro" [the discoverers by sea or land must keep a commentary and memory of everything they see and find . . . and everything should be written down in a book] (494). Furthermore, this daily record would be read to all participants, who would then assess its truthfulness and have the opportunity to add new information: "Despues de asentado se lea en publico cada dia . . . por que se averigue mas lo que pasare y pueda constar de la verdad de todo ello firmandolo de alguno de los principales" [After having been written down, it must be read in public every day . . . so that more can be learned about the events and so that the truth of everything can be confirmed have it signed by one of the officers] (494). Thus, the Nuevas Leyes and the Ordenanzas of 1573 rationalized procedure as well as the production and organization of knowledge. We may question how thoroughly these laws were implemented, but not the effect they had on writing. It would be erroneous to think of the evolving laws and *ordenanzas* as mere ideological subterfuges rather than as forms of rationalizing empire.[6]

The Mediation of the Law

A centerpiece in debates over the legitimacy of the conquest of Amerindian peoples was the *Requerimiento* and its presumption that the pope had the authority to grant the Spanish Crown jurisdiction over the Indies. If jurists, historians, and theoreticians of international law such as Francisco de Vitoria, Domingo de Soto, and Melchor Cano extensively questioned the authority of the pope, they also laid the basis to justify war against the Indians. Thus, in *De los títulos legítimos por los cuales pudieron venir los bárbaros a poder de los españoles* [Of the just titles by means of which the barbarians came to the power of the Spaniards (1539)], Vitoria legitimates war in terms of the natural rights of Spaniards to trade, exploit the natural resources of the New World, and preach Christianity (Morales Padrón 1979: 404–17). Indians had the obligation to trade and to converse with the Spaniards, that is, to place themselves under the civilizing process of asymmetrical contact, as it were, to let themselves be loved by the Spaniards. Only the later Las Casas seems to have evaded the iron logic of love in which the colonizer not only establishes the terms but also defines the language of dialogue— a logic that, by the way, Hernán Cortés mastered though did not invent (see Rabasa 1993b: 83–124). In chapter 1 we saw how Cabeza de Vaca's supposedly unique peaceful conquest in fact followed the Ordenanzas of 1526 to the letter. The *Requerimiento* underlies the staging of dialogue with Amerindians as well as the rationale for war in both Cortés and Cabeza de Vaca. As we will see in chapter 3, the logic of the *Requerimiento* (though nuanced by the language of the Ordenanzas of 1573, that is, under the rubric of pacification) informed Gaspar de Villagrá's account of the massacre of Acoma in his epic poem *Historia de la Nueva Mexico* (1610). Here, I wish to examine in general terms the ways laws mediated the writing of histories and *relaciones*. I draw my examples from the colonization of New Mexico, but the basic concept would apply to other regions or texts.

In the sixteenth century laws determined the modes of producing truth effects in both histories and *relaciones*. As I will point out in chapter 4, in the transition from the crude racism of the early Oviedo and the later critique of Narváez's, Coronado's, and de Soto's excesses, we find less a change of heart toward Native American cultures than the new ethos of violence laid out in the Nuevas

Leyes. But Oviedo remained a constant advocate for the rationalization of the colonial order in his preference for sound business enterprises over the waste and debauchery of gangsters and adventurers like de Soto or dreamers (though as abusive of Indians) like Coronado. Rather than ascribing historians' different positions on colonial policy to sudden revelations about the nature of Amerindians or justice, we ought to trace how imperial policy shaped their texts.

There are two political corollaries to this redefinition of the terms for discussing colonial historiography. The first questions the evolution of the moral attitudes and scientific capacities of the individual historians: evolutionary views of Spanish historiography ultimately propose the West as the privileged knower of the rest of the world. The second addresses the developmentalist model and global occidentalization of the past five hundred years: Spain's colonial project inaugurated a form of modern imperialism that constituted Western civilization as a paradigm to be imposed on the rest of the world. These political corollaries reveal power relations that were first exerted in the sixteenth century but are still in full force today. They imply a postcolonial perspective that enables us to critique the culture of conquest informing developmentalist policies and their implementations through military force — these, obviously, always under the guise of love and truth or, in the lingo of today, of advancing democracy. The centralized policies of the Ordenanzas of 1573 entailed a rationalization of knowledge that promoted developmentalist policies and pastoral forms of power. Laws and *ordenanzas* sought to regulate the subjectivity of both colonizers and colonized, that is, what had to be observed and reported by the colonizers and what could be thought and displayed by the colonized. In the practice of everyday life the colonial divide between Spaniards and Indians was never clearly drawn in binary terms; next to Indian *encomenderos* such as Isabel Moctezuma, who benefited from Cortés's alliances with the Tenochtitlan elite, we find criollos like the poet Francisco Terrazas, who bitterly deplored Cortés's unfair compensation of the conquistadores (see Alvarado Tezozómoc 1992 [ca. 1609]: 156–57; Gibson 1964: 425; García Icazbalceta 1962: 65 and passim). Yet, colonial legislation and its legitimating discourses always articulate a Manichean world, to borrow

Frantz Fanon's term: a divide between the rulers and the ruled, even when the former incorporates the indigenous codes of law and native elites into its ranks (see Fanon 1967, 1968; P. Taylor 1989; JanMohamed 1983).

The dates I have chosen to delimit my discussion of law in the New Mexico corpus correspond to Fray Marcos de Niza's *relación* of the first incursion in 1539 and the publication of Gaspar de Villagrá's *Historia de la Nueva México* in 1610. The texts of the early expeditions—that is, the *relaciones* by Fray Marcos, Coronado, Jaramillo, the *Relación del suceso,* and the *Relación postrera de Zívola*—were written before the promulgation of the Nuevas Leyes; nevertheless, these early texts written after the Ordenanzas of 1526 already emphasize peaceful colonization and the avoidance of warlike situations that would require punishment and consequently hamper evangelization. As Viceroy Antonio de Mendoza put it in his instructions to Fray Marcos: "Ynformandos primero si estan de paz o de guerra los vnos indios con los otros, porque no deys ocasion a que hagan algund desconçierto contra vuestra persona, el cual sera causa para que contra ellos se aya de proceder y hazer castigo" [Find out first if there is peace or war between the Indians, so that you do not give occasion to some action against your person, which would lead to retaliation and punishment] (Craddock 1999: fol. 1v). A pragmatic approach to exploration and settlement informs Mendoza's instructions to avoid war by all means. Little would be gained from creating unnecessary hostilities with Indians, but the *Requerimiento,* the flip side of peaceful conquest, would be readily available if needed.

PEDRO DE CASTAÑEDA'S *Pequeña Obra*

Although Pedro de Castañeda participated in Coronado's expedition, Castañeda wrote his *Relación de la jornada de Cíbola* decades after the event. His *Relación* is exceptional, in comparison to Coronado's, Jaramillo's, the *Relación del suceso,* and the *Relación postrera,* because of its length and its detailed information; it is also valuable because Castañeda writes it to facilitate new incursions: "Se tratara de algunas cosas admirables que se bieron y por donde con mas facilidad se podra tornar a descubrir lo que no bimos que suelo mejor" [Some remarkable things which were seen will be described at the end, and the way by which one might more easily return to discover that better land we did not see] (Winship 1896: 415; 471).[7] At the end of the *proemio,* after indicating that the interval of time between the events and his writing provides him with a historical perspective from which to observe the "rumbos y el aparejo por donde se hallauan" [direction and situation in which they had been], Castañeda alludes to the new projects, "porque tengo entendido algunos de los que de alla binieron holgarian oy como fuese para pasar adelante boluer a cobrar lo perdido" [because I have known several of those who came back from there who amuse themselves now by talking of how it would be to go back and proceed to recover that which is lost] (416; 472). His long experience on the northern frontier, at the Spanish outpost of Culiacan, especially qualifies him to write a *relación* that could inform new expeditions: "Yo al presente escribo esta relaçion y noticia [en esta uilla de culiacan] donde . . . yo y los demás que en esta prouincia paramos no nos ha faltado trabajos apaciguando y sustentando esta tierra, tomando rebeldes y biniendo en probeça y neçesidad y en esta ora mas por estar la tierra probe y alcançada que nunca fue" [I am now writing this account and narrative (in the town of Culiacan) where . . . I and others who have remained in this province, have never lacked tasks in keeping the country quiet, in capturing rebels, and, all the while increasing in poverty and need, and more than ever at the present hour, because the country is poorer and more in debt than ever before] (466; 541). Castañeda dates his *Relación* some twenty years after the event: "como a ueinte años y mas que aquella jornada se hiço" [about twenty years and more since that expedition took place] (415; 471)—sometime in the late 1560s. The original is lost and the only extant copy in the Lenox Collection at the New York Public Library is from 1596. The existence of this copy suggests the value sixteenth-century Spaniards gave to Castañeda's *Relación.*

A rigorous centralization and systematization of knowledge began in 1569 with a set of thirty-seven questions that Juan de Ovando designed and sent to all the officials in the colonies. Between 1569 and 1571 the questionnaire grew to include two hundred questions, and was eventually reduced to fifty in 1577.[8] These homogeneous questionnaires were the matrix of the *Relaciones geográficas*. In addition to this systematic retrieval of information, Ovando named his associate Juan López de Velasco to the post of Cosmógrafo y Cronista Mayor de las Indias (Official Cosmographer and Chronicler of the Indies) (Morales Padrón 1977: 472). Ovando was also responsible for the Ordenanzas of 1573. In the Ordenanzas, a brief version of the questionnaire structures the subject matter that the so-called *pacificadores* were to cover in their *relaciones*. In studying colonial historiography, we must recall that the writing instructions were intended not only to centralize knowledge and to regulate both the behavior of Spaniards as well as the implementation of imperial policy, but also to generalize a scriptural economy in the production of knowledge.[9] This economy of writing is, perhaps, nowhere better expressed than in Joseph de Acosta's judgment on the superiority of the Latin alphabet over Chinese script in the *Historia natural y moral de las Indias:* "Sabe más un indio que ha aprendido a leer y escrebir, que el más sabio mandarín de ellos; pues el indio con veinte y cuatro letras que sabe escrebir y juntar, escrebirá y leerá todos cuantos vocablos hay en el mundo, y el mandarín, con sus cien mil letras, estará muy dudoso para escrebir cualquier nombre propio de Martín o Alonso, y mucho menos podrá escrebir los nombres de las cosas que no conoce" [An Indian who has learned to read and write, knows more than their wisest of mandarins; since the Indian with the twenty-four letters that he knows how to write and join together, will write and read all the words in the world, and the mandarin, with his hundred thousand letters, will have trouble writing whatever proper name of Martin or Alonso, and much less will he be able to write the name of things that he does not know] (Acosta 1979 [1590]: 288). There is an unintended double edge to Acosta's colonialist hubris: on the one hand, we know that the phonetic record of indigenous names and toponyms, though versatile, was hardly uniform and accurate; on the other, Acosta demystifies alphabetical writing by testifying to the fact that Indians learned to use the alphabet overnight. Obviously, Acosta does not limit his *Historia* (as implied by the inclusion of natural and moral phenomena) to recording the name of unfamiliar objects, but overhauls and systematizes sixteenth-century knowledge about the New World. For their part, literate Indians could use their new skill to inscribe knowledge useful to the administration of the colony, to preserve their own traditions, or, for that matter, to decorate paintings, sculptures, and weavings. Thus, Indians could use the alphabet but not necessarily partake of writing as defined by the modern impulse to impose order on the world. The concept of scriptural economy encompasses more than the ability to use alphabetical writing to name unfamiliar objects. Indeed, the writing instructions for *relaciones* were precisely intended to fulfill the task of recording and producing new knowledge. Truth pertained as much to an appropriate ethical colonialist behavior, indeed, of writing one's moral self into history, as to a correct practice of inscription and organization of knowledge. Castañeda defined his *Relación* as "escrebir asi las cosas acaeçidas en la jornada como las cosas que se bieron en aquellas tierras" [writing out the things that happened in the expedition, and the things that were seen in those parts] (Winship 1896: 415; 470). He attributed the questionable character of information available—"tam admirable que pareciera increyble" [so remarkable that it will seem incredible] (415; 470)—to the span of time between the expedition and the writing of his *Relación*. Thus, Castañeda faced the task of both correcting the errors and providing an accurate picture of the territories.

We cannot know for certain if Castañeda followed an early version of questionnaires of the *Relaciones geográficas* when he elaborated his text, but we do know that "personas especulatiuas" (inquisitive persons) pressed him to write his account and that the inquiries were ruled by a will to truth: "Ellos tienen raçon de querer saber la uerdad" [They are correct in wishing to know the truth] (Winship 1896: 414; 470). This will to truth is further reinforced by the rigorous method he follows in what he modestly calls a *pequeña obra*:

Esta pequeña obra . . . ba en tres partes repartida para que mejor se de a entender[:] la primera sera dar noticia del descubrimiento y el armada o campo que hiço con toda la jornada con los capitanes que alla fueron[;] la segunda los pueblos y prouinçias que se hallaron y en que rumbos y que ritos y costumbres los animales fructas y yerbas y en que partes de la tierra. la tercera la buelta que el campo hiço y las ocaciones que ubo para se despoblar aun que no licitas por ser el mejor paraje que ay para se descubrir el meollo de la tierra que ay

en estas partes de poniente como se uera[;] y despues aca se tiene entendido y en lo ultimo se tratara de algunas cosas admirables que se
bieron y por donde con mas facilidad se podra tornar a descubrir lo
que no bimos que suelo mejor. (415)

[This little work . . . will be divided into three parts, that it may be
better understood. The first will tell of the discovery and the arma-
ment or army that was made ready, and of the whole journey, with the
captains who were there; the second, of the villages and provinces
which were found, and their limits, and ceremonies and customs, the
animals, fruits and vegetation, and in what parts of the country these
are; the third, of the return of the army and the reasons for abandoning the country, although these were insufficient, because this is
the best place there is for discovering the essence of the land in these
western parts, as will be seen. And after this has been made plain,
some remarkable things which were seen will be described at the end,
and the way by which one might more easily return to discover that
better land which we did not see.] (471)

Castañeda seems to follow the systematization of knowledge in
the *Relaciones geográficas* and the Ordenanzas of 1573. For instance,
the second part of his *Relación* covers the topics of *ordenanza* 15 in the
same order they are listed there. As for the details of the journey and
the places to establish colonies, Castañeda provides the kind of information requested by *ordenanzas* 16–23. This relationship between
Castañeda's account and the *Relaciones geográficas* and the Ordenanzas could be attributed to language in the Crown's request for a
relación. Laws and questionnaires built their evolving sophistication
and precision from earlier texts by Columbus, Cortés, and Cabeza
de Vaca, who in turn developed their styles and rhetorical strategies in response to the instructions, *capitulaciones,* and laws regulating their expeditions. The explicit directions on writing contained
in the Ordenanzas of 1573 reflect existent technologies for obtain-
ing and recording information that the instructions then generalized for the production of all texts. Maureen Ahern has pointed out
that even though Diego Pérez de Luxán wrote his *diario de campo*
(field journal) during Antonio de Espejo's 1583 expedition to New
Mexico seemingly as a personal record, Luxán followed the Ordenanzas of 1573 in every detail (Ahern 1995a: 154). If it is the case that

Luxán wrote his *diario* as a personal record, he exemplifies the way explorers valued the epistemic grid of the writing instructions regardless of their intent to file their *relaciones*.

Castañeda's "ocaciones que ubo para se despoblar aun que no licitas" [reasons for abandoning the country, although these were insufficient], the subject of part 3, apparently refers to Coronado's excuses for abandoning the pursuit of Quivira. Having fallen from a horse, Coronado recalled a mathematician in Salamanca who had predicted "que se auia de ber en tierras estrañas señor y poderoso y abia de dar una cayda de que no se auia de poder leuantar" [that he would become a powerful lord in distant lands, and that he would have a fall from which he would never be able to recover] (Winship 1896: 459; 532). "Con esta inmaginaçión de su muerte" [with this expectation of death], he decided to return to Nueva Galicia to see his wife and children for the last time. In complicity with his surgeon, "que lo curaua y seruia tambien de chismoso" [who was doctoring him, and also acted as talebearer] (459; 532), he pretended to be sick and convinced the gentlemen and captains of the army to give notarized opinions recommending that they abandon the land and return to New Spain. Castañeda's is hardly a flattering portrait of Coronado. Other *ocasiones para despoblar,* however, could also have included the rebellious Indians and the hardships the camp was enduring: "[Coronado] procuraba en estos comedios apasiguar algunos pueblos de la comarca que estaban no bien asentados y llamar a los de tiguex a paz y buscar alguna ropa de la tierra porque andaban ya los soldados desnudos y mal tratados llenos de piojos y no los podian agotar ni deshechar de si" [During this time (Coronado) endeavored to pacify several villages in the neighborhood which were not well-disposed, and to make peace with the people of Tiguex. He also tried to procure some of the cloth of the country because the soldiers were almost naked and poorly clothed, full of lice, which they were unable to get rid of or avoid] (458; 531). This scene of a shoddy, lice-infested army, exhausted from warring against resistant Indians, would not have been considered a legitimate reason for abandoning a settlement in a frontier where these hardships were expected. The language of "apasiguando y sustentando" is very close to the language of pacification prescribed by the Ordenanzas of 1573. But this might be a mere coincidence in view of the ubiquitous call for love and peaceful colonization in all *capitulaciones* (contracts) between the Crown and explorers drafted after the Ordenanzas of 1526.

LAS CASAS AND SEPÚLVEDA

It is customary to credit Las Casas for the reforms of the 1542 Nuevas Leyes and the Crown's insistence on love and peaceful colonization. As we have seen, this emphasis on peace was reiterated in the Ordenanzas of 1573, where the term discovery is replaced by *pacificación*. The Ordenanzas reinstated the right of the pope to grant the Indies to the Spanish Crown but did not mention the *Requerimiento* (Morales Padrón 1979: 488). They established a series of controls over expeditions and regulated the building of new colonies, all the while underscoring the evangelical mission of Spain's imperial rule. If the insistence on peace recalls Las Casas, the language regulating the foundation, governance, and civilizing mission of the new *colonias* is strikingly Sepulvedan.

Scholars have tended to characterize Sepúlveda's *Democrates Alter* as a reduction of Native Americans to the status of animals. The work of Las Casas, on the other hand, has been viewed as a defense of the Amerindian's potential to be civilized (see, e.g., Pagden 1982; Todorov 1984). This opposition does injustice to both Sepúlveda and Las Casas. Let's take an example of Sepúlveda's rhetoric that casts Amerindians as less human than Europeans. Sepúlveda first asks us to consider whether Amerindian dwellings and commercial exchanges did not prove that they did not lack reason, that they were not bears nor apes: "non esse ursus, aut simia, rationis penitus expertes." Sepúlveda then qualifies this rhetorical question by stating that their lack of private property and their subjection to the arbitrary power of chiefs, a result not of the force of arms but from their own free will, are certain signs of their servile spirit: "Et cuncta haec faciat non vi armis oppressi, sed volentesac sponta sua, certissima signa sunt barbari, demissi ac servilis animi" [The fact that they do all this not because they are oppressed by the force of arms, but willingly and spontaneously, is a certain sign of the servile and beaten spirit of these barbarians] (Sepúlveda 1941 [ca. 1547]: 108–10). But Sepúlveda views the end of empire as leading Indians out of this state of *homunculi* (underdeveloped little men) as he formulates a civilizing process that in the course of time would increasingly free Amerindians from their barbarism, that is, from their incapacity to be free of tyranny: "Nam temporis prograssu cum iidem fuerint humaniores facti, et probitas morum ac religio christiana cum imperio confirmata, liberius erunt liberalliusque tractandi ministri" [And when time itself makes them more human and the probity of custom and Christian religion flourishes among them, they should be given more freedom and be treated more liberally] (173).

Here we have one of the first formulations of tutelage as civilizing mission, one that remains today in neocolonial and internal colonial power relations, in which the ruling elites always retain the criteria for deciding when subalterns are ready to assume their full sovereignty: "when time makes them more human . . . they should be given more freedom." We must note that the call for *pacificación* in the Ordenanzas of 1573 was already central to Sepúlveda's imperial policies. For Sepúlveda, the process of civilization would consist of learning and incorporating Spanish forms of life: "Ac religiosi principis publice datis, tum litterarum ac doctrinarum praeceptoribus, tum morum ac vere religionis magistri" [They have been given public tutors of human letters and sciences, and even more valuable, teachers of religion and customs] (Sepúlveda 1941 [ca. 1547]: 133). This policy approximates what we understand today by development, even though imperial rule has been supplanted by neocolonial forms of intervention.[10] Sepúlveda certainly advocated the right and obligation to make war against those oppressive rulers and nations lacking the appropriate social order and justified committing massacres to punish rebels or as retaliation for damages. Unfortunately, these are still common policies today. The influence of Sepúlveda, which he very likely exerted on the Crown in his capacity as official chronicler of Charles V and as one of the preceptors of Philip II, can be traced in those *ordenanzas* that insisted on the civilizing mission of the colonial order. Take, for instance, the benefits of *pacificación* as expressed in *ordenanza* 141:

Deseles a entender el lugar y el poder en que dios nos ha puesto y el cuidado que por seruirle auemos thenido de traer a su santa fee chatolica a todos los naturales de las Indias occidentales . . . los tenemos en paz para que no se maten ny coman ni sacrifiquen como en algunas partes se hazia y puedan andar seguros por todos los caminos tratar y contratar y comerçiar aseles ensenado puliçia visten y calçan y tienen otros muchos bienes . . . aseles dado vso de pan vino azeyte y otros muchos mantenimientos paño seda lienço cauallos ganados herramientas armas y todo lo demas que despaña han hauido y ensenado los officios y artifiçios con que biben ricamente y que de todos estos bienes goçaran los que vinieren a conocimiento de nuestra santa fee catholica y anuestra obediencia. (Morales Padrón 1979: 516)

[Let them learn of the place and power that God has given us and the care we have taken to serve him by bringing the holy faith to all the natives of the western Indies. . . . We keep them in peace to keep them from killing, eating, and sacrificing each other as it was done in some parts and so they can travel through the roads meeting, negotiating and trading. They have been taught good manners—they dress and wear shoes, and have many other goods. . . . They have been given bread, wine, oil and many other forms of sustenance, flannel, silk, linen, horses, cattle, tools, weapons, and everything else that there has come from Spain and have been taught the trades and arts with which they live richly. All these goods will be enjoyed by those who might come to the knowledge of the holy faith and to our obedience.]

Documents pertaining to Juan de Oñate's governorship, from the *capitulaciones* that include a copy of the Ordenanzas of 1573 to Villagrá's epic poem, manifest an affinity with the imperial policies of Sepúlveda. The *Historia de la Nueva México* presents and defends the massacre of Acoma as an act of extermination in terms reminiscent of the precedents that Sepúlveda draws from the Old Testament to justify the extermination of a people (Sepúlveda 1941 [ca. 1547]: 110 and passim). Sepúlveda, as a good Christian, would insist on giving preference, whenever possible, to Christian charity, which would stop short of committing atrocities. We can further illustrate the ubiquity of Sepúlveda's influence with an often overlooked passage from that most enlightened of Jesuits, Joseph de Acosta: "Y de este género de indios bárbaros; principalmente se trata en los libros *de procuranda indorum salute,* cuando se dice que tienen necesidad de ser compelidos y sujetados con alguna honesta fuerza, y que es necesario enseñallos primero a ser hombres, y después a ser cristianos" [The books in *De procuranda indorum salute* deal with this kind of Indians, when they speak of the need to compel them and subject them with honest force, and states that it is necessary to first teach them how to be men, and then to be Christians] (1979 [1590]: 320).

Whereas these Indians in Acosta's taxonomy of social evolution correspond to savagery, he describes two other stages in the Americas that approximate the nineteenth-century anthropological classifications of barbarism and civilization, namely, *behetría* (chiefdoms) and the "imperial" states of the Incas and the Aztecs (1979 [1590]: 323–24). In this passage from the *Historia natural y moral,* Acosta alludes to evangelical programs he had designed for each of these evolutionary stages in *De procuranda indorum salute* (1984–87 [1588]). Accordingly, the lowest rung would need to be taught first how to be human—clearly, with some "honest" force. Regardless of the advanced stage, the Incas and the Aztecs remain in Acosta's taxonomy at a stage inferior to Europe mainly because they did not "reach" alphabetical writing nor the philosophy and natural doctrine of the Greeks and Romans: "Fuera de la luz sobrenatural, les faltó también la filosofía y doctrina natural" [Beyond supernatural light, they also lacked philosophy and natural doctrine] (1979 [1590]: 216). To explain the origin of New World people in conformity with the Christian dogma that all humans descended from Noah, Acosta speculates that Amerindians migrated to the New World from Asia, and that in the process they lost all their knowledge and degenerated into a state of savagery (45–46, 62–64, 323–24). As Amerindians reinvented culture, they crossed all the evolutionary stages, but Satan hindered their capacity to use natural reason and distorted their knowledge of God. Acosta's anthropological scale recurs in documents pertaining to New Mexico.

Oñate (in a short account of the rebellion of Acoma, which also documents the "muestras de metales mantas otras cosas de lo que alli ay" [samples of metals, blankets, other things there are there]) compares Puebloan urban planning, markets, and textiles to New

Spain (mainly to lend credibility to his colonial program), and then goes on to classify Puebloan political structure as *behetrias:* "Su gobierno es behetría que aunque tienen algunos capitancillos obedescenlos muy mal" [Their government is a chiefdom, where even though they have some minor captains they obey them poorly] (Oñate 1599 [AGI, Patronato 22, ramo 13, fol. 986r]). These *capitancillos* (a derogative diminutive of captain) are ultimately blamed for the massacre of Acoma. For Oñate suggests that the category of *behetria* and the fact that they obeyed their *capitancillos* poorly would counteract the Ordenanzas' instructions to respect Indian sovereignty and to seek consensus. Their rebellion, moreover, had to be repressed to make an example to other Indians who had already pledged obedience to the Crown. Ultimately, the purpose of the massacre was theatrical, to display Spanish force and the power to punish: "que avia fuerças y poder para castigar semejante atrevimiento" [that there was force and power to punish such daring] (fol. 985v). In their testimonies in the *Proceso,* Spaniards of all ranks, mestizos, Blacks, and Indians all insist on the need to set an example. Spaniards generally agreed that unless the Peñol of Acoma was completely destroyed and the Acomans severely punished, no one would be able to live securely anywhere in New Mexico. Because of their legal status, Indians, mestizos, and Blacks do not make these sorts of recommendations in their testimonies. Oñate's account of the violence inflicted leaves no doubt that the intent of the example was to convey that annihilation and slavery would be the consequences of rebellion. After the Acomans fail to respond to the *Requerimientos* of Vicente Zaldívar, the *sargento mayor* (sergeant major) whose brother Juan de Zaldívar had been killed by the Acomans, he "les dio batalla que duro tres dias al cabo delos quales se rindieron aviendoles muerto 800 indios y cautivado 500 de que justicio 80 y abrazo y asolo el pueblo conque quedo toda la tierra paçificada y temorosa" [gave them a battle that lasted three days, at the end of which they surrendered having killed 800 Indians and 500 having been captured, of which he executed 80, and razed and destroyed the town, thereby leaving the land in peace and fear] (fol. 985v).

Following consuetudinary military law, males over twenty-five had one foot cut off and were sentenced to twenty years of personal servitude. Males from twelve to twenty-five and women over twelve were also condemned to twenty years of personal servitude. Two Moquis captured in Acoma had their right hand cut off and were set free to convey the "news" among their people. Children under twelve were handed over to Fray Alonso Martínez and Zaldívar for a Christian upbringing. Sixty of the smaller girls, however, were distributed among convents in Mexico City, never again to see their homelands or relatives. To make the punishments effective as examples, Oñate had the mutilations carried out in Santo Domingo and other surrounding towns on different dates (AGI, Patronato 22, ramo 13, fols. 1084r–1084v). Though this theater of terror was a familiar process to Spaniards and Moors, it was entirely new and shocking to Pueblo Indians.[11] But as Marc Simmons points out, in the end, "the Acomans . . . proved more resilient and slippery than [Oñate] imagined, for within a year or two most of them escaped their servitude, fled back to the rock, and rebuilt a new pueblo that remains occupied to this day" (1991: 146). In passing, let us recall that in January 1998 a group of iconoclasts, perhaps Acomans, continued the rebellion when in the middle of the night they cut off the right foot of a statue of Oñate that had been placed in the town of Alcalde, New Mexico, outside a museum dedicated to Spanish explorers and settlers.[12]

The impact of the laws did not so much affect the specific procedures in the field as it did the documentation that had to be gathered to justify wars, establish settlements, define contracts, and even to write proposals to obtain grants from the Crown authorizing the pacification and colonization of a territory. A quick glance at the competing dossiers compiled by Juan de Oñate and Pedro Ponce de León reveals the extensive research they did on earlier expeditions, documents, maps, and the specific laws regulating settlements, in particular the Ordenanzas of 1573.[13] Of particular interest are those documents that compare Oñate's and Ponce de León's proposals, in which Ponce de León upstages Oñate in just about every item and demands fewer titles and privileges (*HDNM,* 1: 280–92). In the process of evaluation the Crown and the viceroyal authorities questioned the competence of Ponce de León and Oñate. Indeed, the new viceroy, Gaspar de Zúñiga y Acevedo (1595–1603), the Count of Monterrey, expressed doubts regarding Oñate's character. These were further confirmed by "a credible person" and ultimately convinced the Council of the Indies to nullify the *capitulaciones* he had signed with former viceroy Luis de Velasco II and to establish a new contract with Ponce de León. In the end, Ponce de León's failing health, poor finances, and questionable capacity as a Spaniard to recruit an army in New Spain raised serious questions about his ability to fulfill his agreement with the Crown (*HDNM*, 1: 200–207; Simmons 1991: 70–79). But these shortcomings amount to circumstantial factors that had little to do with the quality of his proposal.

The decision to reinstate the contract with Oñate also had the pragmatic end of preventing the anarchy that would result from disbanding his camp. Monterrey recommended retaining Oñate because dispersing the "Machina y gente" (Machine and people) he had already assembled in the north could have grave consequences: "Por ser muchos dellos delinquentes se anden por alla en los Montes como foraxidos y salteadores incitando a los yndios que antes lo heran a que los acompañen en aquel exercicio bolviendo a su antigua costumbre y turbando la paz" [As many of them are delinquents, they will wander there in the mountains like outlaws and bandits, inciting the Indians, who were also formerly such, to accompany them in that exercise, and to return to their ancient custom and disturbing the peace] (*HDNM*, 1: 384; 385). This statement reflects the impact of a series of rebellions that had started with the Mixton War (1541) and lasted for the next fifty years. Though one could argue along with Miguel León-Portilla (1995) that the rebellion of the Coras, Huicholes, Tepehuanes, Zacatecos, Caxcans, and others—their refusal to subject themselves to Spanish or Mexican rule—has lasted to the present.

During his imprisonment in Valladolid, Spain, in the 1550s, Francisco Tenamaztle, one of the Caxcan Indian leaders of the Mixton War, presented a *relación,* apparently written by Las Casas, that traced the origin of the rebellion to abuses and slave raids. These began with Nuño de Guzmán and became intolerable when the governor of Nueva Galicia, Cristóbal de Oñate, hanged "nueve principales señores" [nine principal lords] (León-Portilla 1995: 142). Tenamaztle was taken to Valladolid when he surrendered in 1551, nine years after Viceroy Antonio de Mendoza had defeated them at the Mixton. Earlier, in 1541, Pedro de Alvarado (who had come from Guatemala to aid the settlers in Nueva Galicia) had died during Cristóbal de Oñate's failed assault on the mountainous stronghold of Mixton. León-Portilla underscores the fact that Tenamaztle eventually won the war in the terrain of law and justice in Valladolid, where he articulated principles of human rights that were much later proclaimed at two influential fora: "Ello ocurrió en 1789 cuando la Asamblea Constituyente francesa enunció la 'Declaración de los derechos del hombre y del ciudadano.' Y muchos años más habrían de pasar para que resonara en 1948, en el más amplio de los foros, el de las Naciones Unidas, la 'Declaración universal de derechos humanos'" [This occurred in 1798 when the French Constituent Assembly enunciated the "Declaration of the Rights of Man and of the Citizen." And many years would have to pass before the "Universal Declaration of Human Rights" resonated in 1948, in the most ample of fora, the United Nations"] (15). Similarly, the Zapatista rebellion of 1994 testifies to Indians' ongoing struggle when its communiqués invoke the right of Indians to languages, cultures, and political autonomy as integral to their demands for respect of their human rights (see Rabasa 1997).

Other scholars, such as Philip Powell (1952) and Stafford Poole (1965, 1987), date the end of the rebellion to the 1590s and attribute the pacification, in the words of Powell, to a "'peace by purchase' policy [that] gave an enduring wisdom to Spanish frontier administration on mainland America" (1952: 204). Poole provides a picture in which the peoples from the north were assimilated by the end of the century: "By the year 1600 the people of the Gran Chichimeca had been pacified, converted, and were in the process of amalgamation that would result in the typical Mexican of the central regions. Before that outcome, however, the question of total war had been thoroughly thrashed out before the Third Mexican Provincial Council" (1987: 169). The substance of the policies adopted after the Council follows the Ordenanzas of 1573, which, as we have seen, made settlements key to pacification and contained language that would require a thorough assessment of just causes for making wars of extermination: *guerras a sangre y fuego*. The legality of this kind of war was debated in conferences and councils in a number of opinions. In response to an opinion requested by Philip II, a group of theologians agreed not only that wars of extermination were lawful but, indeed, under certain conditions were an obligation (see Poole 1965: 126–27). In a conference in 1574, most likely prompted by the Ordenanzas of 1573, the consensus among bishops, members of the orders, and lay consultors was that the *guerra a sangre y fuego* against the Chichimeca was justified. During the Third Provincial Council of 1585, the bishops opposed the war in the belief that not enough effort had been made to effect peaceful settlements; in the years following the Council, the viceregal authorities financed mass migrations of Tlaxcaltecas to the North (Powell 1952: 204 and passim). This was consonant with the opinion of the Franciscans and obviously left room for war if settlements did not work. Whereas the Augustinians responded that not enough was known to give an opinion, the Dominicans underscored the obligation to carry out a thorough inquiry and to keep in mind that Indians, in an argument that echoed Las Casas, had inalienable rights and sovereignty over their lands. The lay consultors, on the other hand, agreed that the war of extermination was justified (129 and passim). The issue was (for them, that is) not the legality of extermination wars but whether they were justified in the northern frontier.

In the Crown's assessment of the opinions expressed at the Council, the policy of settling the North with Tlaxcaltecas coexisted with the war of extermination. Indeed, Tlaxcalteca settlements complement war with an equivalent, parallel cultural extermination. Thus, Philip II combines the opinion of the bishops and the lay consultors when, in a letter to Viceroy Marquis of Villamanrique (ca. 1586), he at once subscribes to the opinion of those who recommended the reduction of Chichimeca nomads to settlements and specifies that to carry out this task it would first be necessary to pacify them, that is, to make war "en su avitacion sin aguardar a que ellos salgan a hazerla, y juntamente con los pueblos se fundasen tres o quatro monasterios de frayles para que con blandura los atraxesen después de tenerlos acosados y apretados en las dichas poblaciones" [in their own lands, instead of waiting for them to come out for the same purposes. It is also suggested that together with the settlements three or four monasteries of friars should be founded, for the purpose of attracting the Indians with gentle methods after harassing and constraining them by the use of the settlements] (*HDNM,*

1: 154; 155).[14] Whereas the first part of this recommendation could be taken directly out of Sepúlveda's *Democrates,* the insistence on kindness once more evokes Las Casas's *De unico modo.* Their combination was lethal. The "final solution" involved the destruction of Chichimeca forms of life, as these nomadic peoples would be forced to dwell in towns with Tlaxcaltecas that had been brought north from central Mexico: "Y esto medios se entendia serían los mejores para acavar con los dichos Yndios y los dichos Pueblos se abrian de poblar de naturales de Tlaxcala" [It was thought that these methods would be the best means of doing away with the Indians, and the said towns were to be settled by natives of Tlaxcala] (*HDNM,* 1: 154–56; 155–56).

At the end of his appointment as viceroy, Villamanrique informed the incoming viceroy, Luis de Velasco, that the Chichimecas had been pacified and that this had been achieved through settlements in which friars instructed them in the Christian faith and lay Spaniards taught them sedentary agricultural practices, and that they had become enamored of Spanish products (see Powell 1952: 189–99). Villamanrique's harmonious picture of the northern frontier fails to mention that the Chichimecas had been forced into settlements, and that what his policies achieved was a rationalization of the war effort that curtailed slave raids and other anarchic practices, rather than a zero use of violence. The pacification of the Chichimecas amounts to nothing short of their destruction as a nomadic people; as Michael Murrin has put it: "With the new methods the war quickly died down, and by 1600 the nomadic Chichimecas were already disappearing" (1994: 227). Let's not forget that those who refuse to abandon their nomadic culture, as expressed by Luis de Velazco II in a letter from 1593, are labeled "indios salteadores and matadores" [Indians robbers and murderers] to be punished so that others "se refrenen y tengan miedo y procuren vivir bien" [might restrain themselves and become fearful and seek to live well] (Naylor and Polzer 1986, 1:85). There was not then, nor apparently for some today, a place for nomadic peoples in the colonial telos (see González Arratia 1990). This rationale informed the practice of pacification advocated by the Ordenanzas of 1573, in which war and friars went hand in hand in the destruction of indigenous peoples. Obviously, in the case of ideal "friendly" Indians, strategic uses of war would be avoided by building neighboring settlements of Spaniards and promoting trade that would "enamor" them of Spanish products and ways of life.

The impact of the 1573 Ordenanzas in the writing of contracts cannot be overstressed. Each *capitulación* (contract) drafted between Velasco and Oñate was not only documented by the appropriate *ordenanza,* but subjected to *moderaciones* (i.e., modifications) advanced by Oñate and *conveniencias* (i.e., the appropriateness of the modification) drafted by Velasco. The new contracts were far more complex than the instructions to Fray Marcos de Niza or even the documents regarding Coronado's expedition. By the time Oñate wrote his proposal for the colonization of New Mexico, the Council of the Indies had successfully gained a monopoly over the production of knowledge and, even more important, over the definition of criteria used to authorize further explorations and settlements. Although, in the case of Niza and Coronado, the expeditions were engineered from the colony, the final say would no longer rest on the viceroy but on the Crown. The certifying signatures that underwrote the authenticity and truthfulness of the *relaciones* became more prominent as they crowded the closing pages of documents produced after 1573. One should keep in mind that even if the writing of *relaciones* was never a casual affair with no legal bindings, in the course of the sixteenth century the mediation of the law increasingly regulated the definition and the production of significant knowledge as well as the documentation of the legal intricacies surrounding everyday life.

The systematization of knowledge was so thorough that all the *relaciones* from the second series of expeditions, which followed Chamuscado-Rodríguez's and Espejo's in the early 1580s, reflect a common pattern and organization of topics in their evaluation and description of the land, namely, the site, the agriculture, the cattle, the mines, the channels of communication, the forests, the salubrity, and, of course, the indigenous labor. Gallegos's on Chamuscado-Rodríguez and Luxán's on Espejo are exemplary instances of

112   *Writing Violence on the Northern Frontier*

how the Ordenanzas of 1573 served as a blueprint (see Ahern 1995a, 1995b). As we have seen, these Ordenanzas systematized knowledge-gathering technologies that had been in place at least since, if not before, Columbus. Accounts did include information regarding marvelous kingdoms such as Cibola and Quivira, but these wish horizons were always compatible with recording more immediate needs. Thus, the exploration of the territories and the pursuit of another Tenochtitlan or Cuzco presupposed building a series of settlements that would lend strategic support to further expeditions. Indeed, an important task was to create an infrastructure among the Indians themselves, as shown by Hernando de Alarcón, who, during his expedition of the Colorado River in 1540, "dexóles simientes y gallinas y díxoles cómo las habían de criar" [left behind seeds and hens and instructed them on how to take care of them] (Herrera y Tordesillas 1934–1957 [1601–1615], 13:304).

The discovery of rich ores was hardly the sole end of the expeditions, but often a precondition for colonization because no expedition would draw settlers without gold or silver mines. This precondition was not due to some sort of greedy nature particular to the Spanish character; mines provided the materials for the production in situ of a stable (i.e., universally accepted) monetary form, which, in turn, would enable the settlers to accumulate *some* capital. I italicize some to emphasize that even if the bulk of the colonists dreamt of accumulating a "fortune," in reality the only way to retain settlers on the frontier was with the expectation and the possibility of amassing a small capital through humble but indispensable trades as bakers, farmers, cowboys, carpenters, tailors, and so on.

Thus, settlements on roads to the North established an infrastructure for the wagons carrying camps of women, children, and workers of all trades. The following instruction found in Antonio de Espejo's request for authorization to settle New Mexico in 1584 gives an idea of the size of the caravans: "Han de llevar los dichos cien carros, y para ellos, mil bueyes, para que puedan mudar é ir con mas comodidad el dicho viage; de manera que haya para cada carro, diez bueyes" [They must take the aforementioned one hundred wagons, and for them, one thousand oxen, so they can change them and travel more comfortably on the said journey, such that there are ten oxen for each wagon] (*CDI,* 15:155). These wagons were just for the hundred families of the expedition; it recommends an additional four hundred men but does not specify the number of "friendly" Indians. The caravan would also include one thousand mares, four thousand cows, eight hundred horses, five thousand sheep, ingots of iron for manufacturing picks, hoes, and other tools, bellows and tubes for testing metals, victuals of bread and cured meats—and all at Espejo's expense. Espejo's offer to settle New Mexico was never put into effect, for he died in Havana in 1586 (Hammond and Rey 1966: 238–39). *Ordenança* 25 gives us a good idea as to how closely the king kept an eye on his capital: "Atento que la esperiençia a mostrado en muchos descubrimientos y nauegaçiones *que se han hecho por nuestra quenta se hazen con mucha costa y con mucho menos cuidado y diligençia de los que lo van a hazer procurando mas de se aprouechar de la hacienda real* que de que se consiga el efecto a que van mandamos que ningun descubrimiento nueuo nauegacion ni poblacion se haga a costa de nuestra hazienda" [Having learned from experience that many of the discoveries and navigations *that we have financed have been more costly and more carelessly and less diligently executed, finding that those who carry them out sought more to take advantage of the royal estate* than to achieve the effect for which they were sent, we mandate that no new discovery, navigation or settlement be done at the cost of our estate] (Morales Padrón 1979: 494; emphasis in original).[15]

There is, perhaps, no document that expresses the fact that mines were a precondition to stable settlement than the Viceroy Count of Monterrey's *Discurso y proposición [. . .] tocante á los descubrimientos del Nuevo México* (ca. 1603), an assessment of Oñate's settlements based on reports on the northern frontier that Monterrey had collected for a number of years (*CDI*, 16: 38–66).[16] According to Monterrey, "Si no saliese cierto el haber plata, puesto caso que se hallase forma para que se hallase moneda vellon, y esta corriese y facilitase la contratacion, serviria esto para la provision de aquellos españoles y para sus granjerías en cosas de consideracion; pues no tienen que vender de que haya saca, y todo seria pobreza" [If there does not prove to be silver, a way must be found to have copper money, that it might circulate and facilitate commerce; this would serve for the provision of those Spaniards there and for accumulating substantial profits; otherwise they would have nothing to sell for profit and all would be poverty] (*CDI*, 16:50). Monterrey adds that

Writing Violence on the Northern Frontier

without silver, "no habrá quien vaya á poblar, ni poblado quiera permanecer; porque con solo comer y vestir, nadie vive contento en las Indias" [no one will want to go and settle, nor once settled will want to remain; because no one is content in the Indies with only food and clothing] (16:51). Copper coins would enable some commerce with New Spain, but this solution would merely keep the settlers supplied, because they have nothing to sell with "saca" (profit), no commodities for export, hence, no accumulation of wealth beyond the basic necessities: "Ni el sustento tendrá regalos, ni los vestidos nobleza" [Neither will the sustenance include treats, nor the garments, nobility] (16:51). The *Discurso y proposición* recommends the stimulation of commerce and the overseeing of the value given to money: "Entre tanto que no se descubriere plata ú el cobre que afirman que hay, se pudiere introducir moneda que corra allí y acá, haciéndose alguna en aquella tierra, y dándole bastante bajo valor, que ganasen en ella los mercaderes que tragesen" [As long as the silver or copper that they assert is there has not been discovered, one could introduce money that circulates here and there, minting some in that land, and giving it very low value, so that the merchants who take things make some profit] (16: 48–49). As Monterrey points out, in the Indies settlers expected a standard of living beyond the very basic needs, but this fact does not necessarily imply the "myth-of-the-Spaniard-who-wanted-to-be-a-lord-without-working." On the contrary, his recommendation attests to the capitalist potential of the colony, where there was no longer a place for self-sufficient "traditional" communities among the Spanish immigrants.

Monterrey underscores that unless there are economic incentives, the population of New Mexico will consist solely of "gente violentada por la conservacion de aquella cristiandad" [people motivated by the will to conserve that Christendom] or "hombres condenados por delitos" [men serving sentences for crimes] (*CDI*, 16:51). If the support of committed clergy could be seen as an ideal solution, he finds that "hoy no se que tenga cuerpo ni estado que pueda justificarlo" [today there is not a body or state that could justify it]; as for the second colonial type, these men are "inutiles por sus malas conciencias y costumbres" [useless because of their evil consciences and customs] (16:51). Monterrey concludes the third chapter, which assesses Oñate's and Zaldívar's reports of promising gold and silver mines, with the recommendation that the Real Hacienda subsidize the settlers: "socorrer a los pobladores con algo" (16:51). In spite of economic woes, the Crown should retain the settlements because of the numerous Indian converts. Indeed, the poverty of the land could be used "para confusion de los herejes y aun de los émulos de la Corona de Castilla" [for the confusion of heretics and even of the competitors to the Crown of Castile] by underscoring "que se busca en primer lugar la exaltacion de la fee y propagacion de la Santa Iglesia, la cual se prueba en las Indias cuando se ve que si en unas partes sobra hacienda, en otras suple Vuestra Magestad el gasto" [that the primary end is the exaltation of the Faith and the propagation of the Holy Church, which is proved when one sees that if in some places there is a surplus, in others Your Majesty assumes the cost] (16:47). Thus, New Mexico could lend itself for public relations to cleanse the image of the empire. Monterrey falls short of recommending Oñate's removal from the governorship, though he suggests modifying the original contract, the *capitulaciones,* to limit his authority; the negative tone of the report eventually led the incoming viceroy, the Marquis of Montesclaros, to recommend Oñate's removal in 1605. The Crown ordered Oñate's recall in 1606. By the time the dispatch arrived in New Spain in 1607, however, Montesclaros was no longer viceroy, and, had Oñate not resigned before, his demise would have been the responsibility of the incoming viceroy Luis de Velasco II, who had supported Oñate in 1595 during his first term as viceroy (see Simmons 1991: 177–78).

Discurso y proposición consists of five chapters. The first warns the king that Oñate intends to request the fulfillment of the *capitulaciones* and provides arguments against this request. The second recommends making a *traslado* of documents (establishing a dossier) to evaluate Oñate's and Zaldívar's claims that they had followed the Crown's instructions. Chapter 3 describes the lands and recommends retaining the settlements. Chapter 4 compares Oñate's and Zaldívar's reports with documents pertaining to Cabeza de Vaca, Coronado, Chamuscado-Rodríguez, Espejo, and others. The final chapter dwells on the importance of these territories and compares the accounts discussed in the previous chapter with general and particular maps.

Writing Violence on the Northern Frontier

In chapter 4, Monterrey speaks of collecting and evaluating books and accounts of New Mexico: "Mandé juntar asímismo algunos libros y relaciones de tiempo atras, y comunicóse todo con personas de confianza é inteligencia" [I had books and accounts from former times collected and evaluated, and everything was consulted with trustworthy and intelligent persons] (*CDI*, 16:55). He also consulted a mathematician who tried to define the territories covered by Oñate, but who was unable to do so because of the "oscuridad que trae en su papeles" [obscurity of his papers] (16:55). Monterrey mentions Miguel—an Indian captured during the expedition to Quivira who knew the territories particularly well as he had been a captive of the Indians from whom Oñate had taken him—who at first had resisted collaboration and "estuvo con mucho corage como barbaro" [was very resentful as barbarians would be], but eventually "sin haber aprendido hasta hoy hablar ni entender en lengua ninguna . . . se ha hecho tan ladino, por señas que espanta" [without having learned to speak nor to understand any language to this day . . . became so artful with signs that it is amazing] (16:54). In addition to Oñate's and Zaldívar's *relaciones,* the mathematician was asked to make sense of Miguel's account. For his testimony, "Diligencias tomadas con miguel indio que traxo del nuebo mexico el maese de campo Vicente Zaldívar" (1601), Miguel drew a map (fig. 2) and provided detailed information on distances, natural resources, and other relevant information about the places depicted (Miguel 1601 [AGI, Patronato 22, ramo 4, 211v–217v; Mapas y Planos, México, 50]). Miguel's map was used by the cosmographer Enrique Martínez for his "Razguño de las provincias de la nueua Mexico" in 1602 (fig. 3) (AGI, Patronato 22, ramo 12; Mapas y Planos, México, 49), and there is reason to believe that Martínez is the mathematician consulted by Monterrey.[17] Both maps contain, if not identical information, that most relevant to the rivers and the *caminos* that lead to Quivira. In Miguel's map (if one turns it around) the west appears at the right-hand corner where San Gabriel marks the beginning of the *camino* to the "poblaçion donde lo prendieron," and at the far end on the right he locates a river and lagoon where one finds gold. The legend "no lo a bisto," as in the legend for *rio B* in Martínez's map, establishes that the existence of the river with gold is based on hearsay; the legend in Martinez's map reads:

The Mediation of the Law 117

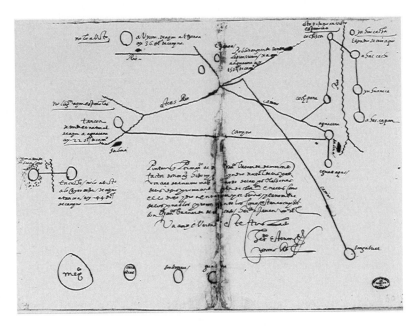

Figure 2. "Mapa de Miguel indio," 1601. Courtesy of the Ministerio de Educación y Cultura. Archivo General de Indias. Patronato 22, ramo 4, Mapas y Planos, México, 50.

"Dizen los indios que es muy poblado y que ai un gran señor y que ai oro, mas nadie de los nuestros lo ha visto ni rastro del" [They say that it is very populated and that there is a great lord and that there is gold, but none of us has seen even a trace of it]. I will come back to Miguel's and Martínez's maps.

For now, let me sum up this discussion of Monterrey by pointing out that the 1573 Ordenanzas' demands for rigorous accounts involved not just drafting proposals and agreements, but also evaluating *relaciones. Discurso y proposición* concluded that Oñate's accounts add very little to what had already been printed regarding the expeditions of Cabeza de Vaca, Fray Marcos de Niza, and Coronado. Besides these well-known cases, Monterrey says: "Hice revolver papeles . . . y se hallaron unas relaciones [del] descubrimiento . . . que hizo Chamuscado . . . y otro . . . que hizo el año siguiente, sin órden y de su autoridad, un Anton de Espejo" [I turned the papers over . . . and found some accounts from the discovery . . . that Chamuscado made . . . and another one made the following year . . .

Writing Violence on the Northern Frontier

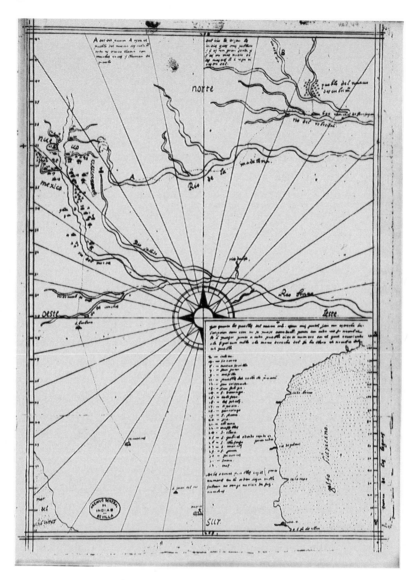

Figure 3. Enrique Martínez, "Razguño de las provincias de la nueua Mexico," 1602. Courtesy of the Ministerio de Educación y Cultura. Archivo General de Indias. Patronato 22, ramo 12, Mapas y Planos, México, 49.

by Anton de Espejo without order nor authorization] (*CDI,* 16:59). After examining these accounts, *Discurso y proposición* arrives at the conclusion that nothing should be expected regarding the supposedly wealthy provinces of Cibola, Quivira, and Totonteac.

If this text was particularly negative regarding Oñate's enterprise, other documents and maps of the time continued to propose establishing settlements to enable the pursuit of legendary kingdoms. The mediation of the law figures as prominently in documents pertaining to the acquisition and codification of information as it does in contracts or justifications of war. The insistence on pursuing other Cuzcos and Tenochtitlans betrays the massive investments behind expeditions and the need to pursue legendary kingdoms to the end. Clearly, it has nothing to do with some sort of weakness among Spanish settlers or a fondness for including fiction in historical texts. Examining documents as literary artifacts has less to do with isolating fiction from fact than with examining rhetorical strategies, narrative structures, and topoi they might share with literary texts (White 1978). Even allegories in maps and texts should be read *as saying one thing but meaning another,* rather than as mere fantasies (Rabasa 1993b: 180–214). The identification of texts as fictive ultimately betrays the projection of contemporary epistemological criteria on texts with different truth values and methods of recording information (Reff 1991, 1995). In the remaining section of this chapter I concentrate on imaginary topoi, both in the spatial and the rhetorical sense, in the cartography of the northern regions, the Indian-Spanish cross-cultural exchanges, and the "discovery" and description of the bison as a wonder in Vicente de Zaldívar's *Relación de la xornada de las bacas.*

Clearly, sixteenth-century explorers valued, if not depended on, earlier accounts as well as established contacts that could be renewed on later journeys. If the testimony of one's travails was a commonplace in *relaciones* (a token of one's desire to serve the Crown), the service, the *servicio* rendered by writing an account was evaluated in terms of the contribution it made to the geographic knowledge of the territories in process of colonization. The measurement of willingness to serve the king ultimately depended on the writer's ability to couch a narrative according to the specifications of the instructions, the contract, and the legal code in force;

the accuracy and truthfulness claimed by *relaciones* were not taken lightly. The investigations of Oñate, Zaldívar, and Villagrá give ample evidence to the rigorous manner in which the Council of the Indies solicited and evaluated testimonies. Thus, Villagrá was as much condemned for taking justice into his own hands when he cut the throats of two deserters as for exaggerating the wealth of New Mexico. Indeed, knowledge of the territories constituted cultural capital that was accumulated and zealously guarded from foreign nations, an effort pursued nowhere more systematically than in the *Relaciones geográficas* through which the Crown established a monopoly over the production and secrecy of information. By placing too much emphasis on fictive elements and mythic-literary echoes in *relaciones,* literary critics tend to lose sight of how territories are invented for colonization (see chapter 1). The literariness of the *relación* and, for that matter, of history, is hardly a question of juxtaposing fiction and fact, but of the production and mediation of meaningful "facts."

IMAGING ACROSS THE COLONIAL DIVIDE

Since Columbus's *Diario* of his first voyage, knowledge of Asia stored in maps, encyclopedias, and European libraries merged with Amerindian understandings of what the European pursued. One cannot and should not underestimate the imaginary dimension that informs the explorations of New Mexico. Michael Taussig's characterization of the colonial communication divide best exemplifies the exchange of products and meanings on the northern frontier: "As such they were in effect new rituals, rites of conquest and colony formation, mystiques of race and power, little dramas of civilization tailoring savagery which did not mix or homogenize ingredients from the two sides of the colonial divide but instead bound Indian understandings of white understandings of Indians to white understandings of Indian understandings of whites" (1987: 109). We can certainly separate the "real" from the "fantastic," the "factual" from the "fictive" from our privileged historical perspective, but in doing so we fail to account for our own particular historical place. Rather than presuming our standpoint as universal we should underscore that from Columbus onward the epistemic impasse was a result of the need to produce referents without antecedents in medieval or ancient travel accounts, where the end product was the invention of a desirable "new world" and not—as the commonplace has it—the description of the new by means of the old (see Rabasa 1993b: 49–82). Given that Columbus never reached the Cathay and Cipango described by Marco Polo (despite his claims to be in the vicinity), he could not simply identify the new with the old. In fact, Columbus faced the task of fabricating new parcels of reality in a new geographic region. As we will see below, the explorers of the northern frontier also carried their copy of Marco Polo. One does find legends (in the Latin sense of *legenda,* things to be read) in Columbus's letters and the *Diario,* but rather than just identifying the allusions to legends (both in Columbus and the accounts of the northern frontier) as an indication of a territory pursued in vain, we ought to trace how the legends are transformed through the descriptions of the places regardless of whether these were (from our historical vantage point) imaginary or real entities.

The transformation of legendary places is, perhaps, nowhere more dramatically seen than in Fray Marcos de Niza's account of his travel to Cíbola (1539).[18] References to Cíbola date back to the medieval legend of the seven bishops that fled the Iberian Peninsula and founded the Seven Cities of Cíbola on the island of Antillia, after Don Rodrigo of Spain lost his kingdom to the Moors in A.D. 714. The Cíbola on the northern frontier, however, bore little resemblance to the medieval legend. Puebloan culture, the desert and the plains, the bison, the cliffs of Acoma define some characteristic traits of the peoples, landscapes, and fauna of the *new Cíbola.* Fray Marco's *relación* is well-known for his "exaggeration" of the size of Hawiku, for Estebanico's enticement of Niza by sending larger and larger crosses, which were meant to denote larger and richer cities, and for Estebanico's miscommunication with the Zuni, who did not receive him as a medicine man but killed him after he insisted on entering the town (see Winship 1896: 361 and passim; Hodge 1895: 142–53). The legal nature of Niza's account is clearly established by Fray Antonio de Ciudad Real's certification of the contract with Antonio de Mendoza and by Antonio de Turcio's legalization of the *relación* (see Craddock forthcoming; *CDI,*

Writing Violence on the Northern Frontier

3:325–29, 350–51). It would be incorrect, however, to see these signatures as validating the veracity of the contents rather than attesting to the official nature of the document (Reff 1991). Coronado was disappointed with Hawiku, which Niza had supposedly seen from a hilltop and had described as larger than Tenochtitlan, but this disillusionment did not keep Coronado from replacing Cíbola with Quivira as the new land of desire. Other marvelous kingdoms were pursued by later explorers. Francisco de Ibarra in 1563 and later on Juan de Oñate both searched for Copala, and the kingdom of Anian was invented in the vicinity of China. The search for a continental connection with Asia also figures prominently in the accounts of New Mexico, and even though imaginary regions remained illusive they were incorporated into the maps of the period. Castañeda's account of Coronado's expedition illustrates the discursive circulation of information from the accounts to the maps and vice versa.

As in the case of modern anthropologists, Castañeda distinguishes two moments in the production of an ethnographic text (Clifford 1988). The first corresponds to dialogue, to the *peregrinaje* (literally pilgrimage, but implying wandering, erring) *en el campo,* (in the field), as it were *a ciegas* (blindly). The second corresponds to a privileged, totalizing perspective, a panopticon: "Ben mas los honbres quando se suben a la talanquera que quando andan en el coso agora que estan fuera cognoçen y entienden los rumbos y el aparejo donde se hallauan" [Just as men see more at the bullfight when they are upon the seats than when they are around the ring, now they know and understand the direction and the situation in which they were] (Winship 1896: 416; 472). This perspective enabled Castañeda to retrace the territories traversed by Coronado and to establish the best routes from within a cartographic representation. Castañeda's empirical framework, however, did not exclude speculation on Quivira and Anian: "Decir sea a que parte cae quiuira ques el rumbo que llebo el campo y a qual parte cae la india mayor que era lo que se pretendia buscar quando el campo salio para alla que agora por aber uillalobos descubierto esta costa de la mar del sur que es por esta uia de poniente" [I will tell where Quivira lies, what direction the army took, and the direction in which the Greater India lies, which was what they pretended to be seeking, when the army started thither. Today, Villalobos has discovered that this part of the coast of the south sea trends toward the west] (464; 539). Although the real Cíbola was a delusion, Quivira remained within the wish horizon, toward the west, in the vicinity of India. Castañeda based his speculations on Ruy Lopez de Villalobos's reconnaissance of the Pacific coast and the "Spice Islands" in 1542–1547.[19] Monterrey's *Discurso y proposición* also locates Quivira to the West: "Ambos [Quivira and Cíbola] los vemos en los mapas generales y particulares, con nombres de reynos ya sentados, no lejos de la costa de la mar del Sur el de Quivira, cerca del cabo Mendocino y Anian, de donde tenia nombre aquel estrecho y el de Cibola en el remate que [los mapas] figuran en la ensenada de las Californias" [We see both (Quivira and Cíbola) on general and particular maps, with their names well established, Quivira not far from the sea, near the cape of Mendocino and Anian, from which comes the name of the strait, and Cibola at the end that they (the maps) depict in the bay of the Californias] (*CDI*, 16:57).

One of the general maps mentioned by Monterrey could very well have been the *Americae sive Novi orbis, nova descriptio* (fig. 4) that Abraham Ortelius first included in his 1589 edition of *Theatrum Orbis Terrarum* and that placed Quivira at the forty-second parallel and Cíbola at the far end of the bay of the Californias, down the Colorado River. Totonteac, which figures prominently in maps, had already displaced Cíbola as the object of desire in Niza's account in which an informant from Cíbola "dixo que a la parte del ueste esta el rreyno que llaman de Totonteac. Dize que es vna cosa la mayor del mundo y de mas gentte y riqueza" [said that the kingdom they call Totonteac lies towards the west. He says that it is an entity in itself, the greatest in the world and more populated and richer] (Craddock forthcoming: fols. 6r–6v). Later on, Fray Marcos adds, "Me dixeron que [Cíbola] hera la menor de las siete ciudades y que Totonteac es mucho mayor y mejor que todas las siette çiudades" [They told me that (Cíbola) was the smallest of the seven cities, and that Totonteac was much larger and better than all the seven cities] (fol. 8v). *Discurso y proposición,* however, contradicts cartographical representations as well as the accounts they were based on: "No se hallaria cierta la relacion aunque se buscasen, como tampoco lo saldria en otros reynos que el fraile refirio oido, que caian cerca llamandolos abucus y totonteas como el mapa los nombra" [Even if

Figure 4. Abraham Ortelius, *Americae sive Novi orbis, nova descriptio,* in *Theatrum orbis terrarum abraham Orteli, quod ante extremum vitae suae diem, postremúm recensuit, nouis tabulis et commentaijs auxit atque illustrauit.* Antverpiae, Ex officina plantiniana, Apud ioannem Moretum, 1601. Courtesy of the Special Collections Library, University of Michigan.

one searched for them, the account would not prove to be true, nor would the other kingdoms that the friar heard of called Abucus and Totonteas as the map names them] (*CDI,* 16: 57). This negative assessment, as we will see later on, did not exclude other, positive opinions nor other expectations of finding rich kingdoms.

New Mexico gained resolution in maps and accounts through the information provided by Indian guides in the field. Although their communication with the guides was not as felicitous as they had hoped, the exchange of information nevertheless entailed a rigorous verification of data. The most well-known—that is, deceptive—Indian guide was Coronado's El Turco (apparently, Spaniards gave him this name because they thought the way this Pawnee Indian wore his hair made him look like a Turk), who led them in pursuit of Quivira all the way to the plains of Kansas (see Winship 1896: 394–99). From Castañeda's rectification of the location toward the west, we get an idea of how much the realization of El Turco's deception must have affected the Spaniards. Indian guides reinvented the "cities" described by the Spaniards, who, in turn, would further reinvent them. The Spaniards' will to believe El Turco makes reading about his garroting seem even more tragic, especially when we learn that Isopete or Sopete, another Indian guide they had picked up in Cicuye (Pecos), had been telling the Spaniards all along that El Turco was lying (395–96). The plains in Kansas and the Wichitas had little in common with the wealth "described" by El Turco:

> El turco . . . deçia que auia en su tierra un rio en tierra llana que tenia dos leguas de ancho a donde auia peçes tan grandes como cauallos y gran numero de canoas grandissimas de mas de ueinte remeros por banda y que lleuaban uelas y que los señores yban a popa sentados debajo de toldos y en la proa una gran aguila de oro[.] deçia mas quel señor de aquella tierra dormia la siesta debajo de un grande arbol donde estaban colgados grand cantidad de caxcabeles do oro que con el ayre le dabã solas[.] deçia mas quel comun seruicio de todos en general era plata labrada y los jarros platos y escudillas eran de oro[.] llamaba el oro Acochis. (432)

> [The Turk said that in his country there was a river in the plains which was two leagues wide, in which there were fishes as big as horses, and large numbers of very big canoes, with more than twenty rowers on a side, and that they carried sails, and that their lords sat on the poop under awnings, and on the prow they had a great golden eagle. He said also that the lord of that country took his afternoon nap under a great tree on which were hung a great number of little gold bells, which put him to sleep as they sung in the air. He said also that everyone had their ordinary dishes made of wrought silver, and the jugs, plates and bowls were of gold. He called gold Acochis. (493)]

From a sixteenth-century Spanish point of view such expectations belonged to the realm of the possible. Although descriptions of

fantastic acc.
possible to them

NB

Writing Violence on the Northern Frontier

Tenochtitlan and Cuzco had redefined the realm of the possible in the Americas, Marco Polo's China continued to be a source of information about the "Far East," as seen in such accounts of the Coronado expedition as the *Relación postrera de Zíbola* (ca. 1541), where bisons and dogs from the plains are compared with similar fauna in the *Divisament duo monde:* "Marco Polo, veneciano, . . . dice que [ha visto] las mesmas vacas, y de la mesma manera en la corcova; . . . Marco Polo, en el capítulo ciento y treinta y cuatro dice que en la tierra de los tártaros, hácia el norte, se hallan canes tan grandes ó poco menos que asnos" [Marco Polo, the Venetian, . . . says that (he saw) the same cows, with the same sort of hump; . . . Marco Polo, in chapter one hundred thirty four, says that in the country of the Tartars, toward the north, they have dogs as large or little smaller than asses] (Winship 1896: 568; 571).

But the expectations derived from Marco Polo also underwent transformations as Indian informants made sense of what the Spaniards would tell them. A passage in Geronimo de Zárate Salmerón's *Relaciones de todas las cosas que en el Nuevo mexico se han visto y sabido, asi por mar como por tierra desde el año de 1538 hasta el de 1626* (1629) describes how an Indian conveyed information to Oñate about boats with sails in Copala, an imaginary land purportedly located in the proximity of Marco Polo's "civilized" Asia:

Señalaron en la tierra el grandor del barco, haciendo en tierra una raya, y [Oñate] comenzó á medir y tenia el barco 70 piés de largo y 20 de ancho, y preguntándoles si aquel barco llevaba paño enmedio, tomó el indio un palo y lo puso en medio del barco que habia pintado, y un indio á la popa haciendo que gobernaba el timon, él entonces tomó un paño y estiendo los brazos en el palo que habia puesto, partió á correr con toda velocidad que pudo, diciendo así corrían los otros por el agua, y mucho más. Lo cierto es que si los indios no lo hubieran visto [el barco de vela], no lo supieran pintar tan perfectamente. (1856 [1629]: 34)

[They traced on the ground the size of the boat, drawing on the ground a line, and (Oñate) measured it and the boat was 70 feet long and 20 wide. When he asked them whether the boat had a sail, the Indian took a stick and placed it in the middle of the boat that he had drawn and drew an Indian on the stern as if he was governing the helm. He then took a piece of flannel, tied it to the stick, and started running as fast as he could, telling us that that was how the others ran through the water, and much more. Clearly, if the Indians had not seen it (a sailboat), they would not have been able to paint it so perfectly.]

This passage alternates between a festive scene—a description in which the Spaniards rejoice in the theatricality of the Indian's mode of communication—and an evaluation of the credibility of the informant. According to Castañeda, to test whether El Turco lied they showed him "joyas de alaton y de oliolo y deçia que no era oro y el oro y la plata cognoçia muy bien" [metal ornaments and he recognized and said they were not gold, and that he knew gold and silver very well] (Winship 1896: 432; 493). The least we can say about El Turco is that he learned very rapidly to identify precious metals.

Information regarding sign communication ranges from festive passages with the clear intent of pleasing the reader to the detailed descriptions of indigenous writing and cartographic systems that *ordenanza* 15 requested, wishing to know "si ay entre ellos alguna doctrina y genero de letras" [if there is among them some sort of doctrine and kind of writing] (Morales Padrón 1979: 492). We find information regarding indigenous writing and cartography in accounts such as those of Hernando de Alarcón, who exchanged maps with an old Indian on the coast of the Gulf of California at the mouth of the Colorado River.[20] Herrera's transcription of Alarcón's account in his official chronicle, the *Historia general de los hechos de los españoles* (1601–1615), reads as follows: "Rogó a un indio viejo que llevaba consigo que en una pintura, conforme a su usanza, le pusíese todas las tierras y habitaciones que había en la ribera de aquel río, y holgó de hacerlo, como Hernando de Alarcón le diese pintada la tierra de su propio nacimiento, y así se lo prometió" [He begged an old Indian that he had taken with him to put in a painting, following their style, all the lands and dwellings that existed on the banks of that river, and he was pleased to do it if Hernando de Alarcón would give him a painting of his own birthplace, and so it was promised] (1934–1957 [1601–1615], 13: 304–5). Hakluyt's English version recounts the incident in more detail and elaborates on the form of the *pintura* (1927 [1588–1600], 10: 257–90). We find a description of indigenous representations of space in Antonio de Espejo's *relación* of his expedition to New Mexico in 1582: "Señalandonos los indios de aquellas provincias con rayas que hacian en el suelo, y con las manos, las jornadas que habia de unas provincias á otras, y los pueblos que habia en cada provincia" [Indians in those provinces signified the day's journey between provinces and the towns in each province with lines that they drew on the ground and with their hands] (*CDI*, 15:125). Oñate provides an even more precise description of a similar writing practice in his *Relación cierta y verdadera* (1601): "Todos los yndios pintaron las poblaçiones en esta forma que siendo su rranchería de cinco o seis mil almas las señalaron haciendo un çerco rredondo con diez y siete granos de maiz" [All Indians painted the towns in this form: if the settlement had five or six thousand souls, they would mark it making a circle with seventeen grains of corn] (Oñate 1601 [AGI, Patronato 22, ramo 12, fols. 951v–952r]).[21] Oñate adds that in one town they placed 727 grains of corn for a total of more than two hundred thousand inhabitants. Oñate decided to include this information as an addendum when, after reading the original *relación* to all the captains and soldiers ("todos los capitanes y soldados"), they had found this detail wanting; they certified its truthfulness: "ser toda la verdad."

On the map of Enrique Mártinez (1602) (fig. 3), which, as we have seen, was in part based on the map and account by the Indian named Miguel (ca. 1601) (fig. 2) whom Oñate had captured along the Arkansas River, a legend to the east records as hearsay the abundance of gold in *rio B:* "Dizen los indios que es muy poblado y que ai un gran señor y que ai oro, mas nadie de los nuestros lo ha visto" [They say that it is very populated and that there is a great lord and that there is gold, but none of us has seen it]. Testimonies regarding Oñate's claims about the wealth of the territories vary. Though there were those, like Juan de Escalona, who warned the king, "No es todo como a Vuestra Alteza se lo han pintado" [Not everything is as it has been painted to Your Majesty] (Escalona 1601 [AGI, 22, ramo 12, fol. 930r]), others, like Zárate Salmerón, recall how Miguel's credibility was tested in Philip III's court: "Los plateros de la corte [de Felipe III] le pretendieron engañar con una ensalada de todo genero de metales picados y no pudieron porque luego conocía lo que era oro puro" [The goldsmiths at the court (of Philip III) tried to deceive him with a mixture of all kinds of oxidized metals and they failed because right away he would identify pure gold] (Zárate Salmerón 1856 [1629]: 28). Miguel's reputed knowledge of metals had already been recounted in the "Diligencias tomadas con miguel indio" (1601) [AGI, Patronato 22, ramo 4, fols. 212r–212v, 214v–215r]); Monterrey, however, remains skeptical of Miguel's report of the lagoon with gold: "Esto del oro, no tiene mas fundamento que el dicho" [On the said gold, there is no more foundation than this statement] (*CDI*, 16: 55). Regarding Miguel's map, Zárate Salmerón cites the favorable opinion of Fray Francisco de Velazco, a cousin of Oñate who participated as a chaplain on the expedition to Quivira: "En casa del duque . . . está un mapa que el dicho Miguel hizo de todos aquellos reinos y provincias de su nación y las circumvecinas á ellas, con tan gran primor como podía un cosmografo" [In the house of the duke . . . there is a map of all those kingdoms and provinces of his nation and the neighboring ones that the said Miguel drafted with as much beauty as a cosmographer] (1856 [1629]: 28; see Simmons 1991: 157–62).

The *primor,* the beauty, of the *cosmógrafos* suggests a judgment as to the precision of Miguel's map, however, not its aesthetics. Sixteenth-century cartography embellished the frames of maps with allegorical representations of the elements, the celestial spheres, and the continents, but these figures should not be seen as merely exterior to the actual cartographic representation inasmuch as they record codes of mapmaking, anthropological schema, and historical narratives that lend significance to depictions of the different regions of the world, otherwise homogenized by parallels and meridians (see Rabasa 1993b: 180–214). In regions where knowledge was wanting, as on the northern frontier of New Spain, legends provided information derived from ancient and medieval texts or from more recent speculations. To characterize these unknown (not yet colonized) territories, cartographers would insert drawings of representative fauna, flora, or cultural practices (e.g., scenes of cannibals in America and nomadic Tartars in Asia). These natural and cultural images, which were drawn from medieval or New World sources, would lend an aesthetic dimension to maps, but their beauty was inseparable from their epistemological and historical import as evinced by conquistadors and settlers traveling on the

Writing Violence on the Northern Frontier

northern frontier with their Marco Polo in hand. Doing fieldwork with old texts has remained a common practice among such modern anthropologists as Lévi-Strauss, who walked into the field with Jean de Léry's *Histoire d'un voyage faict en la terre du Brésil* (1578): "In my pocket I carried Jean de Léry, the anthropologist's breviary" (1977: 76). Modern ethnography still inevitably resorts (often quite consciously) to rhetorical and literary strategies to convey field experience and to circumvent Eurocentric devices and categories that colonialist discourses have deposited in Western culture (see, e.g., Clifford 1988; Clifford and Marcus 1986; Geertz 1988; Taussig 1987; Marcus and Fischer 1986).

As I pointed out in chapter 1, the culture of conquest is not an ideological component that we can separate from some sort of objectivist discourse, but indeed is part and parcel of the production of colonial knowledge. As in the case of allegories and vignettes depicted in maps, the *relaciones* contain imaginary (i.e., literary, rhetorical, artistic, ideological) components intended to delight readers. Vicente de Zaldívar's *Relacion de la xornada de las bacas* exemplifies an aesthetic resolution to an account of a failed enterprise (1599 [Patronato 22, ramo 13, fols. 1029r–1032v]). Failure did not imply absence of knowledge or irregular behavior, for Zaldívar writes his accounts to document how he and Oñate had followed the Ordenanzas of 1573 to the letter.

In his *relación*, Zaldívar identifies the campsite of Antonio Gutiérrez de Humaña and Francisco Leyva de Bonilla—who had explored the northern frontier without authorization in 1593—and alludes to the route followed by "Dorantes, Caueza de Vaca y el negro" (1599, 1029v). Colonial ventures depended on knowledge recorded in the accounts of earlier explorers and information derived from testimonies by Indian informants, who often happened to be the only survivors of the expeditions. Thus, Zaldívar traveled with Jusepe or Jusepillo, who had formed part of the Humaña and Leyba expedition (1593) and served as an interpreter, "vn ynterprete y lengua que lleuaua llamado Clementillo yndio de los que traxeron Vmayña y Leyua" (1029r); the name Clementillo is most likely an error because the other two extant copies of the *relación* name him Jusepillo.[22] Jusepillo or Jusepe Gutiérrez was questioned in the course of the inquiry regarding the expedition to Quivira and his "Declaración que Jusepe Indio dio de la salida a esta tierra del nuevo Mexico de Antonio de Umaña y del capitan Francisco Leyua y lo que sucedio" (Jusepe 1599 [Patronato 22, ramo 13, fols. 1019v–1021r]) contains the few details we possess on Humaña's killing of Leyba. Jusepe also provided information on a large settlement that apparently inspired Oñate's expedition to Quivira in 1601.[23] Beyond following the trails and identifying Humaña and Leyba's campsite, Zaldívar's *relación* includes ethnographic tidbits on Indian forms of address: "Para pedilla [la amistad] es estender la mano derecha hazia el sol y luego boluerla a la persona con quien quieren amistad" [In order to ask for it (friendship) they raise their right hand towards the sun and then turn to the person with whom they want friendship] (fol. 1029v); the use of bows and arrows: "gente de muchas fuerzas, lindos flecheros" [very strong people and beautiful archers] (1029r); dogs of burden: "Vsan un perrillo mediado lanudo los dichos yndios que les sirue de mula" [The said Indians use a medium-sized shaggy dog as a mule] (1031r); and table manners: "El tasajo en la vna mano y la manteca elada en la otra y vocado en el y en ella, crianse luzios y fornidos y valietes" [The meat in one hand and the hard lard in the other and alternately biting from one and the other, they grow healthy and sturdy and brave] (1032r). However, the bulk of Zaldívar's account centers on an extended description of the bison, which assumes a festive tone as it describes how they failed to domesticate it.

ZALDÍVAR'S WHIMSICAL BISON

Zaldívar first tells us that the members of his expedition constructed a large corral that would hold up to a thousand head, but in picturing themselves as great cattle ranchers they were soon disappointed when they realized that the bison was untamable: "Tentaronse mill modos en algunos dias para enzerrarlo o para hazer rodeo del y por ninguna via fue posible y no es de espantar porque esta notablemente zimarron y feroz, tanto que nos mato tres cauallos y nos hirio quarenta muy mal" [We tried a thousand ways to enclose them and to round them up, but to no avail, and there is no reason to wonder about this because they are so notably wild

Writing Violence on the Northern Frontier

and fierce, so much so that they killed three of our horses and badly wounded forty others] (1599 [Patronato 22, ramo 13, fol. 1030v]). This failure, however, did not keep Zaldívar from preferring bison lard of this "bull" over that of pigs and asserting that "la carne del toro [excede] a la de nuestras vacas y la de la vaca yguala con nuestra muy tierna ternera y carnero" [the meat of the bulls (exceeds) that of our cows and the one from the cows equals that of our very tender calves and sheep] (1031r). Nor did it keep him from speculating on the possibility of domestication by separating and feeding calves with cow's milk: "Creen que si no son recien nacidas y a la querenzia de nuestras vacas, no se podran traer hasta que el ganado amanse mas de lo que esta" [It seems that unless they are the newly born and suckled by our cows, one will not be able to bring any back until they become tamer] (1031r). There seemed to be no economic benefits apart from the immediate provision of food to the camp, but Zaldívar does praise the leather—rather, its treatment by the Indians: "El adobo [es] tan lindo que avnque llueua a cantaros no las passa [a las tiendas] ni se endureze el cuero; antes en secandose queda tan blando y tratable como antes" [The leather (is) so beautiful that even in a pouring rain the water would not pass through, moreover, when it dries it remains as soft and pliable as before] (1030r). Zaldívar also comments on the lightness of the leather, but all in all the bison proves to be a disappointment, which nevertheless does not keep him from delighting in writing the description, nor laughing about the dreams of grandeur they had entertained on their way to the "land of the bisons." The festive tone reaches its peak in the following detailed description of the bison, which I find worth giving in its entirety:

Cuyos cuernos son negros del tamaño ya dicho de vna tercia que parecen de bufallo; los ojos pequeños, rrostro y oçico y pesuñas de la misma forma de nuestras vacas, saluo que es muy barbado el toro y la uaca como cabrones, llenos de tanta lana que les cubre los ojos y cara y el copete, casi todos los cuernos. Llegales esta esta lana larga y muy tratable y blanda hasta casi el medio cuerpo y de halli halla es el pelo mas pequeño. Sobre las agujas tienen tanta y sube tanto el lomo que parecen corcoruados aunque en rrealidad de verdad no lo son mucho porque estacados los cueros, seles quita la corcoua muy facilmente.

Son mayores en comun que nuestro ganado, la colilla de la misma manera que vn puerco con pocas cerdillas al cauo, muy corta y que las rretuerce arriba quando corren. En las rodillas tienen unas naturales ligabanbas de pelo muy largo; de las ancas que son como de mula son derrengados y cazcoruos y asi corren de la manera dicha a saltos y mucho en espezial cuesta auajo. Son todos de vna color negros algo leonados y a partes rretinto el pelo. Esta es su forma que a la vista es harto mas feroz que puede significar la pluma. (103[1]v)

[Whose horns are black, of the said length of a foot, and resemble those of a water buffalo; their eyes are small; the face, snout and hoofs have the same shape as in our cows, except for the heavy beard; the bulls and the cows are so hairy that it covers their eyes and the forelock almost all of the horns. The wool is long and very treatable and soft, and hangs almost halfway down their body and from there on the fur is shorter. There is much wool over their ribs and the hump is so high that they resemble hunchbacks, even though in reality they are not since when the leather is staked the hump easily disappears. They are generally larger than our cattle; their tail is like a pig's, with few bristles at the end, very short, and they raise it when they run. At their knees they have natural garters of very long fur. Their haunches, which are like those of a mule, slope down as though broken; their hind legs are bowed, hence they run as described above, by leaps, especially when going downhill. Their hair is all black, somewhat tawny and in parts reddish. This is their semblance, which in real life is much more ferocious than the pen can signify.]

This extended description of the bison apparently had no other end than that of pleasing the reader. Zaldívar's *relación* includes a drawing (fig. 5) that further reinforces this witty verbal description as it accentuates the laughable rather than the ferocious.[24] Surely this visual image sought to be precise, but the slanted eyes, indeed crossed eyes, and round mouth, as if in a smile, seem to evoke a widespread festive mood that prevailed among the Spaniards during their first sightings of the bison: "Cuya hechura y forma es tan marauillosa y de rreyr o espantarse que el que mas vezes lo vee mas desea verlo y ninguno sera tan melancolico que si cien vezes lo vee al dia no se rria muy de gana otras tantas y se admire de ver animal tan fiero" [Their shape and form is so marvelous and comical

Writing Violence on the Northern Frontier

Figure 5. "A bison," in Vicente de Zaldívar, *Relacion de la xornada de las bacas,* 1598. Courtesy of the Ministerio de Educación y Cultura. Archivo General de Indias. Patronato 22, ramo 13, Estampas, 1.

or astonishing that the more you see them, the more you desire to see them, and no one would be so melancholic that if one saw them a hundred times every day one would very willingly laugh each of these hundred times and marvel at the sight of such a fierce animal] (1031r). Zaldivar recreates by means of the pen what is marvelous and ferocious, fearsome and laughable—a source of delight even for the melancholic.

These visual and verbal representations of the bison bear an imaginary component that has very little to do with the chimeras of the medieval Cíbola. The images of the bison, on the contrary, lead readers to wonder at the novelty of the animal. As the bison emerges as marvel (without antecedents in medieval literature, in spite of possible references to Marco Polo's buffalo), it displaces legend (things to be read), that is, the medieval repertoire of imaginary (and real) beings associated with the Seven Cities of Cíbola.

But this verbal and visual play also entails forms of discursive violence characteristic of the culture of conquest. Zaldívar's description of the bison concludes with a laconic statement on butchering them: "Podrase matar cuanto ganado quisieren traerse a estas poblazones" [One could kill as much cattle as one desires to bring back to these settlements] (1031r). The 1573 Ordenanzas were not particularly interested in descriptions of, let alone in respecting, the seminomadic culture of bison hunters; in fact, they prescribed the reduction of nomads to settlements. The mentality underlying Zaldívar's observation on the plentiful head for butchering will eventually lead to the extermination of the herds that roamed the Great Plains along with the destruction of the indigenous cultures that lived according to their migratory patterns.

Implicit in this Western hostility toward nonsedentary forms of life is Acosta's classification of social stages—savagery, barbarism, and civilization—and its recommendation to first turn "savages" into men before converting them to Christianity. The epistemological violence implicit in Acosta's evolutionary model would call for military violence when a culture refuses to move up the scale of "history." For all the recommendations on peaceful colonization and evangelization, Spain's civilizing mission was never questioned in the Ordenanzas. In this regard, the legacy of Las Casas's critique of the imperial project ended up being neutralized by Sepúlveda's insistence on Spain's obligations and rights to subject Amerindians to a civilizing process. In the colonial telos of pacification, all Indians were summoned to give their *obediencia* to the Crown, that is, to live under Spanish rule. Those unwilling to accept Spanish law were tricked into listening to clerics and lay officials, and military force was used against those who resented and opposed the invasion of their lands, which occurred under the pretence of peaceful settlement. To refuse the gifts of Spain and to abandon nomadic forms of life—as it were, to choose to remain homunculi, little men, in Sepúlveda's parlance (1941 [ca. 1547]: 110)—would in the end meet the harshest of punishments: extermination.

As we will see in the next chapter, the massacre of Acoma by the forces of Juan de Oñate was not only legitimized in Gaspar de Villagrá's epic poem, the *Historia de la Nueva Mexico* (1610), but civilized through an aesthetic rendition that drew from the prescriptions, topoi, and motifs of a long-standing Western epic tradition. The epic form ultimately embodied a primordial Manichean mode of subjugating non-Western cultures through art. Villagrá's *Histo-ria* is the story of a particular event, the rebellion and destruction of Acoma, that attains universal significance as an exemplary in-stance of the ideals of conquest put forth by the Ordenanzas of 1573. Peaceful colonization would be complemented with a war of ex-termination when, as in the case of Acoma, Indians would rather die cursing the Spaniards than subject themselves to the Crown. For Villagrá's indomitable Acomans leave war *a sangre y fuego* as the only way to settle New Mexico. During Oñate's and Zaldívar's trials in 1614, the court was not convinced with the evidence the two provided on the justness of the war against Acoma. But the court's doubts had less to do with the nature of that war or, perhaps, even with the subsequent enslavement and mutilation of the Aco-mans (customary law would legitimate mutilation, enslavement, and banishment as integral to war *a sangre y fuego*), than with the character of Oñate and Zaldívar, who were accused of other crimes ranging from abuses of women to presenting false testimonies and murder (see Craddock 1998; Murrin 1994: 222). Villagrá was also banished for exaggerating the wealth of New Mexico and execut-ing two deserters without giving them a fair trial. Questions had come up regarding Zaldívar's and Oñate's actions and claims about New Mexico ever since Monterrey's investigation, but these did not keep the Crown from embracing Villagrá's aesthetic rendition of the massacre. Thus, art constitutes a form of appropriating and claiming possession of territories. In colonial epics such as Villa-grá's (which I will discuss in detail in chapter 3) as well as Alonso de Ercilla's *La Araucana* (1569–1589) and Juan de Castellanos's *Elegías de varones ilustres* (1589–ca. 1607), idealized Indians constitute a back-drop for the narrative of imperial triumph as their physical prowess and curious (the Spanish term would be *peregrino*) barbaric wisdom is praised only to be debunked.[25] If the *relación* enables Spaniards to write themselves as moral subjects with legitimate claims and justi-fiable behavior through the mediation of the law, the epic makes the legal beautiful as it provides aesthetic modes of civilizing unspeak-able (even if sanctioned) tortures and atrocities.

CHAPTER 3

Aesthetics of Colonial Violence:

The Massacre of Acoma in Gaspar de Villagrá's

Historia de la Nueva México

They struggled with their feet for a little, not for very long.
—Homer, *Odyssey*

Sacamos conclusiones de que lo importante era organizar al pueblo
para que el pueblo no tuviera que sufrir lo mismo que nosotros, la película negra que tuvimos con mi hermanito.—Rigoberta Menchú, *Me
llamo Rigoberta Menchú y así me nació la conciencia*
[We concluded that the most important thing was to organize the
people so that they wouldn't have to suffer the way we had, see that horror film that was my brother's death.]—Trans. Ann Wright

These epigraphs from opposite ends of the historical spectrum
provide points of entry for a discussion of the origins and the ends
(dissolution implied) of the aesthetics of colonial violence. Homer's
passage manifests an aesthetic that addresses an audience that
would derive pleasure from or be fascinated by representations of
horror, a perspective presumably initiated in Western literature by
the *Iliad*. Rigoberta Menchú's voice invades the space of the long-
standing epic of Western colonialism with a radical questioning
of the historical horizon of modernity. Menchú's appropriation of
non-Indian forms of political organization (the formation of a
trade union, the Comité de Unidad Campesina) and artistic expression (the horror film, *película negra*) voices a curse of the "vanquished" that the epic tradition has evoked only to erase. Gaspar de
Villagrá's epic poem *Historia de la Nueva México* (1610) is pertinent to
these epigraphs not only because the events it narrates are situated
between these two ends of Western history—the moment in which

European expansionism (already a trait of the *Odyssey,* e.g., 9.39–43 and 105–41) invades Menchú's ancestors—but also because it exemplifies the suppression of voices of resistance and an aesthetic of violence that anticipates an audience that will derive pleasure from descriptions of horror.

Although Odysseus had initially asked Telemachus to behead the twelve women slaves, Telemachus granted them an especially hateful form of death because of their reversion to prostitution (22.437–72). Homer compares the hanged slaves to birds caught in a net. After this passage, Homer describes how they cut off Melanthios's nose and ears and tore off his genitals and fed them to the dogs. But these mutilations lack the cold empirical measurement of the span of the slave women's death: "They struggled with their feet for a little, not for very long." In *The Dialectic of Enlightenment,* Max Horkheimer and Theodor Adorno made an observation that sums up the force of these lines in the *Odyssey:* "The precision of the descriptive artist, which already exhibits the frigidity of anatomy and vivisection, is employed to provide evidence of the dying convulsions of the subjected who, in the name of the law and justice, were cast into that realm from which Odysseus the judge escaped" (1973: 79). The artist partakes of a will to truth that measures the gasp of death in the company of king and torturer.

The aesthetics of violence suppresses the body in pain of the slave women as it situates a disinterested gaze that would delight in the precision of the passage; thereby nonaesthetic (and ultimately nonscientific) criteria become irrelevant for the evaluation of the description.[1] Walter Benjamin's observation, apropos of art under fascism, that "self-alienation has reached such a degree that [humankind] can experience its own destruction as an aesthetic pleasure of the first order," is applicable to the whole Western epic tradition (1968: 244).[2] The renditions of massacres and tortures remain aesthetic to the degree that they keep the audience from empathizing with suffering. Any reference to the materiality of pain would call forth ethicopolitical considerations that question the disinterest of aesthetic values. The description of the hanging women presumes an audience—that is, an intersubjective basis of judgment—that would not only partake of the gaze, but also value the measured span of death for its artistic worth. At stake is not a choice of images but the intersubjectivity that the aesthetic of colonial violence takes for granted.

Rigoberta Menchú's call for action follows the detailed account of the display of her brother's tortured body (among others) in the plaza of the town of Chajúl. Both understandings of the concept of representation (i.e., as political and aesthetic; in Marx's terms, as *Vertretung* and *Darstellung*)[3] are evoked in this call to resistance. Menchú seeks to organize her people precisely to prevent any future repetitions of what she calls a *película negra*. The English version translates this as "horror film," which indeed is what the Army was seeking in the public display and anatomical dissection of parts of the body that had been the target of torture. Though there is no internal audience in the *Odyssey,* an analogous theatricality of terror seems to underlie the hanging of the twelve women slaves; one must note that the death of the slaves is not prolonged, as is that of Melanthios (see *Odyssey,* 22.171–200). Menchú would also seem to have in mind this sort of will to measure the span of death in her description of the Army's drawn-out murder of her brother in the plaza of the town of Chajúl. I am not going to engage here in the polemic over whether these events happened as told or if they were a fabrication of Rigoberta Menchú.[4] My point in quoting Menchú is to draw the limits of the aesthetics of colonial violence. If aesthetics implies a derivation of pleasure (or fascination, for that matter) from artistic description, hers is a counteraesthetic that describes the cold distance of the Army—that is, the epic model—with an intensity that curtails our separation from the events.[5] We do not have, as in the case of Homer, a consolation that the events occurred a long time ago (cf. Horkheimer and Adorno 1973: 80). The vividness of Menchú's testimony makes us complicitous, if not in events of the past, in those of the present and the future. Here we find a subaltern implementing both a political and a counteraesthetic representation of her people. As Sara Castro-Klarén (1996a) has pointed out, Menchú's scene of her brother's torture deploys a rhetoric of pathos that foregrounds the unspeakable cruelty of his suffering in terms that parallel Christ's *via dolorosa.* This intertextuality with the gospel attests to the appropriation and use of the Bible as one of the *weapons of the weak* that the oppressed indigenous peoples of the Americas have deployed since European colonization in the sixteenth century.

The aesthetics of colonial violence had a particularly significant moment in Western history during the European invasion of the New World. In what follows I isolate some variations of epic modes of representing violence. My main source, as already noted, is Gaspar de Villagrá's epic poem, *Historia de la Nueva México*. Both Homer and Menchú, however, provide points for comparison. In the spirit of Rigoberta Menchú, this essay aims to read through and thus counteract the aesthetics of colonial violence.

Villagrá's *Historia de la Nueva México* was published in 1610, three years after Juan de Oñate renounced the governorship of Nuevo México.[6] Clearly, Villagrá seeks to vindicate Oñate and all those who participated in the massacre of Acoma. His epic poem aspires to be a monumental history that would preserve the memory of the deeds of those who entered Nuevo México to conquer and convert its people: "hechos de aquellos esforçados, que en la nueva México entraron, à la conversion de tantas gentes" [the deeds of those brave men, who entered New Mexico, to convert so many peoples] (Villagrá 1900: n.p.; my translation). However, not all the opinions on this event in the history of New Mexico agreed on the legitimacy of the war, much less on the destruction of Acoma. Even though Oñate's position progressively deteriorated in the long judicial processes that culminated in 1614 with his banishment in perpetuity from New Mexico, Villagrá's *Historia* retains for the Crown a usefulness ulterior to that of testifying for Oñate—that is, to praise the heroism of the Spanish deeds in the Indies. Villagrá's exaltation lends legitimacy to Spanish claims over territories in the north of New Spain, claims that were questioned at this time by France and England. And it is perhaps in the context of a restitution of the name of Spain and the Spaniards that we ought to read his identification of the pen with the spear in the last lines of the poem.

Villagrá's *Historia* has a twofold purpose. The most obvious is to legitimize the war against Acoma. On a second plane, however, the ideological validation of the massacre is complemented by a colonization of the body and subjectivity of the Acomans in the representation of their "barbarism." Both intentions counteract the ethics and aesthetics of what has been called the *leyenda negra* (black legend).

Bartolomé de las Casas's *Brevíssima relación de la destruyción de las Indias* (1552) is generally considered the originator of a corpus of texts and images that have exposed and denounced the atrocities committed by the Spaniards in the New World. The term *leyenda negra* betrays a position that judges Las Casas's denunciations as exaggerations that ultimately fed into the hispanophobia of such protestant pamphleteers as Théodore de Bry and sons, who included a set of engravings in their 1593 Latin edition of the *Brevíssima* (see chapter 6). To counteract the *leyenda negra,* apologists of the conquest have underscored the sense of justice and evangelical mission of Spain's imperial project. Representative of this position, also dating back to the sixteenth century, are Juan Ginés de Sepúlveda's treatise on the just causes of waging war against the Indians, the *Democrates Alter* (ca. 1547), and his panegyric, the *Hechos de los españoles en el Nuevo Mundo y México* (1562).[7] The justification of wars in the New World in both historical and epic texts (as well as in legal treatises) depends on the representation of Indians as indomitable barbarians that leave the Spanish no alternative but war (see chapter 2). Nowhere is the Manichean colonial order, which Frantz Fanon analyzed in *Black Skin, White Masks* and *The Wretched of the Earth,* more clearly manifest than in colonial epics.[8] Epics may draw motifs (e.g., noble savages vs. greedy Spaniards) from the black legend to condemn the behavior of individuals who have deviated from the colonial legal order (i.e., the interests of the Crown), but in the end the true Christian knight must prevail over the gangsterlike conquistador and the barbarian Indian. The classic text where these negotiations can be observed is Alonso de Ercilla's *La Araucana* (1569–1589). But it can also be traced in, for instance, Juan de Castellanos's treatment of Lope de Aguirre's expedition to El Dorado in his *Elegías de varones ilustres de Indias* (1589–ca. 1607), where Lope de Aguirre's defeat makes way for praise of the Christian character of the criollo elite. Even though Spaniard might be pitted against Spaniard, in the final analysis, the colonial order in the epic always reproduces the binary "European civilization" versus "Indian savagery."[9]

In Villagrá's *Historia,* the "barbarity" of the Spaniards, that is, the massacre of Acoma, is "civilized" by an epic treatment. The constitution of the massacre as an aesthetic object implies a language that at first seems to praise the behavior of the women and men of Acoma, but under closer inspection manifests one more means of domination. Those passages representing the women of Acoma are particularly revealing of the discursive violence effected in the aesthetic rendition of the massacre.

Sargento Vicente de Zaldívar leads the assault on the Peñol of Acoma. The massacre is a consequence of the Acomans' killing of Vicente's brother, Juan de Zaldívar. There was no consensus, however, on the need to make war against Acoma, nor do all the sources grant the followers of Oñate impunity. Fray Juan de Escalona, in a letter to Viceroy Count of Monterrey, has left a testimony of why, in the first place, the Acomans rebelled against Juan de Zaldívar: "Para sacar el maíz de sus casas contraminan y rompen las paredes y para pedirles las mantas acaese a la pobre india que no tiene mas de la con que esta cubierta quitarsela al redopelo y dexarla en cueros llorando y echa ovillo por quedar en cueros con su hijo en los brazos y de aqui se levantó la guerra de Acoma" [They (the Spanish) destroy and break their walls to get their corn out of their houses. They solicit blankets by forcibly removing them from poor Indian women, who often do not have any other; women are left crying and curled up naked with a child in their arms. This is the reason why Acoma went to war] (Escalona 1601 [AGI, Patronato 22, ramo 12, 930v]). This image of a naked Indian woman, curled up with her child, harassed by Spanish terror, seeks to affect the emotions of the reader by acting directly on the senses. Whatever the cause of the uprising of Acoma, the Spaniards, in view of this sort of terrorism, had no justification for unleashing a massacre. But this is neither the sole nor the main point that I would like to make regarding this dramatic scene; I would also like to define this particular form of representing colonial violence.[10] The defenseless woman in Escalona's passage manifests a sentimental aesthetic that we can trace as well in Las Casas's representations of Indian "lambs" being assassinated by Christian "wolves" in the *Brevíssima,* or in the naked and vulnerable bodies of Indians terrorized by armed Spaniards in Théodore de Bry's iconography—in a word, the preferred sensibility of the *leyenda negra.* Because all colonial epics (in the strict sense of the genre) postdate the publication of the *Brevíssima,* they tend to invoke a sentimental aesthetic only to efface its inversion of the Manichean opposition in the end. Sentimental aesthetics seek to call our attention to abuse (as in Las Casas's appeal to Charles V to end destruction) or to displace religious wars to an ideological register (as in de Bry's attacks on the character of the Spanish nation). But however graphic their descriptions might be, neither de Bry nor Las Casas conveys the materiality of pain. Their representation of violence retains an aestheticized form that may be reterritorialized in an epic rendition where the same images would impart delight. As we saw in chapter 2, from a sixteenth-century perspective the mutilations and tortures described in the *Brevíssima* are atrocities only if the reader participates in a sense of justice that condemns *all* violence against Indians; otherwise, one can imagine someone saying "They deserved it!" Las Casas knew this, but, at least in this text, remained trapped in a binary opposition that took little effort to turn over. In chapter 6, I argue that de Bry's illustrations in the 1598 Latin edition of the *Brevíssima* provide images on which viewers can project their hatred of Spaniards rather than empathize with the tortured body of Indians, who ultimately stand for what will happen to Protestants if they let Spain enter their lands. It would not be an exaggeration to say that the Protestant pamphleteers could not care less for the Indians. Las Casas and de Bry share a sentimental aesthetic of colonial violence, though not the political motivations. For obvious reasons both de Bry and Las Casas lack the immediacy, urgency, and pathos of Menchú's deeply personal description.

In passing, I would like to point out that Menchú and Las Casas do share, however, a common strategic use of a paradisiacal first moment narrated in the present tense that foregrounds the account of terror that will follow in the subsequent chapters of their books. Clearly, this strategy was devised by Menchú and is not an editorial intervention by Elizabeth Burgos-Debray. Whether it was placed in the beginning by Menchú or appeared in other parts of her oral account, it is perfectly consistent for her to begin with or allude to a utopian present—a possible restoration of "normal" life in her Quiche community and its paradisiacal landscape: "Mi tierra es casi un paraíso de todo lo lindo que es la naturaleza en esos lugares" [Where I live is practically a paradise, the country is so beautiful]

(Menchú 1985: 22; 1990: 2). As for her association with the *leyenda negra,* as the epigraph points out, hers is a *película negra,* a "horror film"—not a sentimental aesthetic, but a coünteraesthetic that seeks to do away with the aesthetics of colonial violence for good. One may aestheticize the plight of others but hardly the urgency of organizing one's people. The politics of nostalgia should not be confounded with sentimentality. These last comments are not intended to set up an opposition between the political motivations of Las Casas and Menchú, but to underscore the ambiguity, if not the malleability, of a sentimental aesthetic.

Against a sentimental aesthetic, there are at hand a whole series of epic topoi that have circulated in Western literature at least since Homer.[11] Among the places that we can trace in Villagrá, besides the already mentioned hanging of the slaves in the *Odyssey,* are the curse of the defeated (Polyphemus in the *Odyssey*), the virility of the vanquisher as opposed to the femininity of the vanquished (Achilles vs. Hector), and the civilization of war by means of aesthetic rendition in the multiple battle scenes in the *Iliad.* David Quint has shown in a study of voices of resistance in Western epic, precisely after the curse of the Spaniards by the Indians that hang themselves at the end of Villagrá's *Historia,* that the topos of the curse by the "vanquished" does not suggest an alternative history; rather, it fulfills an ideological function that reinforces the epic plot whose ending characteristically establishes and celebrates the triumph of the "vanquishers" (1989b: 111–18). Thus, the curses of Polyphemus, Dido, Adamastor, and the Acomans are, according to Quint, a mode of defining the impotence of the "vanquished" and ultimately of justifying violence. In Villagrá's schema, the curse (which occurs toward the end of the poem) previews a whole series of future rebellions that will have to be suppressed. The curse reads:

> Mas vna cosa ciertos os hazemos,
> Que si bolver podemos a vengarnos
> Que no parieron madres Castellanas,
> Ni bárbaras tampoco, en todo el mundo,
> mas desdichados hijos que a vosotros.
> [But yet one thing we assure you:
> That if we can return for our vengeance,

Castilian mothers shall not bear,
Barbarian either, throughout all the world,
Sons more unfortunate than all of you.]
(1992 [1610]: 302)

This act of rebellion unto death would, in the end, justify the massacre of Acoma. In his poem, Villagrá also juxtaposes the virility of the victor—the preference for war and public spaces—with the femininity of the vanquished—the preference for love and private spaces. In an excellent study of Pedro de Oña's *Arauco Domado* (1596), Elide Pittarello defined this type of contraposition as the "vía erótica de la conquista" [erotic means of conquest] (see 1989: 250–54).

For now I would like to define the topos of the aesthetic civilization of war with a passage from Raphael Holinshed's *Chronicles of England, Scotland and Ireland* (1577). I cite this passage because I find it paradigmatic of how art civilizes horrendous acts, but also because of the parallelisms between Holinshed's description of Welsh women mutilating English bodies and that of Villagrá's Indian women quartering their own men. Holinshed writes: "This was a shrewd discomfiture to the Welsh by the English, on whome sinister lot lowred, at such a time as more than a thousand of them were slaine in a hot skirmish; and such shamefull villanie executed vpon the carcasses of the dead men by the Welshwomen; as the like (I doo belieue) hath neuer or sildome beene practised" (1: 84). Instead of feeling commiseration, says Holinshed, the Welsh women mutilate the bodies in an unheard-of manner: "The women of Wales cut off their priuitie, and put one part thereof into the mouthes of eueri dead man, in such sort that the cullions hoong downe to their chins; and not so contented, they did cut off their noses and thrust them into their tailes as they laie on the ground mangled and defaced" (1: 84). The references to other women in ancient historiography leave no doubt that Holinshed was proud of the novelty and originality of his topic: "Neither the crueltie of Tomyris nor yet of Fuluia is comparable to this of the Welshwomen" (1: 84). Holinshed, moreover, describes earlier accounts of the event as "desultory mention"—as it were, hardly worth considering. And of course he apologizes for narrating these extremely cruel deeds: "Though it make the reader read it, and the hearer to hear it, ashamed: yet bicause it was a thing doone in open sight, and left testified in historie; I see little reason whie it should not be imparted in our mother toong to the knowledge of our owne countrimen, as well as vnto strangers in a language vnknowne" (1: 84). This scene would apparently define the barbarism of the Welsh women. I say apparently because Holinshed himself separates the Welsh from "barbarian" peoples, "a verie ignominious déed, and a woorsee not committed among the barbarous" (1: 84). It remains unsaid who are the "true" barbarians.[12]

Even more important, the reference to classical texts gives an aesthetic dimension to the Welsh women, as he constitutes them as a novel topic to be drawn on by future historians, if not by playwrights such as Shakespeare, who alludes to Holinshed's passage in Act 1 of the *First Part of Henry IV*:

> Upon whose dead corpses there was such misuse,
> such beastly shameless transformation,
> by those Welshwomen done, as may not be
> Without shame retold.
> (I.i.43–46)

This unspeakable memorableness testifies to the commonplace nature of Holinshed's account. The intended artistry with which he describes the mutilated bodies makes this passage ambivalent if not sympathetic to the rage of the Welsh women. On the other hand, the mutilation of the bodies of the vanquished was hardly an act of barbarism, rather, an acceptable and civilized practice in the sixteenth century. The corpses of tyrants, rebels, and mutineers were cut apart and denied burial. Thus, the legal codes as well as the aesthetic rendition would, in the end, civilize the supposed act of barbarism; in Holinshed's rendition, the Welsh women's profanation of the English is not only acceptable behavior but a fascinating tableau. This passage suggests that battle scenes, beyond celebrating the deeds of epic characters, may transform barbarism into civilization by means of art. Someone might object that from within the contemporary paradigm the applicability of the legality of quartering and defiling the enemy would not apply to women ("a sex pretending the title of weake vessels," in Holinshed's words). As it were, only "civilized" men could afford such deeds. But this question, in turn, ultimately begs for a definition of what makes an act civilized in the first place. In the end, the legality of the act has no bearing; one could enjoy this "beastly shameless transformation," to borrow Shakespeare's phrase, because the virility of Welsh women works against Welsh men.

We must recall that Villagrá's *Historia de la Nueva México* is a panegyric of the Spaniards' behavior. As such, he has first to justify the war against Acoma and then raise the massacre to an epic stage. We can only assume that Fray Juan de Escalona's letter attributing the rebellion of Acoma to the abuses of the Christians was "lost" in the archives of the Crown (actually, in the files compiled by the Count of Monterrey to evaluate Oñate's and Zaldívar's reports; see chapter 2) when the censors enthusiastically endorsed the publication of Villagrá's *Historia*. Thus, we find a censor praising the *Historia* as a heroic poem that "alentara y dara gusto, a todos generos de gente, a vnos a imitallos, y a otros para estimallos, y assi es bien que ande en las manos de todos" [will inspire and move, all kinds of people, some to imitate it, and others to value it, and thus it is good that it is available to all] (Villagrá 1900, n.p.). It remains unclear, however, whether the censor praises this work because it will inspire others to imitate the doggerel verses of Villagrá or, even worse, to commit similar atrocities in the name of justice. Undoubtedly, this censor considered the rationale given in the poem to justify the war to be well founded.

After consigning to a text written in prose (which unlike verse certifies its documentary value) the response of the commissar and other priests to Oñate's question regarding the criteria for just war, Canto 25 goes on to evaluate the case of Acoma:

> Con cuios pareceres, bien fundados
> En muchos textos, leyes y lugares
> De la escritura santa, luego quiso,
>
> . . . .
>
> Cerrar aquesta causa y sentenciarla,
> Mandando pregonar, a sangre y fuego,
> Contra la fuerza de Acoma, la guerra.
> [With whose opinions, well founded
> On many texts, laws and places

In holy Scripture, then the Governor,

. . . .

. . . . wished

To close that case and give sentence,
Ordering war, with fire and blood,
Proclaimed against the fort of Acoma.]
(Villagrá 1992 [1610]: 224)

Acomans deserved war primarily because they had destroyed the
established rule of law by killing Spaniards:

De donde total quiebra se se guía
De la paz vniversal que ya la tierra
En sí toda tenía y alcanzaba.
[Whence there had followed total breach
Of that peace universal which the land
Had possessed and attained throughout.]
(225)

The *paz universal* is a coded term for the *obediencia,* that is, the Acomans' fully conscious acceptance of Spanish rule and the consequences that followed from pledging *obediencia*. Beyond Acoma, the
rebellion questions the legitimacy of Spanish rule. The Peñol of
Acoma had to be razed to the ground. Indeed, in the commissar's
opinion, before the war could be waged legitimately, the Acomans
would be given the opportunity to first surrender to the Spaniards
those who incited the rebellion and then willingly to accept the
destruction of their town and resettle in the valley (see chapter 2).
Thus, Acoma has the alternative of turning in those responsible for
the death of the Spaniards or of having young and old massacred,
"sin que chico ni grande se escapase" [without one, great or small,
escaping him] (226). The curse at the end of the poem is neutralized
before it even occurs: all future (already anticipated) rebellions will
be answered by massacres. But Villagrá adds an emotional note to
this abstract argument:

Demás del gran peligro manifiesto,
De tantos niños, todos inocentes,
Tiernas donzellas con sus pobres madres.
[Besides the great danger, most manifest,

Aesthetics of Colonial Violence   149

Unto so many innocent children
And tender damsels with their poor mothers.]
(226)

Obviously, these children and maidens are not those of Acoma, but of the Spaniards. There was a general consensus among Spaniards that were consulted in the *Proceso* on the rebellion of Acoma that unless the Peñol was destroyed the Spaniards would abandon the land (AGI, Patronato 22, ramo 13, fols. 1086r–1131v). Let us now observe how the *Historia* moves from this ideological justification of the massacre to the elaboration of an aesthetic of colonial violence.

In the likeness of Alonso de Ercilla's *La Araucana,* Villagrá represents the Acomans engaged in harangues and contests for political power. They differ, however, in that Villagrá renders a degraded image of the Acomans. By this I do not want to suggest that *La Araucana* remains unburdened by the weight of the orientalist topoi that the Western epic has devised for representing non-European contenders. We must recall, moreover, that Ercilla's primary concern is to defend the interests of the Crown, and thus the Araucanians provide a counterpart to condemn the behavior of the *encomenderos*.[13] Ercilla also knows how to subordinate the Araucanians and to transform horror into an object of art. Toward the end of the poem, Caupolicán, the most courageous among the Araucanians, converts to Christianity and is given a less than honorable death by the Spaniards:

No el aguzado palo penetrante
por más que las entrañas le rompiese
barrenándole el cuerpo, fue bastante
a que al dolor intenso se rindiese

. . . .

En esto seis flecheros señalados,
que prevenidos para esto estaban
treinta pasos de trecho desviados
por orden y de espacio le tiraban.
[Not even the sharp and penetrating stick
though it was rupturing his innards
as it drilled his body, was sufficient
to have him surrender to the intense pain

Writing Violence on the Northern Frontier

   .   .   .   .

     Meanwhile six appointed archers
     who had been prepared for this
     were standing thirty steps away
     shooting at him in an orderly and slow fashion.]
     (1979 [1569–1589]: 3.34.28, 29)

Although Caupolicán has embraced Christianity, he undergoes a most degrading death as he is placed on a sharp stick that perforates his insides. Ercilla's vivid description neutralizes our empathy for the body in pain as it highlights the warrior's indomitable courage. This particularly cruel execution ends—is civilized—with a set of archers that shoot him in "an orderly and slow fashion." The description aestheticizes the torture of Caupolicán, but Ercilla also makes sure to let the reader know that he was not present:

     Que si yo a la sazón allí estuviera
     la cruda esecución se suspendiera.
     [If I had been there when it occurred
     I would have suspended this crude execution.]
     (3.34.31)

One wonders what was the purpose of providing a detailed description of an execution that he did not witness, if it was not to verbally violate Caupolicán's body. Indeed, a quick glance at Canto 14, which narrates the deeds of Francisco Villagrá, reveals a disparity between the fixed gaze on the face of the Indian corpses and a respectful avoidance of the same in the case of the Spaniards. As Quint has pointed out, Villagrá not only modeled his poem on Ercilla's, but "was a relation of Don Francisco de Villagrá, the conquistador of Chile, who is one of the heroes of Ercilla's poem" (1989b: 113). In Villagrá, there is no glimpse of pity toward the defeated Acomans, however, but a sustained defilement of their bodies and character. Take, for instance, the following passage where the Acomans plot to capture Spanish maidens as prizes of war:

     Y a ti fuerte, Gicombo, yo te mando,
     No obstante que Luzcoija es muy hermosa,
     Doze donzellas bellas Castellanas.

[To you, strong Gicombo, I give,
Though Luzcoija is most beautiful
Twelve beautiful Castilian maidens.]
(Villagrá 1992 [1610]: 235)

Luzcoija and Gicombo reappear in Canto 30, where Villagrá celebrates their love in terms not unlike those of Muley and the beautiful Jarifa in the *Abencerraje*. Israel Burshatin has shown that the apparent praise of Muley's love and courage in that Moorish novel is, in the end, one more means of dominating and constituting the Moor as an "other" (see Burshatin 1984). Echoing Hector (*Iliad,* 6.521–33), Gicombo languishes as he bids farewell to Luzcoija:

Que ya no me es posible que me escuse,
De entrar en la batalla contra España.
[That now I cannot make excuse,
From going to battle against Spain.]
(Villagrá 1992 [1610]: 261)

To this fatalism and amorous context, Villagrá juxtaposes a parallel scene in which, while Gicombo muses on love, the "caballeros de Christo valerosos" [valiant knights of Christ] listen to Mass and receive the blessings of the commissar, Fray Alonso (262). Thus, Villagrá builds an opposition between an Indian who bids farewell to his wife in the private space of the home and the Christians who forge a war community in the public space of the Mass. But beyond this obvious feminization of Gicombo (the Orient as feminine is an epic commonplace at least since Virgil's *Aeneid,* if not since Hector's fatalism and long farewell to Andromache and his child in book 6 of the *Iliad*), in Canto 32, the discourse of love gives way to a representation of the "barbarism" of the Indians (see Quint 1989a).

Surrounded by the Sargento and several soldiers, Gicombo kills Luzcoija to avoid her being rescued by the Spaniards:

Y assomando Luzcoija el rostro bello,

. . . .

Sugeto la espaciosa y ancha frente
Al rigor de la maza poderosa
Que los dos más hermosos ojos bellos,

Writing Violence on the Northern Frontier

Le hizo rebentar del duro casco.
Nunca se vio en solícito montero
Contento semejante cuando tiene,
La codiciosa caça ya rendida
Como el que el bárbaro tomó teniendo
A su querida caza ya sugeta
Y de todos sentidos ya privada.
[And Luzcoija's beauteous face showing,

. . . .

Offered her broad, spacious forehead
To the force of the powerful mace
That caused her two most beauteous eyes
To spring from out her solid skull.
Never was seen in the eager hunter
Greater content when he possessed
His longed-for game, already caught,
Than this barbarian had having
Now quite destroyed his dearest pledge
And deprived her of all feeling.]
(282)

There is a slight sense of admiration for the love and death of Luz-coija that, nevertheless, Villagrá qualifies as barbarian and com-pares to a hunting scene. The clichéd "hard skull" belies the ideal-ization of Luzcoija and counteracts the "soft beauty" (classical) as it inevitably calls to mind a commonplace racist association with "thick intellect." As we will see in chapter 4, Oviedo elaborates a connection between what he describes as the thick skulls of Amer-indians and a corresponding limited intellect. This description, moreover, desecrates the body of Luzcoija. As opposed to cus-toms that might, out of respect, close the eyes of the dead, Villa-grá derives pleasure in distorting them: "Que los dos mas hermo-sos ojos bellos,/ Le hizo rebentar del duro casco" [That caused her two most beauteous eyes,/ to spring from out her solid skull]. If at first the behavior of Gicombo led Vicente Zaldívar to offer him peace and friendship, the Sargento now sees himself forced to kill Gicombo to save the other Indian women who were with Luzcoija.

The recognition of Gicombo's nobility changes immediately into a degradation. In the end, Villagrá praises the virtue of the Sargento who saves the Acoman women from the evil Indian.

Thus, Indian women function as a sort of wild card for defining male virtue as identified with the Spaniards. Villagrá deprives the women of subjectivity as their value and significance depend on the battling positions of the male counterparts. They are, moreover, cast as animal; Luzcoija dies like an animal in a hunting scene, and the rescued women flee like cattle without recognizing their Christian savior. This usage of women is in itself a variation of another commonplace in colonialist justifications of conquest: if the usual run is "brown little folk and women must be saved from abusive brown men," the spin here is that by representing them as animal-like, Villagrá ultimately legitimizes the massacre—instead of a lofty civilizing mission.

Even in those passages that attempt to show the valor of the Acoman women who prefer death over slavery, Villagrá robs them of their heroism by means of grotesque images. When Zutancalpo (one of the more moderate Indians) dies, his mother, in despair over seeing her lineage destroyed, tears her face apart, pulls out her hair, and throws herself into a fire. After her, Zutancalpo's four sisters do the same (Villagrá 1992 [1610]: 277). This scene of despair and "savage" love is complemented with a description of their bodies writhing in the flames:

> Y qual suelen grosíssimas culebras
> O ponzoñosas víboras ayradas
> Las vnas con las otras retorcerse
> Con aprretados ñudos, y enrroscarse,
> Assí las miserables se enlazaban.
> [And like to the most monstrous snakes
> Or poisonous, deadly vipers,
> Who with each other intertwine
> In clinging knots and twist about,
> So these poor wretches were entwined.]
> (278)

The despair of mother and daughters and their writhing in the fire fulfill an ideological function quite apart from the satisfaction of violent impulsions. The image is an implicit condemnation of the Acoman rebellion, as their burning like snakes inevitably evokes images of hell.

This sustained gaze at the women agonizing in the flames conveys an empirical bent of mind similar to the measure of death in the epigraph from Homer: "They struggled with their feet for a little, not for very long." Language in Villagrá, however, is not just used to describe, but to mutilate. Villagrá's use of language does not allude to violence offstage; as it were, it defaces the bodies. We may liken this attention focused on the face of death to that other violation of the sacred in early modern Europe represented by the empirical gaze of science on Mother Earth (Certeau 1988: 232). But as Horkheimer and Adorno have underscored in their study of the *Odyssey,* there is already a dialectic of enlightenment in myth. If we were to pursue a utopian moment before the birth of modern rationality, it ought to be beyond the patriarchal order and the Olympian religion of Homer.[14] There is nonetheless a historical break in the Renaissance when the opening of the world to observation is an instrument of European expansionism. It is ironic that the same society that deplored the loss of the gods and the ensuing alienation destroyed societies that for all practical purposes were embodiments of agricultural religions intimately bound to the sacred, as were the Pueblo Indians massacred at Acoma.[15] The sense of a loss of the gods is not expressed in colonial documents, but it is implied in the opening lines of Las Casas's *Brevíssima,* where after parodying celebrations à la Gomara of the uniqueness of the discovery of America, Las Casas enumerates the unheard-of atrocities committed in the New World. The general attitude, however, is akin to Villagrá's praise of European bravado. Villagrá's desecrating descriptions of corpses are not only representative of an epic expansionist élan, but also of scientific inquiry. As a result, the death of the Acomans is never a mere representation of havoc, but rather a systematic profanation (a dissective description) of corpses:

> Con gran suma de cuerpos ya difuntos,
> Por cuias fieras llagas temerarias
> Terribles quajarones regoldaban,
> Témpanos y sangraza nunca vista,

Aesthetics of Colonial Violence

A bueltas del sustento mal digesto
Que por allí también despedían,
Por do las pobres almas escapaban.
[And a great store of bodies of the dead,
From whose deep, terror stricken wounds
Terrible clots of blood emerged,
Congealed and liquid blood unheard of, too,
And bits of undigested food, as well,
From whence also had way been made
Through which their poor souls had escaped.]
(Villagrá 1992 [1610]: 276)

Just as the bodies of tyrants, rebels and mutineers are torn after being subjected to the garrote, these grotesque images of wounds, clots, blood, and vomit rob the dead rebels of their dignity. This poetic representation of the corpses fulfills a function analogous to the Welsh women's mutilation of English corpses; both instances entail a profanation of the dead. In Villagrá's poem the body of Zutacapan is desecrated and cut into pieces, but it is the same women of Acoma who carry out the task:

Assí las vimos, todas hechas piña,
A palos y pedradas deshaziendo,
A vn miserable cuerpo.

. . . .

Alborotadas todas, nos dixeron:
"Varones esforzados, generosos

. . . .

Dejadnos acabar lo comenzado,
Aquí Zutacapán está tendido

. . . .

Este causó las muertes que les dimos
A vuestros compañeros desdichados.
[So we did see them, gathered in a knot,
With sticks and blows of stones smashing
A miserable body.

. . . .

And all excited, did cry out to us:
"Ye valiant and generous men.

. . . .

[L]et us finish what we have commenced,
Here Zutacapan lies stretched out

. . . .

He caused the deaths which we have dealt
To your unfortunate companions.]
(296–97)

The Acoman women go on to specify that it was Zutacapan who sowed discord among them, and after contemplating the battlefield covered with corpses from Acoma, they continue to quarter the body of Zutacapan in rage:

Assi con yra, todos rebolvieron,
Y en muy menudas piezas le dexaron.
[So, in their rage they gathered around,
And left him battered into small pieces.]
(297)

Needless to say, the Acoman women differ greatly from the Welsh women; by carrying out the punishment of Zutacapan, they save the Spaniards a burden and, furthermore, subordinate themselves to Spanish rule.

The motif of the burial in the last two cantos takes on an allegorical dimension: the poem, by means of the word, quarters the Acomans and then denies them burial. While, in a funeral oration, the Sargento constitutes the Peñol of Acoma as the sepulcher of his brother Juan de Zaldívar, the corpses from Acoma lie without burial, "Y de sus mismos perros comidos" [And eaten now by their own dogs] (289). The desecration of the corpses is a constant that repeats itself until the end of the poem, when Villagrá describes the faces of the cursing Acomans who hang themselves:

Saltando en vago, juntos se arrojaron,
Y en blanco ya los ojos, transtornados,

. . . .

Virtiendo espumarajos, descubrieron
Las escondidas lenguas, regordidas
Y entre sus mismos dientes apretadas.

Aesthetics of Colonial Violence   157

[Together they both leapt out into space,
And now their eyes, turned back, displayed the whites,

. . . .

Spurting out foam they discovered
Their hidden tongues, now all swollen
And tightly clenched between their teeth.]
(302)

Thus, Villagrá's poem exemplifies an aesthetic of colonial violence that draws its legitimacy from an ideology of just war against
Indians, but whose force of representation resides in the use of
grotesque images that rob indigenous peoples of all dignity, even
in death. Though the epigraph from Homer provides a distant
measurement of the span of death by hanging, he stops short of
fixing his gaze on the distorted faces of the hanged women. On
the other hand, Rigoberta Menchú's sustained description of her
brother's tortured body arrests the characteristic detached view of
epic representations of violence. I have not cited Menchú's passage to avoid the objectivism that would tend to make us forget
the *fact* of her brother's suffering or mitigate the pain expressed by
her over having had to witness the *película negra*.[16] Villagrá's ideological justification of the massacre is clearly an instance of the
leyenda blanca (white legend). But we must now underscore that the
white legend does not counter the representation of atrocities committed by Spaniards (ones that feed into the *leyenda negra*) with colonial idylls, but rather with grotesque forms of denigrating the "vanquished." The sentimental aesthetic of Escalona, Las Casas, and de
Bry is countered by Villagrá's faces of death. Between *leyenda negra*
and *leyenda blanca,* what changes are not the facts but the aesthetics
of colonial violence. Everyone agrees that Acoma was destroyed.
Villagrá's difference resides in the poetic process that "civilizes"
the "savagery" of the massacre, its "total" destructive furor. At
first, falling into the rhetoric of conquest, I was tempted to assume
the complete destruction of Acoma, but during a visit to Acoma
Pueblo, our Indian guide made sure to correct such a misconcep-
tion: "Acoma was never completely destroyed," she responded to a
query from a participant on the tour.

CHAPTER 4

Violence in de Soto Narratives:

Moralistic Terrorism in Oviedo's

Historia general

She—Courage is strength—and you are vigilant, sagacious, firm besides. But I am beautiful—as "a cane box, called petaca, full of unbored
pearls." I am beautiful: a city greater than Cuzco; rocks loaded with
gold as a comb with honey. Believe it. You will not dare to cease following me—at Apalachi, at Cutifachiqui, at Mabila, turning from the
sea, facing inland. And in the end you shall receive of me, nothing—
save one long caress as of a great river passing forever upon your sweet
corse. Balboa lost his eyes on the smile of the Chinese ocean; Cabeça de
Vaca lived hard and saw much; Pizarro, Cortez, Coronado—but you,
Hernando de Soto, keeping the lead four years in a savage country,
against odds, "without fortress or support of any kind," you are mine,
Black Jasmine, mine.—William Carlos Williams, *In the American Grain*

Otro día, martes treinta del mes de septiembre, llegaron a Agile, sub-
jeto de Apalache, e tomaronse sus mujeres; e son tales, que una india
tomó a un bachiller, llamado Herrera, que quedaba solo con ella e atrás
de otros compañeros, e asióle de los genitales y túvolo muy fatigado
e rendido, e si acaso no pasaran otros cristianos que le socorrieran, la
india le matara, puesto que él no quería haber parte con ella como libidinoso, sino que ella se quería libertar e huir.
[On the next day, Tuesday, 30 September, they arrived at Agile, subject
to Apalache and some women were captured; they are of such stuff that
one Indian took a *bachiller* called Herrera, who had stayed behind and
remained alone with her, and grabbed him by his genitals and had him
so worn out and weakened that if other Christians had not come by and
rescued him, the Indian woman would have killed him, since he did not

desire her sexually, but rather she wanted to get free and run away.]—
Gonzalo Fernández de Oviedo, *Historia general y natural de las Indias*[1]

A recent special issue of *Archaeology* dedicated to Hernando de Soto's expedition to Florida published a series of articles documenting the extremely violent nature of this tentative conquest.[2] In a later issue of this Journal, a letter by a Hispanic woman (who makes reference to her "Spanish ancestors") denounced the documentation of the violence as one more repetition of the *leyenda negra* (black legend) by "Anglos."[3] There is no question that the editors of *Archaeology* committed a gross impropriety when they decided to illustrate the article using the same images that William R. Hearst used to promote the war against Spain in 1898, especially as they made no attempt to analyze them or even to identify their source. The outraged reader also reminds us that "Anglos" have shed no less Indian blood. We should not forget, however, that there are plenty of romantic images of the Conquistador (with capital letters, indeed) Hernando de Soto, both in North American popular culture and, no less, in modern historiography (in Spanish as well as in English).[4] I have juxtaposed as epigraphs to this chapter two passages from very different kinds of sources that will enable me to problematize a bit this business of the uses of the *leyenda negra* by "Anglos." Obviously, I do not intend to deny that hispanophobia feeds into "Anglo" condemnations of the Spanish conquest; I simply wish to complicate the picture. I quote both William Carlos Williams, who, inspite of a middle name that evokes Hispanic ancestry, is the poet par excellence of Anglo America, and Gonzalo Fernández de Oviedo, who has been seen as having contributed indirectly to the *leyenda negra,* when in fact he was busy vindicating Spain—though not necessarily all the conquistadores who acted in her name.

How Oviedo used Hernando de Soto in his *Historia general y natural de las Indias* (1535–1547) is ultimately the subject of this chapter. By framing Oviedo between examples of North American high and popular culture, I seek to curtail squabbles over the relative horrors of "Hispanic" versus "Anglo" violence against Native Americans, or over which form of colonization is more truly representative of the significance of America in (Western) history. Such debates re-

Writing Violence on the Northern Frontier

tain a thoroughly colonialist position. I will read Hernando de Soto here from a postcolonial perspective (i.e., one that neither privileges European culture as a frame of reference nor proposes colonization as a "civilizing" factor), by addressing first sixteenth-century juridicolegal prescriptions on wars of conquest, and then moving on to analyze the aesthetics of violence in Oviedo's portrayal of one such war.

In addition to Oviedo's version of de Soto's attempt to conquer and establish a settlement in Florida (which Oviedo draws from Rodrigo de Ranjel's account), there are two other texts that were written by members of the expedition. I set aside Garcilaso de la Vega's *La Florida del Inca* (1605) as a case of its own, in part because Garcilaso did not participate in de Soto's expedition, but mainly because the value of Garcilaso's history resides in its self-conscious literary rendition of the events (see chapter 5; cf. Rodríguez-Vecchini 1982). The *Relaçam verdadeira dos trabalhos q̃ ho gouernador dõ Fernãdo de Souto e certos fidalgos portugueses passarom no descobrimẽto da prouincia da Frolida* (1557) is a long account written by the anonymous Portuguese author known as the Fidalgo de Elvas. As a Portuguese participant in the expedition, Elvas did not respond to Spanish law in writing the *Relaçam*. Thus, his descriptions of terror are strikingly candid. In the strict sense of the term, the only primary source (leaving aside the so-called Cañete fragment) is Luis Hernández de Biedma's short account, *Relación del suceso de la jornada del cap. Soto, y de la calidad de la tierra por donde anduvo* (1544).[5] Biedma's is a straightforward account written in his official capacity as the expedition's royal factor. Later on in this chapter I examine the language of terror in Biedma and the Fidalgo de Elvas and compare it with Oviedo's moralistic stance.

My reading of Oviedo is at odds with that of Martin and Ivana Elbl, who interpret Oviedo's moralizing (vis-à-vis the absence of moralizing in the *Relaçam* by the anonymous "Gentleman of Elvas") as an example of a perspective that is "black" (Elbl and Elbl 1997: 61). On the other hand, Patricia Galloway (1990) has argued that by condemning de Soto as incompetent, Oviedo was attempting to atone for having fabricated lies in the first part of his *Historia general y natural de las Indias,* lies for which he was denounced by Bartolomé de las Casas, in other words that Oviedo had a "change of heart." I argue that Oviedo's condemnation of de Soto has less to do with a "change of heart" toward the Indians than with the new legal framework introduced by the Nuevas Leyes of 1542. Three contextual frames tend to accompany Oviedo's allusions and references to the Nuevas Leyes: (1) a condemnation of the behavior of Spaniards (especially those he does not hold in high regard to begin with); (2) an implicit questioning of the reformist program in the Nuevas Leyes by laying the blame for the Indians' deaths on their idolatry, sodomy, and weak intellects; and (3) a direct critique of the power of the Dominican order (in concrete, Bartolomé de las Casas) (see *HGN*, 1:267–8; 2:161; 4:264). Thus, the Nuevas Leyes function as a code he grudgingly accepts, but that he uses to advance his own policies. In the final analysis, Oviedo's denunciation of de Soto reproduces, on a symbolic level, the same violence that he condemns. The categories that legitimate the subordination of Amerindians to the Spanish Crown remain unaltered in Oviedo's condemnation of de Soto. His is the story of "good" versus "bad" conquistadores that never addresses the Spaniards' right to colonize the Americas.

As implied by the title to this chapter, I am interested in taking Oviedo's and Williams's passages as points of entry to an analysis of the culture of terror, whose mechanism de Soto knew well—as can be inferred from the different accounts of the expedition. My point is to suggest that beyond blatant material forms of terrorism (slavery, war, mutilations, etc.), there are corresponding rhetorical forms that exert violence. In the introduction and earlier chapters of this book, we have seen that the language of conquest has at its disposal a whole series of speech acts (both in the modalities of racist hate speech and the love speech of peaceful colonization) that register, as Judith Butler has put it, "a certain force in language, a force that both presages and inaugurates subsequent force" (1997a: 9). Whereas the *Requerimiento*'s threat of violence prefigures in language the subordination that physical violence will make effective if the summoning is not heeded, the aestheticization of violence in colonial epics structures the impulsions of violence that will materialize future massacres. The Crown devised a language of love and peaceful colonization in the Nuevas Leyes of 1541 and the Ordenanzas of 1573 to overcome the contradiction inherent in the *Requerimiento*'s interpellation of Indians to recognize Spanish sovereignty and the 1526 Ordenanzas' explicit denunciation of using violence against Indians. As I pointed out in chapter 1, Las Casas exposed this contradiction in *De unico modo:* "Et quia nemo infidelium sua sponte velit se Christiani populi vel alicuius principis eius ditioni submittere, potissime infidelium reges, esset profecto necesse devenire ad bellum" [And since no infidels would willingly subject themselves to the dominion of a Christian people, or a Christian prince, especially the kings of infidels, there would inevitably have to be war] (Las Casas 1988 [ca. 1534]: 378; 1992b: 117).

De unico modo's contention that love was the only valid approach to evangelization and exposition of the Crown's contradictory policies, which—as we saw in the introduction and chapter 2—also included the Crown's obligation to restore sovereignty and to compensate Indians for damages, eventually led Las Casas to realize in the course of his career that the legal reform of Spain's colonial enterprise in the Indies was a futile passion. The Crown censured the language of violence, but the terms *pacificación* (pacification) and *asentamiento* (settlement), which replaced *conquista* (conquest), entailed a rearticulation of force in a language of love that prescribed (indeed, provided formulas for) seducing Indians with European products and establishing consensual lines of communication; on the historical horizon, this peaceful mode of colonization meant Indians willingly (but also inevitably) pledging *obediencia* (obedience) to Spain (see chapter 2). Violence invariably looms on the horizon for those who choose not to be loved. But in the same way that hate speech and love speech may miss their mark, the denunciation of the violence one assumes inherent in hate or love speech may strengthen the same discourse one sets out to critique. The effectiveness, the violence, of hate or love speech is proportional to the subordination hate or love speech wishes to implant. This last issue ultimately addresses the following questions: How can one write about or even against violence without being terroristic? In what ways is terrorism articulated in aesthetic representations (albeit moral reprobations) of violence? To properly address these issues we must attend to the rhetoric as well as the politics of writing about the New World.

The passages from Williams and Oviedo offer us two perspectives on Amerindian women. They provide the materials to reflect on what it means to write *against* violence. The first represents an allegorical character who, beyond embodying indigenous culture, initially expresses (to eventually debunk) the idealized view of de Soto that has made him the predilect conquistador in North American culture: consider Williams's ambivalent if not ironic reference to de Soto's corpse lying on the bottom of the Mississippi: "you are mine, Black Jasmine, mine." But as may be seen in an earlier chapter dedicated to Ponce de León, "She" (América) is one of the voices that, according to Williams, inhabit the soul of North Americans: "History begins for us with murder and enslavement, not with discovery. No we are not Indians but we are men of their world. The blood means nothing: the spirit, the ghost of the land moves in the blood, moves the blood. It is we who ran to the shore naked, we who cried, 'Heavenly Man!' These are the inhabitants of our souls, our murdered souls that lie . . . agh. Listen!' (1956: 39). This passage conveys Williams's notion of writing history against the grain. He never hesitates to demythologize the colorful Ponce de León, who, according to the legend, was searching for the fountain of youth when in fact he was primarily concerned with capturing slaves for his plantation, then in decline due to a lack of laborers. Williams is more cautious with de Soto. After all, this "favored son" has lent his name to streets, restaurants, shops, and a popular car in the forties and fifties, and the image of an armored conquistador nowadays marks the DeSoto Trail in several southeastern states. Williams rewrites the story of de Soto by juxtaposing the paragraphs that express the voice of "She" with subjectless passages that are increasingly negative (for the most part derived from the accounts of Oviedo and Elvas). But in a key moment, it is "She," the dreamlike, enticing *América* ("You will not dare to cease following me"), who provides a starkly revealing profile of de Soto: "Follow me, Señor, this is your country. I give it to you. Take it. Here are carriers for your burdens; here are girls for your beds; my best men for adversaries." To this submission of *América,* as is already suggested by the gift of "my best men," de Soto responds with terror: "At the sight of your men in armor, terror strikes them" (54). Williams draws a feminine representation of America that avoids a generalized tendency to denigrate Amerindian cultures by means of negative feminine traits. At once, at least in my reading, "She" both undoes a misogynist conception of the feminine and dismantles the romanticized view of de Soto. In spirit, Williams aims to write an "Indian-centered" history, but the voice of America remains bound to a long series of allegories of America that inevitably haunt the "She" with associations of noble or ignoble savagery (see Rabasa 1993b: 23–48; cf. Hegeman 1989).

Let us now examine the quotation from Oviedo in the context of the *Historia general*. Oviedo has a grudge against de Soto that dates back to the expedition of Pedrarias Dávila to Castilla del Oro in 1514, when Oviedo first came to America as "veedor de minas": "Este gobernador era muy dado a esa montería de matar indios, desde el tiempo que anduvo militando con el gobernador Pedrarias Dávila en las provincias de Castilla del Oro e de Nicaragua, e también se halló en el Perú y en la prisión de aquel gran principe Atabaliba, donde se enriquecio" [This governor was much given to hunting and killing Indians, from the time he participated in military expeditions with Pedrarias Dávila in the provinces of Castilla del Oro and Nicaragua. He was also present in Perú, where he became wealthy, and at the imprisonment of that great Prince Atabaliba] (*HGN*, 2:156). Oviedo considers de Soto to be little more than a murderer. This passage also exemplifies the moral commentaries that Oviedo inserts in rewriting the accounts (in this case, Rodrigo Ranjel's account of de Soto's expedition) that he collects for the *Historia general*. Oviedo, however, does not identify this statement on de Soto's character as his own by presenting himself here as *el historiador*. Thus, this passage gains credibility, if not authority, by using the "story-telling-itself" device with no overt narrator.

In other sections of his rewriting of Ranjel's account, Oviedo makes reference to himself as *el historiador* or *el cronista* to testify to his fidelity to Ranjel's account or to emphasize its veracity. Thus Oviedo cites his eyewitness to highlight the limitations of providing an exhaustive report: "Otros indios hicieron otras hazañas muchas que no se podrían acabar de escribir, segund al historiador dijo el que presente se halló" [Other Indians did many other deeds which one could never fully describe, as he who was present told the historian] (*HGN*, 2:161). He furthermore defines the task of *el cronista* as one of ordering Ranjel to provide him with a written account: "Le mandó e encargó que por escripto dijese e me diese a mi razón de todo, para que como cronista de Sus Majestades destas historias de Indias se acumulase y se pusiese en el número dellas" [He was asked and charged with giving me an account in writing of everything, so that, as chronicler for Your Majesties of these histories of the Indies, information regarding this expedition might be gathered and included in the history] (2:167). Ranjel's report is especially valuable and reflects his wisdom (read trustworthiness) because he supposedly wrote down everything that happened on a daily basis: "Queriendo entender lo que vía e cómo se le pasaba la vida, escribía a la jornada, a vueltas de sus trabajos, todo lo que les sucedía, como sabio, y aun por su recreación" [Desiring to keep a record of what he saw and the course of his life, he wrote daily, at the end of his labors, everything that happened, like a wise man, and even for his leisure] (2:167). The epigraph to this chapter exemplifies these journal-like entries. Oviedo collects accounts that, even as they delight readers, will also instruct them so they will not become carried away by irresponsible governors like de Soto, "pues tantas novedades e peregrinas materias concurren para deletación del prudente letor, e aviso de muchos que por estas Indias se vienen a perder tras un gobernador que así dispensa de vidas ajenas, como por estas mis vigilias y renglones paresce" [since so many novelties and strange matters would be a delight for the judicious reader, and a warning for many who are likely to lose their lives in these Indies following a governor who thus dispenses the lives of others, as is apparent in these studies and writings of mine] (2:167).

AESTHETIC MORALISM

Oviedo not only selects accounts but also elaborates an aesthetic vision and extracts moral lessons by working over the "primary" sources. The castrating woman in my epigraph undoubtedly reflects an aestheticist intent to please a European audience avid for novelty. As for the moralistic intent, it can also be found in his account of the earlier Pánfilo de Narváez 1528 expedition to Florida, in which he insists once more on the blindness of those Spaniards who allowed themselves to be led by false promises: "Querría yo que me dijesen qué les predicaron esos frailes e Pánfilo de Narváez a aquellos españoles que tan ciegos se fueron dejando sus patrias tras falsas palabras" [I wanted them to tell me what those friars and Pánfilo de Narváez preached to those Spaniards that led them to venture so blindly, leaving their fatherland in pursuit of false words] (*HGN*, 4:290). Oviedo's denunciation of de Soto's rampages in Castilla del Oro convey more than a mere bias. Indeed, as we will see later on, a colonial policy that regulates violence lies behind his moralism.

These statements on the aesthetic and moral dimensions of the *Historia general* clearly differentiate the rhetoric of the *relación* type of historical writing from that of the *crónica* and the *historia*. The writer of the *relación* must provide a truthful account of particulars, but not speculate over the meaning or significance of events. As Crown-appointed *cronista*, Oviedo must select and collect the most trustworthy accounts of the Indies. The separation between the task of the *cronista* and that of the *historiador* cannot be so clearly defined. In theory, the *Historia general* is a *historia* and not just a *crónica*: the task of collecting the totality of accounts is already a history inasmuch as the collection itself would ultimately convey the meaning of the whole enterprise and the designs of Providence. Thus, the *Historia general* attains its quality of *historia* precisely in those passages where the *cronista/historiador* reflects on and draws a moral significance from particular events. In the passage quoted above, Oviedo highlights his labor in editing the accounts: "como por estas mis vigilias y renglones paresce" [as manifest in these studies and writings of mine] (2:167). Similarly, in the chapters on Narváez's failed expedition and Cabeza de Vaca's subsequent journey across the continent, Oviedo underscores his work on the "primary" materials, saying, "Es cosa [Narváez's failure] que aunque no tiene remedio ni enmienda, tiene alguna parte aviso, o le causará esta relación" [Although Narváez's failure does not have a remedy or correction, it does hold a lesson, or this account will bring it forth] (4:291).[6] If the account is not exemplary in itself, Oviedo will make sure he extracts its significance. As he makes reference to how "le causará esta relación" [this account will bring it forth], Oviedo draws a thin line between those places where he expressly marks his interventions in the text and those modifications he introduces in the process of

Violence in de Soto Narratives   167

"transcribing" the accounts. Thus, attributions of comment to the *relaciones* he edits would not simply imply a transcript of Ranjel's diary or the *Joint Report* (by Cabeza de Vaca, Castillo, and Dorantes; see chapter 1), but *this rendition.* These different modes of writing history, then, imply a deployment of specific rhetorics that dictate the nature of their historical "truth," rather than just providing form to an actual set of facts.

The example of the castrating woman in the epigraph suggests the exotic as a dominant trope in the *Historia general,* in which it is found both in commentary and in rewritten source materials. Oviedo's exoticism is particularly visible in his detailed and playful descriptions of American nature, but also informs his representations of Amerindian men and women in both the *Historia general* and the *Sumario de la natural historia de las Indias,* a short treatise written for Charles V in 1526. Thus, attributes of sexual freedom and the refusal to submit to the Crown led Oviedo to speculate on Indians' physiology. In the *Sumario,* Oviedo portrays Amerindian women as lascivious, voracious, and vain. Wavering between aesthetic representation and moral opprobrium, he explains that they abort out of fear "[que] se les aflojen las tetas, de las cuales mucho se precian, y las tienen muy buenas" [(that) their breasts, of which they are very proud and have very good ones, would droop] (1986 [1526]: 79). As for the Indian women's vaginas, Oviedo remarked that, after giving birth, "según dicen los que a ellas se dan, son tan estrechas, que con pena los varones consumen sus apetitos, y las que no han parido estan que parecen vírgenes" [according to those who give themselves to them, they are so tight that males can barely satisfy their appetites, and (they make) those who have not given birth seem (like) virgins] (79). These observations and others on the anatomy of women fulfilled an analogous function to that of mugshots illustrating twentieth-century handbooks of anthropology.

Oviedo's description of Indian men's skulls is no less offensive, however objective in spirit: "Estos indios . . . tienen el casco de la cabeza más grueso cuatro veces que los cristianos. E así, cuando se les hace la guerra y vienen con ellos a las manos, han de estar muy sobre aviso de no les dar cuchillada en la cabeza, porque se han visto quebrar muchas espadas, a causa de lo que es dicho, y porque además de ser grueso el casco, es muy fuerte" [These Indi-

ans . . . have skulls four times thicker than those of Christians. Consequently, those who make war on them and come into hand-to-hand combat should be forewarned not to strike them in the head because we have seen that many swords break, due to this fact, and moreover because their skulls are not only thick, but very strong] (1986 [1526]: 91). The *Historia general* further elaborates this passage on the skull with a moral component: "Es nación muy desviada de querer entender la fe católica; y es machacar hierro frío pensar que han de ser cristianos, sino con mucho discurso de tiempo, y así se les ha aparecido en las capas, o, mejor diciendo en las cabezas" [This is a nation that is very unfit and unwilling to understand the Catholic faith; and it is idle to presume that they will become Christians, except after a long period of time, and thus has been seen in reference to their skulls, or, better said to their heads] (*HGN*, 1:111). In responding to such issues as sexual mores, rites and ceremonies, and armed resistance, Oviedo sets up an opposition between savagery and civilization, a polarization that also implies biological difference. Oviedo's emotional reaction to cultural differences is not extraneous to his ethnography, but rather serves the integral function of registering physiological "truths"—with racist overtones, of course.

Despite these racist overtones, Oviedo's binary oppositions were never entirely stable, but were applicable to both Spaniards and Indians. Thus, in the *Sumario's* discussion of the *tuyra* (translated by Oviedo as *el demonio,* the devil), he did not fail to mention that the Indians from Tierra Firme (Main Land) referred to Christians by this name. Moreover, he found the term *tuyra* appropriate "porque han pasado a aquellas partes personas que, pospuestas sus conciencias y el temor de la justicia divina y humana, han hecho cosas no de hombres, sino de dragones y de infieles" [because, as a result of putting aside their conscience and fear of divine and human justice, some of the people that have gone to those places have committed deeds not of humans, but of dragons and infidels] (1986 [1526]: 81). Obviously, here Oviedo is denouncing the greed of the conquistadores, who had destroyed and depopulated the land. Oviedo's ideal colonizers would have been hardworking settlers whose own industry would be enhanced by Indian labor. This utopian order implies a condemnation of the behavior of Indians and conquistadores alike, because both contradict the European work ethic. From the comments above that declare that the Indians would require prolonged teaching (due to the thickness of their skulls) before being able to comprehend Christianity, we may assume that Oviedo favored the perpetual subordination of Indians to a life of labor on the *encomiendas*. In these speculations on the best imperial policy for the colonies, Oviedo dwells in that other modern historiographical space we generally identify with Machiavelli's *The Prince* and the *Discourses*.

Though the passage on the castrating woman is a historical trifle, a speck in de Soto's historiography, it invests the Amerindian woman with a paradigmatic quality: "e son tales" [and they are of such stuff]. This is Oviedo's first mention of a systematic capture of women slaves. Oviedo disapproves of the subjection of women to sexual abuse. According to a witness whom he does not name (we must presume that it is not Ranjel), whereas men were captured to serve as *tamemes* ("porters" in Nahuatl), women were captured and baptized for sex: "para sus sucios usos e lujuria, e que las hacían baptizar para sus carnalidades más que para enseñarles la fe" [for their dirty use and lust, and had them baptised for their carnality rather than for instructing them in the Faith] (*HGN,* 2:172). We may wonder, however, how many Christians were victims of crushed testicles. The fact that Oviedo portrays the woman in the epigraph as not wanting to let the *bachiller* loose and him as not desiring her sexually ("puesto que él no quería haber parte con ella como libidinoso") ought to make us suspicious of Oviedo's characterization of the indigenous woman as well as of his condemnation of the sexual commerce. Oviedo's moralism seems to have more to do with a Catholic modesty than with a respect for the humanity of Amerindian women; his depiction of lascivious and castrating Amerindian women feeds into the culture of rape by putting the blame on their voracious and indomitable nature, "e son tales." A similar sentiment underlies his criticisms of de Soto's greed and cruelty. Oviedo's vaunted moralism ultimately conveys compliance with the Crown's insistence on not abusing Indians, and in particular the new set of rules under the Nuevas Leyes of 1542, rather than a sympathy for the plight of Amerindians. Moreover, moralism colors his descriptions of particular acts of violence by specific individuals; as we will see below, torture by some is exemplary, by others condemnable. Again, violence per se does not signify atrocity in sixteenth-century texts. Mutilations, massacres, and torture become atrocity only on the basis of commentary that establishes their illegal or unjust nature. But moralism makes Oviedo's documentations and commentaries all the more useful for a reading of the culture of terror as it was practiced by Christians in different parts of America.[7]

We can already trace this sort of juridicolegal meditation in Oviedo's *Sumario de la natural historia de las Indias,* published in 1526. Take, for instance, the passage where, after declaring that the term "to pacify" actually means "to destroy" ("más que pacífico, lo llamo destruído"), Oviedo goes on to praise the Ordenanzas of 1526, just approved by the Council of the Indies: "Con acuerdo de muchos teólogos y juristas y personas de altos entendimientos, [el Emperador] ha proveído y remediado con su justicia todo lo que ha sido posible, y mucho más con la nueva reformación de su real consejo de Indias" [Following the advice of many theologians and jurists and learned people, with his justice (the Emperor) has provided for and corrected all that has been possible, and even more with the new reforms of his Council of the Indies] (1986 [1526]: 82). One must note that his reference to the wisdom of Charles V is framed by other paragraphs in which he describes Indian women as lascivious, warns Spaniards about using their swords against the "thick skulls" (*cascos duros*) of the Indians, condemns the ritual anthropophagy of the Caribs, and reduces Amerindian cultures to a series of diabolical practices. The difference between his account and that of Bartolomé de las Casas (and the reason why Las Casas opposed the publication of the *Historia general*) resides precisely in Oviedo's attitude toward ritual anthropophagy, sacrifice, and indigenous knowledge and religion.[8]

BESTIAL OBJECTIVITY

Before examining the uses of terror in Oviedo, let us observe how violence is represented in the other two main accounts of de Soto's expedition. Both Elvas's *Relaçam verdadeira dos trabalhos q̃ ho gouerna-*

dor dõ Fernãdo de Souto e certos fidalgos portugueses passarom no descobrimẽto da prouincia da Frolida (1557) and Biedma's *Relación del suceso de la jornada del cap. Soto, y de la calidad de la tierra por donde anduvo* (1544) corroborate the violence documented by Oviedo based on Ranjel's account. The *Relaçam* confirms the systematic use of violence and the capture of slaves without going into the details related by Oviedo. Biedma is less explicit in his account of how porters and women were taken or demanded from caciques. In all three, though with different degrees of intensity, one can hear the noise of the chains of the thousands of men and women who were drawn from one place to another by de Soto's armada (e.g., in the *Relaçam,* just in the course of one week, four hundred slaves were taken in Ocute and seven hundred more in Patofa; see Elvas 1940 [1557]: 52–54). Martin and Ivana Elbl have produced a very useful appendix that annotates variations as well as absences in these accounts (1997: 74–85). My point here, however, is not to compare different versions of events, but to draw from the *Relaçam,* and to a lesser extent from Biedma, an attitude—and even perhaps an aesthetic sensibility— toward conquest and violence.

In the 1557 edition of the *Relaçam* the opening epigraph by Fernão da Silveira gives us a clue as to how violence was read and the type of pleasure that was derived from its narration and description. On the one hand, this epigraph constitutes a minute prism that reflects the sensibility of the anonymous author and his readership; on the other hand, it promotes the "objectivity" of the text. By objectivity I do not mean that the author was impartial, but rather that the rhetoric of the representation in the *Relaçam* is geared primarily toward creating the appearance of a literal description rather than toward elaborating a "figure." Certain passages might lend themselves to an allegorical reading; however, it is worthwhile recalling that by definition allegories include a literal meaning. The epigraph itself reproduces this double structure. Written in two columns in the original, it reads as follows:

Quem quer ver o novo mundo,

Nós abitã-

o Polo Aureo segundo,

mos o polo ártico seten-

trional,

e aquelas

gentes habi-

tam o Polo

antártico aus-

tral.

Disse Polo

Aureo porque

é terra rica.

outros mares, outras terras,

façanha grandes e guerras

e cousas tais empr'ender

que 'spantan e dão prazer,

poem terror e dão dulçor

leia poraqueste autor,

é historia deleitosa

e verá não fabulosa,

digna de ser estimada

usada, lida e tratada.

Finis. (Elvas 1940 [1557]: fol. iv)

[We inhabit the Northern Pole, and that people inhabit the Southern Antarctic Pole. / Golden Pole is used because the region is rich. // He who would see the New World, / the Golden Pole, the second, / other seas, other lands, / achievements great, and wars, / and such things attempted / that alarm and give pleasure, / strike terror and lend delight;— / read of the author this pleasing story, / where nothing fabulous is told, / all worthy of being esteemed, / read, considered, used.] (Bourne 1922, 1:1)

The left-hand column opens with a fanciful geographical location (both Portugal and Florida are in the Northern Hemisphere) of the territories inhabited by "nós" (we) and "aquelas gentes" (that people). Nevertheless, this column reiterates a commonplace that associated southern latitudes with gold as it explains the "obscure" reference to Polo Aureo in the right-hand column. The didactic intent of the marginal annotation ends up obscuring the straightforward description of the book in the second column. This column begins with an allusion to the Polo Aureo and ends by underscoring that the *Relaçam* is delightful and useful. What is true, of course, does not exclude the beautiful; as Horace would put it, the *Relaçam* is *dulce et utile*. As all people are fond of listening to and seeing new things, especially from foreign and remote lands, an account is even more delightful if it is a "historia deleitosa" that narrates and vividly describes events "que 'spantan e dão prazer, / poem terror e dão dulçor" [that alarm and given pleasure, / strike terror and give delight]. Paradoxically, the epigraph characterizes the land as a Polo Aureo, when in the end the *Relaçam* is the testimony of a failed, albeit systematic and tenacious search for gold and opulent provinces. Nevertheless, the mirage of a rich "Orient," in the vicinity of Florida, remains intact.

The epigraph seems to tell us that the pleasure of reading resides precisely in the story of how de Soto's expedition followed a mirage of wealth, and no less in the description of the size of the armada, of its power—in short, of the slave raids and military incursions. The *Relaçam* dwells to a lesser extent (say, in comparison to Oviedo) on the exotic topos of the "savage Indian." We find instead an example of the "gallant Indies" topos in, for instance, the descriptions of the cacica of Cutifachiqui (or Cofitachequi in Oviedo) and even more pronouncedly in those of the cacique of Coça: "Saiu o Cacique a receber dous tiros de béstea de povo em um andor que seus principais aos hombros traziam, assentado em um coxim e cuberto com uma roupa de martas de feição e tamanho de um manto de mulher; trazia na cabeça um diadema de pena e ao redor de si muitos índios tangendo e cantando" [The Cacique came out to receive them at the distance of two crossbow shots from the town, borne in a litter on the shoulders of his principal men, seated on a cushion, and covered with a mantle of martenskins, of the size and shape of a woman's shawl: on his head he wore a diadem of plumes, and he was surrounded by many attendants playing upon flutes and singing] (Elvas 1940 [1557]: 69; Bourne 1922, 1:81).

In the *Relaçam* this "gallant" image is a preface to the detention of the cacique and the subsequent massacre in Mavilla (Mabila in Oviedo); thus from the start, the mirage of gold is accompanied by the abuse of Indians. The first news of a rich land is of Cale, where men supposedly marched to war wearing golden helmets: "traziam de ouro seus sombreiros, á maneira de celadas" (Elvas 1940 [1557]: 36). From this point on in the narration, Indian leaders are systematically held hostage. In the *Relaçam* there is a complete absence of any meddling that would legitimize de Soto's abuses; it never mentions a reading of the *Requerimiento*. It simply tells what happened: de Soto's men enter, destroy, and take captives. The author does not moralize or place the actions in a legal framework; to punish and set an example are the only ends of these actions. Violence ensures control. Thus, the *Relaçam* exemplifies the particular nature of imperialist wars of conquest as that of pursuing the permanent occupation of a territory and subjection (if no enslavement) of a people — at least for a tutelary period defined by the new rulers. A bestial (i.e., amoral) objectivity runs through the *Relaçam*. Occasionally, the author looks back and tells us that the lands were destroyed and that those who passed through them again faced extreme difficulties: "Chegaram a Caliquem com muito trabalho porque at terra por onde o Governador havia passado quedava destruida e sem maís" [They reached Caliquen after much suffering because the land over which the governor had passed lay wasted and without maize] (Elvas 1940 [1557]: 40; Bourne 1922, 1: 40). Like a plague of locusts the armada had combed the region for corn: "O Governador mandou encerrar todo o maís que havía sêco pelo campo, que bastava para três meses" [The Governor ordered all the ripe grain in the fields, enough for three months, to be secured] (37; 1:37). The destruction of lands by armies is a commonplace in sixteenth-century documents of both European and American military campaigns; in the case of de Soto as told in the *Relaçam*, however, there is no concern whatsoever for the land's fate. These towns were not, after all, the great provinces of de Soto's dreams.

When the Fidalgo de Elvas expresses his opinion, he limits himself to direct observations. Take, for instance, his commentaries on de Soto's decision to abandon Cutifachiqui: "E ainda que pareceu erro deixar aquela terra . . . não houve quem cousa alguma lhe dissesse, sabida sua determinação" [For though it seemed an error to leave that country . . . there were none who would say a thing to him after it became known that he had made up his mind] (1940 [1557]: 60; Bourne 1922, 1: 69). The Fidalgo deplores the treatment of the cacica: "O Governador la mandou pôr em guarda e a levou consigo, não con tão bom tratamento como ela merecia. . . . E assim a levava a pé com suas escravas" [The Governor ordered that she be placed under guard and took her with him . . . which was not the proper treatment she deserved . . . and thus she was carried away on foot with her female slaves] (61; 1:70). Thus, de Soto takes on the semblance of a conquistador who is ruled only by greed, to such an extent that he destroys the very source of wealth that would make colonization of the land possible. De Soto's expedition is without doubt an example of "the-myth-of-Spaniards-enthralled-in-dreams-of-dorados." Indeed, his behavior at times borders on the irrational. For instance, going by some towns he wanted to "befriend," de Soto cut down and destroyed large cornfields: "lhes talou e destruiu grandes maísais" (65). Recent scholarship has pointed out that the Amerindian cultures de Soto invaded in the Southeast never recuperated from the destruction of their crops and the epidemics that followed. The destruction was such that by the middle of the seventeenth century, when contact was renewed, the indigenous cultures lacked the splendor attributed to them by some of the accounts of the de Soto expedition.[9]

The *Relaçam*'s rhetorical objectivity entails a representation of Indians in their own terms. An uprising is seen as a refusal to be subjected and enslaved, without passing value judgments. This perspective, obviously, does not exclude the interpretation of uprisings as acts of rebellion against the authority of the Crown. Indians retain their dignity in the narration of the events, but the punishments by the (Christian) victor are told impassively by Elvas: "Seriam por todos duzentos índios; foram todos subjugados e alguns dos mais moços deu o Governador aos que tinham boas cadeias e recado para que se lhe não fossem, e todos os mais mandou justiçar amarrados a um esteio no meio da praça e os flecharam os índios de Paracoxi" [Those who were subdued may have been in all two hundred men: some of the youngest the governor gave to those (Christians) who had good chains and were vigilant; all the rest were ordered to be executed, and, being bound to a post in the middle of the town yard, they were shot to death with arrows by the people of Paracoxi] (1940[1557]: 42; Bourne 1922, 1:44). Here de Soto uses the Paracoxi, Indian "allies," who were unbound by now, "já soltos andavam" (42). This passage suggests that from the time of their initial contact with the Spaniards, the Indians of Paracoxi had directed the Christians toward Cale and Caliquen to bring harm to an old enemy.

All three accounts describe a systematic use of terror that is characterized by the *aperreos,* mutilations, and burning alive of women and men. The whole purpose is to set an example. Let us take some passages from the *Historia general,* which, by the way, also further illustrate the "fine line" separating overt intervention from apparent transcription of events. Oviedo glosses Ranjel with a definition of *aperreo* to underscore the violence of the conquest: "Ha de entender el letor que aperrear es hacer que perros le comiesen o matasen, despedazando al indio" [The reader must understand that *aperrear* means to have the dogs eat them or kill them, thus tearing the Indian to pieces] (*HGN,* 2:156). The burning of Indians to gain information is also systematic, though unsuccessful, from what the following "transcript" of Ranjel would suggest: "Nunca quiso ninguno conoscer el pueblo del señor ni descobrirlo, aunque quemaron uno dellos vivo delante de los otros, y todos sufrieran aquel martirio, por no descobrirlo" [Not one ever showed any knowledge of his lord's town nor disclosed its location, although they burnt one of them alive before the others, and all suffered that martyrdom, for not disclosing it] (2:166). Disobedience is punished by cutting off hands and noses, and Oviedo likens the Indians' impassive reception of the penalty to the Roman Stoics: "Si a algunos cortaban las manos y narices, no hacían más sentimiento que si cada uno dellos fuera un Mucio Scévola romano" [If they cut the hands and noses of some, these showed less feeling than if each of them was a Mucio Scévola of Rome] (2:162).

Thus, all three accounts celebrate the Indian's stoicism and refusal to submit to slavery. Oviedo speaks of four-year-old children who fought next to their parents at the battle of Mavilla, or Mabila, where young Indians chose to hang themselves or jump into fires rather than be subjected to slavery: "Las mujeres y aun muchachos de cuatro años reñían con los cristianos, y muchachos indios se ahorcaban por no venir a sus manos, e otros se metían en el fuego de su grado" [Women and even boys of four years of age fought against the Christians, and the boys hanged themselves in order not to come into their hands, while others jumped into the fire willingly] (2:175). This heroism is matched by the Spanish valor: "E todos los españoles pelearon como varones de grandes ánimos" [And all the Spaniards fought like men of great spirit] (2:175). Thus, in spite of his moralistic diatribes against de Soto, Oviedo also knows how to complement Ranjel's account by praising the Spaniards. In the *Relaçam,* the tragic end of Mavilla is told in a less heroic, but perhaps more realistic tone: "E depois de os cristãos entrar entre êle ás cutiladas, vendo-se mui afrontados, sem reparo algum, muitos fugindo, nas casas ardendo se entraram, onde uns sôbre outros se afogavam e morreram queimados" [And as the Christians came among them with cutlasses, and finding themselves surrounded on all sides, many, fleeing, dashed headlong into the flaming houses, where they were smothered, and, heaped one upon another, burned to death] (Elvas 1940[1557]: 81; Bourne 1922, 1:97). It is never a question of belittling the Indian's courage, but of describing the battle without singling out the courage of the Christians. Both accounts, however, concur that it was a massacre. The *Relaçam* estimates that two thousand Indians died in the battle; Oviedo sets the number at three thousand.

In Biedma's account, the victory assumes a grotesque dimension as it describes the Spaniards' use of Indian fat to cure themselves: "Curámonos aquella noche con el unto de los mesmos indios muertos, que no nos había quedado otra medicina" [We cured ourselves with the fat of the dead Indians, since we had no other medicine] (*CDI,* 3: 427). Garcilaso also mentions the extraction of fat,[10] but neither Oviedo nor the *Relaçam* include the detail. However, elsewhere in the *Historia general* Oviedo mentions and justifies the fact that Cortés caulked thirteen boats with the fat of Indian enemies: "el unto de los indios enemigos" (*HGN,* 4:152; cf. Gerbi 1985: 308). This justification of the use of fat to caulk brigantines is juxtaposed with a description of how the Indians ate the innumerable corpses that lay on the ground after the fall of Tenochtitlan. Thus, the Conquest of Mexico was justified even under the strictures of the Nuevas Leyes; in fact, this account belongs to the second part of the *Historia general* and thus bears the imprint of the new legislation.[11] If Oviedo had known of this use of fat after the massacre he would have mentioned it; he knew all too well that the extraction of

Writing Violence on the Northern Frontier

fat from corpses was a customary medicinal practice in European wars. Notwithstanding its commonplaceness, however, it is a sinister and symbolic act. It provides, therefore, a window on the manner in which terror exercises power over the life and death of the Indians.

De Soto had already used fat for medicinal purposes in Peru and, according to Michael Taussig, this practice gave rise to rumors among the Indians of a systematic extraction to send back to Spain. In the sixteenth century these rumors led to the revolt of Taqui Onqoy or the Dance of Sickness.[12] In our century, it takes the form of the phantom called Nakaq, which usually appears in the form of a White or a mestizo who amasses Indian fat "to sell either to pharmacies where it is used in medicines or to people who use it to grease machines, cast church bells, or shine the faces of the statues of the saints" (Taussig 1987: 238). Whether for military or medicinal purposes, the use of fat constitutes a desecration of the body of the vanquished, and perhaps even a modality of cannibalism — an appropriation of the power of the enemy. As Taussig points out, "the Frazerian principles of sympathetic and contagious magic are clear: with the fat of those who have wounded me I will heal that wound" (237). The use of fat is an act of terror that would have affected at once the survivors and the Indian slaves that were part of de Soto's camp. It asserts the absolute right over the body of the Indians whom the act of conquest reduces to slavery; the extraction of fat implies a total exploitation of Indians as one more natural resource. Hence, we can trace an economy of terror that articulates its principles on the life and death of the slave's body. In spite of Foucault's gnomic expression, "in the 'excess' of torture a whole economy of power is invested," we should state with Taussig that "there is no 'excess,'" where war, torture, and terror are an arbitrary, generalized practice and no longer a means to punish or even avenge a particular injury or disloyalty (see Taussig 1987: 27; 1989; Foucault 1979: 3–31).

In the *Relaçam* it is clear that for both de Soto and Moscoso (who led the expedition after de Soto's death), torture and violence constitute a spectacle where mutilated bodies are displayed. In passing, I should mention that it is somewhat ironic that Oviedo's version stops precisely with de Soto's death. According to the *Relaçam* and

Biedma, Moscoso does not deviate from de Soto's use of violence; there is hardly a case to make for the unique cruelty of the latter. Violence is a fundamental part of the theater of war and conquest—needless to say, on the part of both combatants. Take the infliction of wounds explicitly carried out to set an example in the following military encounter, which occurs right before de Soto's death: "Foram ali mortos cem índios, pouco mais ou menos, e muitos foram feridos de grandes lançadas, que os deixavam ir para que pusessem espanto aos que ali não se haviam achado" [About one hundred men were slain; many were allowed to get away badly wounded, that they might strike terror into those who were absent] (Elvas 1940[1557]: 126–27; Bourne 1922, 1:157). According to the *Relaçam,* the Christians generated so much fear that the cries of the women and children were deafening: "Os gritos das mulheres e meninos eram tantos que atroavam os ouvidos dos que os seguiam" [The cries of the women and children were such as to deafen those who pursued them] (126; 1:157). This is one of those few passages where the *Relaçam* deplores this abuse by the Christians: "Huve ali homens tão crueis e carniceiros que velhos e moços e quantos topavam diante matavam sem pouco nem muito haverem resistido" [Some persons were so cruel and butcher-like that they killed all before them, young and old, not one having resisted little or much] (126; 1:157). One infers that some derived pleasure ("tão crueis e carniceiros" [so cruel and butcher-like]) from the cruelty and injury of helpless young and old Indians. Yet even this lamentation is more in tune with the things that alarm and thereby give pleasure, "que'spantan e dã o prazer, / poem terro e dão dulçor," expressed in the epigraph, than with some sort of abstract moral disapproval. The *Relaçam,* furthermore, reiterates that in the course of the massacre Indians were purposefully wounded but not killed so that they would display their injuries: "Rompiam os índios, derribando muitos com os estribos y peitos dos cavalos, e a alguns davam una lançada e assim os deixavam ir" [They broke through the crowds of Indians, bearing down many with their stirrups and the breasts of their horses, giving some a thrust and letting them go] (126; 1:157–58). The *Relaçam* concludes this war scene by leading us to understand that the Christians achieved the intended effect: "E mui admirados do que ilhe haviam visto fazer com os índios da Nilco,

tudo como passou, com grande espanto a seu Cacique disseram"
[And greatly astonished at what they had seen done to the people
of Nilco, they recounted to their cacique with great fear everything
that had happened] (127; 1:158). The Fidalgo was not present when
the cacique of Nilco was informed, but his assumption that the extreme cruelty would provoke fear implies a practice and rationale
for violence and terror as ends in themselves, that is, unabashed arbitrary violence. This lesson is perhaps what the epigraph means by
an exemplary history, "digna de ser estimada/usada, lida e tratada"
[all worthy of being esteemed, / read, considered, used].

These last examples raise questions regarding the strategic function of terror and its theatricality in the colonial drama itself. It
is worth insisting that torture, cruelty, and terror are not unique
to the sixteenth-century Spanish conquistadores; they prevail even
among twentieth-century "civilized" nations. I do not believe this
is the place to enumerate the atrocities that have been committed
in our very recent past and others that unfortunately belong to the
present. But if we were to draw a parallel with the present, the terror practiced by de Soto's armada or the concept of war *a sangre y
fuego* has closer parallels to Latin American death squads terrorizing
civilians and annihilating the opposition than with ethnic cleansing
in Yugoslavia, where extermination or expulsion do not partake of
a will to establish political dominance over another group. Recent
reflections on the nature of war and terror, however, prove useful
for an understanding of de Soto's invasion of Florida and its narrative variations.

The dominant theoretical model of warfare in the West has been
the confrontation of two individuals in a struggle to death. As has
been pointed out by Elaine Scarry, among the classical theoreticians of war only Clausewitz has clearly seen the deficiency of a definition where the outcome of "a military contest carries the power of
its own enforcement."[13] Clausewitz describes a whole series of wars
that manifest a disparity between the abstract objective of war to
disarm and thus obtain a total victory, and peace treaties that were
signed before one of the antagonists could be considered impotent.
According to Scarry, the schema changes substantially when we
change from a model based on two individuals locked in a struggle
to one where two multitudes come face to face. In this instance, the

notion of a total victory would be tantamount to genocide, slavery, or a permanent occupation. Scarry furthermore argues that the annihilation of a people is a fundamental characteristic not of war but of atrocity (see 1985: 99–108). The European invasion of America, however, was carried out by men who believed that its outcome would carry the power of its own enforcement. Given de Soto's objective of finding a "Dorado" (the conquest of a kingdom as rich or more so than Cuzco and Tenochtitlan), the apparently irrational capture of caciques, burning of villages, and razing of cornfields is, perhaps, wholly consistent with the end of a total victory—that is, permanent occupation and enslavement.

The primordial objective of conquest, like that of warfare, is to injure, or more precisely, to out-injure the enemy.[14] In some instances we find that the Amerindians from Florida, as the different accounts put it, came in peace: "venían de paz." "Peace by surrender" does not imply an absence of injury, but rather unidirectional injuring of the Indians by the Spaniards. This is, indeed, the structure of the *Requerimiento* where the threat of violence demands the subordination of the Indians to the Spanish Crown. But the passage from Las Casas, cited in the introduction, in which mutilated hands were identified with a "letter" bearing the power that will enforce the new regime of law, exemplifies a more "primitive" form of interpellating Indians. The use of terror to convey the news was, in fact, de Soto's preferred method, rather than the more formalistic approach of the *Requerimiento* that was prescribed by the 1526 Ordenanzas (see chapters 1 and 2). Indians, anticipating the injuries that would result from war, would choose to submit to de Soto. Of course, this "surrender" could very well be the Spanish interpretation of Indian traditions and practices of hospitality—or even forms of entrapment. Whether in the mode of the *Requerimiento* or of the mutilated hands as letters, the message of the Spaniards is unequivocal: subordination or war. Such "surrendering" obviously does not imply that the Indians remain uninjured, for the Indians are forced to forsake their sovereignty, to share their foodstuffs, and to provide the Christians with porters and concubines, that is, with slaves. Under these circumstances it is practically impossible to distinguish symbolic or mental injuries from physical violence.

For terror need not be directed at the body to be less effective or physically painful.

If they happened to be evangelized, the destruction of their consciousness, that is, of their interior culture, would complement the destruction of their persons and material culture. The subordination to de Soto already implies a loss of "national" identity and an alteration in the native view of the organization of the world (see Scarry 1985: 92). The Franciscan conception of evangelization as a *conquista espiritual* is neither arbitrary nor a pacifist variation (*avant la lettre*) of Clausewitz's maxim "War is the continuation of politics by other means" (quoted in Glucksmann 1969: 36). The spiritual conquest continues the process set in place by the *Requerimiento*: pledging obedience to the Crown commits Indians not only to obey Spanish law but also to be evangelized. As Clausewitz himself puts it: "A conqueror is always a friend of peace. . . . His ideal would be to enter into our State without opposition" (quoted in Glucksmann 1969: 57). The missionaries knew very well that their spiritual warfare was no less violent and repressive than physical warfare. One has only to refer to the prologues and appendices in Bernardino de Sahagún's *Florentine Codex* or *Historia general de las cosas de la Nueva España,* which explain how, during the first decades of the conquest of Mexico, the Franciscan friars trained *muchachos* who would surveil the religious activities of their elders and terrorize them by surprising and arresting them in the middle of their festivities.[15] If Indians could not be forced to convert to Christianity, they certainly were forced to learn the catechism. The missionaries clearly pursued a deconstruction of the world, in Scarry's parlance, "in the interior of human consciousness itself," and, as we have seen in chapter 2, to accomplish this end, they advocated the forced resettlement of Indians, removed children from families and communities, executed resistant Indians in autos-da-fé by hanging or burning at the stake, and in some instances justified and participated in wars of extermination.

Although we should not conflate the violence of torture and the violence of conversion, in the actual field of action it is difficult to separate (at least from an ethical perspective) the *sanctioning* of wars of extermination (i.e., the Church was complicitous in torture, massacre, genocide) in the name of Christianity from its actual implementation at the hands of soldiers. This was clearly the case in the massacre of Acoma (see chapter 3). The similarity between conquistadores and missionaries also resides in the candor of their narrative descriptions of violence. The candor with which the missionary accounts relate the physical punishments and the extirpation of forms of thinking not compatible with the Christian faith or Western rationality recurs in the de Soto accounts of burning towns, taking slaves, raiding food deposits, sexual abuses, mutilations, *aperreos,* and other means of injuring the Indians. This candor is especially manifest in the *Relaçam* and Biedma's *Relación del suceso;* we will shortly examine Oviedo's moral reservations. The aim of these accounts is not to condemn de Soto. Only Oviedo criticizes de Soto, and more for his greed than for the terrorism he practices. Biedma's account is brief and does not pay great attention to violence. As for the *Relaçam,* it reads more as a manual of what every good conquistador must know than as a juridical document. As a Portuguese writing in 1557, Elvas was under no legal obligation to report to the Spanish Crown.[16]

We have already seen the amoral objectivity of the *Relaçam*'s accounts of terror and violence. In this account, there is no overt indication of the author's intentions. Our only clue as to how to read them is the reception (and horizon of expectations) that Fernão da Silveira anticipates in his epigraph. According to this reading, there is no doubt that the description of violence and destruction in the *Relaçam* will provide pleasure ("que'spantam e dão prazer, / poem terror e dão dulçor"); nothing is farther from this horizon of expectations than a moral condemnation of the conquest of peoples abroad. The last lines of the epigraph, which insists not only on the *Relaçam*'s beauty and truthfulness but its utility ("digna de ser estimada / usada, lida e tratada"), invest the *Relaçam* with a "how-to" quality. Let us now move on to examine how juridicolegal frameworks determine the writing of war and terror in Oviedo's *Historia general.*

Oviedo writes under the demands of the Nuevas Leyes of 1542. As a result of their promulgation, explorers were forced to follow different criteria and rules of action, or at least to tailor their accounts to reflect the new legislation. Because Oviedo's work was never published in its entirety, and therefore never completely revised to reflect a single point of view, these legal changes can also be traced in the different books of his *Historia general,* as well as in the 1535 and 1547 editions of the first part. Moreover, the *Historia general* was requisitioned by Andrés Gasco, the inquisitor of the city of Seville, and turned over to the Council of the Indies in 1563 (see Gerbi 1985: 130). Several reasons have been given for the prohibition of its publication. Among them are two worth mentioning because, as explanations, they belong to different historical moments and represent opposite ideologies. The first is López de Gómara's, who states that it was due to Las Casas's opposition (this in turn apparently because of Oviedo's defamation of Amerindians in more than one place in the *Historia general*); the second is Antonello Gerbi's, who cites the "severe criticism of the clergy and the conduct of the Spanish in the Indies" (129–30). Both are feasible explanations, but Gerbi's must be nuanced; criticism in itself did not worry the Council of the Indies (the Nuevas Leyes call for a report on everything), but if Oviedo's work were to circulate abroad, it would give Spain a bad name. This concern is a trait of Philip II's reign, which was marked by Counter-Reformation rebuttals of Protestant vituperations against Spain's enterprise in the Indies. This new political climate would explain the prohibition of Oviedo's and Las Casas's works under the same pragmatic of 1556 that called for censorship of all books on the Indies (see Friede 1959; cf. R. Adorno 1986). I insist on these historical specificities surrounding the production and publication of the *Historia general* to avoid attributing Oviedo's "new" position on the conquest to a change in his personal opinion. Already in the *Sumario* he condemned the gangster-like behavior of some conquistadores and in the *Historia general* his rantings against de Soto and Narváez hardly manifest an ideological transformation when we compare them to chapters dedicated to others deemed exemplary conquistadores and colonial officials,

Violence in de Soto Narratives

in spite of their terrorism. Racism and exoticism continue to structure Oviedo's representations of Amerindian cultures throughout the *Historia general,* notwithstanding his obligation to "descargar la conciencia" [relieve the conscience of the king] and his preference for a colonial policy that favored settlement over the adventurism of conquistadores such as de Soto. Oviedo promotes a view of the Spanish empire in the Americas where colonists learn to exploit exotic natural resources in profitable businesses; in this utopian model of hard-working Spanish entrepreneurs, because of attributed moral and physical deficiencies Amerindians continue to serve Spaniards in *encomiendas.* It is not so much that de Soto terrorized Indians in Florida that bothers Oviedo, but that de Soto's gangster-like behavior had no place in Oviedo's rationalized view of empire. We ought to consider, moreover, to what extent Oviedo's writing on de Soto reflects the differences between the Nuevas Leyes and the Crown's provision for de Soto's governorship, which preceded them and were informed by the Ordenanzas of 1526.

Under the Nuevas Leyes, slavery was completely forbidden (law 20); they specify that no "discoverer"—the term now preferred over conquistador—could remove Indians from their lands with the exception of up to three or four persons to train as interpreters: "eçepto hasta tres o quatro personas para lenguas" (law 33). The Nuevas Leyes also forbid all forms of pillage, "tomar ni aver cosa contra voluntad de los yndios, si no fuere por rrescate y a vista de la persona el Audiencia nombrare" [to take nor have anything against the will of the Indians, unless it was through exchange and under the supervision of a person appointed by the *audiencia*] (law 33). Before the Nuevas Leyes, it was customary for explorers and conquerors to give an account of their actions, but it was not a legal exigency (see chapter 2). The reading of the *Requerimiento* was the only measure that guaranteed that the Crown's "conciencias quedaran descargadas" [conscience would be relieved], as it is expressed in de Soto's *capitulacion* (contract) with the Crown for the *conquest* of Florida (and not *discovery,* as his invasion would have been termed by the Nuevas Leyes).

De Soto's contract, however, gave him a sufficiently broad field of action in that it licensed such abuses and terroristic practices as military incursions into towns, food raids, the enslavement of

Indians, the pillaging of graves, and the systematic retention of caciques as hostages. Indeed, the provisions go so far as to recommend these procedures and even specify what percentage of the resulting gains will be allotted to the Crown. Take, for instance, the following standard on ransoms: "Segund derecho é Leyes de nuestros Reynos, quando nuestras gentes y Capitanes de nuestras armadas, toman preso algund Principe ó Señor de las tierras donde por Nuestro mandado hacen guerra, el rescate del tal Señor ó Cazique pertenece á nos" [According to the rights and laws of Our Kingdoms, when our people and captains of Our armadas, take as a hostage the Prince or Lord of the land where they make war in Our name, the ransom for such a lord or cacique belongs to us] (Smith 1857 1:144; cf. *CDI,* 22:542). But given the excessive travails of those who wage war in the Indies, exception is made: "[De] todos los tesoros, oro y plata, y piedras, y perlas que se oviere del por via de rescate ó en otra qualquier manera, se vos dé la sesta parte dello y lo demas se rreparta entre los conquistadores sacando primeramente nuestro quinto" [Of all the treasures, gold and silver, and stones, and pearls gained through ransom or other means, a sixth should be given to you and the rest distributed among the conquistadores, first taking out our fifth] (1:144; cf. *CDI,* 22:543). Thus, the *capitulación* foresees de Soto's retention of one cacique after another as hostages. None of the accounts mentions ransoms; the demands for porters, women, and food seem a matter of course, and the pearls of the cacica of Cutifachiqui read more as a gift than a payment of ransom. This provision, then, seems to anticipate the captivity of another Atahualpa, not the preservation of an exact record of "trifles."

On the pillage of graves, the *capitulación* provides that "de todo el oro y plata . . . que se hallaren . . . en los enterramientos . . . se nos [la corona] pague la mitad sin descuento de cosa alguna, quedando la otra mitad para Persona que ansi lo hallare é descubriere" [of all the gold and silver . . . found . . . in the graves . . . half of it should be paid to us (the Crown) without discount, leaving the other half for the person that found and discovered it] (Smith 1857, 1:144; cf. *CDI,* 22:544). Accordingly, the *Relaçam* quite laconically informs of the pillage of graves in a town near Cufitachiqui: "Foran buscadas as daquele povo; acharam-se catorze arrobas de perolas e meninos e aves formados delas" [They examined those in the town, and found fourteen *arrobas* of pearls, and figures of babies and birds made of them] (Elvas 1940 [1557]: 58; Bourne 1922, 1:66). The specific weight of fourteen ounces suggests their removal from the grave. Biedma confirms this supposition, but in a less alluring scene that describes how the pearls have been damaged from lying in the ground and in the fat of the corpses: "Sacamos de allí cantidad de perlas, que serían hasta seis arrobas . . . aunque no eran buenas, que estaban dañadas por estar debajo de la tierra y metidas entre el sain de los indios" [We took from it a quantity of pearls, weighing up to six *arrobas* . . . though they were not good, since they were damaged from lying in the earth and in the fat of the dead] (*CDI*, 3:421). In the *Historia general,* however, de Soto not only prevents the grave from being pillaged, but Oviedo has him expressing a moral maxim: "Déjenlas estar, e a quien Dios se la diere en suerte, Sanct Pedro se la bendiga" [Leave them alone, and to whom God gives by good fortune, may Saint Peter bless him] (*HGN,* 2:168). Considering that in this passage Ranjel proposes pocketing the goods from the grave without letting others know, "Señor no llamemos a nadie" [My Lord, let us not call anyone] (2:168), we may conclude that de Soto's maxim is pure Oviedo vintage—or, less likely, from another informant. Here Oviedo's portrayal of de Soto's restraint could be read as a form of protecting the name of Spain, rather than as an assessment of de Soto's character.

To effect the "descargo de la conciencia" [relief of the conscience] of Charles V, the *capitulación* includes the Ordenanzas of 1526, which demands that the conquistadores read the *Requerimiento.* From all appearances the *Requerimiento* was never read during de Soto's attempted conquest of Florida (at least, none of the accounts explicitly says that it was). If de Soto, or someone concerned with vindicating the enterprise, had written an account, he would not have failed to mention it. Elvas did not have any reason to include this sort of information, but in the case of Biedma's *Relación del suceso* it is a significant silence because he writes his account as official factor of the expedition. Considering that Charles V and the Council of the Indies are Oviedo's most immediate addressees, his own silence amounts to one more denunciation. On the other hand, the "spirit" of the *Requerimiento* underlies the binary categorization of Indians: between those who come in peace and those who resist. How can a people rebel and thus merit "punishment" without having first been subjected by means of the word or arms?[17] The *Requerimiento* would ultimately preface pillage (and the partition of the booty with the Crown) with a "descargo de conciencia."

Oviedo ironically alludes to the Nuevas Leyes when he presents de Soto as praising his own merits and expecting recognition from the Council of the Indies: " '¡Oh válame Dios, y si estovieran aquí aquellos señores del Consejo, para que vieran cómo se sirve Su Majestad!" [Oh my God, if those members from the Council were here to see how we serve Your Majesty!]. After de Soto's exclamation, Oviedo quips: "Y aun porque lo saben, dice el cronista que han mandado cesar las tiranías y crueldades, y que se tenga mejor orden en la pacificación de las Indias" [And because they know this, the *cronista* says that they have ordered the tyrannies and cruelties to cease, and to proceed in a more orderly fashion in the pacification of the Indies] (*HGN,* 2:161). One wonders, however, to what extent the *cronista* Oviedo would have been willing to submit his own activities in the Indies retrospectively to the judgment of the Nuevas Leyes.

One has only to remember that occasion in the Darién, which dated back to the days of Pedrarias Dávila but was written about by Oviedo after the Nuevas Leyes, when Oviedo burnt the cacique Corobari and two other caciques named Guaturo and Gonzalo. Oviedo shows his "humanity" toward Corobari by strangling him first because he wanted to respect his wish to die as a Christian: "Al cual yo mande ahogar primero porque quiso morir cristiano y era baptizado." But he does not forget to underscore the efficacy of bonfires as an instrument of terror: "Esta muerte se le dió porque los indios temen el fuego, e todas las otras maneras de morir no las temen" [This sort of death was given to him because Indians are afraid of fire, and do not fear all other forms of dying] (*HGN,* 3: 272–73). To display Gonzalo's corpse, Oviedo built a gibbet on the hill of Buenavista, "para que los indios de Bea lo pudiesen ver desde las lagunas que están debajo de aquel cerro bien legua y media o dos" [so that the Indians from Bea could see him from the lagoons that are about a league and a half or two below that hill] (3:273). As for Guaturo, he was hanged in the plaza of Darién, while his wife, his two young children, and up to forty Indians were reduced to slavery because they were friends of Cemaco, "que fué un cacique señor del Darién (el cual e su gente e valedores e amigos estaban dados por esclavos por el Rey Católico)" [who was a cacique of the Darién (he and his people had been given as slaves by the Catholic King)] (3:273). This last legal point, that these people had been given to him as slaves by Ferdinand the Catholic, supposedly validates Oviedo's procedures. But it also suggests that his negative judgments of de Soto have more to do with a denunciation of de Soto's adventurism than with a "humanization" of Oviedo's attitude toward Indians. Another example of Oviedo's double standard is the condemnation of de Soto's *aperreos* and his celebration of Alonso Zuazo's wise use of them. According to Oviedo, Zuazo displayed his sagacity ("pareció haberle alumbrado Dios" [God seemed to have enlightened him]) when he threatened two *amantecas* ("que son como agrimensores experimentados" [who are a sort of experienced land surveyors]) with a dog ("qual había aperreado en veces más de doscientos indios por idólatras y sodomitas" [who had been set against more than two hundred Indians for practicing idolatry and sodomy]). The threat was designed to induce the two *amantecas* to an agreement regarding a map, a *pintura,* that established the boundaries of their lands, and it was apparently successful: "Desto los señores y amantecas cobraron tanto temor, que la pintura vino después muy cierta, e las partes la aprobaron" [The lords and the *amantecas* were so filled with fear that they came to agree that the *pintura* was very accurate, and both sides approved it] (*HGN,* 5: 350). Notice that Oviedo offers no objection whatsoever to Zuazo's feeding of "indios por idólatras y sodomitas" [Indians for practicing idolatry and sodomy] to the dogs.

The *Historia general* is, of course, also filled with moralistic diatribes against the excesses of Christians. An exemplary moment is chapter 34 of book 29, where Oviedo deplores the cruelties committed against the Indians and denounces Spain's complicity in tolerating the atrocities of foreigners. But deep down, in this chapter and others, it is not clear whom he deplores more: the Spaniards who have died as a result of failed expeditions or the two million Indians who, according to Oviedo, died unjustly at the hands of conquistadores such as Pedrarias Dávila (see *HGN*, 3: 352–56). In discussing these passages, Antonello Gerbi has attributed an originality to Oviedo's account in comparison with Sepúlveda's *Democrates Alter* (Gerbi 1985: 327–28). Sepúlveda's treatise on the just causes of making war against the Indians, written against Las Casas, denies that Spain can be accountable for the Spaniards' excesses (see Sepúlveda 1941 [1547]: 97; also see chapter 2). In the example cited above, the choice of Pedrarias Dávila should already make us leery of any generalization about Oviedo's sense of justice. Oviedo's originality, according to Gerbi, resides in making Spain responsible for the damage wrought by foreigners. On the contrary, the tenor of these passages from the *Historia general* indicate, in my opinion, that the damages caused by war have been greater because of the large proportion of foreigners among the Spaniards — including even "griegos e levantiscos e de otras naciones" [Greeks and Levantines and from other nations] (*HGN*, 3: 355). Indeed, Oviedo ultimately exculpates Spain and lays the blame on the Indians:

> Todas estas cosas que están dichas, no os espanten letor, porque si habéis leído algunos tractados de guerra e conquistas de otras nasciones, no os maravillaréis de lo que tengo dicho destos indios, donde grandes crueldades entre los orientales e diversas nasciones hay escriptas; e la guerra es la que causa y causará, do quiera que la haya, grandes novedades e notables eventos, en especial, como he dicho, donde se juntan e concurren diversas e diferentes maneras de hombres a militar y seguir la guerra. (3:356)
>
> [The reader should not be shocked by all these things I have spoken about, because if you have read treatises on war or conquest by other nations in which great cruelties among the Orientals and other diverse nations are written, you will not be surprised by what I have said about these Indians; and war is what causes and will be the cause, wherever it happens, of great novelties and notable events, especially, as I have pointed out, where people from diverse and different nations, and different forms of being a warrior and making war, gather together to make war.]

By comparing Indian warfare to the "crueldades entre los orientales" [cruelties among the Orientals], Oviedo is very far from absolving Indians from all guilt. This same attribution of the evils of conquest to the "diversas nasciones" [diverse nations] recurs in chapter 2 of book 45, at which point Oviedo underscores the multiplicity of tongues as the culprit: "Lo cual, en la verdad, es anejo a la guerra, e mucho más en los ejercitos destas partes, porque no son los conquistadores de una lengua" [Truly speaking, this is part of the nature of war, and even more in the armies of these parts, because the conquistadores do not speak one tongue] (*HGN*, 5:27). In fact, Oviedo is primarily concerned with the struggles for power among the Christians (and the responsibility of Spain), and not with the plight of the Indians: "Las culpas de los motines e travesuras e contestaciones todas se atribuyen a los españoles, como es razón, pues que los cabos e los que mandan son de España" [All the blame for the mutinies and the abuses and the disputes rests with the Spaniards, as it must, because the leaders and those who command are from Spain] (5:28). Oviedo recommends keeping foreigners away from the Indies to avoid riots and uprisings among the Christians. Once more, he addresses the Spaniards, not the Indians.

Oviedo's concern for the Spaniards echoes, though somewhat awkwardly, in a commentary on Ranjel's account: "Oid, pues, letor, católico, no lloréis menos los indios conquistados que a los cristianos conquistadores dellos, o matadores de sí y desotros, atended a los subcesos deste gobernador mal gobernado" [Heed, then, Catholic reader, do not lament less for the conquered Indians than for the Christian conquerors, killers of themselves and others, so attend to the actions of this ungoverned Governor] (*HGN*, 2:173). Although he begins by appealing to the Indians' suffering, he goes on to say "atended a los subcesos deste gobernador mal gobernado" [attend to the actions of this ungoverned Governor]. Thus, Oviedo is far from being a pacifist. In the proper place he knows very well how to represent the heroism of the Christian warriors and in particular Ranjel's: "E volviose al gobernador Rodrigo Ranjel, e hízole sacar más de veinte flechas que sobre sí llevaba asidas a las armas" [And Rodrigo Ranjel turned to the Governor, and asked him to remove more than twenty arrows that were stuck to his armor] (2:174). Oviedo complements this portrait of an indomitable warrior covered with arrows by going on to praise the virtue of the conquistadores: "Hobo tanta vertud y vergüenza este día en todos

. . . que pelearon por admiración, e cada cristiano hacía su deber como valentísimo mílite" [There was so much virtue and humility this day in all . . . [who] fought admirably, and each Christian fulfilled his duty as a most valiant soldier] (2:174). He praises them in spite of the injuries they suffered and their participation in the massacre of Mabila, where women and even four-year-old children fought against the Christians: "las mujeres y aun muchachos de cuatro años peleaban con los cristianos." The survivors hanged themselves, choosing death over slavery. The fat of the corpses, as we have seen in Biedma, served to dress the wounds of the Christians.

The passages I have been citing have in common a pairing of Indians and Spaniards, where the evaluation of the Indians depends on the meaning given to the actions of the Christians. To make this point clearer, I cite one more example of how Oviedo makes the Indians responsible for their own destruction. After having attributed the "novelties" (i.e., atrocities) of the wars of conquest in America to the presence of foreigners, Oviedo adds:

> Juntos los materiales de los inconvinientes ya dichos, con los mesmos delictos e sucias e bestiales culpas de los indios sodomitas, idolatrías, e tan familiares e de tan antiquísimos tiempos en la obidiencia e servicio del diablo, e olvidados de nuestro Dios trino e uno, pensarse debe que sus méritos son capaces de sus daños, e que son el principal cimiento sobre que se han fundado e permitido Dios las muertes e trabajos. (*HGN,* 3:355)
> [Along with the materials and inconveniences already cited, the same crimes and dirty and bestial faults of the Indian sodomites and idolaters, who have been so familiar since ancient times with service and obedience to the devil, and as a result forgot our God who is one and three, one ought to consider that their deeds are the cause of their sufferings, and that they are the main foundation on which God has grounded and allowed for their deaths and travails.]

This phantasmagoric and paranoid construction (by the "good" settler) which presents Amerindian culture as being at the service of the devil plays as a refrain (with some variations) whenever Oviedo needs to attenuate the guilt of the Christians. It thus reiterates, on a symbolic level, the same violence that his moralistic diatribes condemn.[18] In fact, the Amerindians portrayed in this invective re-

mind us of the "indios sodomitas e idolatras" [Indian sodomites and idolaters] that Zuazo fed to the dogs, as well as the lascivious women and the thick-skulled irrational men found in other parts of the *Historia general* and the *Sumario* that I mentioned at the beginning of this chapter. It may even remind us of that castrating woman that led Oviedo to refer to Amerindian women, "e son tales" [and they are of such stuff]. These passages that elaborate the semblance of an exotic humanity suggest an irredeemable savagery that in the end would justify extermination campaigns. This portrayal of Indians depends less on facts that Oviedo may have known about Amerindians than on a stock of motifs readily available to represent "savagery" (cf. Bolaños 1994: 151). Their function is primarily rhetorical and should be read in the terms of the sixteenth-century debates over the nature of American Indians and colonial policies (see chapter 2).

Nowhere is Oviedo's position toward Amerindians more clearly shown than in his representation of Indian bodies and voices. Though there are many passages in the *Historia general* that admire the weavings, houses, forts, and other aspects of material culture, there are plenty of others (for the most part made up by Oviedo) that denigrate the Indians' reception of European cultural artifacts. Perhaps to temper the impending gravity of the massacre of Mabila with a comic note, Oviedo portrays the cacique in hardly flattering terms: "Ved qué contentamiento le podían dar esos borceguíes e manteo e levarle a caballo, que pensaba él que iba caballero en un tigre o en un ferocísimo león, porque en más temor estaban los caballos reputados entre aquella gente" [Notice how pleased he was with the buskins and the cloak and the horse ride, that he felt he was mounted on a tiger or a ferocious lion, because this people held horses in the greatest terror] (*HGN*, 2:173–74; cf. Bourne 1922, 2:122). Oviedo transfers to the New World animals from Africa and Asia (for Oviedo, in the Indies, "tigers" are clumsy and "lions" cowardly) to accentuate the "proper colors" of colonial encounters in America: the fear of horses (see 1986 [1526]: 93–98; cf. Gerbi 1985: 302–4).

I would like to conclude with another "comic" portrait, in this case of a Spaniard, which will enable me to define the purpose of Oviedo's criticisms of de Soto's enterprise in Florida. Ranjel (as

testigo de vista [eyewitness], underscores Oviedo) saw Don Antonio Osorio, "hermano del señor marqués de Astorga, con una ropilla de mantas de aquella tierra, rota por los costados, las carnes defuera, sin bonete, la calva defuera, descalzo, sin calzas ni zapatos, una rodela a las espaldas, una espada sin vaina, los hielos y frios muy grandes" [the brother of the Lord Marquis of Astorga, wearing cloth from that land, torn on the sides, his flesh showing, without a cap, showing his bald spot, barefoot, without breeches or shoes, a shield on his back, a sword without a sheath, amidst heavy frost and cold] (*HGN,* 2:176; cf. Bourne 1922, 2:130). Because Don Osorio had received an income of two thousand ducados from the Church before coming to the Americas, his joining de Soto is even more ridiculous: "Yo no pude estar sin reirme cuando le oí decir que ese caballero había dejado la iglesia y renta que es dicho" [I could hardly keep myself from laughing when I heard that this knight had left the Church and the income above mentioned] (2:176). Oviedo cannot resist laughing at this pathetic portrait of a conquistador who had been misled by de Soto. This is one of the few occasions where Oviedo gives us a somewhat flattering profile of de Soto: "Porque conoscí yo muy bien a Soto, y aunque era hombre de bien, no le tenía yo de por tan dulce habla ni maña que a personas semejantes pudiese él encargar" [Because I knew Soto very well, and, although he was a man of worth, I did not suppose that he was so winning a talker or so clever, as to be able to delude such persons] (2:176). Oviedo deplores de Soto's capacity to convince people to follow him to Florida perhaps even more than his venturing into the land without knowledge or experience.

According to Oviedo, all of the three earlier failed governors of Florida were more experienced than de Soto: "Joan Ponce, Garay e Pánfilo de Narváez . . . tenía[n] más experiencia que él en cosas de Indias" [Joan Ponce, Garay and Pánfilo de Narváez . . . had more experience than he in the affairs of the Indies] (2:165). De Soto's earlier experiences in Castilla del Oro, Nicaragua, and Peru are worthless because "era otra manera de abarrajar indios" [it was another manner of attacking and capturing Indians] (2:165). Attacking and capturing Indians, "abarrajar indios," is not the issue, but the right knowledge. Oviedo blames de Soto for daring to take people into Florida without the required experience. In theory, de

Soto would have had an advantage over the earlier conquistadores; he not only had access to their accounts, but also found a ready interpreter in Juan Ortiz, a Spaniard from Pánfilo de Narváez's expedition who had remained in Florida. As incompetent as Ortiz might have been, he must have been of use at least with the people he had lived with for twelve years. Biedma tells us that Ortiz possessed very little knowledge beyond his immediate surroundings: "Tenía tan poca noticia de la tierra, que de veinte leguas de allí no sabía ninguna cosa ni por vista ni por oidas; verdad es que nos dixo en viéndonos que no había punta de oro en la tierra" [He had so little information about the land, that he did not know anything by sight nor by hearsay beyond twenty leagues; however, it is true that he told us when he first saw us that there was no trace of gold in the land] (*CDI,* 3: 415). At least he did not encourage them with false information.

None of the guides promised the de Soto expedition the kind of golden kingdoms of Cíbola, Quivira, and Totonteac that the expeditions of Fray Marcos de Niza and Francisco Vázquez de Coronado were so desperately pursuing during these same years in the Southwest, at times close enough for de Soto and Coronado to have heard of each other from the Indians. Only Biedma mentions a town "que los indios nos lo hacían muy grande, tanto que nos decían que la gente dél, dando gritos, hacían caer las aves que iban volando" [that the Indians described as so large, that the people from the town by shouting could cause the birds (overhead) to fall] (*CDI,* 3: 415; cf. Bourne 1922, 2:5). This fantastic town of Etocale turns out to be, in Biedma's laconical phrase, "un pueblo pequeño" [a small town]. This lack of news of fabulous kingdoms does not keep de Soto from burning guides alive or feeding them to the dogs when he feels that they are lying or refusing to provide him with information, that is, to confirm his fantasies. But Oviedo does not have in mind this sort of abuse when he complains of de Soto's behavior.

If we read beyond the apparent condemnation and compare his denunciations of de Soto's violence with other parts of the *Historia general,* we realize that war and terrorism were forms of exercising power that Oviedo understood only too well. In fact, everything suggests that Oviedo believed it was appropriate to torture and murder Indians guilty of practicing sodomy and idolatry. Oviedo's criticism of the conquistadores aims at rationalizing the colonial regime in America; it is never an abstract condemnation of violence. In Oviedo's ideal society of businessmen and settlers laboring diligently in their assorted trading, farming, and mining enterprises, there is no room for the "irrational" economy of Amerindian cultures, nor, for that matter, for the adventurism of conquistadores like de Soto. This position is very close to that of the Crown, which sought to regiment and control expeditions to avoid the waste of human and material resources that the failed expedition of de Soto represented.[19] In the last instance, Oviedo's main complaints against de Soto were his capacity to fabricate his own mirages and his venturing blindly into the land: "Los indios que llevaban desatinaban, que no sabían camino ni lo españoles tampoco, ni que partido se tomasen, e entre ellos había diversos paresceres . . . e el gobernador propuso, como siempre había seído, que era mejor ir adelante, sin saber el ni ellos en que acertaban ni en que erraban [The Indians did not know where they were going, nor did the Spaniards know the way, or what direction to take, and there were diverse opinions among them . . . and the governor proposed, as he always did, that it was best to go on, none of them knowing if they were guessing right or if they were wandering] (*HGN*, 2:166; cf. Bourne 1922, 2:94).

The conquest of Florida was beyond question one of the most violent military incursions in the New World. But as I have pointed out in this chapter, the *capitulación* with the Crown already articulates a colonizing project that anticipates capturing caciques, pillaging graves, raiding food deposits, and a generalized climate of violence. It requires a reading of the *Requerimiento* for the "descargo de la conciencia" [relief of the conscience] of the king, but this latter document in itself already constitutes an act of war—even though the injuries of such war might be unidirectional. Once Spaniards had read the document and shown their military might, Indians had only war or submission as options. If the *leyenda negra* feeds on these sorts of readings, to deny its reality one would have to deny the existence of documents that propose, when they do not aesthetically celebrate, the practice of terror and warfare in this region of the world that was condemned to be "new." The "histories" that highlight a romantic profile of the conquistador Hernando de

Soto are problematic not so much for their idealization of the conquistador, but because they tend to reiterate a degraded view of Amerindian cultures—that is, to perpetuate a culture of conquest that not only underlay the violence of that time, but is also being perpetuated today against indigenous communities.

CHAPTER 5

"Porque soy indio": Subjectivity in
Garcilaso's *La Florida del Inca*

Inca Garcilaso de la Vega's positioning as an Indian writing in the context of the metropolis calls to mind the "author functions" that colonial subjects could assume in sixteenth-century European historiography of the New World. Clearly, Garcilaso's marginality was inseparable from European ascendancy. To understand the former, we must define the type of subjectivity that underlies Western dominance. As a result, in what follows I move back and forth between the institution of the modern Western episteme and the subjection of indigenous knowledges. In principle, there is no place for an Indian author (i.e., one who writes from the standpoint of an Indian) within a colonial discourse that claims universality for its subjectivity and its history.[1] "The West," "the Western episteme," "Western dominance," and the like are terms that here refer to an always shifting field that defines the legitimacy and rationality, hence the limits, of acceptable contending discourses, rather than a homogeneous entity. For stylistic reasons I avoid a plural form, the "Wests." The "West" may ultimately be understood as *modernity* (even if early) and as the historical horizon that circumscribes both hegemonic and alternative discourses, the cultural space where the *now* is contested.

These are the conditions of representation in which Garcilaso wrote *La Florida*. Indeed, these conditions are decodified in *La Florida*. The quasi-utterance "Porque soy indio" [Because I am an Indian], which, as we will see, constitutes a motif in the work of Garcilaso, places him outside European discourse; it also marks the direction of Garcilaso's "voyage" as the reverse of that taken by Europeans writing about the New World and its corresponding subjectivity as marginal. In this regard, it is highly revealing that Garcilaso always positioned himself as a nonauthor, namely, as the translator of León Hebreo's *Diálogos de Amor,* as the amanuensis of *La Florida del Inca,* and as the glosser and commentator of the *Comentarios reales de los Incas.* These writing practices situated Garcilaso either at the borders or on the margins of discourse. Undoubtedly, writing from the borders and margins paralleled his illegitimacy as a bastard, a mestizo, and an Indian. As Susana Jákfalvi-Leiva (to whom I owe a great deal of what I have to say on Garcilaso's marginality) has stated, "No había ninguna clase en esa estructura que pudiera asimilar como a elemento propio a un indio, mestizo y bastardo" [There was no class in that structure that could assimilate an Indian, mestizo, and bastard as one of its own] (1984: 35).[2] To borrow Abdul JanMohamed and David Lloyd's phrase, we should read Garcilaso as a "minority intellectual," that is, as a border intellectual—a hybrid subjectivity—who had to "begin from a position of non-identity" (1990: 15). Garcilaso was demonstrably capable of appropriating European forms of discourse, but the very borderline social status that would never allow him to cross over and become a Spaniard was also what made him unique in Spanish American letters. Rare has been the Spanish American writer who has identified himself or herself as an Indian and even rarer he or she who has aspired to become an Indian author. One can certainly claim to find the beginnings of a Spanish American tradition in Garcilaso's mastery of Spanish and European culture; however, such a claim should no be advanced at the expense of other border intellectuals who express themselves through indigenous languages or whose mastery (i.e., appropriation) of Western conventions is less apparent.[3] I am not arguing here for what some feminist critics call an "add-and-stir" approach to the canon, but rather for a redefinition of the politics and poetics of canonicity. Merely incorporating those writers who have been excluded from the canon would amount to simply domesticating them along with Garcilaso.

The issue of an alternative authorship and subjectivity in Garcilaso implies questioning the generally accepted notion among poststructuralist critics of "the death of the author." In very broad terms, these critics argue that the concept of the author as originator becomes useless once we understand, as Roland Barthes put it, "that a text is not a line of words releasing a single 'theological' meaning (the 'message' of the Author-God) but a multi-directional space in which a variety of writings, none of them original, blend and clash" (1977: 146). Feminist critic Cheryl Walker, however, has pointed out that questioning the death of the author does not necessarily mean returning to some sort of (patriarchal-)author criticism that would posit an individual as origin of a text; yet "writing is not [as Barthes would have us believe] 'the destruction of every voice' but *the proliferation of possibilities of hearing*" (1990: 568; emphasis in original). Walker goes on to point out that Foucault's concept of the "author function," despite positing what he called the romantic and utopic (read oppressive) disappearance of the author, enables us to examine and apprehend cultural, historical, and gender differences in subjectivities and authorships. It is highly pertinent for us to ask, with Foucault, "What difference does it make who is speaking?"

In "What Is an Author?" Foucault outlined four characteristic traits that define the author function: "(1) The author function is linked to the juridical and institutional system that encompasses, determines, and articulates the universe of discourse; (2) it does not affect all discourses in the same way at all times and in all types of civilization; (3) it is not defined by the spontaneous attribution of a discourse to its producer, but rather by a series of specific and complex operations; (4) it does not refer purely and simply to a real individual, since it can give rise simultaneously to several selves, to several subject-positions that can be occupied by different classes of individuals" (1984: 113). Of these four traits, the one that interests us least in our reading of *La Florida* is the third, which is concerned with how criticism has constructed Garcilaso's identity (see, e.g., Mazzotti 1996; Cornejo Polar 1994; Wey-Gómez 1991; González Echevarría 1990; Zamora 1988; Pupo-Walker 1982, 1985; Ortega 1978; Durand 1976; Miró Quesada 1971; Varner 1968). The first one will be adjunctive to our analysis insofar as we can only conjecture the extent to which the Estatutos de Limpieza de Sangre (Statutes of Blood Purity) determined Garcilaso's problematic authorship; the allusions to *limpieza de sangre, hidalguía* (literally, the condition of being the son of something, i.e., nobility), and belonging to a *nación* will be read here as figures, or rhetorical moves, rather than as signs or symptoms of the specific restrictions imposed by the Statutes of Blood Purity (cf. Shell 1991;

Caro Baroja 1961, 2: 267–96). On the other hand, traits 2 and 4 are crucial to understanding subjectivity and minority discourse in *La Florida*. The fourth trait will lead us to examine the places, and the corresponding natures, of that quasi-utterance "Porque soy indio" that I cite in the title of this chapter; the second will enable us to retrace the historical conditions that determined—and circumscribed—the possibility of Garcilaso's constituting himself as an Indian author.

Let us now sketch the nature of the subject and the object of knowledge in sixteenth-century European historiography of the Americas. Michel de Certeau, in "Ethno-graphy: Speech, or the Space of the Other: Jean de Léry" (1988: 209–43), mapped an epistemic mutation in Jean de Léry's (1975 [1578, 1580]) *Histoire d'un voyage faict en la terre du Brésil*. From Certeau's observations we can derive the premise that in the writing of the New World, Western subjectivity constituted itself as universal, and ethnography defined a set of "fields" where cultural particulars could be inscribed within general categories. As Certeau pointed out, the opposition between orality and writing was the common point of departure for ethnology in Lévi-Strauss, Ampère, and Léry. It is impossible to do justice here to the virtuosity of Certeau's observations on the emergence of ethnography—a reading of Léry in the guise of a Freudian analysis of dream work. I can only reiterate the results of his analysis.

The structural opposition between orality and writing posits a European subjectivity that not only constructs an Other, but privileges itself as knowledge through the practice of writing. This opposition was first expressed in a separation of a "here" from a "there," a break marked literally by the crossing of the Atlantic in the narrative of the transoceanic navigation. A second expression then redefined "the same" and "the Other" in terms of an "exemplary humanity" and an "exotic universe," thereby opening up a space for the translation of culture and the classification of nature. This operation entailed a third transformation, whereby the subject and the object of ethnology could be distinguished. Two planes coexist in the *Histoire:* "On the first is written the chronicle of facts and deeds by the group or by Léry. These events are narrated in a tense: a history is composed with a chronology—very detailed—of actions undertaken or lived by a subject. On the second plane objects are set out in a space ruled not by localization or geographic routes—these indications are very rare and always vague—but by a taxonomy of living beings, a systematic inventory of philosophical questions, etc.; in sum, the catalogue raisonné of a knowledge" (Certeau 1988: 225–26). This distinction between the subject and the object of knowledge defines the conditions of representability of the *Histoire*. However, as in Freudian dream work, a sort of "secondary elaboration" reinstates a series of stable oppositions as a response to a "return of the repressed" that irrupts in the ethnographic text in the mode of eroticized speech: the primitive as a *body of pleasure*. Orality manifests a fascination that gives way to an ideal primitivism: "Facing the work of the West, that is, Western man's actions that manufacture time and reason, there exists in Léry's work a place for leisure and bliss, the Tupi world, indeed a feast for the eyes and ears" (226–27). But this world is also a *body of pleasure*, where noise, frenzy, nudity, voracity, and anthropophagy threaten the rule of law. This excess (whether in its negative or its positive valorization) leads, in turn, to a reinscription of the initial opposition between orality (the object of knowledge) and writing (the subject of knowledge), but here in terms of a stable series of oppositions under the rubrics of "primitive" and "civilized." Thus, in the process of traveling through and writing about the New World, a new subject and a new science emerged in the process of inventing the Savage. In this regard, Léry's *Histoire* is a figure of modernity, a "scientific legenda," as Certeau calls it, that enables us to retrace the formation of the modern picture of the world.

This emphasis on the Savage as invention entails a displacement of the point of departure from a European "self" that, as Tzvetan Todorov would put it, discovers the Other (1984: 3), to a simultaneous and inseparable production of both Europe and its Others. In the process of traveling to America, the modern Western episteme not only established itself as universal but subjected indigenous knowledges by relegating them to the domains of superstition and witchcraft. Accordingly, Otherness must be a product of discourse rather than some form of unmediated alterity that is anterior to the cognitive self. One could further argue, along with Certeau, that the production of Otherness is a historiographical a priori, whether in the form of the past (i.e., of the dead, of what was but perhaps still informs the present) or of ethnography (i.e., of foreign ways of life that are nonetheless still apprehensible as such).

I prefer Certeau's analysis of early ethnography to Margaret Hodgen's (1964) emphasis on a "rhetoric of negativity" (i.e., one that stresses what primitives lack: property, government, clothing, etc.) and to John Elliott's (1970) insistence on an "uncertain impact" (i.e., on Europeans' blindness and silence vis-à-vis the newly found peoples), in that Certeau allows for both an ideal primitivism (and its reversal) and an inscription of "objective" data (cf. Mauroby 1990). Negativity, whether as ideal primitivism or as antiprimitivism, does not preclude a will to truth and knowledge. These transformations of the subject and the object of knowledge can be further corroborated, beyond Léry, in Spanish American sources. There is certainly a great power of objectification along with vituperation toward and praise of Amerindian (Nahua) culture in the ethnography of Bernardino de Sahagún, but also in the history of, say, Gonzalo Fernández de Oviedo.[4] (By objectivity, I mean a consistent and systematic production of objects of knowledge rather than a neutral or "value-free" approach.)

For instance, Sahagún faced the task of devising a method to record Nahua forms of life in their own terms. Although he admired the rhetorical richness of Nahuatl and the Nahuas' forms of government, some of their customs and beliefs led him to perceive the Nahuas as following a different logic, which he defined as irrational and relegated to an earlier historical stage, that is, one rife with superstition and vulnerable to the influence of the devil. According to Sahagún, the Nahuas of the sixteenth century were lying neophytes and, consequently, problematic subjects who continued to practice their rites in secret. Nothing could be further from Sahagunian epistemology than the regime of similarities that, according to Foucault (1973), characterized the sixteenth-century episteme. In fact, Sahagún's epistemology entailed a mutation that enabled him to conceive Nahua forms of life as ruled by their own specific semantic web of resemblances. For Sahagún, such an objectification of Nahua logic was a sine qua non to their complete conversion to Catholicism. Moreover, his work demonstrates a continual reflection on method and on the political circumstances that enabled or obstructed his ethnographic enterprise. Like Léry's *Histoire,* Sahagún's 1579 *Historia general de las cosas de la Nueva España,* also known as the *Florentine Codex,* elaborates both a subject and an object of knowledge.[5] Despite Sahagún's greatness as a pioneering ethnographer, he did not exemplify methodological rigor in Spanish American historiography. In fact, the main traits of this great epistemic realignment, which marks a transition to modernity, had already been displayed by Columbus. And, ultimately, it was by means of metaphors derived from treatises on the art of traveling that in the seventeenth century René Descartes would formulate a universalist method of mapping knowledge (see Klor de Alva 1988; Rabasa 1989a, 1993b; Dorion 1988).

Although Garcilaso cites Oviedo only once, one could claim Oviedo's *Historia general* as a subtext in more than one passage of *La Florida.* Oviedo is especially significant in reading Garcilaso because of Oviedo's anti-indigenist position (or at least the grounds he provides for an anti-indigenism), because of Garcilaso's dislike of moralistic comments in historiography (comments that feature prominently in Oviedo's work), and finally because Oviedo included Rodrigo Ranjel's *Relación* of de Soto's expedition in the *Historia general* (see chapter 4).[6] My reference to Oviedo's anti-indigenist statements in the *Historia general* may disturb those readers who find Oviedo too complex to be reduced to such a position. Indeed, there are certainly passages in Oviedo's work that, as Stephanie Merrim has correctly observed, "could have fueled precisely the Aristotelian arguments used by Las Casas in the *Apologética historia* to qualify the Indians as rational" (1989: 177–78). Merrim goes on to explain Oviedo's negative portrayal of Amerindians as the result of his "vaunting moralism" (180). In chapter 4 we saw the difference between Las Casas's and Oviedo's use of the term *destrucción* to denounce Spanish atrocities in the New World: whereas the former denounces the whole institution and project of the Spanish conquest, the latter singles out individuals, for instance, Pánfilo de Narváez and Hernando de Soto, against whom he often holds a grudge. Moreover, as we will see below, Certeau's reading of Léry suggests a means by which the Las Casas–type statements could have proceeded from the same binary oppositions that informed Oviedo's racist remarks. Oviedo's work manifests a fear of difference, of an excess that cannot be bound by the "jaez de la Historia Natural" [harness of natural history] that he derived from Pliny (*HGN,* 1: 11). For the record, let us recall that Oviedo's allusion to Pliny occurs in the context of giving him proper credit to avoid being accused of plagiarism—a pertinent remark, given the surplus he derived from Pliny, "maxime habiéndose capital de la usura" [especially when one gains capital from the lending] (1:11). Historiography as production entails not only the writing of new objects within the old categories, but a transformation of those same categories in the process of opening new fields of knowledge.

Oviedo's *Historia general* differs from Léry's in design, scope, composition, and intent. We can nevertheless observe within their differences some of the same basic operations and vacillations that constituted and characterized the emergence of modern Western discourse. For instance, the linguistic hiatus that Léry expresses in theological terms between the *unfathomable intentions of the heart* and an *objective nevertheless deceptive religious language* (Certeau 1988: 223) has a corresponding sensualist turn in Oviedo's distinction between the *unspeakable experiences of the flavor, smell, and texture of pineapples* and an *objectification through misnomers* (*HGN,* 1: 239–44). Léry's quotation of Psalm 104, which marks a transition from the hermeneutics of theological language—what is out of this world and unspeakable—to cultural translation, is paralleled by Oviedo's *loores* (eulogies) to Nature, which mediate the passage from ancient and medieval stocks of knowledge to direct description and, consequently, to setting the limits on the representation of New World phenomena. If alterity conveys an excess that leads to a glorification of God, the uncanny lurks at the cultural horizon. We can assume that Garcilaso found insulting Oviedo's physiological characterizations of Amerindians with thick skulls and narrow vaginas that supposedly accounted for the irrationality of men and the lasciviousness of women (see the detailed discussion in chapter 4).

As the appointed chronicler of the Indies, Oviedo organized his *Historia general* not as a voyage in which we can trace the development and discursive transformation of an individual (as in Léry's *Histoire*), but as a collective imperial enterprise in which observations are made and commentaries, corrections, and recommendations offered on matters pertaining to administrative policy and the acquisition of knowledge. Oviedo perceived the writing of the *Historia general* as an endless task. Moreover, this work constituted, at least in principle, a space for objective representation and a corresponding universal subjectivity that structured the task of chronicling the Indies as one that could be continued by future historians. The terms of the binary oppositions would vary from history to history, and the reflections of the historian, that is, those traces that betray the limits of the enterprise and the construction of those binary oppositions, would eventually disappear (though never completely) as ethnography and the natural sciences evolved into objective, "value-free" disciplines. In this same fluidity between the terms of binary oppositions, which allowed Oviedo to criticize greed and debauchery among the Spaniards, lay the potential for writing a counterdiscourse. The goal of such a counterdiscourse, however, would not be to reiterate the same binary logic through a simple inversion of values.

My discussion of Oviedo and Sahagún suggests that the distinction between the colonial subject as colonized and as colonizer is not simply a matter of different narrative focalizations that would restrict themselves to either defending or condemning the conquest of Amerindian cultures (cf. R. Adorno 1988; Bhabha 1986; JanMohamed 1986). Clearly, these Manichean modalities exist. However, less clear-cut expressions present, to my mind, much more interesting forms of counterdiscourse. If, in fact, all inversions of binary oppositions reiterate the logic that informs them, then the reduction of colonial discursive possibilities to "colonized" and "colonizer" positions that mutually represent each other as an absence of culture would ultimately fall into the same trap.

To the lying neophytes of Sahagún and the insatiable women and irrational men of Oviedo we should add one more fiction: the *noble savage* of Bartolomé de las Casas. I highlight the fictive character of Las Casas's noble savage to underscore its utopian function: the construct "noble savage" is not the opposite of "barbarian" because it embodies the terms that define both the barbaric (the savage as uncivilized, not-civilized) and the civilized (the noble as not-savage). The noble savage as a utopian figure is particularly true to the anthropological reflections (where the noble savage is not defined in opposition to [barbaric] Christians) in the *Apologética historia sumaria* (Las Casas 1967 [ca. 1555]), but not to the inversion of the conventional roles of lambs (Christians) and wolves (pagans) in the *Brevíssima relación de la destruyción de las Indias* (Las Casas 1991 [1552]).[7] Neither in the *Apologética* nor in the *Brevíssima,* however, did Las Casas intend his Amerindian noble savages to be understood as empirical phenomena, but rather as rhetorical figures. The difference between these two texts is that the polemical nature of the *Brevíssima* led Las Casas to vilify the Spaniards to underscore the plight of the Indians, whereas the philosophical bent of the *Apologética* led him to emphasize anthropological categories that evaluated Amerindian forms of life positively and, ultimately, to deconstruct the concept of barbarism. The concept of barbarism ends up lacking a real referent other than individual instances of monstrosity, never a whole nation; nor can one categorize a people as barbarian because they lack a particular form of life such as alphabetical writing. In reading Las Casas one has to be especially careful not to read conclusions in statements (e.g., "We may call barbarian a people who lacks a learned language") intended as part of reasoning that proves the contrary of what they assert. As I have argued elsewhere (Rabasa 1989b), the figure of the noble savage in the *Apologética* underwrites a utopian discourse that dismantles the negation of the coevalness of the Other, which, as Johannes Fabian (1983) has argued, is the basis of the production of anthropology's object of study. Thus, Las Casas's utopian ethnology manifests the conditions of possibility of anthropological discourse in general and the semantic field where the "West" defines the "rest of the world" and postulates itself as the universal cultural model in particular. The figure of the noble savage at once anticipates and negates the validity of that inherent tendency in Christian universalism (even in its most tolerant forms) to reduce non-Christians to barbarians (see Shell 1991: 327–35). Even though ideological constraints such as writing as a Dominican friar kept Las Casas from abandoning the universalism of the Roman Catholic Church, he certainly curtailed the range of its corollaries. Furthermore, Las Casas's critique of the opposition "barbarism" versus "civilization" entailed the possibility that the "time of the 'Other'" would invade the temporal fortress of the "West" (Fabian 1983: 35). To paraphrase a recent title, the empire has always written back (Ashcroft, Griffiths, and Tiffin 1989).

Nevertheless, Las Casas never completely shed the tendency to draw Manichean oppositions (manifest in the lambs vs. wolves of the *Brevíssima,* but also in the ironic conjunction of the civilized and the barbarian in the noble savage figure), which suggests that his critique exemplified Louis Marin's (1984) thesis: "Utopia is an ideological critique of ideology." But Marin's point is relevant only within a system that opposes science to ideology (i.e., with utopia prefiguring the social sciences). This valorization, however, has no bearing on minority discourses that draw their *force* precisely from being unscientific, from their marginality, from lack of arts and sciences, as we will see in the case of Garcilaso.

The limitations of Manichean inversions become fully apparent when we compare Garcilaso's idealizations of the conquistadores in *La Florida* with other accounts of massacres and the capture of thousands of slaves, as well as those of *aperreos* (setting dogs on the Indians), mutilation, and torture, that were conscientiously documented by Rodrigo Ranjel and glossed with moralistic diatribes by Oviedo. The two other "primary" sources on de Soto's expedition, Fidalgo de Elvas's *Relaçam verdadeira dos trabalhos q̃ ho gouernador dõ Fernãdo de Souto e certos fidalgos portugueses passarom no descobrimeto da prouincia da Frolida* (1557), in which the massacres and acts of torture are narrated with a "bestial" objectivity, and Luis Hernández de Biedma's *Relación del suceso de la jornada del cap. Soto, y de la calidad de la tierra por donde anduvo* (ca. 1544), with its tone of laconic detachment, neither condemned nor exalted the Europeans (see chapter 4). Garcilaso, on the other hand, idealized both the Spaniards and the Indians. *La Florida* also recorded the atrocities, but it gave a voice to the Indians, who could thereby condemn the random massacres and mutilations that characterized de Soto's expedition. Garcilaso's idealization of both Europeans and Indians, as well as the continual questioning of the criteria for nobility and the means by which European and Indian forms of life were represented, suggests that he was pursuing a deeper truth than a simple inversion of values could yield.

In reading Garcilaso, we must constantly keep in mind his Indian position and a consequently apologetic self-authorization (not without irony) to write history. Thus, in the "Advertencias" to the first part of his *Comentarios reales de los Incas,* he pleads for permission

to alter the then current Spanish spelling of Quechua terms so as to avoid corrupting Quechua any further: "Para atajar esta corrupción me sea lícito, pues soy indio, que en esta historia yo escriba como indio con las mismas letras que aquellas tales dicciones se deben escribir" [In order to forestall this corruption allow me, since I am an Indian, to write this history as Indian with the precise letters which such words ought to be inscribed] (1960 [1609–1617], 2:5). The irony here is that Garcilaso's plea is not appealing to a knowledge of Quechua (i.e., not a plea of a linguist or an otherwise universal subject who seeks objective knowledge), but to his authority as an Indian ("que . . . yo escriba como indio"), one whose subjectivity privileges him as knowledgeable about the correct Quechua phonetics and ultimately about the *incario* (i.e., all things pertaining to the Incas). This sort of appeal to a privileged Indian subjectivity destabilizes, however slightly, the grounds of knowledge in European consciousness.

Beyond asserting a relationship to Inca culture through immanence, Garcilaso's plea seems almost a parody of a parallel passage in Oviedo's *Historia general:* "Si algunos vocablos extraños e bárbaros aquí se hallaren, la causa es la novedad de que se tracta; y no se pongan a la cuenta de mi romance, que en Madrid nascí, y en la casa real me crié, y con gente noble he conversado, e algo he leído, para que se sospeche que habré entendido mi lengua castellana, la cual, de las vulgares, se tiene por la mejor de todas" [If there are some strange and barbaric words, the reason is the novelty of the subject matter; and should not be ascribed to my Spanish, since I was born in Madrid, and bred in royal quarters, and conversed with noble people, and read some, and so there should be no question whatsoever of my understanding of the Castilian language, which, of all the vernacular tongues, is the best] (*HGN,* 1:10). All that is missing in this show of credentials is Oviedo's certificate of *limpieza de sangre,* which, one can assume, along with his biographers, he had, as it was the king himself who had ordered him to write the *Historia general:* "Se escriben por su mandado, y que me da de comer por su cronista destas materias" [You have ordered me to write them, and you feed me as your chronicler of these matters] (1:12). Oviedo's breeding would certainly have guaranteed his mastery of the language and, by extension, of the arts and sciences, a

domain from which Garcilaso was excluded as an Indian: "Las faltas que lleva [*La Florida*] se me perdonen porque soy indio, que a los tales, por ser bárbaros y no enseñados en ciencias ni artes, no se permite que, en lo que dijeren o hicieren, los lleven por el rigor de los preceptos del arte o ciencia, por no los haber aprendido, sino que los admitan como vinieren" [I plead now that this account be received in the same spirit as I present it, and that I be pardoned its errors because I am an Indian. For since we Indians are barbarians and uninstructed in the arts and sciences, it seems ungenerous to judge our deeds and utterances strictly in accordance with the precepts of art or science, which we have not learned, but rather accept them as they are] (Garcilaso de la Vega 1986 [1605]: 69; 1951: xlv). Right after this passage comes one of Garcilaso's autobiographical anecdotes about the poor schooling that Indians and mestizos received in Peru. An overtly rhetorical use of modesty, this *excusatio* suggests not Garcilaso's lack of letters, but rather the pursuit of an alternative discourse. In contrast to Oviedo's need to boast of writing a major work, Garcilaso was apparently quite comfortable with minor genres—not to mention minor roles, such as those of translator, amanuensis, and commentator.

As I have already pointed out, Garcilaso's license to revise the spellings of Quechua terms was not based on identifying himself with a master "scientific" discourse, but rather with a minority position that authorized him to counteract the violence done to Indian culture by a colonizing language. In Oviedo's claiming Spanish as the best of all vernacular languages, one can infer a sense of entitlement to translate indigenous terms and, ultimately, indigenous cultures. Akin to Talal Asad's (1986) recommendation that we soften stronger languages in the process of translating weaker ones, Garcilaso's correctives were aimed at the tone and tenor, not just the phonetics of Quechua expressions: "Es lástima que se pierda o corrompa, siendo una lengua tan galana" [It would be a pity to lose or corrupt it, since it is such an elegant tongue] (1960 [1609–1617], 2: 6). Not coincidentally, it is in the context of these *porque soy indio* expressions (including the variant *pues soy indio* [since I am an Indian]) that Garcilaso indirectly establishes an American audience (if in posterity) as his addressee.

Accordingly, in the *Comentarios,* Garcilaso effectively privileged a

Subjectivity in La Florida del Inca   211

reader versed in Quechua who could appreciate the differences between Quechua and Spanish, Italian, or Latin: "Las cuales [difer-
encias] notaran los mestizos y criollos curiosos, pues son de su len-
guaje, que yo harto hago en señalarles con el dedo desde España los
principios de su lengua para que la sustenten en su pureza" [Such
(differences) will be appreciated by attentive mestizos and criollos,
since they belong to their tongue, and thus I endeavor from Spain
to point out accurately the principles of their tongue so that its
purity is sustained] (1960 [1609–1617], 2: 6). This cultural schema
presupposes that both criollos and mestizos would be Quechua
speakers. When "los indios, mestizos y criollos del Perú" are addressed in *La Florida,* it is to champion a minority discourse and
to underscore the value of writing by those who lack *arte o ciencia*
(art or science): "Y llevando más adelante esta piadosa considera-
ción, sería noble artificio y generosa industria favorecer en mí . . .
a todos los indios, mestizos y criollos del Perú, para que viendo
ellos el favor y merced que los discretos y sabios hacían a su prin-
cipiante, se animasen a pasar adelante en cosas semejantes, sacadas
de sus no cultivados ingenios" [It would be a noble and magnanimous idea to carry this merciful consideration still further and to
honor in me all of the Indians, mestizos, and criollos of Peru, so
that seeing a novice of their own receive the favor and grace of the
wise and learned, they would be encouraged to make advancements
with similar ideas drawn from their own uncultivated mental re-
sources] (1986 [1605]: 69; 1951: xlv). Far from constituting himself or
his "mastery" of Spanish as a model, Garcilaso called for a capital-
ization on marginality. It seems to me that "no cultivados ingenios"
[uncultivated mental resources] suggests both an untapped potential and a reminder not to judge American writers according to "el
rigor de los preceptos del arte o ciencia, por no los haber aprendido, sino que los admitan como vinieren" [the precepts of art or
science, which they have not learned, but rather (to) accept them
as they are]. Their lack of *arte o ciencia* should definitely not keep
"Indians, mestizos, and criollos" from writing.

Thus Garcilaso makes manifest the fact that it was not just the
West that invented itself in the process of writing about the New
World. Cultural identification as an Indian, though certainly a
product of contact, was never solely due to a misnomer borne pas-

sively. Being an Indian conveys the sense of nationality and raciality in *La Florida* that linked Garcilaso with all Amerindians throughout the continent: "Pues decir que escribo encarecidamente por loar la nación porque soy indio, ciertamente es engaño . . . que antes me hallo con falta de palabras para contar y poner en su punto las verdades que en la historia se me ofrecen" [But to say that I exaggerate my praise of the nation because I am an Indian is indeed a falsehood, for . . . I lack sufficient words to present in their proper light the actual truths that are offered me in this history] (1986 [1605]: 192–93; 1951: 159). Garcilaso makes two important points in this statement: the potential for a Pan-Indian identity, and the lack of a rhetoric in which to represent Indian voices. Hugo Rodríguez-Vecchini has quite correctly pointed out that *La Florida* is the story of how to write a credible history of America: "Es la historia de como hacer una historia de América que parezca verdadera" (1982: 588). However, we should modify this statement: *La Florida* is not just the story of how to write a history of America, *but of how to write one from the point of view of an Indian*. Indeed, *La Florida* exposes those motifs and binary oppositions (and their logic of reversals) that have sustained Western discourse on America: precisely those materials that have lent credibility to European histories of America. Garcilaso anticipated that his history would be dismissed as racially biased—and not because readers would question well-established representations of a positive primitivism that were, as we have seen, mere inversions of an equally well-rehearsed de-negation, but because they would doubt the political as well as the literary propriety of Garcilaso's specific version of an ideal primitivism. For this reason, he drew on images, topoi, and rationales from the European storehouse of poetic, political, and historical motifs, comparing, for instance, Vitacucho's speeches to Orlando's in the *Enamorado* and the *Furioso,* and Cofachaqui's pomp to Cleopatra's in Caesar's *Commentaries,* all the while exposing historiography as plagued with circularity (Rodriguez-Vecchini 1982: 613, and passim).

We should not be surprised, then, that the conquistador in *La Florida* is also an ideal type that has fascinated readers and inspired the equally idealized biographies of Hernando de Soto by Miguel Albornoz (1971), R. B. Cunninghame Graham (1912), and John S. C. Abbot (1898). I cannot resist citing here again (see chapter 1) Joseph

Conrad's praise of Cunninghame Graham's biography: "H. de Soto is most exquisitely excellent: your very mark and spirit upon a subject that only you can do justice to—with your wonderful English and your sympathetic insight into the souls of the Conquistadores" (in Watts 1969: 148). In his letter to Cunninghame Graham, Conrad goes on to say that his book has given him "a furious desire to learn Spanish and bury [himself] in the pages of the incomparable Garcilaso—if only to forget all about our modern Conquistadores" (148). This nostalgic looking back to the conquistadores of olden times ignored the fact that Garcilaso was writing against the moralistic posturing of Oviedo's negative portrait of de Soto (see chapter 4).

Quite explicitly eschewing moralizing in historiography, Garcilaso refused, for example, to derive a lesson from the experience of Diego de Guzmán, who chose to remain among the Indians after losing an Indian woman in a gambling match: "Se podrá ver lo que del juego inconsideradamente nace y donde teníamos bien que decir de los que con propios ojos en esta pasión hemos visto, si fuera de nuestra profesión decirlo, mas quédese para los que la tienen de reprehender los vicios" [One may see what is born of reckless gambling; and at this point I might deem it wise, were it my business to do so, to tell what of this passion I myself have seen, but such matters remain for those whose duty (it) is to reprehend vices] (1986 [1605]: 454; 1951: 481). This dislike of moralizing did not prevent Garcilaso from showering us with information on slave raids, *aperreos,* massacres, or the fixation on gold that drove de Soto to roam the country without direction or any ultimate destination. He simply lets the Indians speak for themselves, articulating their own condemnation of such practices: "Tened paciencia, hermanas, y alegraos con las nuevas que os damos, que muy presto os sacaremos del cautiverio en que estos ladrones vagamundos os tienen, porque sabed que tenemos concertado de los degollar y poner sus cabezas en sendas lanzas para honra de nuestros templos y entierros y sus cuerpos han de ser atasajados y puestos por los árboles, que no merecen más que esto" [Be patient, sisters, and rejoice in the news that we bring you, for very soon we are going to release you from the captivity in which you are held by these wandering thieves. For know you that we have agreed to decapitate them and impale their heads on great lances for the glorification of our temples and burial places; and we will cut their bodies into small pieces to be placed on the trees, this being all they deserve] (512–13; 553).

Although this passage expresses Quigualtanqui's sense of justice, it is not he who speaks here but one of his spies. (Quigualtanqui is a cacique who leads a province bearing the same name and comes close to annihilating the Spaniards toward the end of *La Florida*.) We must remember that there was nothing "barbarous" about such calls for retribution; it was, after all, an accepted European practice to cut up bodies as well as to deny burial to traitors and enemies. Quigualtanqui's curse, moreover, subverts a commonplace in Western epics. As David Quint has pointed out, such curses by the "vanquished" in epics do not suggest an alternative history, but an ideological gesture that reinforces the epic plot and its concluding triumph of the "vanquishers" (1989b: 111–18; see chapter 3 above). Accordingly, the curses of Polyphemus, Dido, and Adamastor all ultimately convey impotence and justify violence. In Garcilaso's narrative, however, Quigualtanqui not only survives the de Soto expedition, but is remembered for his courage. Thus, epic topoi, as Bakhtin would put it, are *novelized* in *La Florida* (see Bakhtin 1981). Elsewhere, Garcilaso mentions how Francisco de Mendoza (the son of Antonio de Mendoza, the viceroy, who was also present when the survivors arrived in Mexico City) was fond of praising the great Quigualtanqui every time he recounted the expedition of Florida: "'Verdaderamente, señores, que debía ser hombre de bien Quigualtanqui.' Y con este dicho refrescaba de nuevo las grandezas del indio, [y] eternizaba su nombre" ["Truly, my lords, Quigualtanqui must have been an honest man." And with this remark he revived the grandeur and eternalized the name of that Indian] (1986 [1605]: 543; 1951: 589). One gets the impression that beyond Garcilaso's exaltation of Indian valor, it was the articulate speech and sense of justice that he had in mind when he begged his readers not to be offended by his telling both sides of the story: "Porque la verdad de la historia nos obliga a que digamos las hazañas, así hechas por los indios como las que hicieron los españoles . . . suplicamos no se enfade el que lo oyere porque lo contamos tan particularmente" [Since the facts of history demand that we narrate the brave deeds of the Indians as well as those of the Spaniards . . . we beg that our readers not be offended because we relate this incident in such detail] (439; 460).

The figure of the anonymous oral informant as the author of an account, which Garcilaso transformed into chivalric history in the process of writing it, corresponds to the transition from orally transmitted romances to written chronicles in medieval historiography. Although Garcilaso was always cautious, his aesthetics would seem to have been at odds with the emphasis on pragmatics in Spanish American historiography. We must remember that in the early modern period, writing-as-labor was opposed to orality-as-nonproduction (see Certeau 1984; Rabasa 1993b). Indeed, the adoption of the chivalric model was a self-conscious anachronism that ultimately reveals Garcilaso's understanding of subjectivity in historical writing. Alonso de Carmona and Juan Coles, whose written accounts Garcilaso supposedly used to validate his oral informant, basically confirmed the facts but not the meaning of the events. Though I cannot prove it, the nonexistence of these texts leads me to believe that these sources were invented by Garcilaso and fulfill primarily the taxonomical function of describing the type—as well as the material condition—of the kinds of documents that conform the "archive" (which would include oral testimonies). Accordingly, Garcilaso describes the length and the handwriting of their accounts, and mentions that Coles's had been damaged by termites and mice: "comidas las medias de polilla y ratones" (1986 [1605]: 66). Neither of these accounts is, strictly speaking, history. As Garcilaso put it, neither one arranged his account in a historical manner: "puso su relación en modo historial" (66). These texts nevertheless confirmed the account of his oral informant, who, by the way, was the only one Garcilaso identified as pertaining to the nobility, an "hombre noble hijodalgo" (literally, a nobleman son of something). Thus did Garcilaso subvert the hierarchy with an Indian who wrote history and an *hidalgo* who provided an oral account. In citing his sources, Garcilaso revealed his rhetorical skills, reproducing both the disorganized discourse of Coles and Carmona and the conversational tone of his oral informant. His self-deprecating claim to lack "los preceptos del arte o ciencia" seems highly ironic in conjunction with such obvious writing skills.

Much meaning depends on those European images, topoi, and rationales that paradoxically enabled Garcilaso to invent an Indian subjectivity, namely, one not ruled by the binary logic that informs Western representations and histories of America. Garcilaso's Indian identity and corresponding subjectivity were intimately bound up with the emergence of European history and subjectivity as universals. It is to Garcilaso's credit that he could capitalize on his marginality without resorting to an inversion of values that would merely have reiterated the same logic he set out to overturn.

But to speak of Garcilaso's writing in terms of race or nationality would be to invite the charge of anachronism. The category of race did not exist as such in the sixteenth century, nor, for that matter, does it make sense to speak of Garcilaso as an Indian when he was equally proud of his father's Spanish heritage. But the question here is not so much that of his pride or how he reconciled the two halves of his cultural identity as a mestizo, but of what was at stake when he asserted the impossibility of constituting himself as a reliable author. The quasi-utterance "Porque soy indio," which is associated in his preface with a declaration of his inadequacy as an author given his lack of education, must be read as an allegorization of the system that authorized the writing of history. Beyond attributing his Indian condition to his lacking *arte o ciencia,* Garcilaso's preface suggests a cultural construct that would define his Indianness as an essential trait—a lack of blood purity. If one of the precepts of Renaissance historiography was that only the wise could write history, then it follows that Indians, at least as Indians, could not have been wise, hence allowed to write history (see Mignolo 1981: 369). To write history as an Indian would therefore be to court paradox, to say the least. It seems to me that what was truly at stake in these historiographical negations was the possibility of producing an alternative to the authorized Western account. Garcilaso's alternative historiography in *La Florida* has less to do with factual contradiction than with exposing the codes that define and make historical truths believable.

Because Garcilaso lacked the *limpieza de sangre* that would have certified him as a trustworthy subject, he underscored his informant's trustworthiness: "Volviendo a nuestro primer propósito, que es de certificar en ley de cristiano que escribimos verdad en lo pasado, y con el favor de la Suma Verdad, la escribiremos en lo por venir, diré lo que en este paso me pasó con el que me la daba relación, al cual, si no lo tuviera por tan hijodalgo y fidedigno, como lo es y como adelante en otros pasos diremos de su reputación, no presumiera yo que escribía tanta verdad, como la presumo y certifico por tal" [But returning to our original purpose, to certify upon the word of a Christian that we have written the truth in the past, and that with the favor of the Highest Truth, we shall write it in the future, I shall tell what happened at this point in the story between me and the one who gave me my facts. If I did not hold this man to be such an hidalgo and the trustworthy person he is, as later in other passages I shall speak of him as being, I would not pride myself on having written as much truth as I have, and moreover would guarantee it as such] (1986 [1605]: 193; 1951: 159–60). There is a certain irony to Garcilaso's having testified to the *hidalguía* of an anonymous informant, a status that in turn allowed Garcilaso to claim trustworthiness for his history. Moreover, as Rodríguez-Vecchini would argue, it constitutes a decodification of how historical facts are grounded on circular arguments. But though this passage cries out for an unpacking of the historiographical criteria of truthfulness based on *limpieza de sangre,* this is not the place to undertake such an analysis. However, a cursory look at prefaces to other accounts and at letters from Cabeza de Vaca to Lope de Aguirre will verify how commonly such appeals to illustrious ancestry were used to justify a request to be taken at one's word. On the other hand, it was no coincidence that Garcilaso never identified himself, in plain terms, as a Spaniard. Nor was his *mestizaje* (mestizoness) advanced as some sort of metaphysical identity in need of expression (cf. Cornejo Polar 1994). His identification as an Indian was bound to discrimination and the limitations imposed on him as a colonial subject. We must note that this certification of the nobility of his source follows the passage in which Garcilaso states that his magnanimous representations of Amerindians may be questioned as racially biased: "Pues decir que escribo encarecidamente por loar la nación porque soy indio, cierto es engaño" [But to say that I exaggerate my praise of the nation because I am an Indian is indeed a falsehood].

The juxtaposition of these two passages in which Garcilaso anticipated that his objectivity would be questioned because he praised his *nación* and in which he certified his informant's *hidalguía* and trustworthiness suggests a paradox that we could also find in a number of *converso,* Marrano, and Jewish apologetic works. The predicament of each of these groups is obviously different: whereas *conversos* argued against the Statutes of Blood Purity, which distinguished them from the *viejos cristianos* (old Christians), Jews and Marranos argued for Judaism; the Marranos, furthermore, as Yosef Yerushalmi has pointed out, constituted "the first body of Jewish writers *contra cristianos* to have known Christianity from *within*" (quoted in Shell 1991: 320). As is well-known, in the course of the sixteenth century, *hidalguía* and *limpieza de sangre* came to be identified with the Spanish character. Garcilaso himself testified to that *germanidad* (Germanhood), or Spanish *hermandad* (brotherhood)— *hermandad* is derived from *germanidad*—by which nobility was identified with the Goths, thereby consigning the alternative identities of other nations to a corresponding legacy of negative cultural traits (Shell 1991: 315–16 and passim). I cannot imagine Garcilaso declaring with a straight face that "la nobleza de nuestros españoles, y la que hoy tiene toda España sin contradicción alguna, viene de aquellos godos" [the nobility of those Spaniards and of all the people of present day Spain comes without any question whatsoever from those Goths] (1986 [1605]: 473–74; 1951: 505). As I noted above, in *La Florida* belonging to a nation is an attribute that unites all Indians in America. Garcilaso's continued insistence on the nobility of the Indian nation allows us to read the series of *porque soy indio* statements as a contribution to the debate over the Estatutos de Limpieza de Sangre that differentiated *viejos cristianos* from *conversos.*

Garcilaso's questioning of what constitutes nobility was elaborated through an alternative discourse that emphasized his subjectivity. His was an opinion that lacked *arte o ciencia,* yet Garcilaso was fully conscious of the fact that he was advancing new forms of argumentation, as well as new modes of representing, understanding, and conceptualizing Amerindian cultures. The title *La Florida del Inca* itself highlights the subjectivity of his knowledge—an admittedly untrustworthy history, yet a valid alternative discourse. Toward the end of *La Florida,* Garcilaso further underscored the subjective stance of his text by acknowledging the impossibility of providing an adequate geographic description of de Soto's expedition. He attributed this failing to de Soto's objective, which "no era andar demarcando la tierra . . . sino buscar oro y plata" [was not to mark off the land . . . but to search for gold and silver] (1986 [1605]: 545; 1951: 592). This implicit denunciation of de Soto's greed actually represents an attempt to decolonize historiography, as it displaces Garcilaso's apparent intention of writing a history that would facilitate a new conquest: "Para que de hoy más . . . se esfuerce España a la ganar y poblar" [Our purpose in offering this description has been to encourage Spain to make an effort and acquire and populate this kingdom] (64; xxxviii). *La Florida* is not a text that records information of strategic value, but rather one that vindicates Amerindians by presenting them as magnanimous and capable in all realms of culture. In his repeated insistence on the nobility of spirit expressed by Amerindian discourses, Garcilaso not only provided an idealized vision of Indians, but legitimated himself as an Indian writer of history: an Indian who writes/speaks so eloquently could not be anything less than noble. But this attribute of nobility also went hand in hand with the savage, that is, with lacking *arte o ciencia*. As such are his Amerindians and himself.

Garcilaso simultaneously questioned the category of *limpieza de sangre* as a criterion of nobility and elaborated the semblance of Amerindians that embodied all the attributes of nobility. The eloquence of his Amerindians not only disproved European prejudices, but, in the voice of his informant, Garcilaso asserted that Spaniards familiar with the classics would compare Indian speeches to the most famous ones in Roman histories and would conclude that "los mozos . . . parecían haber estudiado en Atenas cuando ella florecía en letras morales" [the youths . . . seemed to have been trained in Athens when it was flourishing in moral letters] (1986 [1605]: 194; 1951: 160). Obviously, he was not alluding to antiquity in reference to a common paganism, but to ancient cultures and languages as cultural ideals of the Renaissance. Garcilaso was fully conscious of how these allusions to speeches in classical historiography would efface Indian modes of address, and he was careful to signal that his "translations" were not literal but cultural: "Es estilo de los Indios ayudarse unos a otros en los razonamientos"

[It is the style of the Indians to assist each other in discourse] (187; 153). Thus Garcilaso defined cultural differences and underscored another subjective dimension of his history. His role of amanuensis was closer to the collective authorship of Indian discourse, to assisting "unos a otros" in discourse, than to the humanist Author-God. But this evocation of an Indian form of collective discourse also promoted ideological pluralism by questioning the universality of Western subjectivity and history.

Beyond offering a vindication of Amerindians, *La Florida* presented a more general critique of the myth of *limpieza de sangre,* especially as a criterion for nobility. Garcilaso's brief account of the French Protestant corsair who fought for days against a Spanish merchant provided him with a means of extending his critique of blood statutes to the wars of religion that plagued Europe in the sixteenth century. First relativizing, if not democratizing, the concept of nobility, Garcilaso observed, "No se sabe cuál fuese la calidad [del mercader español], mas la nobleza de su condición y la hidalguía que en su conversación, tratos y contratos mostraba decían que derechamente era hidalgo, porque ese lo es que hace hidalguías" [The quality of (the Spanish merchant) is not known, but the nobility of his equipage and the cavalier mien which he displayed in his conversation, manners and business dealings revealed that he was by rights a gentleman, for these are the things which constitute nobility] (1986 [1605]: 94; 1951: 32). *Derechamente* (by rights), both the French corsair and the Spanish merchant behaved like hidalgos. But after describing the ritualism they maintained on the battlefield as well as in their exchanges of gifts during truces, Garcilaso comments on rules that had to be kept in mind with enemies of another religion and nation: "[Los del puerto que se negaron a ayudar al español] no advertían que el enemigo de nación o de religión, siendo vencedor, no sabe tener respeto a los males que le dejaron de hacer, ni agradecimiento a los bienes recibidos . . . como se ve por muchos ejemplos antiguos y modernos" (Those in the harbor who refused to help the Spaniard) did not take into consideration the fact that the enemy of nation or religion, being a victor, knows neither respect for ills withheld nor for good deeds rendered . . . as is proved by examples both ancient and modern] (99; 38). In my reading, this observation conveys a criticism of the meanness of the Spaniards in the port rather than an argument for intolerance or a justification of the wars of religion.

Menéndez de Avilés's 1565 massacre of the French Huguenots in Florida was still a fresh event in the memories of Garcilaso's contemporaries. This massacre spawned a series of Protestant accounts—by Laudonnière, Le Challeux, Gourgues, Haykluyt, and Le Moyne—that denounced the cruelty of the Spaniards in the context of the *leyenda negra* (black legend) (see chapter 6). Toward the end of *La Florida,* Garcilaso mentions that Menéndez de Avilés brought back to Spain seven Amerindians from Florida. As they were passing through a village in Cordoba, Garcilaso's informant hurried out to the countryside to meet them and get news from Florida. Having learned that he had participated in de Soto's armada, the Indians asked him, " 'Dejando vosotros esas tierras tan mal paradas como las dejasteis queréis que os demos nuevas' " ["Having left those provinces as desolate as you did, do you want us to give you news of them?"]. They were so angry, in fact, that they took their bows and shot arrows into the air, "por dar a entender el deseo que tenían de tirárselas y la destreza con que se las tiraran" [in order to make this man realize their desire to shoot arrows at him and the skill with which they might do so] (1986 [1605]: 585; 1951: 641). A few years later, one of the caciques, by then baptized, returned to Florida to aid a group of Jesuits in converting his nation. He and his people ended up killing all the Jesuits. The Amerindians danced, wearing the priests' vestments and ornaments, but three took up a crucifix and, "estándolo mirando, se cayeron muertos" [as they gazed upon it, suddenly fell dead] (586; 642). Although we are not told who witnessed this divine intervention, Garcilaso mentions that Father Pedro Ribadeneyra documented it in writing.

One could argue that if the rule covering war between nations and religions were a universal principle, then the massacre of the Jesuits would have been justified. However, I would rather read a discourse on tolerance in these examples of killings and other cruelties between nations; after all, Garcilaso concludes *La Florida* calling for compassion, "misericordia como la de Cristo Nuestro Señor" [compassion in the manner of Christ Our Lord], and not revenge "como la de Abel" [in the manner of Abel] (1986 [1605]: 586).[8]

Writing Violence on the Northern Frontier

This would not preclude reading Garcilaso's novel argumentation on the nobility of Amerindians as a beautiful vision that could compete with the magnificent watercolors and engravings of John White, Jacques Le Moyne, and Théodore de Bry. In this respect, Garcilaso both performed an intended service to the Crown by rescuing Florida from foreign nations and elaborated an apology for his own Indianness. To the extent that Garcilaso views *La Florida* as an exemplary work, we may also argue that the critique of the intolerance of the Estatutos de Limpieza de Sangre (and, by extension, of the wars of religion) entails an ethics that would ultimately redeem Spain by posing as its representative.

The novelty of Garcilaso's position lies in his having avoided simple inversions of binary oppositions while raising the possibility of a discourse of tolerance. It is well-known that John Locke was an admirer of Garcilaso and had also read (but perhaps not admired) that great thinker on tolerance, Baruch Spinoza. It is thus not idle to presume that the ideal of a tolerant society, which we have come to identify as a Western conception, was actually the invention of the marginalized groups who lived—and were discriminated against—in Western societies. Nevertheless, we must differentiate Garcilaso's and Spinoza's locus of enunciation from that of liberal thinkers. I will return to this question in chapter 6; here, let me point out that for both Spinoza and Garcilaso, the possibility of articulating a true discourse was paradoxically bound up with the acceptability, if not the validity, of their subject positions: Garcilaso's as an Indian historian, Spinoza's as a Jewish freethinker (see Shell 1991: 332–35).

Garcilaso intercalated a wonderful "life-text" in the second part of the *Comentarios* that further illuminates how the colonial situation vexed the project of writing as an Indian who could not claim author*ity:*

Pidiendo yo mercedes a Su Majestad por los servicios de mi padre y por la restitución patrimonial de mi madre . . . el licenciado Lope García de Castro, que después fue por presidente del Perú, estando en su tribunal me dijo: "¿Qué merced queréis que os haga Su Majestad, habiendo hecho vuestro padre con Gonzalo Pizarro lo que hizo en la batalla de Huarina y dádole aquella tan gran victoria?" Y aunque yo repliqué que había sido testimonio falso que le habían levantado, me dijo: "Tiénenlo escrito los historiadores ¿y queréislo vos negar?" Con esto me despidieron de aquellas pretenciones y cerraron las puertas a otras que después acá pudiera haber tenido por mis particulares servicios. (1960 [1609–1617], 3: 360)

[In the process of asking for grants due for the services of my father and the restitution of my mother's patrimony . . . *licenciado* Lope García de Castro, who later on became the president of Peru, told me from his court: "What grants do you want (His) Majesty to give you, since your father did what he did with Gonzalo Pizarro in the battle of Huarina and gave him such a victory?" Although I replied that false testimony had been given on this matter, he told me: "Historians have it in writing and you want to deny it?" With this they turned down my claims and closed the door to others that I could have presented later on for my own services. (My translation)]

Garcilaso resigned himself to being unable to refute the three historians who had testified against his father, alluding to his withdrawal from worldly affairs as described in the preface to *La Florida:* "Como lo dije en el proemio de nuestra historia de la Florida, paso una vida quieta y pacífica, como hombre desengañado y despedido de este mundo y de sus mudanzas" [As I stated it in the preface to my history of Florida, I live a quiet and peaceful life, like that of a man who has been disillusioned and has withdrawn from this world and its inconstancies] (3:360; my translation). There is an element of teasing or parody in this intertextual reference to *La Florida,* as that work also features three witnesses, those who validate his history of de Soto's expedition. Garcilaso ultimately echoed the injunction of Corinthians 13:1: "In the mouths of two or three witnesses shall every word be established" (see Henige 1986: 12). In the life-text of the *Comentarios,* it is writing by historians that gains the upper hand over Garcilaso's oral testimony; *La Florida,* however, is a trustworthy oral history that nevertheless depended on an untrustworthy amanuensis for its validation.

This ongoing elaboration on orality and writing and the insistent repetition of *porque soy indio* suggest an extended metaphor whereby one thing is said and another meant—that is, an ironic allegory of the privileged claim of the "West" to write "the rest of the world."

Close attention to the constitution of an oral "author" for this text, to the corpus of texts that supposedly informed and verified the information in *La Florida* (besides Coles and Carmona, Garcilaso mentions the approval of a *coronista*), and to the silence regarding the written accounts that have survived (Rodrigo Ranjel's account in Oviedo's *Historia general,* the *Relaçam verdadeira* by the anonymous Fidalgo de Elvas, and the *Relación* of Luis Hernández de Biedma) further illuminate Garcilaso's "unscientific legend," or how a minority discourse could inscribe itself in the margins of Western historiography. In the context of sixteenth-century Spanish imperialism, Foucault's question, "What does it matter who is speaking?", is hardly academic. By the same token, in reading Garcilaso, it certainly matters that we read his marginality and practice of writing as the *proliferation of possibilities of hearing.*

CHAPTER 6

Of Massacre and Representation:

Painting Hatred and Ceremonies of Possession

in Protestant Anti-Spanish Pamphleteering

La sabiduría, hoy profesión inocente, fué sobradamente peligrosa en
los pasados siglos, principalmente en países, como España, donde im-
peró el *conservatismo* religioso con toda su cruda fuerza.
[Knowledge, today an innocent profession, was exceedingly dangerous
in past centuries, especially in countries like Spain, where religious *con-
servatism* prevailed with its whole brute force.]
—Genaro García, *Dos antiguas relaciones de la Florida*[1]

This anti-Spanish statement prefaces Genaro García's *Dos antiguas
relaciones de la Florida,* his contribution to the Thirteenth International Congress of Americanists, which met in New York in 1902.
As the title implies, it is an edition of two Spanish texts on sixteenth-century Florida, Bartolomé Barrientos's *Vida y hechos de Pero
Menéndez de Avilés* (1568) and Fray Andrés de San Miguel's *Relación de
los trabajos que la gente de una nao padeció* (ca. 1620). García also includes
a long introduction comprising three chapters: a bio-bibliography
of Barrientos and Fray Andrés, a brief history of the main explorations and colonizations of Florida, and a study of Native Americans under Spanish law. The 1902 meeting of Americanists was the
second occasion this organization had met in the Americas. In the
1890 congress in Paris, the majority of the society expressed strong
opposition to holding sessions in the Americas when New York
and Huelva, Spain, were proposed as the sites for the 1892 gather-
ing, which, by the way, coincided with the fourth centennial of
Columbus's voyage to the New World. Huelva won the vote. At
the 1894 congress in Stockholm, an extraordinary session was con-
ceded to Mexico City for 1895. Five years later (a lapse due to the

1898 Spanish-American War, when the society almost dissolved), during the eleventh congress in Paris, the society agreed that meetings from then on would alternate between Europe and the New World (see Comas 1975: 22–33). This is not the place to sum up the prejudices against the Americans that permeated these debates over the appropriateness of meeting in the New World, but a superficial glance at the proceedings of these years reveals how García's anti-Spanish sentiments contrast with the 1892 Huelva congress, when speakers invariably celebrated the achievements of Spain with rounds of applause after the lectures; the transcript includes such lines as "Grandes y ruidosos aplausos" [Great and noisy applauses], "Bien, Bien. Aplausos" [Well said, well said. Applauses], and just plain "Aplausos" [Applauses] (*Actas* 1894: 17–154).

Given the anticolonial sentiments that derailed plans in the United States to *celebrate* (not commemorate) the 1992 quincentenary, Genaro García's condemnation of Spanish obscurantism might not surprise us. Nevertheless, he could have been accused then, and even today, of propagating the *leyenda negra* (black legend) of the Spanish Conquest, but García apparently had no qualms about perpetuating the prevalent hispanophobia in Anglo-American views of Latin America and, perhaps more insidiously, of the U.S. Southwest.[2] Indeed, we also find in García's anti-Hispanism a gesture of goodwill toward the United States (four years after the Spanish-American War!): "Debo también manifestar que por cortesía hacia la Nación amiga de mi patria, donde la Sociedad Internacional de Americanistas celebra hoy su tredécima sesión, elegí la Historia de la Florida para tema de este libro" [I must also manifest that out of courtesy to this Nation, a friend of my fatherland, and where the International Society of Americanists celebrates today its thirteenth session, I have chosen the history of Florida as the theme of this book] (García 1902: v). Our Mexican positivist historian, moreover, offers a passionate defense of the French tentative colonization of Florida in the sixteenth century. An initial discussion of García's anti-Hispanism will define the *tone* and the *place* from which I write this chapter on symbolism in sixteenth-century anti-Spanish pamphleteering.

García establishes the following binary:[3]

THE SPANIARDS:	THE FRENCH:
arrogant	cheerful
rough	communicative
violent	kind
religious fanatics	friendly religious spirit, if not skeptics
see Indians as beasts	see Indians as robust, agile, beautiful
rape, rob, enslave Indians	treat Indians affably as equals

García's binary reiterates a rhetoric of anticonquest that, since the sixteenth century, has defined a French approach to colonization as one that, by stressing trade and the possession of land, differed from Spain's emphasis on exploiting Indians as a labor force. In our day, the French historian Pierre Chaunu has captured this difference with the laconic statement: "La *Conquista,* à nos yeux, c'est sans doute ce qui s'oppose le mieux à la conquête" [The *Conquista,* according to our view, is without doubt that which best opposes the *conquête*] (1969: 135; also see Lestringant 1990: 15, 170–71 and passim; Seed 1992, 1995).

García's idealized Indians, whom he draws from sixteenth-century Huguenot verbal and visual sources, clearly evoke Rousseau's noble savage and convey the influence of French culture in nineteenth-century Mexico, in particular, of August Comte's positivism on the intellectuals of the Porfiriato, the so-called *científicos* who advised Porfirio Díaz (see Zea 1968). The reference in the epigraph to "sabiduría" [wisdom] as "hoy profesión inocente" [today an innocent profession] refers to a stage in the positivist historical narrative when science has attained autonomy from religion. García's evocation of an innocent profession, a disinterested scientific approach, obviates any reference to the power of knowledge. Positivism enables García, in his introductory comments to Barrientos's *Vida y hechos de Pero Menéndez de Avilés,* to define his historical method as scientific and thus to break away from a Spanish colonial legacy of backwardness: "Dejábase así arrastrar Barrientos por la corriente común de los historiadores españoles, quienes desde un principio atendieron más á halagar al monarca y al pueblo, que á mostrarles sus errores y debilidades y censurar sus vicios ó crímenes, lo que ha sido causa de que varias veces España camine ignorante y confiada hacia la ruina más cierta" [Thus Barrientos

would let himself be led by the common drift in Spanish historians, who from the start paid more attention to pleasing the monarch and the people, than to showing them their errors and weaknesses and censuring their vices or crimes, which has been the cause that Spain often walks ignorantly and trustfully towards its most certain ruin] (1902: xiii). Whereas the lack of self-criticism among Spanish historians figures among the causes that led to Spain's ruin, according to García skepticism and objectivity have defined—at least since the sixteenth century—the national character of the French and the values he emulates in his own work.

This variation of the Spanish/French binary has a parallel formulation in Frank Lestringant's *Le Huguenot et le Sauvage,* in which he sets André Thevet (as exemplary of the history favored by the pro-Spanish Catholic League) in opposition to Urbain Chauveton (as exemplary of the history favored by the Protestant historians): "Chauveton's intervention in someone else's text presented itself as a model of the genre [textual editing]: in fact, through the respect it testified towards the earlier text, and by the modest role it assigns to the critical historian of documents, it appears on all sides as the contrary of the method of savage monopolizing constantly followed by Thevet" (1990: 177).[4] Lestringant, furthermore, underscores the historiographical modernity of the Huguenot corpus on Florida in terms parallel to García's: "This 'new history,' that is born in France at the decline of the Renaissance, certainly is not the exclusive privilege of the Huguenot party [*parti*]. But it finds here a propitious terrain and talented authors that carry out a particularly happy adaptation. As they affirm the primacy of individual conscience, free and sovereign, Calvinist historians guarantee the veracity of testimony while also revindicating a full and whole freedom of consciousness [*liberté d'examen*]" (17). Implicit in Lestringant's assessment of the "new history" are neutrality, hence objectivity, the promotion of religious tolerance, and the definition of a new form of colonization based on peaceful settlements. These all too human, lofty historiographical ideals are too tempting to be left alone. In the spirit of Nietzsche's genealogy of morals, this chapter seeks to elaborate a genealogy of historical objectivity. Writing at the end of the twentieth century from a subaltern studies perspective, I aim not to rewrite the history of modernity—that is, to elaborate a new master narrative that privileges science as the arbiter of truth—but to trace forms of rationality and modernity that have nothing to do with the truth values of the Enlightenment in sixteenth-century verbal and visual texts. Thus, we would not only do justice to subjects existing in other cultures and historical epochs, but also weaken the hold that certain forms of modern rationality have on our late-twentieth-century subjectivities and that are at the root of modes of thinking that subalternize cultures and languages.

The first part of the chapter describes the corpus of Florida both in terms of the political conjunctures that have informed the collections of documents pertaining to the tentative French colonization of Florida between 1561 and 1565, and their implications for sixteenth-century wars of religion.[5] In the second part, I outline a moral economy of violence that links law and aesthetics in representations of massacre, war, and torture. The third part dwells on the representation of violence in verbal and visual texts. A fourth part examines forms of asserting mastery and possession, specifically the connection between the French corpus of Florida and the English imperial projects of both the younger and elder Richard Hakluyt (see E. G. R. Taylor 1967 [1935]: 1–66).

THE CORPUS

Along with Barrientos's account, García published Fray Andrés de San Miguel's *Relación de los trabajos que la gente de una nao padeció* (ca. 1620). For our purposes of examining representations of massacre and revenge in Spanish and French texts, Fray Andrés's *Relación* has no interest, as it does not dwell on these events. García's bibliographical "gift" to the United States clearly counteracts Eugenio Ruidíaz y Caravia's *La Florida su conquista y colonización por Pedro Menéndez de Avilés:* "El país de la Florida . . . pertenece desde 1821, a los Estados Unidos; pero por españoles fue descubierto, por españoles conquistado, España lo poseyó durante muchos años" [The country of Florida . . . has belonged to the United States since 1821; but it was discovered by Spaniards, conquered by Spaniards, and Spain possessed it for many years] (1989 [1893]: 7). Though Ruidíaz, who died in 1896, never witnessed the end of the Spanish empire in 1898, this statement suggests a last gasp of celebrations of Spain's imperial glories and an attempt to vindicate the name of Pedro Menéndez de Avilés. Underlying García's corrosive dismissal of Barrientos's *Vida* is a desire to undermine Ruidíaz's efforts.

In Ruidíaz's collection, Gonzalo Solís de Merás's *Memorial* (1989 [ca. 1574]) constitutes the main, extended account by an eyewitness. Whereas Barrientos's text ends in 1568 with Menéndez de Avilés's return to Spain, Solís de Merás's more "literary" *Memorial* ends in 1574 with the death of Menéndez de Avilés and includes information regarding Dominique de Gourgues's countermassacre of Spaniards in Florida in 1568. The *Memorial* also gives a short account of the martyrdom of Jesuits in 1571 by the Indian cacique Don Luis de Velasco, whom, along with five other Indians, Menéndez de Avilés had taken to Spain in 1568 for indoctrination. (We saw in chapter 5 how Garcilaso's treatment of this martyrdom toward the end of *La Florida del Inca* entailed a discourse of tolerance rather than a diatribe on Amerindian savagery or a justification of the Indians' right to avenge themselves.) In addition, Ruidíaz's collection includes a series of shorter documents that shed light on the Spanish explorations, mappings, and settlements of Florida, among which are several letters by Menéndez de Avilés to Philip II that dwell on the massacre.[6]

The earliest text in the Protestant corpus of texts on Florida is the extant English version of Jean Ribault's lost French account, *The Whole & True Discouerye of Terra Florida* (London 1563 [1964]), which consists of an uneventful exploration and establishment of Charlesfort, named after the twelve-year-old king of France Charles IX.[7] Ribault's Florida is a utopian land of plenty populated with servile Amerindians; this text constitutes as such the first in a series of English Protestant pamphlets, which, starting with the elder Richard Hakluyt's "Inducements to the Liking of the Voyage" in 1585, promoted the colonization of North America in the seventeenth century (see E. G. R. Taylor 1967 [1935]: 327–38). Ribault's purpose, apparently, was to bring the Huguenot settlement to the attention of Queen Elizabeth I at the time he took refuge in England in 1562 due to a renewal of the wars of religion in France. This initial communication between French and English Protestants eventually led to the younger Hakluyt's possession and translation into English of René de Laudonnière's *L'Histoire notable de la Floride*. Martin Basanier first published the *Histoire notable* in Paris in 1586 and Hakluyt the English version in London in 1587. Laudonnière's history covers the French voyages to Florida in 1562 and 1564–1565 and the third voyage of Jean Ribault in 1565, which ended in the massacre of Matanzas Inlet, present-day St. Augustine. Basanier and Hakluyt added an account of Dominique de Gourgues's fourth voyage undertaken to avenge Menéndez de Avilés's massacre. There is another printed version of Gourgues's voyage written by an anonymous author, perhaps Gourgues himself, with the title *Histoire mémorable de la reprinse de l'isle de la Floride* (1568). A fourth French text on the 1565 massacre is Nicolas Le Challeux's *Discours de l'histoire de la Floride* (Dieppe 1566), which describes the massacre by the Spaniards in detail and appended a request to Charles IX calling for vengeance that was written by the widows and orphans of those killed. An English version of the Le Challeux account was published in London in 1566 under the title *A True and perfect description of the last voyage or Navigation, attempted by Capitaine John Rybault*.

Laudonnière's *Histoire notable* was also translated into Latin by Théodore de Bry in *Brevis Narratio eorum quae in Florida Americae Provincia Gallis, Americae Pars Secunda* (1591). Along with Laudonnière, de Bry translated Jacques Le Moyne's eyewitness account and made prints of Le Moyne's drawings and maps of Florida. Hakluyt alludes to Le Moyne's narrative and drawings in his "Epistle Dedicatory to Sir Walter Raleigh," which prefaces the 1587 translation of Laudonnière: "The chiefe things are drawn in colours by the skilfull painter James Morgues . . . which was an eye-witness of the goodness & fertilitie of those regions, & had put in writing many singularities which are not mentioned in this treatise: which he meaneth to publish together with the portraitures before it be long" (in E. G. R. Taylor 1967 [1935]: 373). It must have been around this time that Hakluyt gave Le Moyne's materials to de Bry, who was in London in 1587 (see 43). Elsewhere, in an "Epistle dedicated to Sir Robert Cecil" (1599), the younger Hakluyt reports that the concealment of Laudonnière's *Histoire notable*—for over twenty years by members of the "Spanish faction"—had incensed French magistrates: "Protesting further, that if their King and the Estate had thoroughly followed that action, France had bene freed of their long civill warres, and the variable humours of all sortes of people might have had very ample and manifold occasions of good and honest employment abroad in that large and fruitful continent of the West Indies" (in E. G. R. Taylor 1967 [1935]: 457–58). One cannot overestimate the impact that these French accounts of a failed settlement in Florida had on the course of European expansionism and the definition of both English and French historiographies (see Lestringant 1990: 226–34).

These texts reappear in Urbain Chauveton's translations of Girolamo Benzoni's *La historia del Mondo Nuovo* (1565 [Latin 1578; French 1579]) and La Popelinière's *Les Trois Mondes* (1582). Chauveton and La Popelinière use Thevet's version of Laudonnière's *Histoire notable*. Whereas Chauveton appends to Benzoni's *Historia* Nicolas Le Challeux's *Discours de l'histoire de la Floride* and the call for revenge by the widows and orphans, La Popelinière includes a paraphrase of Gourgues. Both of these authors exemplify what Lestringant calls the "nouvelle histoire." Whereas La Popelinière's *L'Histoire des histoires* (1599) provides a cogent theoretical exposition of the new Protestant historiography, Chauveton manifests his historical acumen when, without knowing the source of Thevet, he singles out the novelty of the chapters where Thevet reproduces Laudonnière (Lestringant 1990: 176). By supplementing Benzoni with Le Challeux, Chauveton further documents Spain's atrocities in the New World, but also identifies Indians and Protestants as victims of Spanish terror, thus underscoring Benzoni's denunciation of Spanish atrocities against Indians by mourning the massacred Huguenots. Memories of Saint Bartholomew's Day massacres in 1572 also infuse a melancholic tone to Chauveton's as well as La Popelinière's histories.[8] As we have already seen in Hakluyt's remarks, the suppression, publication, and republication of these French accounts cannot be understood outside the political climate of the wars of religion in France. On the one hand, Admiral Gaspar de Coligny, the main target of the massacre, had designed and promoted the colonization of Florida (as well as Villegagnon's earlier expedition to and tentative settlement of Brazil in 1555–1560); on the other, the historiographies of Laudonnière, Chauveton, and La Popelinière question Spain's exclusive claim to Florida and denounce Spanish atrocities, while not alienating but, indeed, seeking alliances with French Malcontent Catholics against the pro-Spanish Catholic League.[9]

Next to Chauveton's strategic inclusion of Le Challeux in his translation of Benzoni, the connection between Spanish massacres of Indians and Protestants is nowhere more vividly expressed than in the preface "Au lecteur" to the 1579 French version of Bartolomé de las Casas's *Brevíssima relación de la destruyción de las Indias,* translated as *Tyrannies et cruautez des Espagnols, perpetrees es Indes Occidentales, qu'on dit le Nouveau monde*:[10] "Les desloyautez on este si grandes & si excessives, qu'il ne seroit croyable à la posterité avoir iamas esté au monde une si barbare & cruelle nation que celle là, si, par maniere de dire, nos yeux ne l'ouent veu, & l'auions comme touche de nos mains" [The disloyalties have been so great and excessive that it will not be credible to posterity that there was ever in the world such a barbaric and cruel nation as that one, if, in a matter of speaking, our eyes had not seen it, and had touched it as if with our own hands] (Las Casas 1579: 2r–2v). In these self-referential visual and haptic metaphors, "si, par maniere de dire, nos yeux ne l'ouvent veu, & l'avion comme touche des nos mains" [if, in a matter of speaking, our eyes had not seen it, and had touched it as if with our own hands], we can trace an allusion to the Spanish massacre in Florida, and perhaps also a reference to the influence of the Spaniards on the Catholic League and the slaughter of Protestants in the Saint Bartholomew's Day massacre in 1572. According to the preface, furthermore, the purpose of the translation was to enable Protestants in the Low Countries to see "depeint comme en un tableau quel sera leur estat quand par leur nonchallance, querelles, divisions & partialitez ils auront ouvert la porte à un tel ennemy" [depicted as in a painting what will be their state when, because of their nonchalance, quarrels, division and partialities, they will have opened the gate to such an enemy] (2v). Already in the verses on the title page we find the advice expressed in visual terms,

> Heureux celuy qui devient sage
> En voyant d'autruy le dommage.
> [Fortunate are those who become wise
> Seeing the misfortunes of others.]

There is a wonderful manuscript from 1582 in the Clements Library at the University of Michigan where these visual metaphors become literal through a series of watercolors that illustrate Jacques Miggrode's 1579 translation (see plates I and II). This manuscript was produced by "Guillaume Iulen, a l'enseigne de l'amitie, pres le college de Cambray." The painter of the watercolors most likely had in mind a set of copperplates for a printing—hence mass circulation—of an illustrated translation. As far as I know, this illustrated French version was never published, but Théodore de Bry, in his 1598 Latin edition of the *Brevíssima,* which is a translation from Miggrode's French version, based his copperplates on these watercolors. De Bry also used one of the watercolors for a series of plates representing Pizarro's betrayal of Atahualpa in his Latin translation of Benzoni's *Historia* and Chauveton's addenda in *America, pars sexta* (1594–1596). The multiple temporal planes within one of the watercolors (fig. 6; plate I)—before the production of the corresponding copperplate for de Bry's Latin edition of the *Brevíssima* (fig. 7)—are separated into a sequence of images (figs. 8–11). Thus the tableau hanging on the wall in the background of the watercolor, which represents the scene where Atahualpa is attacked after throwing Vicente de Valverde's Bible to the ground, becomes an individual plate in Figure 8; Pizarro's verbal exchange with Atahualpa in the right-hand corner makes way for Figure 9; the gift of treasures placed in front of them is isolated in Figure 10; and the garroting of Atahualpa is singled out in Figure 11.

This separation of the temporal frames in the watercolor calls for a reading of the images that would set aside cognitive evaluations—these representations *are accurate*—and instead attend to aesthetic criteria—these images *feel right* (Melville and Readings 1995: 11). In making this distinction, I do not want to construct an opposition between cognitive and aesthetic readings, for visual as well as verbal representations can both be accurate and feel right. In opposing these terms we run the risk of introducing other binaries such as the semiotic, sign versus symbol, and the Romantic-aesthetic, allegory versus symbolism (see Todorov 1977). I would like to suggest that (arbitrary) signs (i.e., mere factual accuracy) are never completely devoid of motivation (symbolism), inasmuch as meaning in the most basic acts of perception depends on what the philosopher Alfred North Whitehead (1958 [1927]) called symbolic reference (e.g., the perception of the fruit we have come to call "pineapple" is meaningless outside the plane of reference that allows us to identify it and enjoy it); moreover, lived languages are never completely arbitrary systems of signs, as Saussure's linguistics wants us to believe, but forms of world making particular to cultures (e.g., the words and terms that establish colonialist claims of territorial possession embody deep-rooted national legal traditions; cf. Seed 1992, 1995). Although cultures, like languages, are never stable wholes but processes whose end products we can never fully anticipate, the repetition of forms of life and forms of expression enables us to identify the Indo-European entities we call French, Spanish, and English, as well as the multiple Amerindian linguistic families.

As for the opposition between allegory and symbolism, the Romantic preference for symbolism, which seeks to avoid the simple relationship to a code that identifies the figurative meaning of literal planes in allegories, ultimately betrays a narrow understanding of allegory that ignores Quintilian's definition in terms of irony, whereby "meaning is contrary to that suggested by words" (*Institutio oratoria* 1976: 8.6.54). De Bry's engravings and the watercolors of the 1582 manuscript are allegories insofar as they can be read as saying one thing but meaning another. Ironic allegory lends itself to a figurative meaning that participates in an open-endedness characteristic of symbolism, while at the same time, as in a paradox, it always retains the possibility of a literal reading.[11] For the allegory to work in de Bry's engravings and the watercolors of the 1582 manuscript, the literal must partake of a degree of accuracy that makes the images recognizable as representations of Indians, Spaniards, terror, and so on, even when the criteria defining their accuracy do not depend on external reference points, that is, on descriptions of *real* Indians or philological pertinence.

The conventionality of Spaniards and Indians, which allows the passage from the self-referential *accuracy* to *feels right* in the watercolors and de Bry's plates, conveys the fury of the massacre with little regard for ethnographic correctness or fidelity to the written texts. Whereas Las Casas does not mention Valverde's demand that Atahualpa recognize Spanish sovereignty, limiting himself to stat-

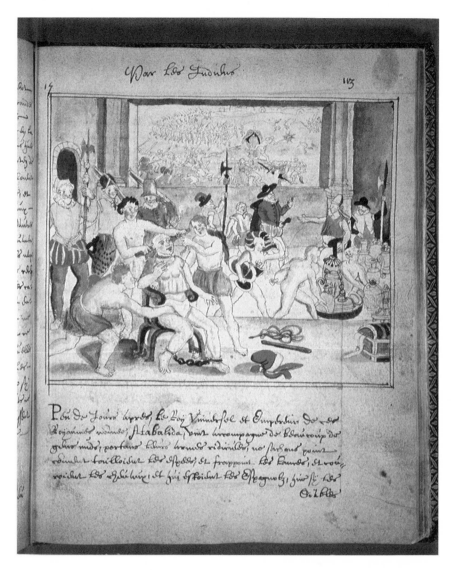

Figure 6. "The garroting of Atahualpa," in Bartolomé de Las Casas, *Tyrannies et cruautez des Espagnols, perpetrees es Indes Occidentales, qu'on dit le Nouveau monde: Brievement descrites en langue Castillane, par l'Evesque Don Frere Bartelemy de Las Casas ou Casaus, Espagnol de l'ordre de sainct Dominique, fidelement traduites par Iacques de Miggrode.* Illustrated manuscript (1582). Courtesy of the Clements Library, University of Michigan.

Figure 7. "The garroting of Atahualpa," in Bartolomé de Las Casas, *Narratio Regionum Indicarum per Hispanos quosdam devastatarum verissima*. Translated and illustrated by Théodore de Bry and Jean Israël de Bry, 1598.

on facing page

(top) Figure 8. *Atabaliba Rex Peruanus à Francisco Pizarro capitur*, in Girolamo Benzoni, *Historia del Mondo Nuovo* (1565), *America, pars sexta*. Translated and illustrated by Théodore de Bry and Jean Israël de Bry, 1594.

(bottom) Figure 9. *Atabaliba de suo litro persolvendo cum Francisco Pizarro paciscitur,* in Girolamo Benzoni, *Historia del Mondo Nuovo* (1565), *America, pars sexta.* Translated and illustrated by Théodore de Bry and Jean Israël de Bry, 1594.

Atabaliba Rex Peruanus à Francisco Pizarro capitur.

Atabaliba de suo litro persolvendo cum Francisco
Pizarro paciscitur.

Atabaliba,fide accepta fe liberatum iri,ad diverfa loca
fuos ablegat adferendi auri & argenti caufa.

Figure 10. *Atabaliba, side accepta se liberatum iri, ad diversa loca suos able-gat adferendi auri & argenti causa,* in Girolamo Benzoni, *Historia del Mondo Nuovo* (1565), *America, pars sexta.* Translated and illustrated by Théodore de Bry and Jean Israël de Bry, 1594.

ing how the Spaniards "matáronle infinitas gente, prendiéronle su persona que venía en unas ancas" [killed innumerable people, capturing his person who was carried on a litter], the tableau offers a perceptual and verbal supplement to the unwritten event, which epitomized, for a Protestant public, the Spanish "misuse" of Christianity in the conquest of America. The verbal description of de Bry's engraving in his edition of Benzoni's *Historia* speaks of how, after Valverde claimed the authority of the pope to grant Spanish jurisdiction over the Indies and presented the Bible as evidence of God's will, Atahualpa failing to "hear" the "word" in the book threw it to the ground. Elsewhere in the chapter on New Spain, however, Las Casas does denounce the absurdity of the *Requeri-miento,* the subtext of the semiotic exchange between Atahualpa and

Francifcus Pizarrus, contra fidem datam, Atabalibæ
gulam laqueo frangi jubet.

Figure 11. *Franciscus Pizarrus, contra fidem datam, Atabalibae gulam laqueo frangi jubet,* in Girolamo Benzoni, *Historia del Mondo Nuovo* (1565), *America, pars sexta.* Translated and illustrated by Théodore de Bry and Jean Israël de Bry, 1594.

Valverde. Thus, the tableau does not so much distort Las Casas as it depicts a scene where Atahualpa and Valverde's alleged verbal exchange must have been drawn from other sources, such as Benzoni's *Historia.*

The breakdown of the events in the watercolor parallels the movement from general to particular maps in such atlases as Mercator's. As in map reading, where one touches places with one's finger, the illustrations promote the haptic dimension already expressed in the prologue to the 1579 French translation of Las Casas. The *feels right* of the representations evokes a having been touched by Spanish terror, while also providing spaces to invest impulses of revenge by touching the object of hatred. As such, the watercolors and the engravings mapped the Spanish character.[12] The

Of Massacre and Representation 241

ubiquity of de Bry's illustrations (more often as adornment than as object of study) in histories of the invasion of the New World further reinforces my argument that judging ethnographic accuracy or textual fidelity is a moot point (see López-Baralt 1990; Duchet 1987; Bucher 1981). Even when, or precisely because, they insult pro-Spanish sensibilities, they manifest their aesthetic power: they *feel right* to a Protestant audience. The transformations of images and their recurrence as accoutrement further attest to their symbolic import.

So, we should ask ourselves: Symbolic of what? What are the meanings and effects of their symbolism? Clearly, there is no single answer to these questions. My end in this chapter is to analyze how de Bry formed part of a concerted effort among Protestant pamphleteers to promote anti-Spanish sentiment while legitimating Protestant claims to the New World and symbolically establishing possession by means of textual and iconographic inscriptions of meanings that defined a new approach to colonization.

Before moving on to a discussion of massacre, I would like to anticipate here some issues concerning representation. It is indeed very difficult to separate the question of *massacre* from its *representation* because it is precisely from verbal and visual representations that we derive the conceptual nature of massacres. The above brief discussion of the relation between Las Casas's *Brevíssima* and Benzoni's *Historia,* the watercolors of the French manuscript and de Bry's later copperplates has complemented my description of the French corpus on Florida by broaching questions pertaining to the poetics and politics of representing violence.

MORAL ECONOMY

"There is, however, a crucial element that differentiates the substantiating function in the two events and partially explains why war has a moral ambiguity torture simply does not have" (Scarry 1985: 139). In many regards Elaine Scarry's *The Body in Pain* helps us understand the nature of violence in sixteenth-century wars of religion, although her differentiation between torture and war needs to be historicized.[13] The antithetical definitions of torture (as morally

Plate I. "The garroting of Atahualpa," in Bartolomé de Las Casas, *Tyrannies et cruautez des Espagnols, perpetrees es Indes Occidentales, qu'on dit le Nouveau monde: Brievement descrites en langue Castillane, par l'Evesque Don Frere Bartelemy de Las Casas ou Casaus, Espagnol de l'ordre de sainct Dominique, fidelment traduites par Iacques de Miggrode.* Illustrated manuscript (1582). Courtesy of the Clements Library, University of Michigan.

Plate II. "Indians in pink," in Bartolomé de Las Casas, *Tyrannies et cruautez des Espagnols, perpetrees es Indes Occidentales, qu'on dit le Nouveau monde: Brievement descrites en langue Castillane, par l'Evesque Don Frere Bartelemy de Las Casas ou Casaus, Espagnol de l'ordre de sainct Dominique, fidelment traduites par Iacques de Miggrode.* Illustrated manuscript (1582). Courtesy of the Clements Library, University of Michigan.

indefensible) and war (as morally ambiguous) are a very recent phenomenon in Western culture (62). Whereas war can be justified in our contemporary political discourse, torture seemingly runs against all the values of Western civilization. For Scarry, the possibility of torture resides in the inexpressibility of the inflicted pain, whereby the torturer can defray death precisely to the extent that pain remains remote, an impenetrable interior state in the midst of a cry. Thus, desire fulfills itself in holding power over the life and death of an individual. Although there seem to be no rules that regiment torture, it betrays disciplined practices and knowledges of how to inflict pain on the edge of life and death. War, on the other hand, cannot be conceived outside a set of principles that define the means and the ends of legitimate violence. Massacre would seem to operate in an intermediate space between torture and war; in modern parlance, war becomes atrocity in massacre. Today, this intermediary space between torture and war suggests that the status of a massacre still depends on a moral economy of violence that links law and aesthetics: the definition of an event as a massacre bars the aesthetic representation of the acts. This moral economy no longer mediates the legal and the beautiful with the candor characteristic of the sixteenth century, when torture and massacre lacked today's unequivocal opprobrium and hence could be *as such* rendered in aesthetic terms once the event was viewed as legal. Let me draw a brief parenthesis that will enable me to elaborate these historical differences further.

The unspeakable status of torture and massacre is commonly accepted today. If it is always others who torture and massacre, the construction of otherness, however, continues to define the limits of terror. Indeed, the bombing of Iraq during the 1991 gulf war, the ethnic wars in Bosnia and Kosovo, and the systematic repression of indigenous communities in Guatemala, just to cite some recent examples, imply no moral progress, in spite of our "enlightened" views. Graphic representations of violence in the media, furthermore, assume a subject who finds gratification in the awakening of aggressive drives. During the gulf war Saddam Hussein's body was identified with the map of Iraq with disregard for the millions of people who suffered the bombings, and, as I revise this statement on 15 November 1998, I fear the press is preparing us for more of the same, though this time with the promise that more advanced technology will ensure the destruction of Hussein's arsenal and regime —with little mention that the wager gambles on how much pain the people of Iraq can endure. On the front page of today's *New York Times* we find an article preparing the U.S. public for massive bombings of Iraq, which inevitably will amount to the massacre of civilians, side by side with an article on Kosovo that speaks of massacre in unambiguous terms. The atrocity of the massive bombings remains invisible in today's paper in much the same way it did when the press was censored in 1991.

On the other hand, the images from Kosovo and Bosnia that circulate in the *New York Times* display cadavers for our prurient examination under the pretext of sensitizing us to the tragedy. This humanitarian pretence has become more evident in a recent article by Felicity Barrienger, "Breaking a Taboo, the Editors Turn to Images of Death" (1998), on the debates over the ethics of publishing photographs of casualties from the bombing of the U.S. embassy in Nairobi. Seemingly, ethical questions have no bearing on the display of corpses from Kosovo or Bosnia, whereas the case of Nairobi warrants a debate over how much of a fragment of a covered body should be displayed in a photograph: a shoeless foot half-covered by a sheet, perhaps also the lower extremities covered with bloody sheets? The strange thing about this article is that traditionally there has been an accusation that the U.S. press and the American "public" care more about massacres and tragedies in places like Bosnia because of an identification with the photos of Europeans, whereas the massacres in Rwanda were second-page news.[14] In the Nairobi coverage, in fact, the bodies were African, but the association of the cadavers with the bombing of the U.S. embassy seems to have not only triggered the debate but also shaped the sensitivity concerning the fragments included in the photographs. Though not those of U.S. citizens, the cadavers were close enough to make full images distasteful. The American casualties had been sent home, and one presumes their bodies would not have been displayed at all.

This discrepancy in sensibilities touches on issues of national identity inasmuch as it is only the display of one's own victims that raises ethical issues. Speaking about policy during World War II,

Writing Violence on the Northern Frontier

but still applicable today, John G. Morris (a former photographer and picture editor for *Life* magazine), put it succinctly: "The rule was: We can show the enemy dead but not our own people. Especially faces" (in Barrienger, 1998). But then again, this specific example drawn from the United States might only be indicative of what the news can display, because it deals with real events, and not of a generalizable sensibility. Fiction films partake of another ethos by which historical distance, as in the case of *Saving Private Ryan* (1998), lends itself to an empathetic and compassionate view of mutilated American bodies while at the same time generating impulsions of violence during scenes depicting the killing of generic Germans. As we will see in the last section of this chapter, sixteenth-century Protestants and Catholics partake of different sensibilities when graphically displaying the victims of massacres.

In discussing the Florida corpus we need to pay attention to how Protestants and Catholics constitute a binary not only in their own terms but vis-à-vis Indians. In denouncing Spanish atrocities, Protestant pamphleteers recur to parallelisms between the fate of Indians and that of Huguenots. But the identity of Indians alternates between subjects whom Europeans either war against or recognize as problematic neophytes and objects that blend into nature as one more item in the theater of hostilities of the warring European nations. Both alternatives deny Indians the status of subjects and the possibility of becoming part of the European community, that is, of possessing what Slavoj Žižek calls "the national Thing" (1993: 201). As collaborators or allies, Indians blend into nature insofar as they facilitate the governance and exploitation of a labor force or constitute a means to gain access to and secure the possession of a territory. They are thus disposable when not useful and form part of what Michel Serres calls *objective* violence, that is, the destruction of the objective world—the theater of hostilities—that results from the *subjective* wars between nations or states (1995: 11).

This lack of "the national Thing" that blends them into the landscape and may justify massacre corresponds to a determination of the Indians as problematic subjects because they lack clean blood (*limpieza de sangre*) in the Spanish case or descend from Ham (the cursed son of Noah, forebear of the Canaanites, an irredeemable "race") in Protestant narratives of salvation. Here we should resist the commonplace that opposes Catholic universalism to Protestant exclusionism, and underscore that these forms recur within each religious group: racial purity plays a role in the imaginary core of the French nation, and the narrative of Ham also haunts Catholic interpretations of the Indians' capacity to convert (see Lestringant 1990: 119). Above all, I am resisting a view that celebrates sixteenth-century Protestant tolerance as progressive (see, e.g., Defert 1987), because all one has to do is pick up Locke's *A Letter Concerning Toleration* (1991 [1689]) to learn how tolerance did no apply to those who did not share "the national Thing"—mainly papists and atheists. Moreover, as Ranajit Guha has pointed out, English liberalism in the colonies translated into an exercise of dominance without hegemony (1989, 1997).

My point is not to deny the value of Locke's contributions to the philosophy of tolerance but to avoid turning the discourse on tolerance into a "national Thing," that is, the hegemony of Northern Europe for the past four hundred years. We must therefore expand the canon on tolerance (include Jewish atheists like Spinoza and Indian Catholics like Garcilaso) as well as transform the spirit of the discussion.[15] Because of their marginality, Spinoza and Garcilaso outline a discourse of tolerance that promotes compassion as an alternative to a moral economy of violence in which the appeal to law and justice lock the contending parties in inescapable cycles of violence. Clearly, for Garcilaso, and I would add for Spinoza as well, it is not an issue of tolerating select groups for the sole purpose of preventing war, but of founding constitutive subjectivities within a horizon of liberation. For Garcilaso, this amounts to providing a historiographical critique that situates Indians, mestizos, and criollos as potential *readers,* hence, historical actors freed from binaries derived from Eurocentric worldviews; for Spinoza, laying the ontologico-metaphysical foundations of a new universalism, hence, a new, completely positive being that would ground the power of the multitude to limit the power of the state. If in *La Florida del Inca* Garcilaso questions *limpieza de sangre,* in the *Comentarios reales de los Incas* he elaborates an eloquent account of the Incas as already embodying Christian values and as an antiquity—equivalent to the Humanists' Rome—for elaborating a political theory (see Castro-Klarén 1996a). I traced in chapter 5 a discourse of tolerance in Garcilaso, who shunned the appeal to invert the terms of the Indian versus European opposition. *La Florida,* moreover, goes beyond a critique of the Indian "condition" by extending its argument to the "inferiority" of Jewish *conversos* and the hatred between Catholics and Protestants. The often repeated *porque soy indio* (because I am an Indian) marks the racial turn in Western history when universality was ethnicized as European. One could argue that Garcilaso pursues a universality that accommodates particularisms. Through this perspective, Garcilaso's histories cannot be reduced to a recuperation of the Inca past. Indeed, he would find unbearable the monument Fanon invokes in *Black Skin, White Mask:*

> On the field of the battle, its four corners marked by the scores of Negroes hanged by their testicles, a monument is slowly being built that promises to be majestic.
>
> And, at the top of this monument, I can already see a white man and a black man *hand in hand.* (1967: 222; emphasis in original)

Like Fanon (who a few pages later states "The Negro is not. Any more than the white man" [231]), Garcilaso aspires to a dissolution of Indianness and Spanishness as opposite terms irretrievably bound to the definition of each. Rather than evoke a glorious pagan past in harmony with Christianity, Garcilaso affirms the historical present, as he puts it in his prologues, of all the "indios, mestizos, y criollos"—thus promoting action, not reaction. Garcilaso's noble savages constitute a utopian discourse that dismantles the Eurocentric criteria that defined Amerindian cultures as less developed. He elaborates his critique of the civilization versus savagery opposition from within the mode of thinking that informs racism (see Balibar 1994: 195) or, as Žižek would put it, by developing "ways to sap the force of [the] underlying fantasy-frame—in short, to perform something akin to the Lacanian 'going through the fantasy'" (1993: 213). Our concern in this chapter, then, is not to condemn or to justify the Spanish massacres or the French countermassacres, but to read through the fantasies that feed hatred. Ultimately, the reconciliation of French Protestants and Catholics would see Spain and the Catholic League as targets of hate and "bad" history, as exemplified in French Protestants' dismissals of Thevet's historiography and Chauveton's addition of the widows and orphans' call for

Of Massacre and Representation　　　247

revenge in his translation of Benzoni's *Historia* (Lestringant 1990: 215 and passim). The appeal to historical objectivity seems to mask a particular consciousness and a violence that confines *others* to lesser degrees of universality.[16] The "hanged negroes" in Fanon's monument could be replaced with massacred Protestants and a French Protestant shaking the hand of a Catholic on top, thereby establishing a place of memory that would mark the transition of universal history from Southern to Northern Europe.

In the trials of history, historical objectivity, as manifest in the "nouvelle histoire" of the Calvinist historians, defines a landmark in the formation of Western culture. The classic formulation of this historical development is, of course, Hegel's *Philosophy of History,* but Lestringant's assessment also seems to confirm this narrative of Northern Europe's ascendancy. Garcilaso responds to Spain's historical supersession and French and English symbolic appropriations of Florida. As for Spain, there have been, up to the present, ongoing defenses of Spain's colonial enterprises in the Indies, in particular, the claims to Florida and the massacre of the Huguenots.

Perhaps the most eloquent is Francisco de Quevedo's *España defendida y los tiempos de ahora,* where he rescues Spain from "defamation" by Protestants, in particular, Chauveton's translation of Benzoni: "Pues aún lo que tan dichosamente se ha descubierto y conquistado y reducido por nosotros en Indias, está disfamado con un libro impreso en Ginebra, cuyo autor fué un milanés, Jerónimo Benzon" [Since even what we have felicitously discovered and conquered in the Indies has been defamed by a book printed in Geneva, whose author was a Milanese, Jerónimo Benzon] (1969 [1609], 1: 491). Quevedo finds especially offensive Chauveton's addition to Benzoni's title, " 'la traición y crueldad que en la Florida usaron con los franceses los españoles' " [the treason and cruelty that the Spaniards used with the French] (1:491). This is not the place to examine Quevedo in detail. Let it suffice that his text elaborates a sketch of Spain that highlights the virtues of his *patria,* his *nación,* in terms of an ideal geographic location, the multiple origins of its people, the virtues of the Spanish language, and a great literary tradition that dates back to Lucan, Quintilian, and Seneca. His references to and refutations of Gerhard Mercator's *Atlas* attest to the uses of cosmography and geography to define the character of nations as well as the impulse of Mercator's *Atlas* to displace Spain as the embodiment of universality.[17] Though we may not share the aesthetic of conquest of Quevedo's patriotism, his political ethos remains of interest insofar as *España defendida* elaborates an apologia of Spain's historical character that does not aim to promote a hatred of foreigners, but to temper their defamatory statements.

Quevedo describes his text as "Memorias, que serán las primeras, que, desnudas de amor u miedo, se habrán visto sin disculpa de relaciones y historia (si este nombre merece), en que se leerán los ojos y no los oídos del autor" [Memorials, which will be the first, that, free of love or fear, have ever been seen without appealing to accounts or histories (if this name they deserve), in which the eyes and not the ears of the author will be read] (1969 [1609]: 489). In the distinction between reading the eyes of the author rather than the ears, we may trace an allusion to Antonio de Herrera y Tordecillas's *Historia general de los hechos de los castellanos en las islas y tierra firme* (1601–1615), where Herrera defines the task of writing a "historia general" as based on the sense of hearing. Tom Cummins has pointed out that "the historical totality that Herrera wishes to achieve is greater than local knowledge and it must be based on the sense of hearing, that is the reading of other texts, so as to be able to reorganize and integrate these particular histories (individual experiences and unrelated places) into a coherent whole (Historia general)" (1994: 21). Cummins makes this observation in the context of a comparative study of Herrera and de Bry as exemplary texts of "the antagonistic differences in Europe between Catholicism and Protestantism, Spain and Northern Europe, nascent capitalism and royal patronage" (17). Quevedo does not address de Bry but Mercator's *Atlas,* perhaps an even more representative text of print capitalism. His preference for sight over hearing suggests a critique of the inefficacy of Herrera's *Historia general* and royal patronage to counteract the power of Mercator's *Atlas*—which was an objectification and naturalization of national boundaries and colonial possessions, alternatively, for Dutch free trade policies and English mercantilism (see Rabasa 1993b: 192 and passim; E. G. R. Taylor 1967 [1935]: 21 and passim).

To address Chauveton's addenda to Benzoni's *Historia,* Le Challeux's vivid description of the Spanish massacre of Huguenots in

Florida and the call for revenge by the widows and orphans, is one of the reasons Quevedo gives for writing his *defensa*. Without appealing to a more accurate version of the events or even a justification, Quevedo's "Memorias," based on reading the author's eyes, seek to confront Chauveton's claims of historical objectivity with a speculative discourse. It is not coincidental, then, that Quevedo critiques Mercator, who also defined his *Atlas* in speculative terms: "(as in a mirror) [it] will set before your eyes, the whole world . . . and so by attayning unto wisedome and prudence, by this meanes leade the Reader to higher speculation" (quoted in Rabasa 1993b: 186). In his "Memorias" Quevedo corrects point by point the entry on Spain in Mercator's *Atlas,* but does not produce an effect of objectivity. The strangeness and beauty of Quevedo's text consist of a negative dialectic that corrects Northern European distortions of Spain but abstains from a universality that would conceal the violence of its particularity.

Thus, *España defendida* reads less as a definition of a "national Thing" than as a deconstruction of the inherently evil Spanish character that feeds the *leyenda negra*. Obviously, Quevedo's text could be (and has been) read as an ultrapatriotic defense, but I find it more timely and meaningful in the context of this chapter to reinscribe him in terms of what, following Michel de Certeau, we may refer to as a heterological tradition in the West (1986). As the subtitle puts it, *De las calumnias de los noveleros y sediciosos* [Of the slander of the newsmongers and the seditious], his defense would make manifest the rhetoric that defames Spain in historicogeographical descriptions like Mercator's *Atlas*. As a defense, Quevedo's text lacks the objectivist logic that measures blame and demands restitution.

We must account for an unspoken moral economy of violence that not only measures the justice implanted through punitive reprisals but also draws differentiations in terms of race, religion, or nationality. The difference between *inimicus* (personal enemy) and *hostis* (public enemy) may be pertinent to the specific treatments Europeans reserve for each other and for Indians. Indeed, the distinction between the God of wrath and of love, between the Old and the New testament, has as much to do with what Nietzsche defined as "the brilliant stroke of Christianity: God's sacrifice of himself for man . . . ; the creditor offers himself as a sacrifice for his debtor" (1956: 225), as with a distinction between *inimicus* and *hostis*.[18] Nietzsche's definition of Christianity is certainly pertinent to Lestringant's characterization of Calvinist history in terms of "the primacy of individual conscience, free and sovereign" (1990: 17). If one forgives an *inimicus* but destroys a *hostis*, the balance (the measure of guilt and debt) assesses damages within a moral economy of revenge. Whereas conflict among Europeans moves from *inimicus* to *hostis*, Amerindians are first conceptualized as *hostis*. Friendliness depends on Amerindian willingness to accept the Christian civilizing drive, the gifts of death: trinkets and self-sacrifice.

Thus Laudonnière's preface to his history of the voyages speaks in terms of profiting, civilizing, and converting: "Pour ceste cause les princes ont faict partir de leurs terres quelques hommes de bonne enterprise, pour s'habituer en pays estranges, y faire leur proffit, civilizer le pays, et si possible estoit, reduire les habitans à la vraye cognoissance de nostre Dieu" [So, monarchs have sent out enterprising persons to establish themselves in distant lands to make profit, to civilize the countryside, and, if possible to bring the local inhabitants to the true knowledge of God] (in Lussagnet 1958, 2: 35; Laudonnière 1975: 5). Laudonnière contrasts this colonial model with those driven by tyrannical and Roman (Spanish implied) ambition. Let us not be deceived by this "civilizing" mission, however, for Laudonnière also views violence as an option for those colonial enterprises that promote "la police universelle de tous les hommes, et taschent de les unir les uns avcques les autres tant par commerces et conversations foraines que par vertus militaires, lors que les estrangers ne veulent entendre à leur tant salutaire devoir" [the universal well-being of all people, and try to bring unity one with the other, more by foreign commerce and communication than by military measures, except when these foreigners do not want to pay attention to their obligations that are so beneficial to them] (2:35; 4–5). One thing is for sure in this globalizing vocation: Whether one succeeds or not in communicating the true knowledge of God, accepting the gift of "civilization" is not a choice but an obligation. There is, moreover, a calculated investment in a patient introduction of Christianity (hence civilization): "Ils ont tousjours prosperé en leurs entreprise, et petit à petit gaigné le coeur de ceux qu'ils avoient surmontez ou pratiquez par quelque moyen" [And so they have always nurtured enterprises and bit by bit gained the hearts of those conquered or won over by other means] (2:35; 5). Insofar as the debt can only be ransomed by the Christian God, Amerindians must accept Europeans as their creditors. They are obligated to feed them, to obey them—out of love. The so-called French (actually drawn from the Portuguese) model of colonization based on trade and peaceful settlements assumes this acceptance of love (see Lestringant 1990: 17–18, 258–61 and passim). In this regard, the French documentation is not that different from Spanish legislation and its insistence on justice (see chapter 2), for in both cases, these "friendly" colonial gestures ultimately function as prefaces to war. Violence plays a role in both *la conquista* (the colonization of minds and bodies for labor) and *la conquête* (the colonization of land that disregards the local inhabitants). In either case, Indians are merely seen as part of the theater of hostilities. For in the scientific conquest of the world as image and in the assessment of one's performance in history, objectivity depends on a disciplining of subjectivity that is proportionate to the power to act and alter the world (see Heidegger 1977). Failure, error, and blame are always on the balance sheet.

Whereas the Spanish sources are very clear and self-righteous as regards the right to massacre and mutilate the corpses of the French intruders in terms that define them as *hostis* because of their Protestantism, the French elaborate a discourse that dwells in the passage from *inimicus* to *hostis,* the moral economy of justice, and the aesthetics of vengeance. Before examining these aspects, let's look briefly into a sacrificial body in Laudonnière's account of the first voyage: the disastrous end of Ribault's idyllic settlement.

The first settlement in Charlesfort fails because Indians refuse to feed the French, a fire destroys the fort and all their material belongings, and a state of anomie sets in which Captain Albert, to retain control, oppresses his own subjects. Captain Albert hangs a soldier named Guernache and banishes another named Lachère. The settlers revolt, kill the captain, elect Nicolas Barré as their commandant, and build a boat to return to France. On their return, as a result of extreme want, they decide that one of them has to be sacrificed to feed the rest. Lachère is killed and his flesh divided equally among his companions, an act of cannibalism that horrifies Laudonnière: "chose si pitoyable à reciter, que ma plume mesme diferé de l'escrire" [a thing so pitiful to recite that my pen is loath to write about it] (in Lussagnet 1958, 2: 79; Laudonnière 1975: 50). Laudonnière immediately moves on to praise *le bon Dieu* for changing their sorrow into joy as they sight land and are rescued by an English rowboat. In this event, as in those passages dwelling on the attack by the forces of Menéndez de Avilés, Laudonnière's account lacks physical details and the tone is characteristically distant.

Clearly, neither the cannibalization of Lechère nor the Spanish massacre of the Huguenots at the end of the third voyage seems to be proper subject matter. Laudonnière provides a brief account of the defense of the fort but abstains from describing the Spanish massacre, perhaps because he did not witness it, though more likely because it was not clear to him who would benefit from gore in a text directed not exclusively to Huguenots but to a general readership of Catholics and Protestants in France. If it is true that a vivid representation of the slaughter might have struck a Catholic reader as biased, as Lestringant has argued (1990: 163–64), it is also compelling to read the restraint as a blocking of his enemies' delight in the blood. A hostile reader could easily transform a text of mourning into one of celebration; martyrologies are not safe from prurient eyes.

Laudonnière solicits the judgment of "lecteurs equitables et non passionez" [objective and clear-thinking readers], and emphasizes that he has followed "la verité de l'histoire" [the truth of history] (in Lussagnet 1958, 2: 185; Laudonnière 1975: 169). His claims of objectivity cannot be dissociated from his responsibility for losing the support of the Indians, for their alliances with the Spaniards, for the loss of Fort Caroline, and, ultimately, for the massacre. His restraint in describing the cruelty of the Spaniards cannot be naïvely attributed to a specifically Protestant form of individual consciousness—a *liberté d'examen,* Lestringant would say—that lends itself to objectivity and value-free historical writing. Needless to say, appeals to veracity and objectivity (both as expressed by authors as well as by the Crown's instructions) are commonplaces in Spanish texts. In the balance is the amount of guilt Laudonnière should be accountable for, rather than a Protestant predisposition for objective truth: "Ce que je pretens discourir en ceste presente histoire avec une vérité si evidente, que la majesté du Roy mon prince, sera satisfaicte en partie du devoir que j'ay faict en son service, et mes calomniateurs se trouveront si descouverts en leur imposture mensongere, qu'ils n'auront aucun lieu pour se mantenir en droict" [All of this I intend to discuss in this account which I am writing, with a truthfulness so evident that my king will be satisfied in my part with the diligence that I have exerted in his service; and so that my enemies will have no place to hide in their untruths] (2: 36; 5).

This moral motivation obviously does not exclude a geographic objectification (renaming capes, rivers, and bays as well as identifying foodstuffs and animals and describing the terrain) nor ethnographic documentation (encoding linguistic, religious, and political orders). Rather than attributing Laudonnière's restraint to a particular vocation for historical objectivity, we ought instead to read a will to scramble previous territorializations by renaming places, peoples, and natural phenomena (and, in the case of Le Moyne, by visual representation). This objectification that seeks to erase previous mappings and thus claim mastery and possession will be the subject of the last section of this chapter.

For now, let us examine the politics and poetics of representations of massacres.

REPRESENTATION

Cruelty and massacre are among the favored terms used in French and English translations of the *Brevíssima,* but one wonders how the two can be singled out, and what their relationship is to torture. The watercolors and de Bry's copperplates dwell on particular passages in Las Casas that detailed the kinds of torture the Spaniards inflicted on the Indians. The illustrations depict scenes of war in the background, but the specificity of the depicted event as massacre seems to reside in its conceptual nature rather than in a particular mode of violence that lends itself to representation; we grasp the massacre in the portrayal of defenseless Indians. Clearly, neither the French nor the English shared Las Casas's anticolonial vehemence; their denunciation of Spanish cruelty ultimately points to the violence inflicted on the Protestants, calling for revenge and territorial rights to the New World. The Huguenot accounts as well as Chauveton's and La Popelinère's histories of Florida and the New World *react* to the massacres; they can hardly be considered *actions* designed to condemn massacre itself, and, furthermore, they also lack any concern about being perceived as resentful. In this light, the *objectivity* of the French historians, as defined by Lestringant, manifests a moral economy of vengeance.

The *force* (at once political and aesthetic) of de Bry's illustrations does not depend on adding information alien to Las Casas, but on how, as supplements, they displace the Indians as the central subject of the *Brevíssima;* rather than expressing compassion for Indians they promote hatred of Spaniards. In some of the plates, we find instances where the background scenes might not correspond to the location of the written text, but this disparity in itself reinforces the rhetorical strategies of the *Brevíssima,* which does not pretend to be a history but a political pamphlet. The lack of names of the Spanish conquerors—amply documented by Las Casas in the *Historia de las Indias*—suggests that the end of the *Brevíssima* was not to denounce the abuses committed by individual conquerors but the colonial enterprise as a whole: "Todos chicos y grandes andan a robar, unos mas, otros menos. Unos pública e abierta, otros secreta y paliadamente. Y con color de que sirven al rey, deshonran a Dios, y roban y destruyen al Rey" [All, young and old, are occupied in pillage, some more, some less. Some publicly and openly, others secretly and stealthily. And with the pretense that they serve the king, they dishonor God, and rob and destroy the king] (1991 [1552]: 80). Written after the failed reform of the 1542 Nuevas Leyes, these closing statements mark a transition to a Las Casas who came to condemn Spain's presence in the New World and colonialism in general.[19] The *Brevíssima* is neither a history nor a learned treatise on canonical law, but an inflammatory tract. Likewise, the visual text does not purport to evince the historical accuracy of verbal descriptions but to buttress the moral outrage expressed in the narrative with a Protestant audience in mind: the illustrations seek to capture the Spanish fury that could devastate the Low Countries, and not this or that maltreatment of particular Indians.

It is not a coincidence that Figure 12 (and plate II) depicts

Figure 12. "Indians in pink," in Bartolomé de Las Casas, *Tyrannies et cruautez des Espagnols, perpetrees es Indes Occidentales, qu'on dit le Nouveau monde: Brievement descrites en langue Castillane, par l'Evesque Don Frere Bartelemy de Las Casas ou Casaus, Espagnol de l'ordre de sainct Dominique, fidelement traduites par Iacques de Miggrode.* Illustrated manuscript (1582). Courtesy of the Clements Library, University of Michigan.

Indians as pink rather than brown nor that the ubiquity of red clothing reinforces the spattered blood. Because watercolors and engravings are independent forms of expression with their own specific vocabulary, the passage from watercolor to copperplate entails a translation primarily concerned with retaining the expressive force of light and color. The luminosity and brilliance of the watercolors had to be reinterpreted in terms of a chiaroscuro with a tonal range between black and white (fig. 13). This translation can also be appreciated in the differences between this copperplate and the black-and-white photograph of plate II, which lacks the dramatic shadings of the copperplate. The artistry and expressiveness of the watercolors must have posed a challenge to the engravers,

Figure 13. "Indians in chiaroscuro," in Bartolomé de Las Casas, *Narratio Regionum Indicarum per Hispanos quosdam devastatarum verissima*. Translated and illustrated by Théodore de Bry and Jean Israël de Bry, 1598.

who faced the task of assessing color values and symbols in terms of lines and tones. The fury expressed by red is conveyed by a somberness defined by tones that range from the light, tormented Indians to the darker Spaniards, who, as they impassively contemplate torture and mutilation, embody irredeemable evil. De Bry compensates for the lack of color with the realism achieved in the photographic quality of the copperplates, where shades, tones, and linear resolution translate luminosity and brilliance, a realism that woodcuts could obviously never achieve. If the physique of the Indians is Greco-Roman, as scholars of de Bry unfailingly indicate, sharpness in bodily definition had its match in the use of color in the 1582 manuscript. In either case, the tortured subjects of the visual texts lose their Indianness, ultimately materializing the visual metaphor on the title page to the 1579 French translation (the manuscript also incorporates the verses into its own title page):

Heureux celuy qui devient sage
En voyant d'autruy le dommage.
[Fortunate are those who become wise
Seeing the misfortunes of others.]

Tom Conley has observed that the nakedness of the Indians codes them as inferior and thus lends the images to a prurient gaze on the details of torture or of nubile Indian women (1992: 108–10). But the nakedness might simply underscore the pain of a tortured body and not necessarily an Indian, especially if we take into account Protestants identifying with the victims. Moreover, if nakedness is a commonplace in paintings of martyrdoms and stripping victims a common practice in torture, it is not uncommon to find the fury of massacre and torture made manifest by representing the executioners naked in, for example, Baccio Bandinelli's *The Martyrdom of St. Lawrence* or Raphael's *The Massacre of the Innocents* (see Hults 1996: 168–70). Furthermore, both the watercolor and de Bry's engravings depict the executioners of Atahualpa partially naked. At any rate, representations of violence are, needless to say, always subject to viewings that might derive pleasure from depictions of subjects in pain. And it is on the basis of a (mis)viewing that Conley identifies de Bry's distortion of Las Casas's message; for instance, I do not see in Figures 12 and 13 the stake that, according to Conley, "enters the victim's rectum" (1992: 110). I am not suggesting that inserting stakes into rectums was not a common torture among Spaniards and other Europeans, as manifest in Ercillas's account of Caupolicán's torture, but that this particular torture is not represented in this image and clearly is not an element of sadism introduced by de Bry, as Conley claims. There is no need to add sadism, for sixteenth-century Europeans simply were openly sadistic when executing massacres and tortures.[20]

It should be evident from the above discussion of massacre and torture that our concern with the watercolors in the 1582 manuscript and the engravings in the 1598 edition of de Bry is not with misrepresentations of the Spaniards, or of the Indians for that matter. I find disingenuous those notions that put too much weight on how power is exercized through some sort of will to misrepresent, to err, as it were. The power of stereotypes resides in their trans-

Writing Violence on the Northern Frontier

parency: they lose their hold once they are perceived as such (see Bhabha 1986). Indeed, we must differentiate between error in representations of the world and willful distortions with a symbolic value that never pretended to mimic external reality. Correcting representations from another era on the basis of present knowledge always runs the risk of mistaking categories, reading aesthetic or symbolic forms in cognitive terms, for instance. Misrepresentation, moreover, presumes a correct or more accurate representation and thus eschews the issue of how knowledge (supposedly more true) buttresses mastery, possession, and domination. The symbolic and the aesthetic are also modes of establishing mastery, but the power of these forms does not reside in a cognitive error but in the specific emotive and psychophysiological effects they seek to engender. Representation is indissolubly bound to objectification, wherein power is coterminous with our will to believe its accuracy or recognize (even if negatively) its appropriateness. It would be a mistake, however, to judge the accuracy of the watercolor on the basis of the Spaniards' red clothing, when redness aims to convey the fury of the massacre and promote hatred for Spaniards. Likewise, the pinkness of the Indians and the classical human forms in the engravings function on a metaphorical plane: the tortured Indians stand for what will happen to Protestants if they let in the Spaniards.

Thus, the illustrations to Las Casas come into play with Protestant martyrologies, not to lament the fate of the Indians, but to imagine a reversal of lots—that is, imagining Spaniards and members of the Catholic League tortured and massacred. An epigraph to the 1656 English translation of the *Brevíssima* conveys this symbolic transference: "Therefore thine eye shall have no compassion; but life for life, tooth for tooth, hand for hand, foot for foot."[21] As for the Protestant denunciations and vivid descriptions of Saint Bartholomew's Day massacres, the call for vengeance could not be more explicit in Simon Goulart's first page to his *Mémoires:* "La souuenance des massacres faits en plusieurs villes de france es mois de aout & septembre 1572 . . . fait desirer à plusieurs que la desloyaute des autheurs de ces massacres ne demuere càchee es tenebres d'oubliance, & que les executeurs des cruautez execrables soyent chastiez selon leur merite" [The memory of the massacres committed in several cities in the months of August and September of 1572 . . . made many wish that the treachery of the authors of these massacres not remain hidden in the shadows of forgetfulness and that the executioners of these abominable cruelties be punished as they deserved] (quoted and translated by Kingdon 1988: 4–5).

Nicolas Le Challeux's *Discours de l'histoire de la Floride* and the request to the king by the widows and orphans, first published in Dieppe in 1566 and included in Chauveton's translation of Benzoni in 1578, falls within this tradition of pamphlets calling for revenge. Because Le Challeux blames Laudonnière for the catastrophic end of Charlesfort, his account has its own claims to objectivity within a moral economy of guilt. Le Challeux does not spare us any details in his description of how Menéndez de Avilés first betrayed the Protestants and then cut their throats, hung them from trees, and, in the case of Jean Ribault, quartered his head and stuck the parts on pikes at the four corners of the fort. Ribault's beard was sent as a missive to the king of Spain. Le Challeux apparently did not witness the massacre, but that did not keep him from adding gory details about how the Spaniards, not content with the execution, went on to pull the eyes from the cadavers, to puncture them with daggers, and afterwards, with cries, howls, and trumpets, to thrust the bodies into the water toward the French, who observed the events from the other side of the river.

The Protestants did not initially view the Spaniards as *hostis*. On the contrary, Le Challeux emphasizes how they followed the instructions of their king to avoid Spanish territories, and condemns the injustice of the massacre on these grounds: "Nous avons gardé et observé inviolablement le comendament du Roy, et ne pouvez dire contre nous, que nous avons esté la cause du massacre que vous avez fait de nos hommes: contre tout usage de guerre" [We have kept and observed without violation the king's orders, and you cannot say against us that we are the cause of the massacre you committed of our men: against all the customs of war] (in Lussagnet 1958, 2: 220; my translation). Though Le Challeux denounces these actions as contrary to all principles of warfare, he does not hesitate to call for vengeance. It was not the cruelty that he condemned, but the legal framework. According to the Huguenot settlers, French claims to Florida were legitimate, and, in conformance with the instruction of their king, they had built Fort Carolina outside Spanish jurisdiction.

The appeal by the widows and orphans also denounces the Spaniards' cruelty for breaking both human and divine law: "La cruauté de Petremelande Espagnol [Pedro Menéndez de Avilés], est contraire à toutes factions de la guerre, et à toutes loix et ordonnances qui jamais ayent esté receuës, ni de Dieu ni des hommes" [The cruelty of Petremelande Espagnol (Pedro Menéndez de Avilés) goes against all proceedings in war, and all the laws and statutes that have ever been received, either from God or from men] (in Lussagnet 1958, 2: 235; my translation). They call for countermassacre to relieve their pain with the sweetness and consolation one derives from taking revenge: "leur assister avecques telle douceur et consolation" [to relieve them with such sweetness and consolation] (2:234). They describe in detail the mutilation of the bodies of men, women, and children and the affront to Ribault in hopes of moving the king to avenge them:

> Parquoy s'il fut jamais memoire d'humanité, compassion et misericorde, les supplians esperent que nostre Dieu par sa bonté en touchera si vivement vostre coeur, que vostre majesté se voudra ressentir de nos justes doleances et pitoyables complaintes, embrassera nostre fait pour en rendre justice, . . . qui sera une oeuvre de pieté, digne de vostre vocation et un effet de charité envers vos povres subjets et fideles serviteurs, pour afin d'adoucir l'amertume de leurs afflictions. (2:239)
> [If there has ever been in the world humanity, compassion, and mercy, the suppliant hope that our God in all His goodness will touch your heart so vividly that your majesty, moved by our just pain and sad complaint, will embrace our cause to bring us justice, . . . which will be a pious deed, worthy of your vocation and an act of charity toward your poor subjects and faithful servants, so that it will sweeten the bitterness of their afflictions.]

Neither Charles IX nor Catherine of Medici were particularly moved by these accounts of the massacre. The 1568 punitive expedition of Dominique de Gourgues was a private Protestant initiative. If Gourgues seems to have been a Catholic during this period of his life, the prayer at the end of the *Histoire mémorable de la reprinse de la Floride* indicates that on this occasion, as put by Charles-André Julien, "[Gourgues] s'entoura de protestant et s'exprima en protestant" [(Gourgues) surrounded himself with Protestants and expressed himself in Protestant] (in Lussagnet 1958, 2: 251).

The *Histoire mémorable de la reprinse de la Floride* recalls the gore of Le Challeux and the widows' call for justice with atrocities worthy of the *Brevíssima:* "Les femme furent ouvertes pour en tirer le fruict, disant qu'ils vouloyent exterminer les Luthériens" [The women were opened up to extract the fruit, saying that they wanted to exterminate the Lutherans] (in Lussagnet 1958, 2: 242; my translation). Thus, the *Histoire mémorable* first instigates hatred and justifies revenge, and then gives an account of the exemplary punishment of the Spaniards to gratify the reader's desire for vengeance.

The version in Basanier's 1586 edition of Laudonnière's *Histoire notable* adds that Gourgues, in the place where Menéndez de Avilés had posted a sign saying, obviously in Spanish, "Je ne fay cecy comme à François, mais comme à Lutheriens" [I do not do this to you as French, but as Lutherans], put up a sign saying, "Je ne fay cecy comme à Espagnols, ny comme à Mariniers, mais comme à traistres, voleurs, et meurdriers" [I do not do this to you as Spaniards, nor as Sailors, but as traitors, thieves, and murderers] (in Lussagnet 1958, 2:197; cf. Solís de Merás 1989: 251). Scholars generally dispute the historicity of these signs, but their significance can be read in terms of the political climate that followed the Saint Bartholomew's Day massacres. This contrast between Menéndez de Avilés's definition of the Huguenots as *hostis* because of their religion and Gourgues's appeal to justice because of the Spaniards' criminal behavior ironically entails a defamation of the Spanish character and a conciliatory message to the Politique Party, which opposed the religious zeal of the pro-Spanish Catholic League (see Lestringant 1990: 230). This passage can be read, then, as a warning of what occurs when one lets the Spaniards into one's country, not unlike Miggrode's advice in the *Tyrannies et cruautez des Espagnols,* where the citizens of the Low Countries will see "comme en vn tableau quel sera leur estat quand par leur nonchallanc, querelles, divisions & partialitez ils auront ouvert la porte à un tel ennemy" [as in a painting what will be their state when because of their nonchallance, quarrels, division and partialities they will have opened the gate to such an enemy] (Las Casas 1579: 2v). This signing and countersigning has an equivalence in the *Histoire mémorable* where justice and its objectivity call for a moral economy of punishment: "Les payèrent de mesme monnoye qu'ils avoyent payé les François" [They paid them with the same coin they had paid the French] (Lussagnet 1958, 2: 248). Here we have a clear and unabashed instance of compensation as a legal warrant entitling one nation to exercise its cruelty against another.

If we are to trace in these texts the origins of modernity in a secular discourse supposedly inaugurated by Protestantism, we must retrace its origins to a moral economy of vengeance and cruelty in the administration of justice and punishment. The Spanish sources, of course, do not spare us the gore and, indeed, expect us to delight in the cunning of Menéndez de Avilés and the execution of the French (Solís de Merás 1989: 162–65). Bartolomé Barrientos's description of the killing of Ribault solicits complicity: "Abiendoselas Atado [las manos] y marchando Vn poco adelante, El capitan sant bicente le dio Vna puñalada En la olla, y gonzalo solis le atraueso por los pechos Con Vna pica que lleuaua, y cortaronle la caueza" [Having tied up (his hands) and walking a bit ahead, Captain Saint Vicente stabbed him on the head and Gonzalo Solís pierced him through the chest with a lance he was carrying, and they cut off his head] (in Solís de Merás 1989: 69). There are apparently no extant Spanish or French visual images of the massacre and countermassacre in Florida. Pictorial renditions of other massacres, in particular of the Saint Bartholomew's Day massacre, enable us to approximate the particular sensibilities of Protestants and Catholics.

Catholics cultivated visual representation in their propaganda campaigns both as victims and as perpetrators of massacres. Take, for instance, Pope Gregory XIII's commission of a series of paintings by Giorgio Vasari for the Sala Regia of the Vatican to celebrate the massacre of Saint Bartholomew (fig. 14). Detailed expressions of terror and pictorial mastery infuse an aesthetic distance that positions the viewer as witnessing a scene from Doomsday. The Greco-Roman helmet and attire of the soldier in the foreground of the panel introduces a mythological dimension that evokes the angel of doom. The panel situates the viewer as a righteous participant in the spirit of the massacre.[22] In contrast to the

Figure 14. Giorgio Vasari,
The Night of St. Bartholomew,
ca. 1572, second panel of the
series commissioned by Pope
Gregory XII for the Sala Regia
in the Vatican Palace. Courtesy
of Fratelli Alinari.

Figure 15. François Dubois d'Amiens, *La Saint Barthélemy à Paris,* ca. 1572. Musée Arlaud, Lausanne. Lithography by A. Duruy (1878). Cabinet des Estampes. Courtesy of the Bibliothèque nationale de France.

immediacy of Vasari's painting, Protestant representations of Saint Bartholomew's Day massacres, such as the painting by François Dubois, a Huguenot survivor who had taken refuge in Switzerland, cluttered the painting with as many individual scenes of treachery as would fit in a broad panorama that includes multiple perspectives and locations in Paris (fig. 15). The viewers are thus forced first to apprehend the totality of the massacre and then to move on to contemplate (and mourn) specific events. As it seeks to capture the fury of the Catholics, it casts the sublime in the mode of a martyrdom, whereby the painting would evoke Divine Providence for the viewer in the mode of a Calvinist moral economy of deserved punishment for sinning—obviously not as a manifestation of God's favor for the Catholic murderers. The murder of Admiral Coligny figures near the center of the painting. By representing Guise pointing at the decapitated body of Coligny, Dubois would have us read the mutilation as ordered by Guise, where a more conciliatory representation would have excluded the decapitation (see Noguères 1962: 83).[23] Dubois's depictions of corpses lying on the floor, dragged with ropes around their neck, piled up in wagons, and thrown into the Seine not only lack the precision and virtuosity of Vasari's panel, but never lend themselves to a detached view as they are overdetermined by the initial perception of the whole scene.

This representation complements the verbal descriptions in texts such as Simon Goulart's *Mémoires* by enabling illiterate Protestants to mourn the massacred. It is perhaps an index of the Protestants' understanding of the power of the printing press that copperplates were never made of this painting, limiting the viewing of it to that accepted by Protestant premises. Note that the lithograph I follow in this discussion is from 1873. On the other hand, Vasari's panels, commemorative medals, and the thanksgiving procession headed by Gregory XIII on 8 September (the massacre took place before dawn on 24 August) indicate that the Catholic authorities as well as the general public were hardly vulnerable to the inflammatory rhetoric of the Protestant pamphleteers.[24]

Jesuit pamphlets such as Richard Verstegan's *Le théâtre des cruautés des hérétiques de notre temps* (1587) and Louis Richome's *La Peincture espirituelle, ou l'Art d'admirer, aimer et lour Dieu en totutes ses ouvres* (1611), who based his engravings on a painting, not in existence today, at the Jesuit novitiate in Rome, celebrate martyrdom (Verstegan 1995 [1587]; Lestringant 1996). Though Verstegan's aquafortes lack the precise details of Vasari's panels, de Bry's engravings, or even Dubois's painting, they anticipate viewers who would appreciate their beauty. Verstegan provides a clue as to why the Jesuits had no qualms about massively circulating these images: "Bienheureux seront ceux à qui Dieu fera cette faveur, car telle mort se tournera en très heureuse vie, cette douleur en plaisir, cette absinthe en miel et ce tourment en très gracieux contentement" [Blessed will be those to whom God gives this grace, since such a death will turn into a very blessed life, such pain into pleasure, such absinthe into honey and such torment into graceful contentment] (62). Because Protestants will surely want to deter Catholics from entering this "theater" ("pource que les hérétique vous dégoûteront d'entre en ce theatre") and will remind Catholics of their own killings on Saint

Bartholomew's Day, Verstegan makes a distinction between the deaths: "La mort de ceux qu'ils appelent leurs frères en impiété, n'a eu rien d'extraordinaire que la mort" [The death of those whom they call their brothers in impiety, holds nothing more extraordinary than death itself] (62–63). A laconic phrase by Richome perhaps best captures the Catholic aesthetic of martyrdom that would neutralize, indeed capitalize on, a potentially hateful Protestant eye: "La mort cause d'allegresse" [Death a source of joy] (in Lestringant 1996: 253).

MASTERY AND POSSESSION

The column is not the same thing as the colossus. Unless they have in common only the fact that they are not things. —Jacques Derrida, *The Truth in Painting*

Where knowledge would no longer imply property, nor action mastery, nor would property and mastery imply their excremental results and origins. —Michel Serres, *The Natural Contract*

By juxtaposing these two passages from Derrida and Serres I want to connect the sublime with the excremental in Le Moyne's watercolor depicting the Indian chief Athore showing Laudonnière the marker column set up by Ribault (fig. 16). The colossal (the sublime as unmeasurable) and the excremental (the setting of boundaries) coexist in this miniature by Le Moyne (180×260 mm). Whereas color is integral to the beauty of the painting, its small dimensions tease a sense of the sublime as unmeasurable not necessarily in size but in concept. Rather than questioning the veracity of the colors or even the ethnographic accuracy of the items depicted, we should see this painting not as a representation of reality but as having no referent beyond the mishmash of apparently contradictory things.

I argue that the painting does not pretend to make a realistic use of color nor even to identify the baskets and fruits as American ("very improbable—really impossible—for Florida," the description in the catalogue of the exhibit reminds us [Le Moyne 1977, 1: 163]), but to inscribe a logic of sacrifice and gift.[25] Not unlike the thin golden frame, which signifies nothing beyond infusing a uto-

Figure 16. Jacques Le Moyne, *Laudonnierus et Rex Athore ante columnam prima navigatione locatam quamque veneratur Floridenses,* ca. 1564. Gouache with metallic pigments. Courtesy of Print Collection, Miriam and Ira D. Wallach Division of Arts, Prints and Photographs, The New York Public Library, Astor, Lenox and Tilden Foundations.

pian aura of brightness into the scene (in the manner of a nimbus), the meaning of colors is symbolic; parallelly we ought to resist seeing the depicted fruits as inaccurate representations of commodities indigenous to the "land." Indeed, these offerings transform the column from a mere marker of possession into a colossal idol, a full sign of mastery. Le Moyne's commentary (which de Bry included in his copperplate engraving and attributed to Le Moyne) reads: "Drawing close they noticed that the Indians were worshipping this stone as if it were an idol. . . . After witnessing the rites of these poor savage people they returned to their comrades with the intent to search out the most suitable site for building a fort" (1: 141). In representing the offerings as idolatrous, Le Moyne invests France's emblematic column with an irresistible, mesmerizing power. The idolatrous behavior would eventually be corrected with a Christian interpretation of French authority and right to possess the land. If Laudonnière's dress and staff of authority seem to further document the Indians' recognition of French signs of mastery, Athore's raised arm, perhaps unwittingly on the part of Le Moyne, establishes—to borrow Derrida's poignant phrase—"the measure of its erection," the limits of the column's magical effect on the Indians.

Following this reading, one could say that the painting juxtaposes a French excremental claim of possession and an Indian celebration of a new pact with the world (see Seed 1995: 58–59). (Let us recall that the word *mojón* in Spanish means both a landmark and a piece of solid excrement.) "Amnesiacs that we are," writes Serres about idolatry, "we believe that they adored the god or goddess sculpted in stone or wood. No: they were giving to the thing itself . . . the power of speech" (1995: 47). Whereas the Indians would reinscribe the column as one more item in their communication with the world, Le Moyne's attribution of idolatry blends them into nature as one more item in the theater of hostilities of the colonial wars between European powers. The illusion of idolatrous behavior as an adoration of the column inevitably bars access to the subjectivity of the Indians, setting in motion a conflict between an economy of gift and one of commodities. Le Moyne's verbal description of Athore as a noble savage introduces a dual register into the watercolor: "an incredibly handsome man, intelligent, reliable, strong, of exceptional height, exceeding our tallest man by a foot and a half, and endowed with a certain restrained dignity, so that in him a remarkable majesty shone forth" (1977, 1: 141). We have seen above how Genaro García praised the French precisely for this sort of representation of the Indians, but here I wish to project an Indian subjectivity that would question Western notions of idolatry and commodity exchange.

Only by resisting the realist impulse to read the painting as a (mis)representation of Indians and products from Florida do we begin to perceive the symbolic import of the objects represented. Those apparent mistakes, the fantastic use of color in the paleness of the Indians (even if the Timucas were [are] fairly light, perhaps coded by Le Moyne's "incredibly handsome man," no source speaks of them as phantomlike),[26] as well as in the blue and gold attire of Laudonnière (which, by the way, matches the colors of the French insignia) and the gilded helmets of the soldiers behind him, for instance, constitute self-referential signs that certify the establishment of a colony: "After witnessing the rites . . . they [the French] returned to their comrades with the intent to search out the most suitable site for building a fort" (Le Moyne 1977, 1: 141). This scene, which legitimates French claims to Florida, forms part of a sequence that narrates the selection of a suitable place to build Fort Caroline. Indians are instrumental as allies, but hardly an end in themselves. The inclusion of an equally fantastic bow with a "bowstring touched with gold" and "a skin quiver, blue outside, yellowish shaded with reddish brown inside, full of arrows," to borrow the catalogue's vivid description, manifests the importance of Indian alliances rather than depicting the gift of a specific Indian weapon (1: 163).

By combining native and European products, Le Moyne projects a land of plenty where Europeans could grow commodities needed in the metropolis rather than record their existence in the New World. Thus, the painting would lend support to the mercantilist policies of the younger Richard Hakluyt's *Discourse of Western Planting* (1584) or the elder's "Pamphlet for the Virginia Enterprise" (1585), where they argue the need to develop colonies in lands with climates that lend themselves to growing products for which England depended on Spain (e.g., wine, olive oil, sugar). In fact, as the elder Hakluyt put it to Queen Elizabeth, the business would go both ways because Virginia, "standing in the same degree that The Shroffe the Olive doth in Spaine, we may win that merchandise, graffing the wilde" (in E. G. R. Taylor 1967 [1935]: 335), would become a market for English manufactured goods: "Receiving the salvage women and their children of both sexes into your protection, and imploying the English women and the others in making Linnen, you shal raise a wonderful trade of benefit, both to carie into England and also into the Islands, and into the main of the West Indies, victual and labour being so cheap there" (336). Though not represented, the invisible "message" of Le Moyne's painting implies that the naked "savages" will become both an inexpensive labor force ("labour being so cheap there") for growing and extracting natural resources to take to England and consumers of English merchandise, as they will dress in English linen. We must recall that the Hakluyts' colonial project builds on Le Moyne's as well as Laudonnière's accounts of Florida. For instance, the younger Hakluyt, in the dedication to Raleigh of his translation of Laudonnière, mentions Le Moyne's paintings as a supplementary source of information: "The skillful painter James Morgues . . . which was an eye-witness of the goodness & fertility of those regions, & hath put downe in writing many singularities which are not mentioned in this treatise" (373). Seen in this light, the painting of Laudonnière and Athore testifies to the fertility of the land, thereby promoting "western planting." Le Moyne's paintings and maps further contributed to Hakluyt's claims of English rights to North America. Insofar as they certified a pattern of settlement, even if by the French, they served to undo Spanish claims of exclusivity. England thus appropriates the documents of what could have been a French colonial enterprise, but Hakluyt also drew information from Spanish sources to debunk the legality of Spain's possessions. Accordingly, in a letter to Raleigh, Hakluyt first establishes "the bay of Chesepians, to wch latitude Peter Martyr, and francisco lopez de Gomara the spaniard confess that our Cabot and English did first discover," and then goes on to claim New Mexico: "antonio de Espejo bringeth yo^w to rich mines in the country in the latitude of 37 1/2" (355).

Although the French never successfully established a colony in Florida, the Huguenot accounts as well as the theoretical writings of La Popelinière and Chauveton proved invaluable to the English. We can only mention this topic here. Both La Popelinière (1582: 50v) and Chauveton (1579: 23) argue that the English have more rights over North America than does Spain, and Chauveton establishes that possession depends on the continuous occupation of the land and not on the donation of the pope, or for that matter the imposition of mastery by force (3–11). Whereas Le Moyne's miniature of Laudonnière and Athore establishes symbolically a memory of possession and occupation, his maps reterritorialize the land with new names for such natural phenomena as rivers, hills, and capes, and his chorographies locate forts and friendly Indian villages that attest to continuous presence and mastery. Hakluyt commissioned

John White to continue this form of appropriation through visual representation: "A skilfull painter is also to be carried with you, which the Spaniards use commonly in all their discoveries to bring the descriptions of all beasts, birds, fishes, trees, townes, &c" (in E. G. R. Taylor 1967 [1935]: 338). Although the Spanish visual archive contains extensive and detailed information about its imperial possessions, the use of watercolors and copperplates defines a particularly Northern European form of symbolic appropriation. It is not simply a question of recording knowledge, but of rendering it in a beautiful manner. Thus Le Moyne's watercolors, but also de Bry's engravings and the watercolors of the 1582 manuscript, testify to aesthetics as a key mode of colonization and appropriation. Garcilaso knew this all too well when he deplored the loss of Florida and sought to regain the territory with equally courageous and gallant Indians and Iberians (his praise especially singled out the Portuguese participants). Garcilaso also knew, or at least sought to establish, that the colonial contest over Florida was actually over the nature of justice and the historical memory of the contending European as well as Indian nations—hence *La Florida*'s relentless questioning of *limpieza de sangre* and *hidalguía* as a deeper current that formulates a discourse of tolerance based on compassion rather than political expediency.

Implicit in Le Moyne's scene of the "contact zone" is a rhetoric of anticonquest that constitutes both Huguenots and Indians as victims of Spanish barbarism (see Pratt 1992). Like the other Protestant sources, Le Moyne's written account described in detail Menéndez de Avilés's treacherous massacre, but abstained from visually representing it. Le Moyne reserves painting for reterritorialization. On the plane of discourse, the massacre could be used to defame Spain and debunk its territorial claims, but what could be a better record of possession and mastery than a chorography depicting Ribault's column (fig. 17) or the painting where Athore embraces Laudonnière as he shows him the monumental marker? These visual representations are clear instances of objectifying devices, but they have little to do with historical objectivity as a form of neutral discourse. The moral economy of vengeance has its complement in a parasitic discourse of possession. In the trials of history, English mercantilism will have the upper hand as an economic policy that led to

Writing Violence on the Northern Frontier

6

IN naves tamen regreßi, & in illis traducta unica nocte, Præfectus limitem columnæ in-
star excisum, in quo sculpta erant Regis Galliæ insignia, in cymbam exonerari jubet, ut eum
amænißimo aliquo loco collocaret: quo peracto, & tria circiter miliaria in Occidentem versus emensi, fluviolum observarunt, quem ingreßi tamdiu navigarunt, ut tandem in majo-
rem fluminis alveum relabi, atque parvam insulam à continente sejunctam conficere, com-
pererint. In hanc descendentes, perspecta ejus summa amænitate, ex Præfecti mandato, columna in nudo quodam tumulo collocata fuit: deinde binos ingentis magnitudinis cervos, præ ijs quos hacte-
nus conspexerunt, invenerunt, quos facile tormentaria pyxide occidißent, nisi Præfectus, singulari eorum
magnitudine delectatus, vetuißet: antequam vero cymbam conscenderent, fluviolo parvam insulam cingenti
Liburni nomen indiderunt. Conscensa cymba, aliam insulam non procul à prima distitam perlustrare vo-
luerunt: sed cùm in ea nihil præter celsißimas cedros, quibus pares in ea regione non viderant, reperißent, Ce-
drorum insulam propterea appellarunt; deinde ad sua navigia reuersi sunt. Parva insula in qua columna
erecta fuit, hac nota F. insignita est.

B

Figure 17. Jacques Le Moyne, *Gallorum Prefectus columnam, in qua Regis
Galliarum insignia, statuit,* in *Brevis narratio eorum quade in Florida quade in
Americae Provincia Gallis, America, pars secunda.* Translated and illustrated
by Théodore de Bry and Jean Israël de Bry, 1591.

the ruin of Spain. But in the interstices of Le Moyne's painting we find, reading against the discourse of idolatry, the celebration of an Indian pact with the world that located the French marker within an economy of the gift. This glimpse at the ritual of gift in a scene of mastery and possession may suggest a reading of history where we no longer privilege science as the arbiter of truth: "Science alone now has all the rights" (Serres 1995: 85). By attending to the symbolic import of visual and verbal representations we avoid the pitfalls of privileging truth values of science, which has led scholars to find errors where the end was not to mimic reality. And this is not to say that symbols do not play a constitutive role in our perception of the world; otherwise, the *leyenda negra* would be just that, a mere *leyenda,* and not an oppressive form of racism.

Epilogue:

Before History

One cannot argue with modern bureaucracies and other instruments of governmentality without recourse to the secular time and narratives of history and sociology. The subaltern classes need this knowledge to fight their battles for social justice. It would therefore be unethical not to make historical consciousness available to everybody, in particular the subaltern classes. When has the International Monetary Fund or the United Nations listened to an argument involving the agency of the gods?—Dipesh Chakrabarty, "The Time of History and the Times of the Gods"

The only pure myth is the idea of a science devoid of all myth.
—Michel Serres, quoted in Bruno Latour,
We Have Never Been Modern

For Dipesh Chakrabarty, one has the ethical and political obligation to make historical consciousness available to subalterns. Only secular history will make sense to organizations such as the International Monetary Fund and the United Nations. Stories told from the perspective of the times of the gods are politically ineffective, but Chakrabarty also seems to exclude the possibility that subalterns learn to tell stories in the language of secular time inasmuch as he makes it the duty of the academic historian to convey the knowledge. Otherwise, why doesn't Chakrabarty specify that *we* (i.e., academics and subalterns alike) must learn to speak to modern bureaucracies? Does this need to speak the language of bureaucrats entail a capitulation of power by confining ourselves to addressing issues only in their terms? Does Chakrabarty's formulation entail that one cannot live in both the times of the gods and the time of history? To what extent does Chakrabarty's binary *times of the gods* versus *time of history* reproduce the imperialist language of the Enlightenment? What are the implications of this historical figure for the historian of the early modern period? Is Chakrabarty's profession of love for the subaltern a twentieth-century version of the violence we have identified in this book as "love speech"?

These questions seek to address the dilemma he poses at the beginning of his essay that we can sum up as follows: In order that writing subaltern history (documenting forms of resistance to oppression in which gods have agency in the world) partakes of the project of making the world more socially just, one must write in the realist mode of the social sciences. The subaltern historian faces two systems of thought, "one in which the world is *ultimately*, that is, in the final analysis, disenchanted, and the other in which humans are not the only meaningful agents" (Chakrabarty 1997: 35). Hence, the historian, as defined by Chakrabarty, faces a system of thought that is not his or her own, a world to be translated into a secular system. We can hardly do justice here to Chakrabarty's argument. I will limit myself to testing the necessity of the dilemma, to questioning the categories that make it a *real* dilemma rather than a paradox that vanishes under analysis.

The history of the epistemological violence that underlies Chakrabarty's definition of secular history dates back to the eighteenth century, when the time of progress aspired to silence all the gods, for good. It is a time when the Enlightenment constituted itself as the arbiter of scientific and historical knowledge and made it its mission to communicate the news on a global scale. For Chakrabarty, that today only secular time makes sense should be a fact obvious to the academic historian. But doesn't this amount to a circular argument insofar as history (the academic discipline) posits itself as the only possible form of understanding history (the incomplete project of capital)? According to Chakrabarty's definition of history, the task is to translate the (plural) times of the gods into secular time. From the point of view of the Enlightenment, the time of history is homogeneous, secular, calendrical, natural—not a particular code of representation. But Chakrabarty is not merely stating the inevitability of secular time, a position that would reiterate an imperialist hegemonic program. As a modality sensitive to cultural difference, the practice of writing subaltern history pursues an ethics and politics that "aims to take history, the code, to its limit in order to make its unworking visible" (Chakrabarty 1997: 58). But then, is *the making of a code of representation unworkable* the knowledge historians are ethically bound to convey to subalterns?

Under this formulation, the consolation of the subaltern historian, that is, of the history of subaltern groups, is that there is always an "outside" of global narratives of capital, an outside that Chakrabarty brilliantly formulates as "something that straddles a border zone of temporality, something that conforms to the temporal code within which 'capital' comes into being while violating that code at the same time" (1997: 57). In its strongest formulation, the times of the gods and the time of history are (theoretically speaking, for Chakrabarty) incommensurable. In a weaker version, translation entails a loss of the temporality of the "gods." Stories of what remains "outside" of capital breach the code of representation; however, the "gods" remain inaccessible to the historian. Ultimately, the subaltern is a figure that calls into question *the code of representation,* a figure of difference "that governmentality . . . all over the world has to subjugate and civilize" (56).

The subaltern as the "outside" of capital that questions the limits of representation, of what resists governmentality, is a negative figure. As negative figures, subalterns cannot be thought of as subjects that unmask outlaw states, as agents of history that embody the ideals of governmentality, as communities that express rightful dissent. Negativity bars subalterns from turning the Enlightenment against its own biases, by arguing the *human right* to live and express oneself in terms of the times of the gods. Under this formulation, the task of secular languages would not be limited to the representation or the translation of the times of the gods or, for that matter, to mapping the violation of the code. Rather, they may take reasoning to its ultimate consequences in the mode of "enlightened de-enlightenment" (see Rabasa 1998). Chakrabarty's definition of subaltern history implies that subalterns cannot be historians; once one drinks from the fountain of secular time, as it were, one is barred from the times of the gods. One of the greatest achievements of the Enlightenment has been to convince us that we can dwell in only one world. His formulation of subaltern history remains caught in a teleology in which there is only one possible *historical* world, even if this world is shot through by other forms of worlding and the end of subaltern history is to blast the

NB

homogeneity of secular time. It presupposes a theory of interpellation that never fails to hit its mark: we confirm the truth of modernity's exclusive claims to history in responding to its hail (see Butler 1997a). Thus, Chakrabarty excludes the possibility that one (a subaltern) may learn the language of secular time to address bureaucrats, priests, and teachers without necessarily abandoning the times of the gods. Chakrabarty's formulation of coexistence is theoretical (this and that world are possible), not existential (individual subalterns may dwell in two or more different worlds).

The coexistence of a plurality of worlds need not entail relativism, but rather (in a logical sense) a weak version of incommensurability. Take the following example: The time of history (as in the origin of Amerindians in Asia) and the times of the gods (as in the origin of the Nahuas in the seven caves of Aztlan) *speak* two different worlds, and do not, as it were, *utter* propositions that contend to make equally valid statements about one same world.[1] The secular historian can certainly reconstruct the route followed by the Nahuas as they migrated from Aztlan to central Mexico, but the experience of "magical" space and time coded in Nahua cartographic histories will always remain inaccessible to the historian and the anthropologist—for that matter, to the language of science. Within this formulation, translation proves to be a futile, indeed a violent task. To translate the times of the gods to the language of the time of history knowing and documenting the violence of translation—in the name of providing a service to subalterns—seems to be the dilemma of the historian who, like Chakrabarty, confines historical work to *representation* and its limits.[2]

One does not need, however, to be a *representational historian*—that is, one who defines the métier as one of reducing the time of the gods to secular time, even if to blast the homogeneity of the code—to think historically, and even less to *make* history. This book has examined the conjunction of writing with violence that grounded the political, ethical, and epistemological conquest of the Americas. The project of *writing violence* consists of analyzing how verbal and pictorial representations exert violence. We have examined historical accounts, an epic poem, legal tracts, and visual images pertaining to the colonization of Florida and New Mexico during the sixteenth century. In unveiling acts of violence in writing and painting, the project of writing violence violates the possibility of claiming value-free objectivity, aesthetic disinterest, peaceful colonization, and universal truths without acknowledging the codes that make these ideals seem natural. As I argued in the introduction and documented in the individual chapters, violence is at once symbolic and physical. Thus, the aim of this book has been to examine how writing produces subalternity, rather than offering a more accurate representation of subalterns. In a similar vein, Chakrabarty's proposal documents the ways in which writing violence continues to be exerted today, even from within the project of subaltern histories. After Frantz Fanon we have learned that the process of decolonization involves more than a mere transference of power from the metropolis to a native elite (Fanon 1967, 1968). We have become sensitive to creeping internal colonialisms that followed independence from European powers, and we have also learned to suspect the objectivity and the scientific claims of history, cartography, anthropology, and sociology. Paradoxically, the force of Chakrabarty's argument resides in making us aware of the violence of history, while insisting that "we cannot avoid writing history" (Chakrabarty 1997: 58).

The histories we have examined in this book were obviously written with historiographical criteria of truth and reality that were different from those of the Enlightenment and the mode of capitalism that consolidated thereafter. For one, the secular and the sacred coexist in their epistemology. Notwithstanding, the conquest of America partakes of a capitalist impulse to colonize the world on a global scale that Pierre Chaunu has traced back to the Portuguese and Spanish explorations of the Atlantic in the fourteenth and fifteenth centuries (see Chaunu 1969). In the process of expanding, Europe invented a whole series of technologies for the objectification of the world, including trade routes, mining methods, sailing ships, the compass, cartographic grids, writing genres, and legal apparatuses. The *objectification of the world* refers to the process of making the world an object of study, and not to the value-free type of history and scientific inquiry that characterizes the legacy of the Enlightenment. Early modern objectifications of the world openly display the interests, ideologies, and colonial failures that history after the Enlightenment erased from the surface of its representations of reality.

If sixteenth-century Europeans also sought to map out and thereby colonize the world on a global scale, the practice of writing history included among its objects of study the ontological reality of magic, the limits if not the impossibility of translating Amerindian "sacred times and spaces" into European "secular" languages, and the historicity of indigenous peoples. The binary "people with history" versus "peoples without history," the time of history versus the times of the gods, had not been formulated yet. Indeed, Divine Providence provided a script that called for a universal dissemination of the gospel, whereby territories were liberated from the devil as the Catholic Church consolidated its power. In this view of expiating the land of demons, however, Protestants and Catholics did no differ much; rather, their differences lay in the narratives they construed by tracing genealogies of Amerindians to one of the three children of Noah. Whereas for the Protestants, Amerindians descended from Ham and hence belonged to an irredeemable race, for the Catholics they descended from Japhet, hence the missionaries' obligation to convert them (see Lestringant 1990: 119–26). In the process, Catholicism's claims of universality constituted the inferiority of all other cultures, and thus placed the newly converted subjects as problematic neophytes. The historicity of Amerindians bound them to an inferior state even after conversion. In Catholic colonialism it was history, not biology, rather biological history that underlay racism. In this respect, the time of history has created the illusion that universalism and racism are opposites. However, as Etienne Balibar has shown, under scrutiny, universality manifests itself as one form of racism (1994). Let the binary universalism versus racism stand as one more instance of how the Enlightenment erases its particularisms, or better, the particularity of the world in which its sciences make sense.

In chapter 5 we traced in Garcilaso's critique of New World historiography an argument for a universalism that exposed the arbitrariness of the Estatutos de Limpieza de Sangre (Statutes of Blood Purity) and suggested a discourse of tolerance that drew its force from a politics of compassion. At the opposite end of Garcilaso, in chapter 6 we found that a moral economy of vengeance structured

NB

Writing Violence on the Northern Frontier

the desire for objectivity (the appropriate reciprocation of hatred and violence) in the Protestant corpus on the 1565 Spanish massacre of Huguenots in Florida. My point was not to oppose Garcilaso's Catholicism to Protestantism, but to propose that the discourse of tolerance (at least in a radical formulation that went beyond tolerating this or that group to avoid war) was an invention of minorities—such as Garcilaso and Spinoza—living in metropolitan centers. This gesture was furthermore informed by my desire to disrupt, even if slightly, the seamless narrative of a movement of universal history from the South to the North that, at least since Hegel, has been identified with the rise of Protestantism. This seamless narrative remains lodged in the secular history that Chakrabarty identifies as the unrefusable *gift* of the Enlightenment: "We cannot avoid writing history" (1997: 58). Perhaps not. Yet, we can certainly turn the Enlightenment against itself and argue that the incompatibility of the time of history and the times of the gods has no rational ground other than the Western desire to destroy all nonmodern cultures. Personal history also figures in the balance. Indeed, biography would seem to verify the effectiveness of imperial violence: "The workers' practices suggesting a belief in gods was no threat to my Marxism or liberalism" (41). One could reverse the phrase and conceive of a worker saying "My Marxism or liberalism was no threat to my belief in gods." And here we would also benefit from Bruno Latour and Michel Serres's reminder, cited above, that *we* (modern thinkers) have never been entirely secular.

In tracing writing violence in the descriptions of terror, massacres, and torture on the northern frontier of New Spain, I have outlined forms of thinking and structures of feeling that, if on the surface seem diametrically opposed to our sensibilities today, also exemplify ways the law (then as well as now) mediates the legitimacy of violence and the propriety of its representation. My critique of the oxymoron "peaceful conquest" (mainly in the introduction and chapters 1 and 2) conveyed the rhetorical finesse of Spanish colonial laws, which consisted of outlawing all use of violence except when unavoidable, and exposed modern historians and literary critics who, in taking the Crown's legislation against violence at face value, upheld a position that entails making a distinction between "good" and "bad" conquistadores. From this perspective (of "bad" and "good" conquistadores) colonialism can be redeemed, and it raises the question of whether one can actually speak of Spanish colonialism in the sixteenth-century Americas. As an oxymoron, the notion of peaceful conquest either ignores its irony or betrays cynicism. In the case of the Spanish laws, the systematization of methods of exploration and programs of settlement linked peaceful processes to productive outcomes. The varieties of interpellating Indians—which included mutilation and terror as "letter," the "Hey you, recognize Spanish sovereignty or I'll kill you" of the *Requerimiento,* and the more sophisticated enticement into pledging obedience to the Crown—all have in common subordination to Spanish rule. I might add that these forms do not cancel each other, in that, as we saw in the introduction, the possibility of using terror as "letter," as exposed in Las Casas's early example of the mutilated hands, remains in the 1573 Ordenanzas.

The concept of writing violence in this book entails an inverted allegory, in which, if the metaphorical pertinence of the utterance "writing is violence" is self-evident, its literal meaning surfaces as undecidable. The literal meaning is undecidable not because we cannot identify writing with violence unequivocably, but because the nature of the injuries that writing exerts cannot be reduced to an all-or-nothing immediate causation of physical pain: the will to injure may very well miss its mark (see Butler 1997a).

Let us take some of the examples from central Mexico of interpellation missing the mark parallel to the texts we examined in the introduction. There we examined two histories of Tlatelolco, the *Historia de Tlatelolco desde los tiempos más remotos* and the *Codex of Tlatelolco,* that exemplified savage literacies and domesticated glyphs. Whereas the *Historia de Tlatelolco* uses the alphabet to write texts for the internal consumption of the Tlatelolcans with no traces of missionary or bureaucratic supervision, the *Codex of Tlatelolco* uses glyphs to establish a position for Tlatelolco within the colonial order. Clearly, the circulation of European forms of life (the Latin alphabet or three-dimensional perspective) is a two-way street in which Indians do things with the alphabet and Renaissance perspective that could not have been anticipated by colonial authorities.[3]

I would like to allude to Amerindian pictorial and written texts that identify different if not contradictory views of evangelization (see Rabasa 1998). Since the beginning of the colonization of the Americas, Amerindians have returned the Spaniards' gaze. In the sixteenth century they used their pictographic writing systems to produce ethnographic studies of the colonial order. The evangelical impulse that sought to extirpate the times of the gods created for the Indians the need to dwell in at least two worlds. The missionaries knew this all too well, and their own ethnographic efforts sought to document how Amerindians lied, concealed the celebration of their gods, and continued to invoke their ancestral warriors. Missionaries also knew that translating the language of the "gods" was a futile task. For instance, the Dominican Diego de Durán expresses this impossibility when in his *Historia de la Nueva España e islas de Tierra Firme* he explains that Nahua "magic" speech amounts to nonsense when translated into Spanish: "Estos conjuros andan escritos y los he tenido en mi poder y pudiéralos poner aquí, si fuera cosa que importara. Pero además de no ser necesario en nuestra lengua, vueltos, son disparates" [These incantations have been written down, and I have had them in my hands, and I could write them down here, if they were important. But aside from not being important in our language, translated, they amount to nonsense] (1984 [ca. 1581], 1: 79). Missionaries at once testified to a failed colonization and betrayed a dependence on Indians in learning their languages and worldviews. The more intimate missionaries became with Indian languages, the more absurd translations seemed to them. In fact, translations that sought to convey intimacy with the other language would amount in the missionaries' frame of reference to undermining the grammaticality, hence the rationality, of Spanish. Talal Asad's recommendation that in translating from a weaker to a stronger language one should invade the stronger one by making it weaker would not only have made no sense (politically speaking) to a missionary such as Durán, but would also have been seen as constituting a useless trompe l'oeil, a mere illusion of gaining access to the minds of the Nahuas (Asad 1986; see also Spivak 1993). In the meantime, Indians argued cases in Spanish courts.

The violence of interpellation that demanded the subordination of Indians to the Crown, the colonial aesthetic that prompted impulsions of violence toward outlaws, the reduction of Indians to one more natural resource in the colonial wars between European nations, the Indian historians who by writing from the point of view of an Indian deconstructed the code of New World histories such as those we have examined in this book, would find their complement in inquisitorial missionary writings that sought to unmask the continuation of pagan practices in order to eradicate the times of the gods and to expose wily Indians who pledged obedience but whose everyday life practices made manifest that interpellation had missed its mark.

These Amerindians who questioned the exclusivity of Christianity (*a-position-of-not-being-really-convinced-of-the-necessity-of-dwelling-in-only-one-world*) are a far cry from the inert and negatively defined subalterns *for whom* Chakrabarty finds an ethicopolitical responsibility to write history. These differences can certainly be explained in terms of the specific colonial and postcolonial histories of India and the Americas, differences that continue to inform the political practices of these regions. Nevertheless, I don't see why we cannot imagine South Asian subalterns addressing modern bureaucracies in a secular language, that is, inhabiting Western forms of life and acting on them, without abdicating the times of the gods. At the very least, Chakrabarty's stance constitutes a form of symbolic violence as it excludes subalterns from the practices of "secular" history, regardless of his honorable intentions. Writing violence cannot be identified with certain practices of "bad" writing vis-à-vis others that are "good" (though shades are important), but with the conjunction between writing and violence that grounded the Spanish conquest of the Americas in the sixteenth century and continues to haunt us all, even today.

Abbreviations

AGI	Archivo General de Indias. Seville, Spain.
CI	*Cartas de Indias.* 2 vols. Ministero de Fomento. Madrid: Imprenta de Manuel G. Hernández, 1887.
CDI	Joaquín Pacheco, et al., eds. *Colección de documentos inéditos, relativos al descubrimiento, conquista y organización de las antiguas posesiones en América y Oceanía.* 42 vols. Madrid: Imprenta de José María Pérez, 1864–1884.
CLD	Manuel Serrano y Sanz, ed. *Colección de libros y documentos referentes a la historia de América.* Vols. 5–6. Madrid: Librería General de Victoriano Suárez, 1906.
HDNM	Charles Wilson Hackett. *Historical Documents Relating to New Mexico, Nueva Viscaya, and Approaches Thereto, to 1773.* 3 vols. Washington, DC: Carnegie Institution, 1923–1937.
HGN	Gonzalo Fernández de Oviedo y Valdés. *Historia general y natural de las Indias.* 5 vols. In *Biblioteca de Autores Españoles,* vols. 117–21, ed. Juan Pérez de Tudela Bueso. Madrid: Ediciones Atlas, 1959 [1535–1547].

Notes

On Writing Violence: An Introduction

1 Ernst Mengin (1939–40) transcribed the Nahuatl text known as the *Historia de Tlatelolco desde los tiempos más remotos* with a German translation. The *Historia de Tlatelolco* is part of a series of texts known as *Unos Anales Historicos de la Nación Mexicana,* which are located at the Bibliothèque Nationale de Paris; there are two versions identified as *Manuscrits mexicains* numbers 22 and 22bis. Mengin also published a facsimile edition (1945). For an edition in Spanish bearing the title *Anales de Tlatelolco,* see Berlin (1948). I provide Mengin's transcript of the Nahuatl version below, followed by Berlin's Spanish version. My English translation follows Berlin's Spanish version. The song, which I isolate in italics (following the convention in Spanish and the German translations), is not graphically marked in the original manuscript, with the exception of the reproduced sound "ayyayyeuaye" (Mengin 1945, fols 16–17).

> 191. nima yc motlatlania y mexica y ciūauaqz catca colhuaca yn icuaua[n] quiuatquiliqz yn imamatlacuilol auh y ciua yn v̂pa oquichuaqz catca yn imoquichva yn imamatlacuilol quiualquiliqz. 192. niman yc[y]e mononotza quitoa câ tiui câ titlamatiui ca vc motinuicquin ma cana tinamvelloti tle [yn] ticchiuaqs yn imamauh ŷ colhuaqz yn otiquiualitquilique ma ticnechicoca ma ticcêtlalica. 193. yn oquinechicoqz muchi amallacuilolli nima ye quitzoualpepechoua yc onca quimamatepetique quitzoualpepechoqz tzaualli quitzôtecôtique yâcuica vnca quinixtiq ima ye quicuicatia acaluapalli quinitequilia ye vncâ quitlalia yn inquic: 194. *yztacaltzincopa yollitiloc tamatepeuh yuh çe youal y yeuaca maytiloc yxtlauacan maytiloc tomatepeuh y cuepa Nanoçiuatzi tetocalzi ayyayyeuaye yxtlauaca maytiloc tamatepeuh.* 195. ŷ coyuna ŷ coluaacatl quiualcalcaqui cenca ŷpâ omoteca cuicatl nima ye yc yaotlatoua tepanecae ma tiquîmôtôpepeuiti cuix oc miequi y mexica yn iztlacaticate ynic ye yaotlatoua. (Mengin 1939–40: 116–18)
>
> 191. Después de esto se examinaron los mexica, cuyas mujeres eran colhuaque: las mujeres trajeron sus escritos de papel de *amate.* Y las mujeres que allá habían tomado marido, trajeron los escritos sobre amate de sus maridos. 192. Después se consultan y dicen: "¿Adónde

vamos? ¿Qué proyectamos, pues todavía no hemos muerto para que podamos haceros saber lo que haremos? Juntad, reunid los escritos (sobre amate) de los colhuaque que trajimos." 193. Cuando hubieron reunido todos sus papeles escritos, rellenaron con masas de bledo (el ídolo hecho de palos), lo envolvieron con papel, le pusieron cabeza y los descubrieron allá por primera vez. Después hicieron música golpeando tablas de canoas y componen allá el siguiente cantar: 194. *Por Iztacaltzinco fue renovada nuestra montaña de papel de corteza, (el idolo) después de haber sido fabricada nuevamente con la mano durante una noche. En una llanura fue fabricada con la mano nuestra montaña de papel de corteza. Regresa otra vez el Nanociuatzin, el de nombre de gente. ¡Allalleuaye! En la llanura nuestra montaña de papel de corteza fue hecha a mano.* 196. El coyouácatl, el coyolhuácatl escuchan la canción, cuyo son se extiende a lo lejos. E inmediatamente llaman a las armas: "¡Oh Tepaneca!, vamos a reprenderlos. ¿Son todavía muchos mexica? Se equivocan al llamar a las armas." (Berlin 1948: 42–43)

2 In the *Vocabulario en lengua castellana y mexicana,* Alonso de Molina translates *amoxtli* as *libro de escritura* (book of writing) (1992 [1571]). The *Historia de Tlatelolco* uses the term *imamatlacuilol,* which can be translated as *pintura* (painting) or *escritura* (writing) on paper. On the misuse of the term *libro* for *amoxtli,* see Mignolo (1995a: 69–80).

3 In studying the mixture of pre-Columbian and European forms of expression and thought, Serge Gruzinski has underscored in *La pensée métisse* that inasmuch as the term *culture* suggests consistency and permanence as well as a substance that would determine "outward" manifestations, it keeps us from understanding the fluidity and improvisation characteristic of *la pensée métisse* (mestizo thought) (1999: 44–45). In this book, the term culture lacks the associations with purity, homogeneity, or instability and the corresponding associations with contamination that have prevailed in anthropology. For a critique of the concept in anthropology and other discreet unities as "language" and "life," see Fabian (1991). "Culture" stands here as shorthand for "forms of life" or "forms of expression" that in their fluidity or nebulosity manifest characteristics we may identify as pre-Columbian or European. Otherwise, we could not speak of hybridity, *métissage* or *mestizaje,* or, for that matter, of mixture. My use of the concept *culture of conquest* refers to deep-seated *habits* that were first developed in the sixteenth century, if not before the Spanish invasion of the Americas, and that still underlie the categories and sensibilities we bring to bear when we reflect on or speak about colonialism. The end is not to discover stable entities or exhaust modalities

of "conquest" but to render certain forms of thought and expression inoperative in the process of their description.

4 I am thinking of a series of texts that build on speech act theory and, more specifically, on the concept of force as developed by J. L. Austin's *How to Do Things with Words* (1962), among which the most influential are Butler (1997a), Derrida (1990), Bourdieu (1987), and Fish (1989).

5 A recent article by Norimitsu Onishi in the *New York Times,* "A Brutal War's Machetes Maim Sierra Leone's Civilians," which included a picture of a man, Mohammed Sesay, after rebels cut off his hands, reminds us that mutilation today still conveys messages: " 'This,' the rebels told him, 'is an example to show the president' " (1999: A1).

6 I have benefited from Butler's critique of Althusser's concept of interpellation and her discussion of hate speech as a form of interpellation that exerts violence: "The utterances of hate speech are part of the continuous and uninterrupted process to which we are subjected, an on-going subjection (*assujettissement*) that is the very interpellation, that continually repeated action of discourse by which subjects are formed in subjugation" (Butler 1997a: 27; see also Butler 1997b: 106–31). Butler connects speech to violence by building on J. L. Austin's distinction between illocutionary (violence is in the speech act itself) and perlocutinary (violence is a consequence of the speech act) performatives.

7 Mignolo (1995a) and Gruzinski (1994) offer invaluable studies of the imposition or the adoption of the alphabet as central to the process of colonization and occidentalization of Amerindians. For a critique of Jack Goody's seminal essays on literacy and its consequences (Goody 1977, 1987; Goody and Watts 1963), see Halverson (1992). Street (1984) has argued that literacy must be thought in tandem with its ideologies. In what follows, I have benefited from Michel de Certeau's deconstruction of transhistorical formulations of the supposedly inherent opposite nature of orality and writing (1984: 131–53).

8 For a comparative study of Western and Amerindian reading and writing cultures, see Mignolo (1995a: 69–122).

9 On the concept of grassroots literacy and reading autochthonous texts, see Fabian (1993: 92). For an account of the clandestine production and circulation of alphabetic texts in sixteenth-century Mexico, see Gruzinski (1994: 55–56).

10 For studies of the genres preferred by different Mesoamerican ethnic groups and the primarily local nature of pre-Columbian history (including histories written in this vein after the conquest), see the essays in Boone and Mignolo (1994), especially Boone (1994), Pohl (1994),

and Leibsohn (1994). See also Quiñones Keber (1995) and Leibsohn (1995).

11 I have already cited Fabian (1993), but also see the other essays on the ethnography of reading in Boyarin (1993).

12 See the reproduction of *Codex of Tlatelolco* in Berlin (1948). For a discussion of *Codex Tlatelolco,* see Gruzinski (1994: 63).

13 One can hardly do justice in a footnote to the literature on postcolonialism that has emerged in the past twenty years. I give proper accreditation in specific places where I discuss the work of these scholars and others associated with postcolonialism, subaltern studies, and the critique of anthropology. See the collection of texts representative of postcolonial studies in McClintock, Mufti, and Shohat (1997) and Ashcroft, Griffiths, and Tiffin (1994). For an exceptional postcolonial theory in English studies that marks the beginning of colonial discourse in the sixteenth century, see Hulme (1987). There is a considerable body of postcolonial studies in the context of the Americas: see, e.g., *Poetics Today* 15 and 16 on the locus of enunciation (Mignolo 1994, 1995b), the collection of essays on subaltern studies in the Americas in Rabasa, Sanjinés, and Carr (1996), and the collection of essays on colonial discourse in R. Adorno and Mignolo (1989). For an assessment of postcolonial theory in the context of Latin American literature and culture, see Colás (1995).

14 In this respect, the forms of internal colonialism that emerged after the nineteenth-century wars of independence in Latin America (in which mestizo and White elites assumed dominant positions) signal major differences with postcolonial Asia and Africa (see García Martínez 1991; Stavenhagen 1963, 1988).

15 For critiques of the concept of colonial discourse, see the essays by Mignolo (1993), Vidal (1993), and R. Adorno (1993) in the special section "Commentary and Debate" of *Latin American Research Review.* These critiques responded to an earlier essay by Patricia Seed, "Colonial and Postcolonial Discourse" (1991). By discourse (from *dis,* about, apart + *currere,* to run), I do not mean exclusively verbal expressions, but also systems of thought and structures of affect operating in different media. Images and sounds, of course, communicate thoughts and affects in particular semiotic modalities. It is also evident that one can respond to images and sounds by producing images and sounds that interact with the thoughts and affects expressed by the first. But there is a danger of confusing *semiosis,* the mode of interaction between subjects, with the systems of thought and structures of affect expressed in mapping, painting, whistling, drumming, speaking, and so on. This definition of the term discourse partakes of

an equivocal dimension similar to a generalized understanding of the term writing, but the etymological sense of *run about, apart* (by extention, to go back and forth, to and fro), often assumed to be a *natural* form of understanding verbal expressions, could be productively used to understand how discourses are constituted inter-semiotically. The fact that I write—not paint or play an instrument—inevitably contaminates with verbal language the things I say about images or sounds. For instance, in my analysis in chapter 6 of Protestant illustrations of Las Casas's *Brevíssima relación de la destruyción de Indias,* I speak of watercolors and copperplates in terms of vocabularies used to translate the affect expressed in color into black-and-white equivalents. These illustrations, in turn, contaminated the reading of Las Casas to the extent that their depiction of the Indians ultimately stood for what Protestants would suffer if they let the Spaniards into their countries. Thereby, they provide a space for the projection of hatred and pulsations of violence. I have found Tom Conley's *The Self-Made Map* (1996) particularly illuminating of how semiotic systems interact with each other in the constitution of cartographic writing and the production of the subject in early modern France.

16 Alonso (1995) argues that the spirit of the frontier can be traced back to Spanish colonization of Chihuahua and lent the north of Mexico cultural characteristics usually associated exclusively with the Anglo-American version of the frontier spirit. For a complex view of the social groups and geographic diversity of Sonora but generalizable to other regions in the far north, see Radding (1997). For a longer historical and broader geographic view, as well as a challenging discussion of claims that the frontier is a particularly Anglo-American phenomenon, see Bannon (1974), Weber (1979, 1982, 1992), and Wyman and Kroeber (1957). For a strategic use of the concept of the U.S.-Mexico border as space to theorize U.S. cultural studies, see Saldívar (1997). I owe this critical view of the term *frontier* to Estévan Rael y Gálvez (n.d.), who prefers not to use it in his own work on the Genizaros of New Mexico.

17 I am thinking of John Searle's distinction: "Brute facts exist independently of any human institution; institutional facts can exist only within human institutions. Brute facts require the institution of language in order that we can *state* the facts, but the brute facts *themselves* exist quite independently of language or any other institution. Thus the *statement* that the sun is ninety-three million miles from the earth requires the institution of language and an institution of measuring distances in miles, but the *fact stated* that there is a certain distance between the earth and the sun, exists independently of any institu-

tion" (1995: 27). I would add that the exercise of violence and power is proportional to the epistemological capacity a *colonialist institution* has of producing (stating) *brute facts*. In a perverse extension of Searle's point, we can further assert that the effectiveness of stereotypes and racism in general is also proportional to their standing as *brute facts*.

18   I owe to Helen Solterer this reference to Aristotle's identification of art and violence.

19   On Villagrá's poetics and information regarding plays performed in Spanish ceremonies of possession, see the essays by Gutiérrez, Lamadrid, and Leal in Herrera-Sobek (1993).

20   For a study of the *Memorial de los Indios de Nombre de Dios, Durango acerca de los servicios al Rey, 1563,* a document written in Nahuatl that documents the alliances among Mexicas, Michoacanos, Zacatecos, and Spaniards in the 1560 war against the Guachichiles, see Ahern (1998). See also Barlow and Smisor (1943).

21   I owe this reference to Patricia Seed.

1. Reading Cabeza de Vaca, or How We Perpetuate the Culture of Conquest

1   The literature that critiques the category of the *literary* is immense; indeed, one could say that it is one of the main staples in today's literary criticism. For a review of recent work on law and literature that raises important questions regarding violence (with particular attention to the work of Derrida and Bourdieu), see Leckie (1995). Key studies in the context of Latin American literary and cultural studies are Cornejo Polar (1994) and Beverley (1993).

2   See Fabian (1983: 109–13 and passim) on topoi of discourse and their function in anthropology.

3   I am thinking in particular of the summaries in Gonzalo Fernández de Oviedo's *Historia general y natural de las Indias* (1535–1547) and Antonio Herrera y Tordecilla's *Historia general de los hechos de los castellanos en las Islas y Tierra Firme del Mar Oceano* (1601–1615). I address Oviedo's account later in this chapter. For studies of the reception and censorship of colonial historiography, see Friede (1959) and more recently R. Adorno (1987). On metaphor, transport, and the motif of shipwreck, see Pranzetti (1993) and Certeau (1984).

4   Mignolo (1986) has drawn an extensive critique of the reduction among literary critics of the multicultural reality of the Americas to Spanish and Western cultural norms.

5 My understanding of the concept of background has benefited from Searle (1995: 125–47).

6 Patricia Seed (1993) has argued, for the most part accurately, that the term *hábiles* (i.e., capacity to understand the gospel and convert to Christianity) has a key function in justifying Spanish sovereignty over the New World. We must, nevertheless, also trace an anthropology in the discourse on *habilidad* that structures different colonialist practices, from persuasion to wars of extermination. There is no legal impediment to prevent conquistadores from at once claiming territorial possession and justifying extermination of the native population. The papal bulls, as it were, obligated the Crown to politically subject in order to convert only *indios* who were *hábiles*.

7 For different versions of the *Requerimiento* and a translation into English, see Morales Padrón (1979: 331–47) and Parry and Keith (1984, 1:288–90).

8 This rough itinerary does not pretend to give the reader the actual trajectory but a feeling for the distances. Cabeza de Vaca's exact route is a highly debated issue involving all sorts of nationalistic feelings; for example, Robert E. Hill, a distinguished geologist working at the University of Texas in the 1930s, felt that to favor a trans-Mexico route would take away Cabeza de Vaca's citizenship. I draw these observations from Chipman's (1987) review of the historiography of Cabeza de Vaca's route across Texas.

9 For the *Naufragios* and the *Comentarios,* as well as other documents pertaining to Cabeza de Vaca's governorship of the Río de la Plata, I am using *Colección de libros y documentos referentes a la historia de América* (1906), vols. 5 and 6, edited by Serrano y Sanz, cited in the text as *CLD.* For the English version of the *Naufragios* I am following, with some modifications, the recent translation by Frances M. López-Morillas (Núñez Cabeza de Vaca 1993). Unless otherwise indicated, all other translations are mine.

10 As William Taylor has pointed out to me in a personal communication, this opposition by literary critics presupposes an understanding of " 'history' . . . as an ideal type—as what objectively happened. Few historians would say that this is what they are able to produce."

11 Gonzalo Fernández de Oviedo first came to America in 1514 as supervisor of the gold-smelting operations on Pedrarias Dávila's expedition to the Darién. Except for a few brief trips to Spain, Oviedo remained in America until his death in 1557 in Santo Domingo, where he had been the *alcalde* (governor) of the fortress since 1533. An edition of the first part of his *Historia general* appeared in 1535, followed

by an expanded version in 1547, but the work was not published in its entirety until the nineteenth century (see chapter 4). The latest internal date in the manuscript of the *Historia general* is 1549, given at the end of part 3, where he announces his intention to write a fourth part. Oviedo tried to publish an edition that would have included parts 2 and 3 but was not granted authorization (see Gerbi 1985: 129–31). In addition to Gerbi's major book, see Avalle-Arce's bio-bibliographical note (1997). Oviedo placed the *Joint Report* and additional information drawn from the *Naufragios* in book 16 of part 2 of the *Historia general*. For an English version, see Gerald Theisen's translation included in a recent edition of Fanny Bandelier's 1905 translation of the 1542 edition of the *Naufragios* (Nuñez Cabeza de Vaca 1972). Theisen left out Oviedo's summary of the *Naufragios* and commentary expressing his preference for the *Joint Report*, under the assumption that one can neatly separate the *Joint Report* from Oviedo's moralistic addenda and other information drawn from the *Naufragios*. See chapter 4 for a detailed discussion of Oviedo's editorial practices in his incorporation of written or oral *relaciones* into the *Historia general*. See also Galloway (1997a: 13–14). Translations of the *Joint Report* are mine.

12 For readings that have drawn ethnographic information from the *Naufragios*, see Newcomb (1983), Campbell and Campbell (1981), and Weddle (1985). After pointing out the limitations of these sorts of studies that give no data on religious belief, Spitta (1995: 40) draws from Mircea Eliade's classic study *Shamanism: Archaic Techniques of Ecstasy* (1964) to identify shamanistic practices in the *Naufragios*. Spitta underscores the disjunction "between his practice as a Native American and his use of a biblical discourse to frame these experiences. The biblical model serves to render Cabeza de Vaca's otherwise incomprehensible experiences in America comprehensible to a European reader. . . . That Cabeza de Vaca could and did appeal to Christian rhetoric in his chronicle was only natural given that he himself was a Christian" (40). The story, then, is how Cabeza de Vaca transculturated Indian shamanism into Christianity. It seems to me that we should distinguish between interpretation of the rhetorical strategies Cabeza de Vaca uses to convey his experience and an interpretation that would domesticate this experience by seeing it as a *transculturación*. Undoubtedly, the content is a transculturation of Indian beliefs; the form, however, tells another story. Also of interest are Goldberg's (1992: 205–17) ethnographic observations on gender among the Native Americans in the *Naufragios* and Cabeza de Vaca's ambiguous gender role as a shaman. One wonders, however, if all shamans had such a fussy gender role, or was it just Cabeza de Vaca?

Leticia González Arratia's (1990) archaeological work on hunters and gatherers in the desert of Coahuila has pointed out the subordinated position women held as the gatherers vis-à-vis the male hunters. The males benefited from the leisure women afforded, not only assuming the position of warriors but, more important for the present discussion of shamans, by healing, which also produced the ideologies that bound the groups. In passing, we should also mention that González Arratia's work on hunter and gatherer societies prompts serious questions as to the appropriateness of the anthropological category of the Indian Paleolithic used to speak of nomadic groups coexisting with sedentary tribes. Knowledge of topography, fauna and flora, and the production of durables manifests forms of thought at least as abstract and complex as the ones entailed in the domestication of plants. González Arratia (1991) has traced this blindness to the knowledge involved in hunter and gatherer societies to the early chroniclers of Northern Mexico. Also see Reff (1996) for a critique of readings of the *Naufragios* where, "despite our explicit cultural relativism, the Indian that comes to mind is other-than-rational, or 'backward' relative of the European" (132).

13 See Rabasa (1995b) for a full development of these ideas. For an approximation of "magic realism" and shamanism, see Taussig (1987: 167). On the *real maravilloso* as an aesthetic in Alejo Carpentier, see González Echevarría (1977). Also see T. W. Adorno (1993: 82–85) on the representation of sociolects from previous epochs in his discussion of the historical novels of Thomas Mann and Hegel's theory of the rationality of the real.

14 For a critique of the exclusive attention Geertz places on language in ethnography, see Fabian (1990). Taussig comes very close to Geertz's formulation when he writes about his study of the Putumayo and the rubber boom: "There was no Theory outside of its being brought to life. Social analysis was no longer an analysis of the object of scrutiny, but of the mediation of that object in one context with its destination in quite another — for instance, Putumayan healers over there and back then, with you engaged with these stained-glass words here" (1992: 6).

15 For bibliographical information on both the *Naufragios* and the *Comentarios,* see Cardozo (1959, 1:133–44), Hart (1974: xi–xix), and Lastra (1984: 150–51).

16 Without pretending to exhaust the bibliography on the debates over Cabeza de Vaca's cures versus miracles, the following provides snapshots of the history of the reigning sensibilities in different historical periods. In the sixteenth century, all references to shamanism

were displaced by interpretations that attributed miracles to divine intervention. This emphasis on the miraculous led Honorius Philoponus to denounce in the seventeenth century the heretical character of Cabeza de Vaca's use of the sign of the cross (*signum Crucis signaverit*) to perform "miracles" on the grounds that he was not a priest: "Quos effetus sacros Religiosos Monachos & Sacerdotes fecisse & non scelestos milites aliunde constat" [Other sources make evident that these effects (healings) were to be done by religious monks and priests and not by roguish soldiers] (1621: 91). This brief though defamatory dismissal of Cabeza de Vaca and his companions as *scelestos milites* (roguish soldiers) led Antonio Ardonio to Cabeza de Vaca's defense one hundred years later in a long disquisition on the nature of miracles and the capacity of Cabeza de Vaca to perform them: "Me estimula à esta Apologia, ò defensa de la historica narracion de los *Naufragios, i peregrinaciones de Alvar Nuñez,* no deseos de arguir, ni apetitos de reprehender la mendaz insolencia, I orgullo de la pluma del Padre Honorio, sino la consideracion [que] salga a su nueva impresion [de los *Naufragios*] sin lunares de legitima contradiccion, I se mantenga indemne al credito de las comunes opiniones" [I am called to this Apology, or defense of the historical narrative of the *Naufragios, i peregrinaciones de Alvar Nuñez,* not out of a desire to debate, nor an appetite to reprehend the mendacious insolence, and pride of Father Honorius's pen, but out of consideration (that) the new printing (of *Naufragios*) might appear without blemishes of legitimate contradiction, and remain undamaged by the credit of common opinions] (1736: 3). At the turn of this century, in the "Advertencia" by Serrano y Sanz, the tone of the polemic is displaced to science and a denunciation of the novelesque character of ethnographic data in the *Naufragios.* After evaluating Ardonio's text as "lleno de pruebas silogísticas y falto de hechos" [full of syllogistic proofs and lacking facts], Serrano y Sanz cites a long passage from a supposedly scientific description of Indians in New Mexico "que hace sospechoza la veracidad de muchos detalles consignados por Alvar Núñez en sus *Naufragios,* hijos, acaso, de su imaginación andaluza y el deseo de aumentar con circunstancias novelescas su expedición" [that throws into question the veracity of many of the details consigned by Alvar Núñez in his *Naufragios,* the offspring, perhaps, of his Andalusian imagination and desire to augment his expedition with novelesque circumstances] (1906, 5: vii, xix). With similar criteria, perhaps as an influence, Adolph F. Bandelier wrote in 1886 in the *Revue d'Ethnographie:* "Without contemporary documentary evidence . . . there might be a tendency to believe that this extraordinary journey is a piece of fiction, and that the four adventurers were simply impostors"; later Bandelier adds: "Cabeza de Vaca's reports are sometime precise, but more often they become confused, under the influence of an imagination overstimulated by long suffering" (1981 [1886]: 45–46). Contemporary literary criticism vindicates these same passages as fictions with a purported literary value. The latter statement continues the tradition that since Oviedo has ascribed lack of clarity to the *Naufragios*. Jacques Lafaye (1984) has studied the reception and the different interpretations the *milagros* have assumed since the first comments in the sixteenth and seventeenth centuries. See also Pupo-Walker (1987).

17　Also see in this essay Ahern's (1993) equally brilliant analysis of the appropriation and semantic transformations of the *calabazo* (a gourd used by shamans) as a sign that would convey indigenous healing powers, function as an evangelical tool, or symbolize a space of death in different communications with indigenous people in Cabeza de Vaca's *Naufragios* and Niza's *Relación*.

18　They performed many miracles now. They would set fire to a house, as if they were burning it, and suddenly bring it back again. Now Xibalba was full of admiration.

　　Next they would sacrifice themselves, one of them dying for the other, stretched out as if in death. First they would kill themselves, but then they would suddenly look alive. The Xibalbans could only admire what they did. Everything they did now was already the groundwork for their defeat of Xibalba. (Tedlock 1985: 150)

19　These time travel metaphors by Lagmanovich and Pupo-Walker exemplify a tendency in Western anthropology to deny the coevalness of the people it studies—that is, to place them in another time, obviously anterior to the observer. For a definition of this denial of coevalness as the allochronism of anthropology, see Fabian (1983: 32). Ferrando, in his edition of the *Naufragios y Comentarios* (Nuñez Cabeza de Vaca, 1984: 17–20), uncritically reproduces allochronic metaphors (such as referring to Amerindians as primitives) and insists on placing the different groups within an evolutionary cultural schema ranging in his case from the Mesolithic to the Neolithic ages. In the face of such prehistorical cultures, Ferrando feels the need to imitate evidence that physical anthropology uses in the study of human evolution by reproducing information on cranial forms, facial shapes, and such other physical data as height. He obviously did not feel the need to provide measurements for Cabeza de Vaca's cranium.

20　I follow the Latin/Spanish bilingual edition by Antonio Castañeda Delgado and Antonio García del Moral. I have modified Parish's translation when I have found it necessary. Also see Agustín Millares Carlo's edition and translation, *Del único modo de atraer a todos los pueblos a la verdadera religión* (Las Casas 1942).

21 Las Casas was born in 1484 and first went to America in 1502. He held an *encomienda* until 1514, when he renounced his claims on the grounds that the institution was unjust. His career as a protector of the Indians, which began in 1515 and lasted until his death in 1566, included the four years (1543–1547) when he was bishop of Chiapas. Las Casas was responsible for two major social experiments, the first one (1520–1521) in Cumana (in present-day Venezuela), and the second (1537–1550) in Verapaz, Guatemala. The *Apologética historia sumaria* (ca. 1555), which postdated these events, represents a theoretical and political transition to the later Las Casas, who condemned the Spanish colonization of the New World outright and called for the full restoration of Indian sovereignty (see Las Casas 1992a; Parish and Weidman 1992; Rabasa 1989b: 273–74). For a study of Las Casas's texts and experiments, see Wagner and Parish (1967). The most complete study of Cumana continues to be Giménez Fernández (1953, 1960). According to Parish, Las Casas finished the first draft of *De unico modo* in 1534 and at an ecclesiastical conference in 1536, "bishops and friars enacted missionary principles that incorporated [Las Casas's] tenets" (in Las Casas 1992b: 36). There were dissenting views, especially among the Franciscans, who sent an envoy to Rome. Dominicans and Augustinians assembled a dossier to advance their position in Rome, which included a copy of *De unico modo*. The main ideas of *De unico modo* were incorporated in the encyclica *Sublimis Deus* (1537), better known for establishing once and for all the humanity of the Indians — that is, the obligation to convert them to Christianity (Parish in Las Casas 1992b: 36–37). The force of Las Casas's argument and its influence in Rome would seem to have undermined the validity of the *Requerimiento,* but not its logic. See chapter 2 for a discussion of the changing language of violence in the Nuevas Leyes of 1542 and the Ordenanzas of 1573.

22 I have modified Parish's translation to reconcile these two passages. In the first, Parish suggests that Las Casas was thinking of making war to prepare the ground for evangelization, but it is clear from the second passage that he has in mind the sort of subjection demanded by the *Requerimiento.* The absurdity of the opposite method resides in the assumption that pagans, especially pagan princes, would willingly surrender to Christian political power. The Spanish version in Castañeda Delgado and García del Moral's edition reads:

> El modo contrario e éste sería si aquellos a quienes incumbe predicar o hacer predicar el evangelio a los fieles, consideraron mas adecuado

y facil de realizar que primero dichos infieles debieran ser sometidos, quiéranlo o no, al dominio temporal del pueblo cristiano. Una vez sometidos, la predicación seguiría de manera metódica. . . .

Pero como ningún infiel por su voluntad quiere someterse al dominio del pueblo crisitiano o de alguno de sus principes, sobre todo los reyes de los infieles, sin lugar a dudas sería necesario llegar a la guerra. (Las Casas 1988: 379)

23 See, for instance, Motolinía's bitter critique of Las Casas in his 2 January 1555 letter to Charles V (documentary appendix to Motolinía 1971).
24 See, e.g., R. Adorno (1991), Pastor (1989: 141–42), and Molloy (1987: 439–49) for different conceptualizations of Cabeza de Vaca's manipulation of ignorant Indians. The most systematic critique of this explanation of disease and cure can be found in Reff (1996). Reff traces what he views as epidemics of psychosomatic illness in Cabeza de Vaca's narrative to knowledge of the fall of Tenochtitlan, the devastating epidemics of infectious diseases (small pox, measles, malaria) that followed, and the slave raids on the northern frontier. There is no room, however, in Reff's essay for Cabeza de Vaca undergoing initiation and training into shamanism: "Nowhere in the *Relación* does Cabeza de Vaca speak of shamanism with respect or real understanding" (131).

2. The Mediation of the Law in the New Mexico Corpus, 1539–1610

1 For a review of recent work on law and colonialism, see Merry (1991). This otherwise useful article needs to be complemented with studies on the Americas. The classic studies on juridical institutions in Colonial Spanish America are Zavala (1971 [1935]) and Hanke (1949), just to mention two I consider indispensable. Patricia Seed is currently working on a three-volume study of how national legal traditions shaped English, Spanish, French, Portuguese, and Dutch colonial enterprises in the New World and how these distinct forms of establishing possession are still influential in the United States and Latin America. As of this writing, only the first volume of her study has appeared (1995). See also Seed (1992).
2 The *Historia* was not published until last century. For a discussion of Las Casas's prohibition and history of its publication, see Hanke (1965, 1: ix–lxxxviii; esp. xxxviii).
3 Sepúlveda in fact builds his arguments on the authority of Oviedo. See, e.g., Sepúlveda and Las Casas (1975 [ca. 1550–51]: 61). For bio-

bibliographical information on Oviedo, see note 3 in chapter 1. Juan Ginés de Sepúlveda (ca. 1490–1573) never traveled to America and drew extensively from Oviedo and others who promoted denigrating images of Native Americans that served to legitimate declaring war against them, if not their extermination. Sepúlveda was the official chronicler of Charles V and one of the preceptors of Philip II. At one point in his career he was the official papal translator of Aristotle. In addition to his translations of and commentaries on Aristotle, Sepúlveda wrote law, political philosophy, theology, letters, and history (see Ramírez de Verger 1987).

4   Only the *Brevíssima* was published during Las Casas's lifetime, in 1552. See note 21 in chapter 1.

5   Also see the copy of the *Proceso* in *AGI* Patronato 22, ramo 13, fols. 1086r–1131r. Here, as in many other places in this chapter, I have benefited from Jerry R. Craddock's ongoing transcriptions and comparisons of copies. Under the auspices of an NEH Collaborative Research Grant (1997), Craddock and his collaborator, Barbara De Marco, have been working on editions and translations into English of documents pertaining to the early Spanish colonization of New Mexico that for the most part have not been available in Spanish.

6   It is important to note that the Ordenanzas emphasized naming the whole territory as well as the individual provinces, cities, towns, rivers, and mountains not only because this information was indispensable for mapmaking, but also because for the Spanish empire naming was a symbolic mode of claiming possession over territories. Linguistic and legal differences as to how nations named and what possession meant often led to insurmountable conflicts over the territorial claims. Chapter 6 examines one of the conflicts between French Huguenots and Spaniards in Florida. For a discussion of the linguistic differences and the specific legal traditions that informed sixteenth- and seventeenth-century European colonial projects and rationalizations of empire, see Seed (1992, 1995).

7   I am following George Parker Winship's *The Coronado Expedition, 1540–1542* (1896), a bilingual edition of documents pertaining to the Coronado expedition. I have modified Winship's translations when I have felt it necessary.

8   For a discussion of the *Relaciones geográficas* and the questionnaires, see Morales Padrón (1979) and Cline (1972). Mignolo (1989; 1995a: 281 and passim) has studied the maps in the *Relaciones geográficas* as hybrid cartographies. On the other hand, Gruzinski (1993) has analyzed the adoption of alphabetical writing and Western pictorial conventions as processes of acculturation. Whether we place the emphasis on hy-

bridity or on acculturation, the *Relaciones geográficas* instituted a practice that affects both the kind of knowledge and the type of subjectivity they required to answer the questions.

9 I follow Michel de Certeau's understanding of scriptural economy as a modern, capitalist form of producing knowledge in the process of appropriating past writings as well as data derived from the external world: "I designate as 'writing' the concrete activity that consists in constructing, on its own, blank space (*un espace propre*) — the page — a text that has power over the exteriority from which it has first been isolated" (1984: 134).

10 To a great extent, readings of Las Casas as a partisan of the Indians as "educable" races in opposition to Sepúlveda have been informed by nineteenth-century developmentalist ideologies of progress that have prevailed until very recently (see, e.g., Pagden 1982; Hanke 1949, 1965). For a critique of developmentalism as the imaginary of our time, see Escobar (1992).

11 Ahern (1995a, 1995b) has documented how Chamuscado (1581–1582) and Espejo (1583) violated sacred space to terrorize Puebloans; as Luxán puts it: "y corrio la nueua de Puala en todas las provincias e temblaron en tanta manera que todos nos serbian" [and the news of Puala got around all the provinces and all trembled in such a degree that all served us] (quoted in Ahern 1995a: 160). On the inner sacred spaces as distinct from the outside space of war in Pueblo culture, see R. A. Gutiérrez (1991).

12 See *New York Times,* 9 February 1998, A10. I owe this reference to Craddock (1998).

13 These documents have been published and translated in the first volume of Charles Wilson Hackett's *Historical Documents Relating to New Mexico, Nueva Vizcaya, and Approaches Thereto, to 1773* (1923–37). I have modified Hackett's translations when I have felt it necessary.

14 Hackett mistakenly dates this letter 19 June 1566. This is clearly an error because the Marquis of Villamanrique was viceroy of New Spain from 1585 to 1590. Dr. Juan Bautista de Orozco had actually proposed the policy of establishing Tlaxcalteca and Spanish settlements as a means of pacification in a letter from 1576; and because it is difficult to make war against Indians in the places where they take refuge, Orozco recommends "acudir a la fuente que es poblar sus propias tierras" [to go to the source which means to settle in their own lands] (Naylor and Polzer 1986, 1: 61).

15 It is interesting to note that in the *Discourse of Western Planting* (1584), the younger Richard Hakluyt argued that the success of the enterprise would hinge precisely on the investment by the Crown: "A brefe Col-

lection of certaine reasons to induce her Majestie and the state to take in hande the westerne voyadge and the plantinge there" (in E. G. R. Taylor 1967 [1935]: 313; see chap. 6 below).

16 Monterrey indicates that he instructed the factor Francisco Valverde to compile and supervise the *traslado* of *relaciones* on the voyage to Quivira (*CDI*, 16: 55), which Valverde compiled under the file: "Ynformacion que por comission del Virrey Conde de Monterrey hyzo de officio el factor don Francisco de Valverde sobre el nuevo descubrimiento que el governador Juan de Oñate hizo hazia la parte norte mas adelante de las prouincias de Nuevo Mexico" [Information gathered by factor don Francisco de Valverde at the request of Viceroy Count of Monterrey on the new discovery that governor Juan de Oñate made toward the most northern part beyond the provinces of New Mexico] (1601 [AGI, Patronato 22, ramo 4, fols. 159r–217v]). For an English version of Valverde's file and Monterrey's *Discurso*, see Hammond and Rey (1953). See also Simmons (1991: 177), Bannon (1974: 38), and Hammond and Rey (1938: 31).

17 For a reading of Miguel's map from an ethnographic perspective, see Newcomb and Campbell (1982).

18 For an analysis of the appropriation and different meanings of the *calabazo* (a gourd used by shamans) — means to healing, evangelical tool, or symbol of death — in communications with different indigenous people in Cabeza de Vaca's *Naufragios* and Niza's *Relación*, see Ahern (1993). Also see Ahern (1989) for a study of how in Niza's *Relación* geographic, cultural, and mythic space become one. On the other hand, Reff (1991) has critiqued readings of Niza that reduce his *relación* to fiction (i.e., lies).

19 On Ruy López de Villalobos's armada, see the letter from Cochin by Fray Geronimo de Santisteban to Antonio de Mendoza, 1547 (*CDI*, 14: 151–65).

20 For a study of Fernando de Alarcon's *relación* of his parallel exploration of the Gulf of California to Coronado's inland expedition, see Ahern (1994). As Ahern points out, the original version in Spanish has been lost; Herrera's version is a summary that transforms the subject of enunciation from the first to the third person. An Italian version appeared in the third volume of Giovanni Battista Ramusio, *Navigationi et Viaggi* (1556), and an English version in volume 10 of Richard Hakluyt, *The Principal Navigations* (1588–1600).

21 Also see Farfán de los Godos's testimony on his expedition to the mines, where he describes Indians drawing maps on the ground using grains of corn to denote the size of populations (AGI, Patronato 22, ramo 13, fols. 1025r–1025v).

22 I owe this information to Craddock, who has compared the three copies in his transcription of the version of Zaldívar's *relación*. I have also benefited from John Poltz's translation which accompanies Craddock's unpublished edition. Zaldívar's *relación,* which has never been published in Spanish, has been translated by Bolton (1916: 223–32) and Hammond and Rey (1953, 1: 398–405). But as Craddock has argued in this paper and elsewhere (1996), both Bolton's and Hammond and Rey's English translations of documents pertaining to sixteenth-century New Mexico are unreliable and Spanish editions are not yet available.

23 For an English version of Jusepe's account, see Hammond and Rey (1966).

24 Zaldívar's is not the first description of a bison. The following are notable earlier descriptions: Cabeza de Vaca describes them on the basis of a hide with horns; in the Coronado corpus Castañeda has the most elaborate descriptions; Oviedo included a painting along with his verbal description in the *Historia general* (1535–47); Gallegos has several chapters on Chamuscado's pursuit of the bisons (1580–81); and, outside of Spanish sources, André Thevet's drawing in *Les Singularitez de la France Antartique, autrement nommé Amerique* (1557) approximates Zaldívar's whimsical bison.

25 For Murrin these idealizations of Amerindians in colonial epics compensated for their lack of advanced military technologies. One commonplace is the use of the *furioso* to characterize Indians, indeed, of "bad" *furioso* types (1994: 168).

3. Aesthetics of Colonial Violence

1 For a study of the expression of pain in war and torture, see Scarry (1985).

2 For a review of recent discussions of aesthetics and politics, see Jay (1992).

3 See the definition of these terms in the context of subaltern studies in Spivak (1988).

4 Since I first wrote this essay, the anthropologist David Stoll (1999) has published a book dedicated to discrediting Rigoberta Menchú's version of the war of extermination the Guatemalan Army conducted against indigenous peoples and leftist guerrillas in the 1970s and 1980s. Menchú's accounts of torture and terror in Guatemala partake of a collective witnessing of unspeakable atrocities compared to which her testimony pales. How would one go about telling of and

depicting the torture and massacre of thousands of Indians that the independent Historical Clarification Commission has estimated at more than 200,000 civilians killed? We should also note that if guerrillas were responsible for some of the killings, the commission has traced 90 percent of the human rights abuses to the Army and paramilitary groups (see Navarro, 1999). See John Beverley (1992) for an early account of this polemic. Also of interest in this context is the polemic between Beverley and Robert Carr, who in that same issue criticizes an earlier essay by Beverley (1989) for aestheticizing Menchú's *testimonio* by categorizing it as an instance of "magic realism" (Carr 1992: 78).

5   In *Aesthetic Theory,* Theodor Adorno has pointed out in reference to prose writings such as Kafka's *Metamorphosis* and *Penal Colony,* which "seem to call forth in us responses like real anxiety," that "art renounces happiness for the sake of happiness, thus enabling desire to survive in art" (1986: 18).

6   Unless otherwise indicated, all English versions of Villagrá are from Fayette S. Curtis's 1920 translation, now published for the first time in the bilingual edition prepared by Encinias, Rodríguez, and Sánchez (Villagrá 1992). Unfortunately, their edition does not include Villagrá's dedication to Philip III, his prologue, nor the approvals by the censors. Of modern editors, only Luis González Obregón includes these materials (Villagrá 1900). As Mercedes Junquera points out in the introduction to her edition of the *Historia,* because of the mediocrity of its verses, Villagrá's epic has for the most part been ignored by literary critics (Villagrá 1989: 68–69). Historians, however, have depended on Villagrá in their historical refigurations of the events surrounding the massacre of Acoma (see, e.g., Gutiérrez 1991).

7   See note 3 in chapter 2 for bio-bibliographical information on Sepúlveda.

8   For a discussion of Fanon's views on the colonial Manichean world and his analyses of colonial violence and counterviolence, see JanMohammed (1983) and P. Taylor (1989). JanMohammed underscores that African novels subvert Manichean colonial binaries by providing a just, hence alternative, picture of indigenous culture, and not just an inversion of the opposition (4–8). Taylor, on the other hand, underscores Fanon's linkages to the work of Nietzsche, specifically to Nietzsche's critique of resentment and "a movement beyond reactive ethics" (71). Rigoberta Menchú's testimony provides at once an alternative picture of Quiche culture and a counteraesthetic that does not merely invert (i.e., react to) the colonial binary but binds ethico-political considerations to aesthetic questions. The ethics and aesthet-

ics of the *leyenda negra* are limited responses to colonialist discourses precisely insofar as their inversion of the Manichean binary does not provide an alternative view of indigenous culture. Las Casas's Amerindian "noble savage," as depicted in the *Brevíssima* (as well as in the illustrations of de Bry), remains within the colonial system of representation, and therefore does not elaborate new forms of understanding Amerindian societies and cultures. Las Casas, however, overcomes this limitation in his *Apologética historia sumaria* (ca. 1555) where he transvalues Amerindian cultures (e.g., anthropophagy and sacrifice are instances of religiosity and the value of human life among Amerindians) and uses the noble savage figure within utopian discourse that makes manifest the semantic field underlying the opposition between "civilization" and "savagery" (see Rabasa 1989b).

9 For David Quint, the *Araucana*'s "nonending plot" follows the epic model in Lucan's *Pharsalia* and would thus destabilize the binary opposition (Quint 1993: 157). I would add that colonial epics could not be but open-ended mainly because the narrated events correspond to the historical present. Contrary to the absolute past that Bakhtin (1981) attributes to the epic genre, the colonial epic articulates a political now. In this regard, colonial epics are clear instances of what Bakhtin calls the novelization of pure genres. *La Araucana* is an open-ended epic to the extent that the Araucanos, in spite of their defeat, recovered their forces (an ambiguous open-endedness, as their "indomitable" nature would call for extermination), but, perhaps more insidiously, because García Hurtado de Mendoza (for Ercilla, a despicable character with little to offer the Spanish empire) was appointed viceroy (Pittarello 1989). In Castellanos's *Elegias,* the imperial project also lacks closure because worthy conquistadores and their Criollo descendants, in spite of their moral qualities, have not been sufficiently rewarded. Villagrá's could also be considered an open-ended story, but one that augurs that history will vindicate Oñate, Zaldívar, and Villagrá himself. Even when open-ended, the plot of the epic requires a binary and a story of triumph. The open-ended plot of these colonial epics suggests the plot structure of the comedy in which the disruption of order, whether due to greedy *encomenderos* or rebellious Indians, would be resolved within a historical telos. In the case of Villagrá's descriptions of terror there is a comic streak that balances the intensity of participating in the violent impulses with a detachment afforded by laughter. For a discussion of the comic in Camões's description of the Hottentot slaughter in *Os luisiades,* see Quint (1989b: 127–35).

10 Michael Murrin questions whether the credibility of testimonies like

Escalona's and others, bent on discrediting Oñate, provides a sympathetic view of Oñate, Zaldívar, and Villagrá, and questions the validity of referring to the war against Acoma as a massacre (1994: 216–28). Murrin seeks to revise versions like Forbes's *Apache Navajo and Spaniard* (1960: 89–94), that, in his opinion, give uncritical credence to what he calls the anti-Oñate party. My use of the term massacre follows Villagrá, who presents Oñate as ordering the war to be *a sangre y fuego* (by blood and fire) (Villagrá 1992 [1610]: 224). Villagrá reflects the language used in the trials against the Indians of Acoma, *Proceso que se hizo . . . contra los yndios del pueblo de Acoma,* which makes clear that war was waged against Acoma after the Acomans had been summoned to surrender those responsible for killing Juan de Zaldívar, to abandon their town in the mesa (which would be burned down), and to resettle in the valley, and had refused to comply (AGI, Patronato 22, ramo 13, fols. 1086r–1131r). See Hammond and Rey (1953) for an English version of the trial.

11   These topoi as they relate to empire have been studied by Quint (1989a).

12   I owe this reference to Raphael Holinshed's chronicle to Jody Mikalachi, who presented this passage in a workshop on "Representations of Women in Early Modern English Historiography" during the symposium "Attending to Women in Early Modern England," 8–10 November 1990, organized by the Center for Renaissance and Baroque Studies at the University of Maryland.

13   In this regard, I am following Jaime Concha's indication that before praising Ercilla's representations of the Araucanos we ought to understand the social situation of the poet in the process of conquest (Concha 1969; cf. Quint 1993: 166). For a suggestive reading of *La Araucana* as the first instance of a new Spanish American consciousness, see Pastor (1988 [1983]: 563). Also see my discussion of the colonial epic and, in particular, of the *Araucana* in note 9.

14   The classical reference to the utopian heroic world of Homer is, of course, the initial study of the epic form in Georg Lukács, *Theory of the Novel* (1978). In *The Dialectic of Enlightenment* (1973), Horkheimer and Adorno's critique of Enlightenment (already manifest in myth) seeks to debunk this privileging of Western culture in Lukács. Mikhail Bakhtin, on the other hand, privileges the novel as a genre that breaks away from the closure of the epic and thus introduces the carnivalesque into "high" culture (1981: 26). Both Lukács and Bakhtin share a privileging of Western cultural forms and thus exemplify an instance of the dialectic of Enlightenment, which, as Horkheimer and Adorno incessantly remind us, is totalitarian by nature. Under the

dialectic of Enlightenment the subaltern not only cannot speak, but indeed must be taught how to speak. The principle of the dialogic in Bakhtin suggests an opening of this closure; however, the dialogic does not imply the possibility that the subaltern can speak but rather provides a representation of the subaltern speaking—at best, a suspension of one's privileged perspective, a provision for one's inscription. The symbolic violence, the force of law, that keeps subalterns from speaking (i.e., from being understood and listened to) in "actual" historical situations also haunts the representation of believable subaltern speaking subjects and the limits of meaningful discourse in fiction.

15   See R. Gutiérrez (1991: 39–44) for a study of how a Spanish patriarchal order was imposed on the Pueblo religious organization along matrilocal patterns and the religious preeminence of the Corn Mothers.

16   Again, we should ask ourselves if it really matters that the torture and death of her brother did not happen exactly as told by Menchú. For a detailed discussion, see note 4. My answer is a categorical No! Her brother, who was murdered, is but one frame of the *película negra;* the independent Historical Clarification Commission estimated that more than 200,000 civilians were killed. Here I can only touch on the issue of different testimonial genres which, at the very least, would include the sort of dry account of facts that commissions on human rights collect to argue cases in court and those deeply personal accounts like Menchú's. They not only fulfill different purposes (whereas one seeks empathy, the other calls for logical analysis) but also partake of different criteria that define truth. Testimonies are given for a variety of reasons that cannot be limited to providing evidence for legal cases: for example, for building solidarity, for creating spaces to mourn, for overcoming one's experience of terror, and for the simple record of an atrocity that should never happen again. For a study of torture and the dangers of objectivist discourse of the kind collected by human rights commissions for arguing legal cases ("we neutralize the FACT of the agony for these women, woman by woman"), see Bunster-Burotto (1986: 308).

4. Violence in de Soto Narratives

1   Unless otherwise specified, all English translations of Oviedo and other texts on Hernando de Soto are my own. I have consulted and benefited from Buckingham Smith's translations of Oviedo, Luis Hernández de Biedma, and the Fidalgo de Elvas in *Narratives of the*

Career of Hernando de Soto in the Conquest of Florida, 2 vols., edited by Edward Gaylord Bourne (1922).

2   See "Hernando de Soto: Scourge of the Southeast," special section, *Archaeology* 42:3 (1989): 26–39.

3   See *Archaeology* 42:5 (1989): 10.

4   Cf., e.g., Abbot (1898), Graham (1968 [1912]), and Albornoz (1971). All these romantic versions base their narratives on Garcilaso de la Vega's *La Florida del Inca.* Chapter 5 below offers a reading of Garcilaso's cultural politics and questioning of the modern Western episteme.

5   For editions of Biedma's *Relación,* see *CDI,* 3: 414–41; Smith (1857, 1: 47–64). On Biedma as primary source, see Altman (1997). Patricia Galloway (1990, 1997a) has argued that neither Ranjel nor the *Relaçam* can be considered primary sources. See also Elbl and Elbl (1997). For the Cañete fragment, see Eugene Lyon, "The Cañete Fragment" (n.d.).

6   See my discussion in chapter 1 of these generic distinctions in Cabeza de Vaca's *Naufragios* and the *Joint Report.*

7   Murrin is of the opinion that descriptions of atrocities are in themselves critiques of violence. The following comment on Ercilla illustrates his assumption that readers would readily condemn acts on the basis of detailed depictions: "Ercilla, who rejects total war, emphasizes the violence by making his audience see the dying, mutilated, and wounded. For him such visualization achieves more than any moralizing discourse" (1994: 215). Does Ercilla condemn total war in all situations? To what extent did Ercilla intend the aesthetic rendition of death to delight, even while the surrounding discourse on the actors involved colored the event as unchivalrous? Moreover, in the passages on which Murrin bases his comment, Ercilla does not interrupt the description of the massacre after "No puedo proseguir, que me divierte/ tanto golpe, herida, tanta muerte" [I cannot go on because so great a blow, wound, and so much death distract me], but instead goes on to provide aesthetically pleasing gruesome details (Murrin 1994: 215; Ercilla 1979 [1569–89]: 3.32.10). In the end, Ercilla blames Caupolican for the massacre, while he also praises other Araucano leaders who refused to follow Caupolican, "visto que el General usado había de fraude y trato entre ellos reprobado" [having seen that the General had used fraud and ways condemnable among them] (3.32.10). At the very least the reader is left wondering whether fraud deserves massacre. See the discussion of the aesthetics of violence in chapter 3 above. As for Oviedo, in one passage he condemns violence, whereas in other the same action is celebrated.

8   One must, therefore, not place these historians under the same histo-

riographical traditions, as Manuel Ballesteros (the modern editor of the *Sumario*) has done in an editorial note to this passage, simply on the grounds that both use the term *destrucción* (see Oviedo 1986 [1526]: 82). Obviously, Ballesteros's note is alluding to Las Casas's *Brevíssima relación de la destruyción de Indias* (1552). Cf. Stephanie Merrim (1989). On the utopian character of Las Casas's ethnology, see Rabasa (1989b).

9 See the articles dedicated to this topic in the special issue of *Archeology* 42: 3 (1989). On massacres and in particular the archaeological "King Site," see Robert L. Blakely (1988). Also see the chapters dedicated to de Soto in Jerald T. Milanich and Susan Milbrath (1989) and the chapters on the expedition and Indian history in Galloway (1997b).

10 "Otros se ocuparon en abrir indios muertos y sacar el unto para que sirviese de ungüentos y aceites para curar las heridas" [Others worked on opening the bodies of the dead Indians and extracting the fat that would serve as unguents and oils to heal the wounds] (Garcilaso de la Vega, 1986 [1605]: 370).

11 The dialogue between Oviedo and Joan Cano at the end of chapter 54 of book 33, dedicated to the conquest of Mexico, specifically addresses the issue of the Nuevas Leyes and criticizes Las Casas (see *HGN*, 4: 259–64).

12 For a study of the dance in the colonial period and twentieth-century Peru, see Castro-Klarén (1993).

13 I owe to Elaine Scarry (1985) the observations that follow on the concept that military contest carries the power of its own enforcement. Also of interest is André Glucksmann's (1969) reading of Clausewitz.

14 See Scarry (1985: 63–64), where she argues that even though to injure is the main objective and end of making war, historical and strategic discourses on war tend to use a whole set of metaphors that conceal or completely omit this self-evident fact: it disappears from view.

15 "These boys were very useful in this task. Those from the house helped much more in uprooting the idolatrous rituals which were held at night . . . for these boys, by day, spied out where something of this sort was to be performed at night. . . . The fear which the common people felt of these boys who were reared with us, was so great that, after a few days, it was not necessary to go with them when some feast or orgy took place at night. For if we sent ten or twenty of them, they seized and bound all those of the feast or orgy, even though there might be a hundred or two hundred" (Sahagún 1950–82 [ca. 1579], 1: 80).

16 For a reconstruction of the sources of the *Relaçam* and their transformation into a literary text, see Galloway (1997a); see also Elbl and Elbl (1997).

17 Miguel Albornoz's argument that the "fact" that de Soto never read the *Requerimiento* demonstrates his realism, is an example of how de Soto has been idealized by modern historians: "De Soto era un hombre realista; pese a las disposiciones del Consejo de Indias se había abstenido del inútil formalismo del 'requerimiento' y así había dado instrucciones a sus hombres para toda la expedición" [De Soto was a realist man; in spite of the dispositions of the Council of the Indies he had abstained from the useless formalism of the 'requerimiento' and thus he had instructed his men for the whole expedition] (1971: 289). See chapter 1 above for a discussion of the *Requerimiento* in the context of Cabeza de Vaca and Pánfilo de Narváez.

18 On the contemporary use of these sorts of phantasmagoric constructs in the images of the underworld in the press and its link to the appearance of death squads, see Taussig (1989: 13). Also see Bolaños (1994) for a study of Fray Pedro de Simon's rhetoric in his account of the war against the Pijaos and how the same stereotypes continue to inform twentieth-century anthropological, medical, and sociological explanations of violence in Colombia.

19 It is worth remembering that if the Crown listened to Las Casas, it is because he too sought to represent its interests: his call for the dissolution of the *encomienda* is couched in terms that benefited the Crown; that is, the *encomiendas* would revert to the Crown. See, e.g., the *memorial* by Bartolomé de las Casas and Domingo de Santo Tomás in García Icazbalceta (1971 [1866], 2: 231–36).

5. "Porque soy indio"

1 Inca Garcilaso de la Vega (1539–1617) was the illegitimate son of Sebastian Garcilaso de la Vega, one of the first Spanish conquerors of Peru, and Chimpu Ocllo (baptized as Isabel Suárez), a descendant of Inca nobility. Garcilaso's father recognized him in his will as a natural son and left him an inheritance of four thousand pesos so that he could study in Spain. Baptized Gómez Suárez de Figueroa, Garcilaso adopted his father's surname when he established himself in Spain. He arrived in Spain in 1560 and settled in the Andalusian village of Montilla, where he lived for most of his life. His first publication was a Spanish translation from Italian of the *Dialoghi di amore* by Jehudah Abarbanel (better known in Spain as León Hebreo), which was published in Madrid in 1590 and entitled *La traducción del Indio de los tres Dialogos de Amor de León Hebreo, hecha de Italiano en Español por Garcilaso Inga de la Vega natural de la gran Ciudad de Cuzco, cabeza de los Reynos*

y provincias del Piru. Although it is common knowledge that, as early as this first publication and later in his other two main works, Garcilaso identified himself in his titles as well as in numerous passages as an Indian, or "the Inca," insufficient attention has been paid to how these self-referential statements express a problematic authorship. Two notable exceptions to this rule are Nicolás Wey-Gómez (1991) and Jákfalvi-Leiva (1984). Garcilaso's other main works were *La Florida del Inca* and the *Comentarios reales de los Incas* (in two parts). *La Florida del Inca* first appeared in Lisbon in 1605 under the title *Historia del Adelantado Hernando de Soto, Gobernador y capitan general del Reyno de la Florida, y de otros heroicos cavalleros Españoles è Indios.* The first part of the *Comentarios,* which covers precontact Peru, appeared in Lisbon in 1609 as *Primera parte de los Comentarios Reales, que tratan del origen de los Incas, Reyes que fueron del Perú, y de su idolatría, leyes y gobierno en paz y en guerra: de sus vidas y conquistas, y de todo lo que fue aquel imperio y su Republica, antes que los españoles passaran a el. Escritos por el Ynca Garcilaso de la Vega.* The second part, which covers the conquest and the subsequent civil wars among the Spaniards and which was supposed to be entitled *Segunda parte de los Comentarios Reales,* first appeared posthumously in 1617 as *Historia general del Perú. Trata del descubrimiento dél; y cómo lo ganaron los españoles. Las guerras civiles que hubo entre Picarros y Almagros, sobre la partija de la tierra. Castigo y levantamiento de tiranos; y otros sucesos particulares que en la Historia se contienen. Escrita por el Ynca Garcilaso de la Vega.* For a biography of Garcilaso, see John Grier Varner (1968). See also the English translation of *La Florida del Inca* by John Grier Varner and Jeannette Johnson Varner (Garcilaso de la Vega 1951 [1605]), from which I quote here, with some modifications.

2   More recently, Castro-Klarén (1996a), Sommer (1996), Mazzotti (1996), Rabasa (1994b, 1995b), and Cornejo Polar (1994, 1995) have emphasized the tensions in Garcilaso's mestizo identity rather than a harmonious synthesis of the two cultures. Cornejo Polar and Mazzotti take the discussion of harmony in different directions. Cornejo Polar traces in Garcilaso a hegemonic (indeed, tragic) will to harmonize the European and Quechua traditions in the *Comentarios,* and in so doing to legitimize his condition of mestizo and, consequently, to advance a homogeneous view of Andean culture (1994: 93 and passim). On the other hand, Mazzotti traces Quechua voices, that is, Andean origins in the *Comentarios* that raise questions regarding Garcilaso's purported will to homogenize Andean culture and also regarding the influence of European sources on Garcilaso. Castro-Klarén has elaborated a comparison of Garcilaso and Giovanni Botero in which she suggests a reading of the *Comentarios* as a political tract where his

commentaries on the Andean history are a close parallel to Machiavelli's comments on Livy in the *Discourses*. Sommer finds in Garcilaso's translation of León Hebreo a rehearsal of a style that weaves in and out of Spanish and Quechua cultures. Beyond a reference to his racial or even his cultural hybridity, his self-reference as mestizo or *indio* point to his position of marginality, to the place from which he writes. The *porque soy indio,* then, is not a gesture that aspires to validate an identity, but a rhetorical move that exposes hegemonic discourses and thus serves as a marker of an alternative historiography. I view these references to being an *indio,* as well as those that speak of himself as mestizo or Spaniard, as a baroque-like production of a *superject* (i.e., an emergent self), a discursive product, rather than a stable, essential mestizo *subject-author* that would underlie the process of a certain kind of mestizo writing. My reading points to how Garcilaso disrupts the categories that lend solidity and permanence to hegemonic selves. Otherwise, we run the risk of reading Garcilaso as anachronistically responding to the Cartesian subject. A baroque exuberance seems to me a more appropriate description than a Renaissance humanism in the likeness of Michel de Montaigne because Garcilaso lacks the introspection and convolution of the latter's writing self. Garcilaso's style is delightfully superficial, but nonetheless profound. On the notion of the baroque superject, see Deleuze (1988), who derives this concept from Whitehead (1969 [1929]).

3 Castro-Klarén (1996b) has elaborated a comparison of Garcilaso's and Guaman Poma's modes of writing subalternity that avoids establishing an opposition between them. For studies that oppose Garcilaso and Guaman, see, e.g., Seed (1991) and Wachtel (1971).

4 For extended discussions of Spanish historiography of the New World, the modern Western episteme, and the formation of Eurocentrism, see Rabasa (1993b).

5 Bernardino de Sahagún was the most accomplished ethnographer among the Franciscans in sixteenth-century Mexico. He arrived in New Spain in 1529 and remained there until his death in 1590. Sahagún was an active member of the Colegio de Santa Cruz de Tlaltelolco, where the sons of the indigenous elite were trained to read and write Latin, Spanish, and Nahuatl. These trilingual students assisted Sahagún in the collection of materials, the Roman alphabetic transcription of oral reports, and the various tasks involved in producing the *Historia general de las cosas de la Nueva España.* The *Florentine Codex* is the most finished version of a series of texts that Sahagún developed over the years. For a discussion of Sahagún's methods, the different texts, and the stages in the production of the *Historia,* see Klor de Alva

(1988). Recent editions of the *Historia* include a Spanish one by Angel María Garibay K. (Sahagún 1956 [1579]) and an English bilingual edition of the Nahuatl version and the Spanish prologues by Arthur J. O. Anderson and Charles E. Dibble (Sahagún 1950–82). For a facsimilar edition of the *Florentine Codex,* see Sahagún (1979).

6   For bibliographical and biographical information on Oviedo, see note 11 in chapter 1.

7   For biographical and bibliographical information on Las Casas, see note 21 in chapter 1.

8   I thank Anna More for making this observation in the course of a seminar.

6. Of Massacre and Representation

1   Unless otherwise indicated, all translations from Spanish and French texts are my own.

2   For studies on the black legend, see, e.g., Juderías (1917), Carbia (1943), Maltby (1971), Powell (1971), Robinson (1973), and Sánchez (1990).

3   "Los españoles, de carácter soberbio, rudo y violento, bastante exacerbados por sus largas y sangrientas luchas contra los moriscos, fuertemente movidos además de insaciable ambición y exaltados hasta grado sumo por crudelísimo fanatismo; veían en los indios á seres 'más semejantes á bestias feroces que á criaturas racionales,' y como á tales les trataban: crían que por ser gente sin fé, podían indiferentemente violar á sus mujeres é hijas, 'matarlos, cautivarlos, tomarles sus tierras, posesiones y senoríos é cosas, é dello ninguna conciencia se hacía.' Los Franceses, de carácter alegre, comunicativo y amable, un tanto desprendidos y de espíritu religioso amable, cuando no escépticos, miraban en los naturales á seres humanos inteligentes, más robustos, más agiles y hermosos que ellos, y no les despojaban de su riqueza, ni les arrebataban su libertad, ni estupraban á sus mujeres é hijas, ni tampoco les asesinaban, sino que les trataban afablemente como á iguales" [The Spaniards, with an arrogant, rough, and violent character, greatly exacerbated by the long and bloody struggles against morisco, moved by ambition and exalted by crude fanaticism, saw in the Indians beings "more like ferocious beasts than rational creatures," and as such they treated them: they believed that because they were people without faith, they could indifferently rape their wives and daughters, "kill them,

captivate them, take their lands, possessions and sovereignty and things, and without blame." The French, with a cheerful, communicative, and kind character, somewhat detached and with a friendly religious spirit, when not skeptics, saw in the natives intelligent human beings, more robust, more agile and beautiful than they, and would not take their wealth, nor seize their freedom, nor rape their women and daughters, nor murder them, rather treated them affably as equals] (García 1902: lxxviii)

4　Also see Lestringant (1990: 167–71) for a discussion of Thevet's method as "phagocytic" and lacking critical distance vis-à-vis the "respectful" historiography of the Huguenots and Hakluyt. For a detailed discussion of Protestant attacks on Thevet's historiography, see Lestringant (1991, esp. 236–46).

5　My use of the term "the corpus of Florida" differs from Marcel Bataillon's (1974: 45) definition exclusively in terms of the French Huguenot texts on the New World. Here the corpus comprises Spanish and French texts as well as any materials that might connect the Spanish conquest of the New World, in particular the massacres in Florida, to the wars of religion plaguing Europe. See Lestringant (1990, 1991, 1996) for exhaustive studies of the corpus as defined by Bataillon.

6　The *edición principe* of Ruidíaz's collection consists of two volumes. Volume 1 includes several maps, a history of the exploration, a biography of Pedro Menéndez de Avilés, a short biographical sketch of Solís de Merás, and the *Memorial*. Volume 2 consists of twelve appendices that collect the letters and memorials of Menéndez de Avilés, titles, instructions, and several accounts by other participants, and other documents. José M. Gómez-Tabanera's 1989 publication of this collection includes fewer documents than the second volume, but adds the main French accounts (Rudíaz y Caravia 1989 [1893]). Gómez-Tabanera's "edition" of the French documents is somewhat of a scandal because he merely translates Suzanne Lussagnet's edition (1958), including footnotes, without giving proper credit! When Gómez-Tabanera adds anything to the footnotes, his comments emulate Ruidíaz's panegyric introduction to the 1893 edition. Because of the inaccessibility of Ruidíaz's edition, all citations from the Spanish sources are from Gómez-Tabanera's edition. For a recent biography of Menéndez de Avilés that, as the author claims, "examined all possible primary material which might bear upon sixteenth-century Spanish Florida or its founder," see Lyon (1974: v).

7　A recent article by John Noble Wilford (1996) reporting on the excavations and the location of the fort made the front page of the *New*

York Times: "The site of the fort is under a golf course on the Marine training base at Parris Island, near Beaufort, South Carolina." According to the article, the finding has triggered differing evaluations of the significance of the site. I will just cite Ivor Noël Hume's somewhat baffling statement: "No longer will France in the New World be epitomized only by Quebec and New Orleans" (A13). The parallelism between this archaeological site buried under a golf course with these two major cities is not only bizarre, but also obscures the significance of French accounts of the colonization of North America. (I am afraid there is some nationalistic motivation in this statement that might have to do with the generally accepted claim that St. Augustine was the first permanent European settlement in what is today the United States.)

8 Lestringant gives "Une Saint Barthélemy Américaine" as the title to one of his chapters in *L'Expérience huguenote au Nouveau Monde* (1996: 229–42).

9 On Protestant pamphleteers seeking alliance with Malcontent Catholics against the pro-Spanish Catholic League, see Kingdon (1988: 201).

10 The full title is *Tyrannies et cruautez des Espagnols, perpetrees es Indes Occidentales, qu'on dit le Nouveau monde: Brievement descrites en langue Castillane, par l'Evesque Don Frere Bartelemy de Las Casas ou Casaus, Espagnol de l'ordre de sainct Dominique, fidelement traduites par Iacques de Miggrode* (Anvers: F. Raphelengius, 1579).

11 For a discussion of open-endedness and self-reference in paradox, see Colie (1966: 38). Also see Rabasa (1993b: 34).

12 Tom Conley has defined this engaged reading of maps and paintings in terms of the psychoanalytic concept of the *perspectival object:* "This concept has to do with positioning and mapping of the self in and about the world in its ongoing construction of psychogenesis, and it is tied at once to aesthetics, the history of perspective, and clinical practice. . . . [I]t designates a series of junctures between a viewer and what he or she sees, projects, fantasizes, and remembers, but also what always eludes containment" (1996: 13). Also see Alpers (1983: 119–68).

13 The literature on violence and the wars of religion is immense. I have found Natalie Zemon Davis's understanding of the Saint Bartholomew's Day massacres as ritual forms of social cleansing particularly useful (1975: 152–87). Davis criticizes Estebe's view of the Catholics' emasculation of Protestant men and the killing of pregnant women as seeking to exterminate "une race haïe et maudite" [a hated and damned race], but in view of recent events in Bosnia the term "ethnic cleansing" seems to me more appropriate (Davis 1975:

160; Estebe 1968: 197). Also see Estebe (97) and Kingdon (1988) on the degrees of premeditation and planning of the massacres by the royal authorities.

14 I thank Anna More for this observation.

15 The scholarship on tolerance goes well beyond the objectives of this chapter. Here I will limit myself to recent scholarship that has expanded the canon as well as the topics of the debates; see Laursen and Nederman (1998), Nederman and Laursen (1996), and Remer (1996). In light of these studies, which take us back to antiquity, the Middle Ages, and the early modern period, the discourse of tolerance should no longer be limited to the history of liberalism as embodied by the tradition that goes from John Locke to John Stuart Mill and thereafter. In what follows I have benefited from Negri's interpretation of Spinoza (1991).

16 It is somewhat ironic that when we consult Spanish sources we also often find claims of objectivity and measure. Elsewhere I have traced the invention of modern historiography in Columbus, Cortés, Oviedo, and Sahagún, among other Spanish texts on the New World (Rabasa 1993b). This genealogy of modern historiography critiqued the emergence of European history and subjectivity as universal rather than celebrating an intellectual accomplishment. My concerns in this chapter are to connect the will to objectivity with the moral economy of violence manifest in representations of massacres and torture. On objectification as a specific form of modernity, see Heidegger (1977).

17 For an assessment of Mercator and de Bry's book printing enterprises as examples as well as emblems of the economic emergence of Northern Europe as world power, see Rabasa (1993b: 180–209) and Cummins (1994, esp. 24–27).

18 Derrida draws this distinction from Carl Schmitt in *The Gift of Death:* "Carl Schmitt . . . emphasizes the fact that *inimicus* is not *hostis* in Latin and *ekhthros* is not *polemios* in Greek. This allows him to conclude that Christ's teaching concerns the love that we must show to our private enemies, to those we would be tempted to hate through personal or subjective passion, and not to public enemies. . . . As he reminds us, no Christian politics ever advised the West to love the Muslims who invaded Christian Europe" (1995: 103). Derrida underscores a broader frontier between *inimicus* and *hostis* than Schmitt allows. Distinctions based on ethnicity, nationality, or religion haunt the neatness of the opposition between *hostis* and *inimicus:* "And the opposition between the mediocre salary of retribution or exchange and the noble salary that is obtained through disinterested sacrifice or

through the gift also points to an opposition between two peoples, ours, to whom Christ is speaking, and the others, who are referred to as *ethnici* or *ethniko,* the races, therefore, in short, the peoples, those who are only peoples, collectivities (goyim in Chouraqui's French translation, pagans in Grosjean's and Léturmy's Bibliothèque de la Pléiade's version)" (105-6).

19 Las Casas's denunciations of Spanish atrocities led to the Nuevas Leyes of 1542 that sought, needless to say unsuccessfully, to abolish slavery and the *encomienda.* Eventually Las Casas, in his *Tratado de las "Doce dudas,"* demanded that Spaniards abandon the Indies and expressed the opinion that the Indians had the right to erase the Spaniards from the face of the earth: "La octava [conclusión] que las gentes naturales de todas partes y de qualquiera dellas donde havemos entrado en las Indias tienen derecho adquirido de hazernos la guerra justissima y raernos de la haz de la tierra y este derecho les durara hasta el dia del juyzio" [The eighth (conclusion is) that the native people of these and all parts where we have entered in the Indies have the right to make a most just war against us and to erase us from the face of the earth, and they hold this right until doom's day] (1992a, 11.2: 218). Spaniards should be read as a shorthand for Europeans and certainly not as an attribution to the nation of some inherently evil nature. In a recently rediscovered text from 1546, "De exemptione sive damnatione," Las Casas threatens Prince Philip of Spain with eternal damnation if he does not stop the atrocities in the Indies (see Parish and Wiedman 1992).

20 Given the French origin of de Bry's illustrations, we must qualify Conley's observation that in de Bry's edition, "A double symbolical efficacy is obtained insofar as each image can both distill a pertinent unit of description in the surrounding text and provide a lesson for deciphering of the Latin" (1992: 125). Conley furthermore connects this "Berlitz-like immersion into Latin" with a "subterranean genre that runs from hagiography and martyrology to CIA manuals of torture: the pictures tell us to strengthen our souls at the sight of excess, but only in such a way that we are told that we have to see it in order to know it" (125). This might explain Le Moyne's reticence to visually represent the Florida massacres. But I would add that verbal descriptions can also lend themselves to sadistic readings and prurience. Would the CIA make Menchú's description of her brother's tortured body required reading for future torturers?

21 *The Tears of the Indians: Being an Historical and true Account Of the Cruel Massacres and Slaughters of above Twenty Millions of Innocent People; Committed by the Spaniards In the Islands of Hispaniola, Cuba, Jamaica, & also,*

in the continents of Mexico, Peru, & other Places of the West Indies, to the total destruction of those Countries. Written by Casaus, an eye-witness of those things; And made English by J. P. London, Printed by J. C. for Nath. Brook, at the Angel in Cornhil. 1656.

22 For a detailed description of Vasari's panel that highlights its disturbing effect from the perspective of a twentieth-century viewer, see Fehl (1974). Commemorative medals of Saint Bartholomew's Day massacres, made in Rome in 1572, convey this same sense of the sublime in their depictions of the angel of history executing the Protestants. The effigy of Gregory XIII, on the reverse, further certifies the providential significance of the atrocity, with corpses lying at the feet of the angel (see Erlanger 1960). For descriptions of medallions produced in France, see Goulart (1578: 386r–387v). Goulart describes one in which "Dorat poëte, escriuit des vers Latin, où il se mocque de ce corp mutilé" [Dorat the poet wrote verses in Latin where he laughs at this mutilated body] (386r).

23 For instance, the recent film *La Reine Margot* (Berri 1995) limits itself to having Guise kick the head of Coligni, in itself a disputed incident among witnesses of the slaughter. Given the anti-emigrant rhetoric in France today and the emergence of French minority culture in the suburbs of Paris as exemplified by another recent film (*La Haine*, Kassovitz 1995), we cannot fail to associate *La Reine Margot* with Fanon's monument—a statement on French national identity.

24 The title of a pamphlet describing the procession leaves no doubt as to the celebratory ambience in Rome: "Ordine della solennissima procession fatta dal sommo pontifice nell'alma citta di Roma, per la fellicissima noua dell destruttione de la setta Vgonotana" [The order of the most solemn procession made in the heart of the city of Rome by the Sovereign Pontiff, on account of the most felicitous news of the destruction of the Huguenot sect] (Nicholson n.d.).

25 Considering the "monumentality" of the scene as represented in the miniature, Laudonnière's account is very brief and uneventful, describing the offerings as merely consisting of "petits panniers de mil" [little baskets of corn] (in Lussagnet 1958: 87; Laudonniére 1975: 61). Le Moyne does not mention this event in his narrative, leading me to assume that the representation of the scene is a symbolic form of certifying possession in painting rather than a record of a particularly significant event in the second voyage (see Le Moyne 1977, 1: 120–38). The commentary under de Bry's engraving speaks of "various offerings of fruits of the district and roots that were either good to eat or medically useful dishes full of fragrant oils, and bows and arrows" (1: 141). We cannot ascertain to what extent these words were Le Moyne's,

but clearly they reinforce the realism of the copperplate, which thus loses the imaginary dimension conveyed by the fantastic use of color. De Bry's commentary marks the beginning of a series of descriptive readings that have subjected this watercolor and other allegorical representations of America to realistic interpretations of accuracy (see Rabasa 1993b: 23–48).

26 I thank Patricia Seed for this reminder. Jean Ribault describes them as of "tawny collour, hawke nosed and of pleasant countenance" (1964 [1563]: 69). Lussagnet (1958: 10) has pointed out that only Fray Andrés de San Miguel addresses their skin color and compares them to Indians from Mexico and indicates that the women were lighter (see also García 1902: 194).

Epilogue: Before History

1 See my essay on the Zapatistas in Chiapas for examples of plural-world dwelling in a subaltern insurrection (Rabasa 1997). For a philosophical formulation of the coexistence of a plurality of worlds in the experience of one subject, see Spinosa and Dreyfus (1996). Also see Goodman (1978).

2 In passing I would like to point out that what Chakrabarty calls translation would be more aptly understood as the reduction of one world (the times of the gods) to another (the time of history) by means of representation. The work of translation implies drawing parallel identities, even if it involves invoking the times of the gods in a world in which they no longer speak. Chakrabarty draws a distinction between translation in the mode of barter, as in the Hindi term *pani* for the English term *water,* and translation in the mode of commodity exchange, in which a third term participates in a general economy of exchange. For the latter, Chakrabarty gives as an example the Hindi term *pani* and the English term *water* mediated by H_2O. Yet, within this "higher" form of translation looms the specter of reification—indeed, of fetishized general categories. Concepts such as H_2O, abstract labor, culture, language, religion, superstition, and idolatry all have the capacity (in some instances, bear the imperialist élan) to reduce plurality to one. They also privilege an order and clarity that might have more to do with the psychological needs of the scholar than with the object of study. Concepts such as H_2O lack a corresponding phenomenological experience. In fact, they shelter us from the contingencies of the world of experience and the indeterminacy of forms of life, which, by the way, may be closer to chaos theory in

physics than to the Newtonian model Chakrabarty invokes to ground his belief in the capacity of language to represent reality (Chakrabarty 1997: 38). Examples like H_2O mediating *pani* and *water* (unless conceived in the ethereal world of the laboratory) have less to do with translation than with representation. The relationship between *thing* and *concept* is analogous to the relationship between landscape A and its representation in painting B, in which it is true to say that A is in B, but not that B is in A. If there is a loss of the phenomenal world (temporality and experience) in the *reductions* the sciences draw, and Chakrabarty acknowledges this, why should we continue to think of general concepts in terms of translation, which is based (ideally speaking) on identity, and not acknowledge a difference between translation and representation? We can thus embrace the richness of scientific inquiry in its ongoing reconsideration of its categories in the different and *differing* disciplines (the one is also plural) without abandoning the opaqueness as well as the translucent experience of the singular. We may further this line of questioning by asking whether under the sign of reification and fetishization the time of history would not amount to one more instance of the times of the gods, indeed, to a most unforgiving and jealous "god"?

3 For detailed discussions of Indians using Western forms of life in ways that could not be anticipated by missionaries and colonial authorities, see Gruzinski (1999).

Bibliography

Abbot, John S. C. 1898. *Ferdinand De Soto.* New York: Dodd, Mead.

Acosta, Joseph de. 1984–87 [1588]. *De procuranda Indorum salute.* Bilingual edition. L. Pereña, ed. Madrid: Consejo Superior de Investigaciones Científicas.

———. 1979 [1590]. *Historia natural y moral de las Indias.* Ed. Edmundo O'Gorman. Mexico City: Fondo de Cultura Económica.

Actas de la novena reunión del Congreso Internacional de Americanistas. 1894. Madrid: Los Hijos de M. G. Hernández.

Adorno, Rolena. 1994. "Peaceful Conquest and Law in the *Relación* (Account) of Alvar Núñez Cabeza de Vaca." In *Coded Encounters: Writing, Gender, and Ethnicity in Colonial Latin America,* ed. Francisco Javier Cevallos-Candau, et al. Amherst: University of Massachusetts Press. 75–86.

———. 1993. "Reconsidering Colonial Discourse from Sixteenth- and Seventeenth-Century Spanish America." *Latin American Research Review* 28(3): 135–45.

———. 1992. "The Discursive Encounter of Spain and America: The Authority of Eyewitness Testimony in the Writing of History." *William and Mary Quarterly* (s3) 49: 210–28.

———. 1991. "The Negotiations of Fear in Alvar Núñez Cabeza de Vaca's *Naufragios.*" *Representations* 33: 163–99.

———. 1988. "El sujeto colonial y la construcción cultural de la alteridad." *Revista de Crítica Literaria Latinoamericana* 14(28): 55–68.

———. 1987. "Literary Production and Suppression: Reading and Writing about Amerindians in Colonial Spanish America." *Dispositio* 11:1–25.

Adorno, Rolena, and Walter D. Mignolo, eds. 1989. *Colonial Discourse.* Special issue of *Dispositio* 14, nos. 36–38.

Adorno, T. W. 1993. *Hegel: Three Studies.* Trans. Sherry Weber Nicholsen. Cambridge, MA: MIT Press.

———. 1986. *Aesthetic Theory.* Trans. C. Lenhardt. New York: Routledge and Kegan Paul.

Ahern, Maureen. 1998. "Fronteras mudables: Un informe náhuatl de la Guerra Chichimeca, 1563." In *Indigenismo hacia el fin del milenio. Homenaje a Antonio Cornejo-Polar,* ed. Mabel Moraña. Pittsburgh: Instituto Internacional de Literatura Iberoamericana, Serie Biblioteca de América.

———. 1995a. "Testimonio oral, memoria y violencia en el diario de Diego Pérez de Luxán: Nuevo México 1583." *Revista de Crítica Literaria Latinoamericana* 21(41): 153–63.

———. 1995b. "La relación como glosa, guía y memoria: Nuevo México 1581–1582." *Revista Iberoamericana* 61(170–71): 41–55.

———. 1994. "The Articulation of Alterity on the Northern Frontier: The *Relatione della navigatione & scoperta* by Fernando de Alarcón." In *Coded Encounters: Writing, Gender, and Ethnicity in Colonial Latin America,* ed. Francisco Javier Cevallos-Candau et al. Amherst: University of Massachusetts Press. 46–61.

———. 1993. "The Cross and the Gourd: The Appropriation of the Ritual Signs in the *Relaciones* of Alvar Núñez Cabeza de Vaca and Fray Marcos de Niza." In *Early Images of the New World: Transfer and Invention,* ed. Jerry Williams and Robert Lewis. Tucson: University of Arizona Press. 215–44.

———. 1989. "The Certification of Cibola: Discursive Strategies in *La relación del descubrimiento de las siete ciudades* by Fray Marcos de Niza (1539)." *Dispositio* 14: 303–13.

Albornoz, Miguel. 1971. *Hernando de Soto: El Amadís de la Florida.* Madrid: Ediciones de la Revista de Occidente.

Alonso, Ana María. 1995. *Thread of Blood: Colonialism, Revolution, and Gender on Mexico's Northern Frontier.* Tucson: University of Arizona Press.

Alpers, Svetlana. 1983. *The Art of Description: Dutch Art in the Seventeenth Century.* Chicago: University of Chicago Press.

Altman, Ida. 1997. Hernando de Soto. In *Hernando de Soto,* ed. Patricia Galloway. Lincoln: University of Nebraska Press. 3–10.

Alvarado Tezozómoc, Fernando. 1992 [ca. 1609]. *Crónica Mexicáyotl.* Trans. Adrián León. Mexico City: Universidad Nacional Autónoma de México.

Ardonio, Antonio. 1736. *Examen apologético de la histórica narración de los naufragios, peregrinaciones, i milagros de Alvar Núñez Cabeza de Vaca, en las tierras de La Florida y Nuevo México.* Madrid: Imprenta Juan Zúniga.

Aristotle. 1966a [1928]. *Etica Nicomachea.* In *The Works of Aristotle,* vol. 9. Trans. W. D. Ross. London: Oxford University Press.

———. 1966b [1928]. *Politica.* In *The Works of Aristotle,* vol. 10. Trans. W. D. Ross. London: Oxford University Press.

———. 1966c [1928]. *The Works of Aristotle.* 12 vols. Trans. W. D. Ross. London: Oxford University Press.

Asad, Talal. 1986. "The Concept of Cultural Translation in British Social Anthropology." In *Writing Culture: The Poetics and Politics of Ethnography,* ed. James Clifford and George E. Marcus. Berkeley and Los Angeles: University of California Press. 141–64.

Ashcroft, Bill, Gareth Griffiths, and Helen Tiffin. 1989. *The Empire Writes Back: Theory and Practice in Post-Colonial Literatures.* New York: Routledge.

———, eds. 1995. *The Postcolonial Studies Reader.* New York: Routledge.

Austin, J. L. 1962. *How to Do Things with Words.* Ed. J. O. Urmson and Marina Sbisà. Cambridge, MA: Harvard University Press.

Avalle-Arce, Juan Bautista de. 1997. Gonzalo Fernández de Oviedo y Valdés: Chronicler of the Indies. *Hernando de Soto,* Galloway, ed. Pp. 369–79.

Bakhtin, M. M. 1981. "Epic and Novel." *The Dialogical Imagination.* Michael Holquist, ed. Austin and London: University of Texas Press. 3–40.

Balibar, Etienne. 1994. "Racism as Universalism." *Masses, Classes, Ideas: Studies on Politics and Philosophy Before and After Marx.* Trans. by James Swenson. New York: Routledge. 191–204.

Bandelier, Adolph F. 1981 [1886]. *The Discovery of New Mexico by the Franciscan Monk, Friar Marcos de Niza in 1539.* Trans. Madeleine Turrell Rodack. Tucson: University of Arizona Press.

Bannon, John Francis. 1974. *The Spanish Borderlands Frontier 1513–1821.* Albuquerque: University of New Mexico Press.

Barlow, R. H., and George T. Smisor, eds. 1943. *Nombre de Dios, Durango: Two Documents in Náhuatl Concerning Its Foundation. Memorial of the Indians concerning their services, c. 1563; Agreement of the Mexicans and the Michoacanos, 1585.* Trans. R. H. Barlow and George T. Smisor. Sacramento, CA: The House of Tlaloc.

Barrera, Trinidad. 1985. Introducción to *Naufragios,* by Núñez Cabeza de Vaca. Madrid: Alianza Editorial. 7–55.

Barrera, Trinidad, and Carmen Mora. 1983. *Los Naufragios* de Alvar Núñez Cabeza de Vaca: Entre la crónica y la novela. *Actas de las II Jornadas de Andalucía y America.* Seville: Escuela de Estudios Hispano-Americanos de Sevilla. 331–64.

Barrienger, Felicity. 1998. "Breaking a Taboo, the Editors Turn to Images of Death." *New York Times,* 25 October 1998. Week in Review sect., p. 1.

Barrientos, Bartolomé. 1902 [1568]. *Vida y hechos de Pero Menéndez de Avilés.* In *Dos antiguas relaciones de la Florida,* ed. Genaro García. Mexico City: J. Aguilar Vera. 3–149.

Barthes, Roland. 1981a. *Camera Lucida: Reflections on Photography.* Trans. Richard Howard. New York: Hill and Wang.

———. 1981b. "The Discourse of History." In *Rhetoric and History: Comparative Criticism Yearbook.* Ed. E. S. Schaffer. Trans. Stephen Bann. Cambridge, England: Cambridge University Press. 7–20.

―――. 1977. "The Death of the Author." In *Image, Music, Text.* Trans. Stephen Heath. New York: Hill and Wang. 142–48.

Bataillon, Marcel. 1974. "L'Almiral et les 'nouveaux horizons' français." In *Actes du Colloque 'L'Almiral et son temps' (octobre 1972).* Paris: Société de l'histoire du protestantisme française. 41–52.

Benjamin, Walter. 1986. "Critique of Violence." In *Reflections: Essays, Aphorisms, Autobiographical Writings.* Ed. Peter Demetz. Trans. Edmund Jephcott. New York: Schocken Books. 277–300.

―――. 1968. "The Work of Art in the Age of Mechanical Reproduction." In *Illuminations: Essays and Reflections.* Ed. Hannah Arendt. Trans. Harrt Zohn. New York: Schocken Books. 217–51.

Benzoni, Girolamo. 1565. *La historia del Mondo Nuovo.* Venice: F. Rampazetto.

Berlin, Henrich, ed. 1948. *Anales de Tlatelolco: Unos annales históricos de la nación mexicana,* and *Códice de Tlatelolco.* Annotated version in Spanish by Heinrich Berlin with a summary of the *Anales* and an interpretation of the *Codex of Tlatelolco* by Robert H. Barlow. Mexico City: Robredo.

Berri, Claude. 1995. *La Reine Margot.* Coproduced by Renn Productions, France 2 Cinema, D.A. Films (Paris), NEF Filmproduktion GmbH/Degeto for ARD/WMG (Munich), RCS Films & TV (Rome).

Beverley, John. 1993. *Against Literature.* Minneapolis: University of Minnesota Press.

―――. 1992. "Introducción." Special issue on *Testimonio, Revista de Crítica Literaria Latinoamericana* 18(36): 7–18.

―――. 1989. "The Margin at the Center: On Testimonio (Testimonial Narrative)." *Modern Fiction Studies* 35(1): 11–28.

Bhabha, Homi. 1986. "The Other Question: Difference, Discrimination and the Discourse of Colonialism." In *Literature, Politics, and Theory,* ed. Francis Barker, Peter Hulme, Margaret Iversen, and Diane Loxley. London: Methuen. 148–72.

Biedma, Luis Hernández de. 1864–1884 [1544]. *Relación del suceso de la jornada del capitan Soto, y de la calidad de la tierra por donde anduvo.* In *Collección de documentos inéditos relativos al descubrimiento, conquista y organización de las antiguas posesiones en America y Oceanía.* 42 vols. Madrid: Imprenta José María Pérez. 3: 414–41.

Bishop, M. 1933. *The Odyssey of Cabeza de Vaca.* New York: Century.

Blakely, Robert L., ed. 1988. *The King Site: Continuity and Contact in Sixteenth-Century Georgia.* Athens: University of Georgia Press.

Bolaños, Alvaro Félix. 1994. *Barbarie y canibalismo en la retórica colonial. Los indios pijaos de Fray Pedro Simón.* Bogota: Cerec.

Bolton, Herbert. 1916. *Spanish Exploration in the Southwest, 1542–1706.* New York: Charles Scribner's Sons.

Boone, Elizabeth Hill. 1994. "Aztec Pictorial Histories: Records with-out Words." In *Writing without Words,* ed. Elizabeth Hill Boone and Walter D. Mignolo. Durham, NC: Duke University Press. 50–76.

Boone, Elizabeth Hill, and Walter D. Mignolo, eds. 1994. *Writing without Words: Alternative Literacies in Mesoamerica and the Andes.* Durham, NC: Duke University Press.

———. 1994. "Aztec Pictorial Histories: Records without Words." In *Writing without Words,* ed. Elizabeth Hill Boone and Walter D. Mignolo. Durham, NC: Duke University Press. 50–76.

Bourdieu, Pierre. 1987. "The Force of Law: Toward a Sociology of the Juridical Field." *The Hastings Law Journal* 38: 805–53.

Bourne, Edward Gaylord, ed. 1922. *Narratives of the Career of Hernando de Soto in the Conquest of Florida.* 2 vols. New York: Allerton Book.

Boyarin, Jonathan, ed. 1993. *The Ethnography of Reading.* Berkeley: University of California Press.

Bruce Novoa, Juan. 1993. "Shipwreck in the Seas of Signification: Cabeza de Vaca's *La Relación* and Chicano Literature." In *Reconstructing a Chicano/a Literary Heritage: Hispanic Colonial Literature of the Southwest,* ed. María Herrera-Sobek. Tucson: University of Arizona Press.

Bucher, Bernadette. 1981. *Image and Conquest: A Structural Analysis of De Bry's "Grands Voyages."* Chicago: University of Chicago Press.

Bunster-Burotto, Ximena. 1986. "Surviving beyond Fear: Women and Torture in Latin America." In *Women and Change in Latin America: New Directions in Sex and Class,* ed. June Nash and Helen Safa. South Hadley, MA: Bergin & Garvey. 297–326.

Burshatin, Israel. 1984. "Power, Discourse, and Metaphor in the Abencerraje." *MLN* 99: 195–213.

Butler, Judith. 1997a. *Excitable Speech: The Politics of the Performative.* New York: Routledge.

———. 1997b. *The Psychic Life of Power: Theories of Subjection.* Stanford: Stanford University Press.

Calderón, Héctor, and José David Saldívar. 1991a. "Editors' Introduction: Criticism in the Borderlands." In *Criticism in the Borderlands,* ed. Héctor Calderón and José David Saldívar. Durham, NC: Duke University Press. 1–7.

———, eds. 1991b. *Criticism in the Borderlands: Studies in Chicano Literature, Culture and Ideology.* Durham, NC: Duke University Press.

Campbell, T. N., and T. J. Campbell. 1981. *Historic Indian Groups of the Coke Canyon Reservoir and Surrounding Area, Southern Texas.* San Antonio: Center for Archaeological Research, University of Texas at San Antonio.

Cárbia, Rómulo D. 1943. *Historia de la leyenda negra hispanoamericana.* Buenos Aires: Ediciones Orientación Española.

Cardozo, Efraín. 1959. *Historiografía paraguaya.* 2 vols. Mexico: Instituto Panamericano de Geografía e Historia, Comisión de Historia, 83.

Caro Baroja, Julio. 1961. *Los judíos en la España moderna y contemporánea.* 3 vols. Madrid: Ediciones Arion.

Carpenter, Ronald H. 1983. *The Eloquence of Frederick Jackson Turner.* San Marino, CA: The Huntington Library.

Carr, Robert. 1992. "Representando el Testimonio: Notas sobre el cruce divisorio Primer Mundo/Tercer Mundo." Trans. John Beverly and Ileana Rodríguez. *Revista de Crítica Literaria Latinoamericana* 18(36): 73–94.

Carreño, Antonio. 1987. "Naufragios, de Alvar Núñez Cabeza de Vaca: Una retórica de la crónica colonial." *Revista Iberoamericana* 53: 499–516.

Cartas de Indias. 1887. *Cartas de Indias.* Published by Ministerio de Fomento. Madrid: Imprenta Manuel G. Hernández.

Castañeda, Pedro de. 1886 [ca. 1560]. *Relacion de la jornada de Cibola compuesta por Pedro de Castañeda de Naçera. Donde trata de todos aquellos poblados y ritos, y costumbres, la cual fue el año 1540.* In *The Coronado Expedition,* ed. George Parker Winship. Washington, DC: Government Printing Office. 414–546.

Castellanos, Juan de. 1962 [1589–ca. 1607]. *Elegías de varones ilustres de Indias.* Ed. Isaac J. Pardo. Caracas: Biblioteca de la Academia Nacional de la Historia, 57.

Castro-Klarén, Sara. Forthcoming. "Historiography on the Ground: The Toledo Circle and Guamana Poma." In *Citizenship and Ungovernability,* ed. Iliana Rodríguez. Durham, NC: Duke University Press.

———. 1996a. "Garcilaso's Theory of the State and Giovanni Botero." Paper presented at the 1996 MLA Convention, Washington, DC.

———. 1996b. "Writing Subalternity: Guaman Poma and Garcilaso, Inca." In *Dispositio/n* 46: 229–44.

———. 1993. "Dancing and the Sacred in the Andes: From Tiqui-Oncoy to Rasu-Ñiti." In *New World Encounters,* ed. Stephen Greenblatt. Berkeley: University of California Press. 159–76.

———. 1992. "The Litbody or the Politics of Eros in *Lumperia.*" *Indiana Journal of Hispanic Literatures* 1(1): 41–52.

Certeau, Michel de. 1988. *The Writing of History.* Trans. Tom Conley. New York: Columbia University Press.

———. 1986. *Heterologies: Discourse on the Other.* Trans. Brian Massumi. Minneapolis: University of Minnesota Press.

———. 1984. *The Practice of Everyday Life.* Trans. Steven Rendall. Berkeley: University of California Press.

Chakrabarty, Dipesh. 1997. "The Time of History and the Times of the Gods." In *The Politics of Culture in the Shadow of Capital,* ed. Lisa Lowe and David Lloyd. Durham, NC: Duke University Press. 35–60.

Chaunu, Pierre. 1969. *Conquête et exploitation des nouveaux mondes.* Paris: Presses Universitaires de France, "Nouvelle Clio."

Chauveton, Urbain. 1579. *Histoire Nouvelle du Nouveau Monde . . . Extraite de l'Italien de M. Hierosme Benzoni Milanois . . . Ensemble, Une petite Histoire d'un Massacre commis par les Hespagnols sur quelques François en la Floride.* Geneva: Eustache Vignon.

———. 1578. *Novae Novi Orbis Historiae . . . Ex Italicis Hieronymi Benzonis Mediolanensis . . . His ab eodem adjunta est, De Gallorum in Florida expeditione, et insigni Hispanorum in eos saevitiate exemplo, Brevis Historia.* Geneva: Eustache Vignon.

Chipman, D. E. 1987. "In Search of Cabeza de Vaca's Route across Texas: An Historical Survey." *Southwestern Historical Quarterly* 91: 127–48.

Clifford, James. 1997. *Routes: Travel and Translation in the Late Twentieth Century.* Cambridge, MA: Harvard University Press.

———. 1988. *The Predicament of Culture: Twentieth-Century Ethnography, Literature, and Art.* Cambridge, MA: Harvard University Press.

———. 1986. "On Ethnographic Allegory." In *Writing Ethnography: The Poetics and Politics of Writing Ethnography,* ed. James Clifford and George Marcus. Berkeley: University of California Press.

Clifford, James, and George Marcus, eds. 1986. *Writing Culture: The Poetics and Politics of Ethnography.* Berkeley: University of California Press.

Cline, Howard F., ed. 1972. *Guide to Ethnohistorical Sources.* Vol. 12 of *Handbook of Middle American Indians.* Austin: University of Texas Press.

Colás, Santiago. 1995. "Of Creole Symptoms, Cuban Fantasies, and Other Postcolonial Ideologies." *PMLA* 110(3): 382–97.

Colie, Rosalie Littel. 1966. *Paradoxia Epidemica: The Renaissance Tradition of Paradox.* Princeton, NJ: Princeton University Press.

Collier, George A. 1994. *Basta! Land and the Zapatista Rebellion in Chiapas.* With Elizabeth Lowery Quaratiello. Oakland, CA: Institute for Food and Development.

Comas, Juan. 1975. *Cien años de Congresos Internacionalistas de Americanistas.* Mexico City: Universidad Nacional Autónoma de México.

Concha, Jaime. 1969. "El otro Nuevo mundo." In *Homenaje a Ercilla.* Concepción: Universidad de Concepción. 31–82.

Conley, Tom. 1996. *The Self-Made Map: Cartographic Writing in Early Modern France.* Minneapolis: University of Minnesota Press.

———. 1992. "De Bry's Las Casas." In *Amerindian Images,* ed. René Jara and Nicholas Spadaccini. Minneapolis: University of Minnesota Press. 103–31.

Cornejo Polar, Antonio. 1995. "El discurso de la armonía imposible. (El Inca Garcilaso de la Vega: discurso y recepción social)." *Revista de Crítica Literaria Latinoamericana* 19(38): 73–80.

———. 1994. *Escribir en el aire: ensayo sobre la heterogeneidad socio-cultural en las literaturas andinas.* Lima: Editorial Horizonte.

Craddock, Jerry R. Forthcoming. "Fray Marcos de Niza, *Relación* (1539): Critical Edition and Commentary." *Romance Philology.*

———. 1998. "Aspectos del legado jurídico español en Nuevo México." *España 1898: Un legado para el mundo.* Jornadas celebradas en la Universidad de Córdoba, 17–20 de marzo.

———. 1996. "Philological Notes on the Hammond and Rey Translation of the 'Relación de la Entrada que hizo en el Nuevo México Francisco Sánchez Chamuscado en junio de 1581' by Hernán Gallegos, Notary of the Expedition." *Romance Philology* 49: 351–63.

Cummins, Tom. 1994. "De Bry and Herrera: 'Aguas Negras' or the Hundred Years War over an Image of America." In *Arte, historia e identidad en América: Visiones comparativas,* ed. Gustavo Curiel, Renato González Mello and Juana Gutiérrez Haces. XVII Coloquio Internacional de Historia del Arte. Mexico City: Universidad Nacional Autónoma de México. I: 17–31.

Cunninghame Graham, R. B. 1968 [1924]. *The Conquest of the River Plate.* New York: Greenwood Press.

———. 1912. *Hernando de Soto.* London: Heinemann.

Davis, Natalie Zemon. 1975. "The Rites of Violence." In *Society and Culture in Early Modern France.* Stanford: Stanford University Press. 152–87.

De Bry, Théodore. 1594–1596. *Americae Pars Quarta, Quinta et Sexta. Sive Insignis et Admirata Historia de reperta primum Occidentali India à Christophoro Columbo Anno* MCCCXCII. *Scripta ab Hieronymo Benzono Mediolanense.* Frankfurt: Théodore de Bry.

———. 1591. *Brevis Narratio eorum quae in Florida Americae Provincia Gallis acciderunt, secunda in illam Navigatione, duce Renato de Laudonniere classis Praefecto; Anno* MDLXIIII. *Americae Pars Secunda.* Frankfurt: J. Wechel.

Defert, Daniel. 1987. "Collection et nation au XVIe siècle." In *L'Amérique,* ed. Michèle Duchet. Paris: Centre National de Recherche Scientifique. 47–67.

Delacampagne, Christian. 1983. *L'invention du racisme: Antiquité et Moyen Age.* Paris: Fayard.

Deleuze, Gilles. 1988. *Le pli: Leibniz et le Baroque.* Paris: Minuit.

Derrida, Jacques. 1995. *The Gift of Death.* Trans. David Wills. Chicago: University of Chicago Press.

———. 1992. "Force of Law: The Mystical Foundation of Authority."

In *Deconstruction and the Possibility of Justice.* Ed. Drucilla Cornel, Michael Rosenfeld, and David Gray Carlson. New York: Routledge. 3–67.

———. 1990. "Force of Law: The 'Mystical Foundation of Authority.'" *Cardozo Law Review* 11: 919–1045.

———. 1987. *The Truth in Painting.* Trans. Geoff Bennington and Ian McLeod. Chicago: University of Chicago Press.

Dorion, Normand. 1988. "L'art de voyager: Pour une définition du récit de voyage à l'époque classique." *Poétique* 73: 83–108.

Dowling, Lee. 1984. "Story vs. Discourse in the Chronicle of Indies: Alvar Núñez Cabeza de Vaca's Relation." *Hispanic Journal* 5: 89–99.

Duchet, Michèle. 1987. *L'Amérique de Théodore de Bry: Une collection de voyages protestants de xvie siècle: Quatre études d'iconographie.* Paris: Centre National de Recherche Scientique.

Durán, Diego de. 1984 [ca. 1581]. *Historia de las Indias de la Nueva España e islas de la Tierra Firme.* 2 vols. Ed. Angel María Garibay K. Mexico City: Editorial Porrúa.

Durand, José. 1976. *El Inca Garcilaso, clásico de América.* Mexico City: Sep Setentas.

Echevarría, Nicolás. 1989. *Cabeza de Vaca.* Produced by Producciones Iguana in coproduction with Instituto Mexicano de Cinematografía and Televisión Española.

Elbl, Martin Malcolm, and Ivana Elbl. 1997. "The Gentleman of Elvas and His Publisher." In *Hernando de Soto,* ed. Patricia Galloway. Lincoln: University of Nebraska Press. 45–97.

Eliade, Mircea. 1964. *Shamanism: Archaic Techniques of Ecstacy.* Trans. Willard R. Trask. London: Routledge and Kegan Paul.

Elliott, John Huxtable. 1970. *The Old World and the New, 1492–1650.* Cambridge, England: Cambridge University Press.

Elvas, Fidalgo de. 1940 [1557]. *Relaçam verdadeira dos trabalhos q̃ ho gouernador dõ Fernãdo de Souto e certos fidalgos portugueses passaron no descobrimẽto da prouincia da Frolida.* Facsimilar edition by Frederico Gavazzo Perry Vidal. Lisboa: Divisão de Publicacões e Biblioteca Agência Geral das Colónias.

Ercilla, Alonso de. 1979 [1569–1589]. *La Araucana.* 2 vols. Ed. Marcos A. Morinigo and Isaías Lerner. Madrid: Editorial Castalia.

Erlanger, Phillipe. 1960. *Le massacre de la Saint-Barthélemy, 24 août 1572.* Paris: Gallimard.

Escalona, Fray Juan de. 1601. "Carta de sobre los excesos cometidos por el gobernador D. Juan de Oñate en el descubrimiento de Nuevo México" (15 de octubre de 1601). Archivo General de Indias (Seville, Spain), Patronato 22, ramo 12, fols. 930r–932v.

Escobar, Arturo. 1992. "Imagining a Post-Development Era? Critical

Thought, Development and Social Movements." *Social Text* 31–32: 20–56.

Estebe, Janine. 1968. *Tocsin pour un massacre: La saison des Saint-Barthélemy.* Paris: Editions du Centurion.

Fabian, Johannes. 1993. "Keep Listening: Ethnography and Reading." In *Ethnography of Reading,* ed. Jonathan Boyarin. Berkeley: University of California Press. 80–98.

———. 1991. "Culture, Time and the Object of Anthropology." In *Time and the Work of Anthropology.* Philadelphia: Harwood Academic Publishers. 191–206.

———. 1990. "Presence and Representation: The Other and Anthropological Writing." *Critical Inquiry* 16(4): 753–72.

———. 1983. *Time and Its Other: How Anthropology Makes Its Object.* New York: Columbia University Press.

Fanon, Frantz. 1968. *The Wretched of the Earth.* Trans. Constance Farrington. New York: Grove Press.

———. 1967. *Black Skin, White Mask.* Trans. Charles Lam Markmann. New York: Grove Press.

Fehl, Phillip P. 1974. "Vasari's 'Extirpation of the Huguenots': The Challenge of Pity and Fear." *Gazette des Beaux Arts* 116(1270–1271): 257–84.

Fish, Stanley. 1989. "Force." In *Doing What Comes Naturally: Change, Rhetoric, and the Practice of Theory in Literary and Legal Studies.* Durham, NC: Duke University Press. 503–24.

Forbes, Jack D. 1960. *Apache Navajo and Spaniard.* Norman: University of Oklahoma Press.

Foucault, Michel. 1984. "What Is an Author?" In *The Foucault Reader.* Ed. Paul Rabinow. New York: Pantheon Books. 101–20.

———. 1982. *This Is Not a Pipe.* Trans. and ed. James Harkness. Berkeley: University of California Press.

———. 1979. *Discipline and Punish: The Birth of the Prison.* Trans. Alan Sheridan. New York: Vintage Books.

———. 1973. *The Order of Things: An Archaeology of the Human Sciences.* New York: Vintage Books.

Frazer, J. G. 1911. *The Golden Bough: A Study of Magic and Religion. Part 1: The Magic and Evolution of Kings.* Vol. 1. 3d. ed. London: Macmillan.

Freud, Sigmund. 1955 [1919]. "The 'Uncanny.'" In *The Standard Edition of the Complete Psychological Works of Sigmund Freud.* Trans. James Strachey. Vol. 17. London: Hogarth Press. 217–52.

Friede, Juan. 1959. "La censura española del siglo XVI y los libros de historia de América." *Revista de Historia de America* 47: 45–94.

Galloway, Patricia. 1997a. "The Incestuous Soto Narratives." In *Hernando de Soto,* ed. Patricia Galloway. Lincoln: University of Nebraska Press. 11–44.

————. 1990. "Sources for the Soto Expedition: Intertextuality and the Elusiveness of Truth." Paper presented to the Meeting of the Society for Spanish and Portuguese Historical Studies, New Orleans.

————, ed. 1997b. *The Hernando de Soto Expedition: History, Historiography and "Discovery" in the Southeast.* Lincoln: University of Nebraska Press.

Gandía, Enrique de. 1932. *Indios y conquistadores en el Paraguay.* Buenos Aires: Librería de A. García Santos.

García, Genaro. 1902. *Dos antiguas relaciones de la Florida.* Mexico City: J. Aguilar Vera.

García Icazbalceta, Joaquín, ed. 1971 [1866]. *Colección de documentos para la historia de México.* 2 vols. Nendeln, Liechtenstein: Krauss Reprint.

————. 1962. *Francisco Terrazas y otros poetas del siglo XVI.* Madrid: Edicones J. Porrúa Turanzas.

García Martínez, Bernardo, ed. 1991. *Los pueblos indios y las comunidades.* Mexico City: El Colegio de México.

Garcilaso de la Vega, Inca. 1986 [1605]. *La Florida del Inca.* Ed. Sylvia L. Hilton. Madrid: Historia 16.

————. 1960a [1609]. *Obras completas.* Vol. 2. *Primera parte de los Comentarios Reales de los Incas.* Madrid: Ediciones Atlas.

————. 1960b [1617]. *Obras completas.* Vols. 3–4. *Segunda parte de los Comentarios Reales de los Incas.* Madrid: Ediciones Atlas.

————. 1951. *The Florida of the Inca.* Trans. John Grier Varner and Jeannette Johnson Varner. Austin: University of Texas Press.

Geertz, Clifford. 1988. *Works and Lives: The Anthropologist as Author.* Stanford: Stanford University Press.

Gerbi, Antonello. 1985. *Nature in the New World: From Christopher Columbus to Gonzalo Fernández de Oviedo.* Trans. Jeremy Moyle. Pittsburgh: University of Pittsburgh Press.

Gibson, Charles. 1964. *The Aztecs under Spanish Rule.* Stanford: Stanford University Press.

Giménez Fernández, Manuel. 1960. *Bartolomé de las Casas, volumen segundo: Capellán de S.M. Carlos I, poblador de Cumaná, 1517–1523.* Seville: Escuela de Estudios Hispano-Americanos de Sevilla.

————. 1953. *Bartolomé de las Casas, volumen primero: Delegado de Cisneros para la reformación de las Indias, 1516–1517.* Seville: Escuela de Estudios Hispano-Americanos de Sevilla.

Glantz, Margo. 1993a. "El cuerpo inscrito y el texto escrito o la desnudez como naufragio." In *Notas y comentarios,* ed. Margo Glantz. Mexico City: Editorial Grijalbo. 403–34.

————, ed. 1993b. *Notas y comentarios sobre Alvar Núñez Cabeza de Vaca.* Mexico City: Editorial Grijalbo.

Glucksmann, André. 1969. *El discurso de la guerra.* Trans. M. Martí Pol. Barcelone: Editorial Anagrama.

Goldberg, Jonathan. 1992. *Sodometries: Renaissance Texts, Modern Sexualities.* Stanford: Stanford University Press.

González Arratia, Leticia. 1991. "La mujer recolectora en la reproducción material. Los grupos cazadores-recolectores del desierto del norte de México." *Antropología: Boletín oficial del Instituto Nacional de Antropología e Historia.* Nueva época. 34(Abril/Junio): 2–21.

————. 1990. "El discurso de la conquista frente a los cazadores recolectores del norte de México." *Antropología: Boletín oficial del Instituto Nacional de Antropología e Historia.* Nueva época. 29(Enero/Marzo): 2–15.

González Echevarría, Roberto. 1990. "The Law and the Letter: Garcilaso's *Comentarios.*" In *Myth and Archive: A Theory of Latin American Narrative.* Cambridge: Cambridge University Press. 43–92.

————. 1977. *Alejo Carpentier, the Pilgrim at Home.* Ithaca, NY: Cornell University Press.

Goodman, Nelson. 1978. *Ways of Worldmaking.* Indianapolis: Hackett.

Goody, Jack. 1987. *The Interface between the Written and the Oral.* Cambridge, England: Cambridge University Press.

————. 1977. *The Domestication of the Savage Mind.* Cambridge, England: Cambridge University Press.

Goody, Jack, and Ian Watts. 1963. "The Consequences of Literacy." *Comparative Studies in Society and History* 5(3): 304–45.

Gossen, Gary H. 1999. *Telling Maya Tales: Tzotzil Identities in Modern Mexico.* New York: Routledge.

Goulart, Simon. 1578. *Mémoires de l'estat de France sous Charles neufiesme. Contenant les choses plus notables, faites et publiées tant par les Catholiques que par ceux de la Religion, depuis le troisiesme édit de pacification fait au mois d'Aoust 1570, iusque au regne de Henry troisiesme. Reduit en trois volumes, shascun desquels a un indice des principales matiere y contenues.* 2nd ed. revue, *corrigée, et augmentée des plusieurs particularitez et traitez notables. Par Henrich Wolf.* Geneva: Vignon.

Gourgues, Dominique de. 1958 [1568]. *Histoire memorable de la reprinse de l'isle de la Floride par les François sous la conduite du capitaine Gourgues gentilhomme Bourdelois le 24. et 27. d'avril de ceste année 1568.* Imprimé noevellement 1568. In *Les Francais en Amérique,* ed. Suzanne Lussagnet. Paris: Presses Universitaires de France. 241–51.

Gruzinski, Serge. 1999. *La pensée métisse. Paris:* Librairie Arthème Fayard.

————. 1993. *The Conquest of Mexico: The Incorporation of Indian Societies into the Western World, 16th–18th Centuries.* Trans. Eileen Corrigan. Cambridge, England: *Polity Press.*

Guha, Ranajit. 1997. *Dominance without Hegemony: History and Power in Colonial India.* Cambridge, MA: Harvard University Press.

———. 1989. "Dominance without Hegemony and Its Historiography." *Subaltern Studies 6.* New Delhi: Oxford University Press. 210–309.

Gutiérrez, Jusepe. N.d. "Declaracion que Jusepe Indio dio de la salida de la tierra del nuevo Mexico de antonio de Humaña y del capitan francisco Leyva y lo que sucedio en el viaje." Archivo General Indias (Seville, Spain), Patronato 22, ramo 15, fols. 1019r.–1022v.

Gutiérrez, Ramón A. 1993. "The Politics of Theater in Colonial New Mexico: Drama and the Rhetoric of Conquest." In *Reconstructing,* ed. María Herrera-Sobek. Tucson: University of Arizona Press. 49–67.

———. 1991. *When Jesus Came, the Corn Mothers Went Away: Marriage, Sexuality, and Power in New Mexico, 1500–1846.* Stanford: Stanford University Press.

Hackett, Charles Wilson, ed. 1923–1937. *Historical Documents Relating to New Mexico, Nueva Vizcaya, and Approaches Thereto, to 1773.* 3 vols. Washington, DC: Carnegie Institution.

Hakluyt, Richard. 1967 [1935; 1584]. *Discourse on Western Planting. A particuler discourse concerning the great necessitie and manifold commodyties that are like to growe to this Realme of Englnde by the Western Discoveries lately attempted, Written in the yere 1584. by Richarde Hackluyt of Oxforde at the request and direction of the righte worshipfull Mr. Walter Raghly, before the comynge home of his twoo Brakes: and is divided into xxj chapiters, the Titles whereof followe the nexte leaf.* In *The Original Writings and Correspondence of the Two Richard Hakluyts,* ed. E. G. R. Taylor. Originally printed as volumes 76–77 of the Richard Hakluyt Society. Nedeln/Liechtenstein: Krauss Reprint. 211–326.

———. 1927 [1588–1600]. *Hakluyt's Voyages.* Vol. 10. London: J. M. Dent and Sons.

Hakluyt, Richard (the elder). 1967 [1935; 1585]. "Pamphlet for the Virginia Enterprise. Inducements to the liking of the Voyage intended towards Virginia in 40. and 42. degrees of latitude, written 1585. by M. Richard Hakluyt the elder, sometime student of Middle Temple." In *The Original Writings and Correspondence of the Two Richard Hakluyts,* ed. E. G. R. Taylor. Originally printed as volumes 76–77 of the Richard Hakluyt Society. Nedeln/Liechtenstein: Krauss Reprint. 327–38.

Halverson, John. 1992. "Goody and the Implosion of the Literacy Thesis." *Man* (n.s.) 27: 301–17.

Hammond, George P., and Agapito Rey, eds. 1966. *The Rediscovery of New Mexico 1580–1594: The Explorations of Chamuscado, Espejo, Castaño de Sosa,*

Morlete and Leyva de Bonilla and Humaña. Albuquerque: University of New Mexico Press.

———. 1953. *Don Juan de Oñate, Colonizer of New Mexico.* 2 vols. *Coronado Cuarto Centennial Publications, 1540–1940,* vols. 5 and 6. Albuquerque: University of New Mexico Press.

———. 1940. *Narratives of the Coronado Expedition 1540–1542.* Albuquerque: University of New Mexico Press.

———. 1938. *New Mexico in 1602: Juan Montoya's Relation of the Discovery of New Mexico.* Albuquerque: Quivira Society.

Hanke, Lewis, ed. 1967. *History of Latin American Civilization: Sources and Interpretation.* 2 vols. Boston: Little, Brown.

———. 1965. "Las Casas historiador." In *Historia de las Indias,* by Bartolomé de Las Casas, ed. Agustín Millares Carlo. Mexico City: Fondo de Cultura Económica. ix–lxxxviii.

———. 1949. *The Spanish Struggle for Justice in the Conquest of America.* Philadelphia: University of Pennsylvania Press.

———. 1942. Introducción to *Del único modo,* by Bartolomé de Las Casas, ed. Agustín Millares Carlo. Mexico City: Fondo de Cultura Económica. 21–60.

Hart, B. T. 1974. "A Critical Edition with a Study of the Style of *La Relación* by Alvar Núñez Cabeza de Vaca." Ph.D. diss., University of Southern California.

Hegeman, Susan. 1989. "History, Ethnography, Myth: Some Notes on the 'Indian-Centered' Narrative." *Social Text* 23: 144–60.

Heidegger, Martin. 1977. "The Age of the World Picture." In *The Question Concerning Technology and Other Essays.* Trans. William Lovitt. New York: Harper Torchbooks.

Henige, David. 1986. "The Context, Content, and Credibility of *La Florida del Ynca.*" *The Americas* 43: 1–23.

Herrera-Sobek, María, ed. 1993. *Reconstructing a Chicano/a Literary Heritage: Hispanic Colonial Literature of the Southwest.* Tucson: University of Arizona Press.

Herrera y Tordesillas, Antonio. 1934–1957 [1601–1615]. *Historia general de los hechos de los castellanos en las Islas y Tierrafirme del Mar Oceano.* 17 vols. Ed. A. Ballesteros y Beretta et al. Madrid: Real Academia de la Historia.

Historia de Tlatelolco desde los tiempos más antiguos. 1948 [ca. 1528]. In *Anales de Tlatelolco,* ed. Henrich Berlin. Mexico City: Robredo.

Hodge, F. W. 1895. "The First Discovered City of Cibola." *The American Anthropology* 8: 142–52.

Hodgen, Margaret T. 1964. *Early Anthropology in the Sixteenth and Seventeenth Centuries.* Philadelphia: University of Pennsylvania Press.

Holinshed, Raphael. 1577. *Chronicles of England, Scotland, and Ireland. 1577,*

the firste volume of the chronicles of England, Scotlande, and Irelande: conteyn-
ing the description and chronicles of England, from the first inhabiting vnto the
Conquest: the description and chronicles of Scotland, from the first originall of
the Scottes nation, till the yeare of our Lorde 1571: the description and chronicles
of Yreland, likewise from the first originall of that nation, vntill the yeare 1547.
2 vols. London: Imprinted for Iohn Hunne.

Homer. 1992. *The Odyssey of Homer.* Trans. Richard Lattimore. New York:
Harper and Row.

———. 1991. *The Iliad.* Trans. Robert Fagles. New York: Penguin.

Horkheimer, Max, and Theodor Adorno. 1973. *The Dialectic of Enlighten-*
ment. Trans. John Cumming. London: Allen Lane.

Howard, David A. 1997. *Conquistador in Chains: Cabeza de Vaca and the*
Indians of the Americas. Tuscaloosa: University of Alabama Press.

Hudson, Charles, and Carmen Tesser, eds. 1994. *The Forgotten Centuries.*
Athens: University of Georgia Press.

Hulme, Peter. 1987. *Colonial Encounters: Europe and the Native Caribbean,*
1492–1797. London: Methuen.

Hults, Linda C. 1996. *The Print in Western History: An Introductory History.*
Madison: University of Wisconsin Press.

Iglesia, Cristina, and Julio Schvartzman. 1987. *Cautivas y misioneros: Mitos*
blancos de la Conquista. Buenos Aires: Catálogos Editora.

Invernizzi, Lucía. 1987. "Naufragios e Infortunios: Discurso que trans-
forma fracasos en triunfos." *Revista Chilena de Literatura* 29: 7–22.

Jákfalvi-Leiva, Susana. 1984. *Traducción, escritura y violencia colonizadora: un*
estudio de la obra del Inca Garcilaso. Syracuse, NY: Maxwell School of
Citizenship and Public Affairs.

JanMohamed, Abdul R. 1986. "The Economy of Manichean Allegory:
The Function of Racial Difference in Colonialist Literature." In *"Race,"*
Writing and Difference, ed. Henry Louis Gates. Chicago: University of
Chicago Press. 78–106.

———. 1983. *Manichean Aesthetics: The Politics of Literature in Colonial*
Africa. Amherst: University of Massachusetts Press.

JanMohamed, Abdul R., and David Lloyd. 1990. "Introduction: Toward
a Theory of Minority Discourse: What Is to Be Done." In *The Nature*
and Context of Minority Discourse, ed. Abdul JanMohamed and David
Lloyd. New York: Oxford University Press. 1–16.

Jara, René, and Nicholas Spadaccini, eds. 1992. *Amerindians Images and*
the Legacy of Columbus. Hispanic Issues 9. Minneapolis: University of
Minnesota Press.

———. 1989. *1492–1992: Re/Discovering Colonial Writing.* Hispanic Issues 4.
Minneapolis: Prisma Institute.

Jay, Martin. 1992. "The Aesthetic Ideology; or, What Does It Mean to Aestheticize Politics?" *Cultural Critique* 18(3): 41–61.

———. 1988. "Scopic Regimes of Modernity." In *Vision and Visuality*, ed. Hal Foster. Dia Art Foundation Discussions in Contemporary Culture, Number 2. Seattle: Bay Press. 3–23.

Joseph, Gilbert M., and Daniel Nugent. 1994a. "Popular Culture and State Formation in Revolutionary Mexico." In *Everyday Forms of State Formation*, ed. Gilbert M. Joseph and Daniel Nugent. Durham, NC: Duke University Press. 3–23.

———, eds. 1994b. *Everyday Forms of State Formation: Revolution and the Negotiation of Rule in Modern Mexico*. Durham, NC: Duke University Press.

Juderías, Julian. 1917. *La leyenda negra*. Barcelona: Casa Editorial Araluce.

Jusepe, indio. 1599. "Declaración que Jusepe indio dio de la salida a la tierra de nuevo mexico de Antonio de Umaña y del capitan Francisco Leyva y lo que sucedio en el viaje." Archivo General de Indias (Seville, Spain), Patronato 22, ramo 13, 1019v.–1021r.

Kassovitz, Matthieu. 1995. *La Haine*. Produced by Productions Lazennec.

Kessel, John. 1979. *Kiva, Cross, and Crown: The Pecos Indians and New Mexico, 1540–1840*. Washington, DC: National Park Service, U.S. Department of the Interior.

Kingdon, Robert M. 1988. *Myths about the St. Bartholomew's Day Massacre, 1572–1576*. Cambridge, MA: Harvard University Press.

Klor de Alva, J. Jorge. 1995. "The Postcolonization of the (Latin) American Experience: A Reconsideration of 'Colonialism.' " In *After Colonialism: Imperial Histories and Postcolonial Displacements*, ed. Gyan Prakash. Princeton, NJ: Princeton University Press.

———. 1988. "Sahagún and the Birth of Modern Ethnography: Representing, Confessing, and Inscribing the Native Other." In *Bernardino de Sahagún: Pioneer Ethnographer of Sixteenth-Century Aztec Mexico*, ed. J. Jorge Klor de Alva, H. B. Nicholson, and Eloise Quiñones Keber. Albany, NY: Institute of Mesoamerican Studies. 31–52.

Kobayashi, José María. 1974. *La educación como conquista*. Mexico City: El Colegio de México.

Laclau, Ernesto. 1996. "Why Do Empty Signifiers Matter to Politics?" In *Emancipation(s)*. New York: Verso.

Lafaye, Jacques. 1984. "Los milagros de Alvar Núñez Cabeza de Vaca (1527–1536)." In *Mesías, cruzadas, utopías: El judeo-cristianismo en las sociedades ibéricas*. Trans. Juan José Utrilla. Mexico City: Fondo de Cultura Económica. 65–84.

Lagmanovich, David. 1978. "Los *Naufragios* de Alva Núñez como construcción narrativa." *Kentucky Romance Quarterly* 25: 23–37.

Lamadrid, Enrique. 1993. "*Entre Cíbolos Criado:* Images of Native Americans in Popular Culture of Colonial New Mexico." In *Reconstructing,* ed. María Herrera-Sobek. Tucson: University of Arizona Press. 159–200.

La Popelinière, Lancelot Voisin de. 1582. *Les Trois Mondes, par le Seigneur de la Popelinière.* Paris: Pierre L'Huillier.

———. 1599. *L'Histoire des Histoires: Avec l'Idée de l'Histoire accomplie.* Paris: M. Orry.

Las Casas, Bartolomé de. 1992a. *El tratado de las "Doce dudas."* Ed. J. B. Lassegue. In *Obras completas,* vol. 11.2. Madrid: Editorial Alianza.

———. 1992b. *The Only Way.* Ed. Helen Rand Parish and Francis Patrick Sullivan. Mahwah, NJ: Paulist Press.

———. 1991 [1552]. *Brevíssima relación de la destruyción de las Indias.* Ed. Andrés Moreno Mengibar. Seville: Colección Er de Textos Clásico e Instituto Italiano per gli Studi Filosifici.

———. 1988 [ca. 1534]. *De unico vocationis modo omnium gentium ad veram religionem.* Ed. Paulino Castañeda Delgado and Antonio García del Moral. In *Obras completas,* vol. 2. Madrid: Alianza Editorial.

———. 1967 [ca. 1555]. *Apologética historia sumaria.* 2 vols. Mexico: Universidad Nacional Autónoma de México.

———. 1965 [1527–1563]. *Historia de las Indias.* 3 vols. Ed. Agustín Millares Carlo. Mexico City: Fondo de Cultura Económica.

———. 1942 [ca. 1536]. *Del único modo de atraer a todos los pueblos a la verdadera religión.* Ed. Agustín Millares Carlo. Mexico City: Fondo de Cultura Económica.

———. 1656. *The Tears of the Indians: Being an Historical and true Account Of the Cruel Massacres and Slaughters of above Twenty Millions of Innocent People; Committed by the Spaniards In the Islands of Hispaniola, Cuba, Jamaica, & also, in the continents of Mexico, Peru, & other Places of the West Indies, to the total destruction of those Countries.* Written by Casaus, an eye-witness of those things; And made English by J. P. London, Printed by J. C. for Nath. Brook, at the Angel in Cornhil.

———. 1598. *Narratio Regionum Indicarum per Hispanos quosdam devastatarum verissima.* Illustrated and trans. by Théodore de Bry and Jean Israël de Bry. Frankfurt: Théodore de Bry and J. Sauer.

———. 1582. *Tyrannies et cruautez des Espagnols, perpetrees es Indes Occidentales, qu'on dit le Nouveau monde: Brievement descrites en langue Castillane, par l'Evesque Don Frere Bartelemy de Las Casas ou Casaus, Espagnol de l'ordre de sainct Dominique, fidelement traduites par Iacques de Miggrode.* Illustrated manuscript. Clements Library, University of Michigan.

————. 1579. *Tyrannies et cruautez des Espagnols, perpetrees es Indes Occidentales, qu'on dit le Nouveau monde: Brievement descrites en langue Castillane, par
l'Evesque Don Frere Bartelemy de Las Casas ou Casaus, Espagnol de l'ordre
de sainct Dominique, fidelement traduites par Iacques de Miggrode*. Anvers:
F. Raphelengius.

Lastra, P. 1984. "Espacios de Alvar Núñez: Las transformaciones de una
escritura." *Cuadernos Americanos* 3: 150–64.

Latour, Bruno. 1993. *We Have Never Been Modern*. Trans. Catherine Porter.
Cambridge, MA: Harvard University Press.

Laudonnière, René de. 1975. *Three Voyages*. Trans. Charles E. Bennett.
Gainesville: University of Florida Press.

————. 1587. *A Notable Historie containing foure voyages made by certayne
French Captaynes to* FLORIDA . . . *by Monsieur Laudonniere* . . . *Newly trans-
lated out of French into English by R[ichard] H[akluyt]*. London: Thomas
Dawson.

————. 1586. *L'Histoire Notable de la Floride . . . à laquelle a esté adjousté un
quatrieme voyage fait par le Capitaine Gourgues. Mis en lumiere par M. Basanier,
gentil-homme François Mathematicien*. Paris: Guillaume Auvray.

Laursen, John Christian, and Cary J. Nederman, eds. 1998. *Beyond the
Persecuting Society: Religious Toleration before the Enlightenment*. Philadelphia:
University of Pennsylvania Press.

Leal, Luis. 1993. "Poetic Discourse in Pérez de Villagrá's *Historia de la
Nueva México*." In *Reconstructing*, ed. María Herrera-Sobek. Tucson:
University of Arizona Press. 95–117.

Le Bot, Yvon. 1997. *Le rêve zapatiste*. Paris: Seuil.

Leckie, Barbara. 1995. "The Force of Law and Literature: Critiques
of Ideology in Jacques Derrida and Pierre Bourdieu." *Mosaic* 28(3):
109–36.

Le Challeux, Nicolas. 1958 [1566]. *Discours de l'histoire de la Floride, contenant
la cruautee des Espagnols contre le subjet du Roy en l'an mil cinq cens soixante
cinq. Redigé au vray par ceux qui en sont restez. Chose autant lamentable à ouïr
qu'elle a éste proditoirement et cruellement executee par lesdits Espagnols Contre
l'autorite du Roy nostre sire à la perte et domage de tout ce Royaume. Item, une
Requeste au Roy faites en forme de complainte par les femmes vefves, petits enfants
orphelins et autres leur amis, parens et alliez de ceux qui ont esté cruellement en-
vahis par les Espagnols en la France anthartique, dites la Floride*. De Dieppe
ce 22. de may, 1566. In *Les Francais en Amérique*, ed. Suzanne Lussagnet.
Paris: Presses Universitaires de France. 201–38.

————. 1922 [1566]. *A True and perfect description of the last voyage or Navia-
gation, attempted by Capitaine John Rybaut, deputie and generall for the French
men, into Terra Florida, this yeare past, 1565: truly set forth by those that returned
from thence, wherein are contayned things as lametable to heare as they haue bene*

cruelly executed. Imprinted in London for Henry Denham, for Thomas Hacket, and are to be solde at his shop in Lumbard streate. Photostat reproductions by the Massachusetts Historical Society, no. 13, Boston.

Leibsohn, Dana. 1995. "Colony and Cartography: Shifting Signs on Indigenous Maps of New Spain." In *Reframing the Renaissance: Visual Culture in Europe and Latin America 1450–1650,* ed. Claire Farago. New Haven: Yale University Press. 264–81.

———. 1994. "Primers for Memory: Cartographic Histories and Nahua Identity." In *Writing without Words,* ed. Elizabeth Hill Boone and Walter D. Mignolo. Durham, NC: Duke University Press. 161–87.

Le Moyne, Jacques. 1977. *The Work of Jacques Le Moyne: A Huguenot Artist in France, Florida and England.* 2 vols. Ed. Pault Hulton. London: British Museum Publications.

León-Portilla, Miguel. 1995. *La flecha en el blanco: Francisco Tenamaztle y Bartolomé de las Casas en la lucha por los derechos de los indígenas 1541–1556.* Mexico City: Editorial Diana.

Léry, Jean de. 1975 [1578, 1580]. *Histoire d'un voyage faict en la terre du Brésil.* Facsimile edition of the 1580 edition by Jean-Claude Morisot. Geneva: Librairie Droz.

Lestringant, Frank. 1996. *L'Expérience huguenote au Nouveau Monde (XVIe siècle).* Geneva: Librairie Droz.

———. 1991. *André Thevet: Cosmographe des derniers Valois.* Geneva: Librairie Droz.

———. 1990. *Le Huguenot et le Sauvage.* Paris: Aux Amateurs de Livres.

———. 1982. "Les Séquelles littéraires de la Floride française: Laudonnière, Hakluyt, Thevet, Chauveton." *Bibliothèque d'Humanisme et Renaissance* 44: 7–36.

Lévi-Strauss, Claude. 1977. *Tristes Tropiques.* Trans. John Weightman and Doreen Weightman. New York: Pocket Books.

———. 1967. *Structural Anthropology.* Trans. Claire Jacobson and Brooke Grundfest Schoepf. New York: Anchor Books.

Lewis, R. E. 1982. "Los *Naufragios* de Alvar Núñez: Historia y ficción." *Revista Iberoamericana* 48: 681–94.

Lippard, Lucy R. 1990. "Andres Serrano: The Spirit and the Letter." *Art in America* 78(April): 239–45.

Locke, John. 1991 [1689]. *A Letter Concerning Toleration.* Ed. John Horton and Susan Mendus. London: Routledge.

Lockhart, James, and Stuart B. Schwartz. 1983. *Early Latin America: A History of Colonial Spanish America and Brazil.* Cambridge, England: Cambridge University Press.

Long, Haniel. 1973 [1939]. *The Marvelous Adventures of Cabeza de Vaca.* Preface by Henry Miller. New York: Ballantine Books.

López-Baralt, Mercedes, ed. 1990. *La iconografía política del Nuevo Mundo.* Río Piedras, Puerto Rico: Editorial de la Universidad de Puerto Rico.

Losada, Angel. 1977. "Observaciones sobre la 'Apología' de Fray Bartolomé de las Casas (respuesta a una consulta)." *Cuadernos Americanos* 212(3): 152–62.

Lowe, Lisa, and David Lloyd, eds. 1997. *The Politics of Culture in the Shadow of Capital.* Durham, NC: Duke University Press.

Lukács, Georg. 1978. *Theory of the Novel: A Historico-Philosophical Essay on the Forms of Great Epic Literature.* Trans. Ana Bostock. London: Merlin Press.

Lussagnet, Suzanne. 1958. *Les Français en Amérique pendant la deuxième moitié du xvie siècle.* 2 vols. Paris: Presses Universitaires de France.

Lyon, Eugene. 1974. *The Enterprise of Florida: Pedro Menéndez de Avilés and the Spanish Conquest of 1565–1568.* Gainesville: University Presses of Florida.

———. N.d. "The Cañete Fragment." Unpublished ms.

Machiavelli, Niccolò. 1950. *The Prince* and *The Discourses.* New York: The Modern Library.

Maltby, William S. 1971. *The Black Legend in England: The Development of Anti-Spanish Sentiment, 1558–1660.* Durham, NC: Duke University Press.

Mannheim, Bruce, and Krista Van Vleet. 1998. "The Dialogics of Southern Quechua Narrative." *American Anthropologist* 100(2): 326–46.

Marcus, George, and Michael Fischer. 1986. *Anthropology as Cultural Critique: An Experimental Moment in the Human Sciences.* Chicago: University of Chicago Press.

Marin, Louis. 1984. *Utopics: Spatial Play.* Trans. Robert A. Vollrath. Atlantic Highlands, NJ: Humanities.

Maura, Juan Francisco. 1995. "Veracidad en los Naufragios: La técnica narrativa de Alvar Núñez Cabeza de Vaca. In *Literatura colonial I. Identidades y conquista en América,* ed. Mabel Moraña. *Revista Iberoamericana* 170–71: 187–95.

———. 1989. Introducción to *Naufragios,* by Alvar Núñez Cabeza de Vaca. Ed. Juan Francisco Maura. Madrid: Ediciones Cátedra. 11–72.

Mauroby, Christian. 1990. *Utopie et primitivisme: Essai sur l'imaginaire anthropologique à l'âge classique.* Paris: Editions du Seuil.

Mazzotti, José Antonio. 1996. *Coros mestizos del Inca Garcilaso: Resonancias andinas.* Mexico City: Fondo de Cultura Económica.

McClintock, Anne, Aamir Mufti, and Ella Shohat, eds. 1997. *Dangerous Liaisons: Gender, Nation, and Postcolonial Perspectives.* Minneapolis: University of Minnesota Press.

Melville, Stephen, and Bill Readings, eds. 1995. *Vision and Textuality.* Durham, NC: Duke University Press.

Menchú, Rigoberta. 1990. *I, Rigoberta Menchu an Indian Woman in Guatemala*. Ed. Elizabeth Burgos-Debray. Trans. Ann Wright. London: Verso.

―――. 1985. *Me llamo Rigoberta Menchú y así me nació la conciencia*. Ed. Elizabeth Burgos-Debray. Mexico City: Siglo XXI.

Mengin, Ernst. 1945. *Unos annales históricos de la Nación Mexicana*. Facsimilar edition of *Manuscrits mexicains* 22 and 22bis of the Bibliothèque Nationale de France. Havnia, Denmark: E. Munksgaard.

―――. 1939–1940. *Unos annales históricos de la Nación Mexicana*. Bilingual edition in Nahuatl and German of *Manuscrits mexicains* 22 and 22bis of the Bibliothèque Nationale de France. Berlin: D. Reimer.

Merrim, Stephanie. 1989. "The Apprehension of the New in Nature and Culture: Fernández de Oviedo's *Sumario*." In *Re/Discovering*, ed. René Jara and Nicholas Spadaccini. Minneapolis: Prisma Institute. 165–99.

Merry, Sally Engle. 1991. "Law and Colonialism." *Law and Society Review* 25(4): 890–922.

Mignolo, Walter D. 1995a. *The Darker Side of the Renaissance: Literacy, Territoriality and Colonization*. Ann Arbor: University of Michigan Press.

―――. 1993. "Colonial and Postcolonial Discourse: Cultural Critique or Academic Colonialism?" *Latin American Research Review* 28(3): 130–31.

―――. 1989. "Colonial Situations, Geographic Discourses, and Territorial Representations: Towards a Diatopical Understanding of Colonial Semiosis." *Dispositio* 14: 93–140.

―――. 1986. "La lengua, la letra, el territorio (o la crisis de los estudios literarios coloniales)." *Dispositio* 11: 137–60.

―――. 1981. "El metatexto historiográfico y la historiografía indiana." *MLN* 96: 358–402.

―――, ed. 1995b. *Loci of Enunciation and Imaginary Constructions: The Case of Latin America*, II. Special issue of *Poetics Today* 16(1).

―――, ed. 1994. *Loci of Enunciation and Imaginary Constructions: The Case of Latin America*, I. Special issue of *Poetics Today* 15(4).

Miguel, Indio. 1601. "Diligencias tomadas con miguel indio que traxo del nuebo mexico el maese de campo Vicente Zaldivar." Archivo General Indias (Seville, Spain), Patronato 22, ramo 4, 211v.–217v.

Milanich, Jerald T., and Charles Hudson. 1993. *Hernando de Soto and the Indians of Florida*. Gainesville: University Press of Florida.

Milanich, Jerald T., and Susan Milbrath, eds. 1989. *First Encounters: Spanish Explorations in the Caribbean and the United States*. Gainesville: University of Florida Press and Florida Museum of Natural History.

Miró Quesada, Aurelio. 1971. *El Inca Garcilaso y otros estudios garcilasistas*. Madrid: Ediciones Cultura Hispánica.

Mitchell, W. J. T. 1994. *Picture Theory.* Chicago: University of Chicago Press.

Molina, Alonso de. 1992 [1571]. *Vocabulario en lengua castellana y mexicana compuesto por el muy Reuerendo padre Fray alonso de Molina, de la Orden del bienaventurado Padre sant Francisco. Dirigido al muy excelente sennor Don Martin Enriquez, Visorrey desta nueva España.* Mexico: Casas de Antonio de Spinosa. Facsimile edition. Mexico City: Editorial Porrúa.

Molloy, Silvia. 1987. "Alteridad y reconocimiento en los *Naufragios* de Alvar Núñez Cabeza de Vaca." *Nueva Revista de Filología Hispánica* 35: 425–49.

Morales Padrón, Francisco. 1979. *Teoría y leyes de la conquista.* Madrid: Ediciones Cultura Hispanica del Centro Iberoamericano de Cooperación.

Motolinía, Toribio de Benavente. 1971. *Memoriales o libro de las cosas de la Nueva España y de los naturales de ella.* Mexico: Universidad Nacional Autónoma de México.

Murrin, Michael. 1994. *History and Warfare in Renaissance Epic.* Chicago: University of Chicago Press.

Navarro, Mireya. 1999. "Guatemala Study Accuses the Army and Cites U.S. Role." *New York Times,* 25 February. A1.

Naylor, Thomas H., and Charles W. Polzer, eds. 1986. *The Presidio and Militia on the Northern Frontier of New Spain: A Documentary History.* Vol. 1: *1570–1700.* Tucson: University of Arizona Press.

Nederman, Cary J., and John Christian Laursen, eds. 1996. *Difference and Dissent: Theories of Toleration in Medieval and Early Modern Europe.* Landham, MD: Rowman & Littlefield.

Negri, Antonio. 1991. *The Savage Anomaly: The Power of Spinoza's Metaphysics and Politics.* Trans. Michael Hardt. Minneapolis: University of Minnesota Press.

Newcomb, William W. 1983. "Karankawa." In *Handbook of North America.* Vol. 10: *Southwest,* ed. Alfonso Ortiz. Washington, DC: Smithsonian Institution.

Newcomb, William W., and Thomas N. Campbell. 1982. "Southern Plains Ethnohistory: A Re-examination of the Escanjanes, Ahijados, and Cuitoas." *Oklahoma Anthropological Society* 3: 29–43.

Nicholson, Edward W. B., ed. N.d. "Ordine della solennissima procession fatta dal sommo pontifice nell'alma citta di Roma, per la fellicissima noua dell destruttione de la setta Vgonotana." London: Bernard Quaritch.

Nietzsche, Friedrich. 1956. *The Birth of Tragedy* and *The Genealogy of Morals.* Trans. Francis Golffing. New York: Doubleday Anchor.

Noguères, Henri. 1962. *The Massacre of Saint Bartholomew.* Trans. Claire Eliane Engel. London: George Allen and Unwin.

Núñez Cabeza de Vaca, Alvar. 1993. *Castaways: The Narrative of Alvar Núñez Cabeza de Vaca.* Ed. Enrique Pupo-Walker. Trans. Frances M. López-Morillas. Berkeley: University of California Press.

————. 1992. *Los Naufragios.* Ed. Enrique Pupo-Walker. Madrid: Editorial Castalia.

————. 1986a. *Naufragios.* Ed. Juan Francisco Maura. Madrid: Ediciones Cátedra.

————. 1986. *Relación de los Naufragios y Comentarios* de Alvar Núñez Cabeza de Vaca. Ilustrado con varios documentos inéditos. In *Colección de libros y documentos referentes a la historia de ameerica.* Vols. 5–6. Ed. Manuel Serrano y Sanz. Madrid: Librería General de Victoriano Suárez.

————. 1985. *Naufragios.* Ed. Trinidad Barrera. Madrid: Alianza Editorial.

————. 1984. *Naufragios y comentarios.* Ed. R. Ferrando. Madrid: Historia 16.

————. 1972. *The Narrative of Alvar Núñez Cabeza de Vaca.* Trans. Fanny Bandelier. With Oviedo's version of the lost *Joint Report* presented to the Audiencia of Santo Domingo, trans. Gerald Theisen. Barre, MA: Imprint Society.

Oña, Pedro de. 1944 [1596]. *Arauco domado.* Madrid: Ediciones Cultura Hispánica.

Onishi, Norimitsu. 1999. "A Brutal War's Machetes Maim Sierra Leone's Civilians." *New York Times,* 25 January. A1.

Oñate, Juan de. 1601. "Relación cierta y verdadera de los subcesos que hubo en la entrada que hizo el adelantado y gobernador don Juan de Oñate, en nombre de su magestad desde estas primeras poblaciones de la Nueva Mexico." Archivo General Indias (Seville, Spain), Patronato 22, ramo 12, fols. 946r–953v.

————. 1599. "Relación delo q Don Juan de Oñate governador de las provincias del nuevo mexico envia de lo sucedido en su jornada a 2 de marzo del año de 99 con retiros y muestras de metales mantas otras cosas de lo que alli ay." Archivo General Indias (Seville, Spain), Patronato 22, ramo 13, fols. 985r–986v.

Ortega, Julio. 1978. "El Inca Garcilaso y el discurso de la cultura." *Revista Iberoamericana* 44 (104–5): 507–13.

Oviedo y Valdés, Gonzalo Fernández de. 1986 [1526]. *Sumario de la natural historia de las Indias.* Ed. Manuel Ballesteros. Madrid: Historia 16.

————. 1959 [1535–1547]. *Historia general y natural de las Indias.* 5 vols. In *Biblioteca de Autores Españoles,* vols. 117–21, ed. Juan Pérez de Tudela Bueso. Madrid: Ediciones Atlas.

Pacheco, Joaquín, et al., eds. 1864–1884. *Colección de documentos inéditos, relativos al descubrimiento, conquista y organización de las antiguas posesiones en América y Oceanía.* 42 vols. Madrid: Imprenta de José María Pérez.

Padilla, Genaro. 1991. "Imprisoned Narrative? Or Lies, Secrets, and Silences in New Mexico Women's Autobiography." In *Criticism,* ed. Hector Calderón and José David Saldívar. Durham, NC: Duke University Press. 43–60.

Pagden, Anthony. 1982. *The Fall of Natural Man: The American Indian and the Origins of Comparative Anthropology.* Cambridge, England: Cambridge University Press.

París Lozano, Gonzalo. 1984. *Guerrilleros de Tolima.* Bogotá: El Ancora.

Parish, Helen Rand, and Harold E. Weidman. 1992. *Las Casas en México: Historia y obra desconocida.* Mexico City: Fondo de Cultura Económica.

Parry, J. H., and R. G. Keith, eds. 1984. *New Iberian World: A Documentary History of the Discovery and Settlement of Latin America.* Vol. 1. New York: Times Books.

Pastor, Beatriz. 1989. "Silence and Writing: The History of the Conquest." In *Re/Discovering,* ed. René Jara and Nicholas Spadaccini. Minneapolis: Prisma Institute. 121–63.

———. 1988 [1983]. *Discursos narrativos de la conquista de América.* Rev. ed. Hanover, NH: Ediciones del Norte.

Philoponus, Honorius. 1621. *Nova typis transacta navigatio. Novi Orbis Indiæ Occidentalis admodum reverendissimorum PP. ac FF. Reverendissimi ac Illustrismi Domini. Dn. Buellii Cataloni abbatis montis Serrati, & in vniversam Americam, sive Novum Orbem sacræ sedis Apostolicæ Romanæ â latere legati, vicarij, ac patriarchæ : sociorumque monarchorum ex Ordine S.P.N. Benedicti ad suprà dicti Novi Mundi barbaras gentes Christi S. Evangelium prædicandi gratia delegatorum sacerdotum dimissi per S.D.D. Papam Alexandrum VI. Anno Christi. 1492. Nunc primum e varijs scriptoribus in vnum collecta, & figuris ornata,* Linz.

Pittarello, Elide. 1989. "*Arauco Domado* de Pedro de Oña o la vía erótica de la conquista." *Dispositio* 14(36–38): 111–41.

Pohl, John M. D. 1994. "Mexican Codices, Maps, and Lienzos as Social Contracts." In *Writing without Words,* ed. Elizabeth Hill Boone and Walter D. Mignolo. Durham, NC: Duke University Press. 137–60.

Poole, Stafford. 1987. *Pedro Moya de Contreras: Catholic Reform and Royal Power in New Spain.* Berkeley: University of California Press.

———. 1965. "'War by Fire and Blood': The Church and the Chichimecas 1585." *The Americas* 13(2): 115–37.

Powell, Philip Wayne. 1971. *The Tree of Hate: Propaganda and Prejudice Affecting United States Relations with the Hispanic World.* New York: Basic Books.

————. 1952. *Soldiers, Indians and Silver.* Berkeley: University of California Press.

Pranzetti, Luisa. 1993. "El naufragio como metáfora." In *Notas y comentarios,* ed. Margo Glantz. Mexico City: Editorial Grijalbo. 57–73.

Pratt, Mary Louise. 1992. *Imperial Eyes: Travel Writing and Transculturation.* New York: Routledge.

Pupo-Walker, Enrique. 1992. Introducción to *Los Naufragios* by Núñez Cabeza de Vaca. Madrid: Editorial Castalia. 9–174.

————. 1987. "Pesquisas para una nueva lectura de los *Naufragios,* de Alvar Núñez Cabeza de Vaca." *Revista Iberoamericana* 53: 517–39.

————. 1985. "*La Florida,* del Inca Garcilaso: notas sobre la problematización del discurso histórico en los siglos XVI y XVII." *Cuadernos Hispanoamericanos* 47: 91–111.

————. 1982. *Historia, creación y profecía en los textos del Inca Garcilaso de la Vega.* Madrid: Porrúa Turanzas.

Quevedo y Villegas, Francisco de. 1969 [1609]. *España defendida y los tiempos de ahora.* In *Obras completas,* 2 vols. Madrid: Aguilar. 1: 488–526.

Quint, David. 1993. *Epic and Empire: Politics and Generic Form from Virgil to Milton.* Princeton, NJ: Princeton University Press.

————. 1989a. "Epic and Empire." *Comparative Literature* 41(1): 1–32.

————. 1989b. "Voices of Resistance: The Epic Curse and Camões's Adamastor." *Representations* 27: 111–41.

Quintilian. 1976. *The "Institutio Oratoria" of Quintilian.* 4 vols. Trans. H. E. Butler. Cambridge, MA: Harvard University Press.

Quiñones Keber, Eloise, ed. 1995. *Codex Telleriano-Remensis: Ritual, Divination, and History in a Pictorial Aztec Manuscript.* Austin: University of Texas Press.

Rabasa, José. 1998. "Franciscans and Dominicans under the Gaze of a Tlacuilo: Plural-World Dwelling in an Indian Pictorial Codex." *Morrison Library Inaugural Lecture Series 14.* University of California at Berkeley.

————. 1997. "Of Zapatismo: Reflections on the Folkloric and the Impossible in a Subaltern Insurrection." In *The Politics of Culture,* ed. Lisa Lowe and David Lloyd. Durham, NC: Duke University Press. 399–431.

————. 1996. "Pre-Colombian Pasts and Indian Presents in Mexican History." In *Subaltern Studies in the Americas,* ed. José Rabasa, Javier Sanjinés, and Robert Carr. Special issue of Dispositio/n 46: 245–70.

————. 1995a. "De la *allegoresis* etnográfica en los *Naufragios* de Alvar Núñez Cabeza de Vaca." Literatura colonial I. Identidades y conquista en América. Special issue, ed. Mabel Moraña. *Revista Iberoamericana* 170–71: 176–81.

———. 1995b. " 'Porque soy indio': Subjectivity in *La Florida del Inca.*"
Poetics Today 16(1): 79–108.

———. 1994a. "Allegory and Ethnography in Cabeza de Vaca's *Naufragios* and *Comentarios.*" In *Violence, Resistance and Survival in the Americas,*
ed. William B. Taylor and Franklin Pease. Washington, DC: Smithsonian Institution Press.

———. 1994b. "On Writing Back: Alternative Historiography in *La
Florida del Inca.*" In *Latin American Identity and Constructions of Difference,*
ed. Amaryll Chanady. Hispanic Issues 10. Minneapolis: University of
Minnesota Press. 130–48.

———. 1993a. "Aesthetics of Colonial Violence: The Massacre of
Acoma in Gaspar de Villagrá's *Historia de la nueva México.*" *College Literature* 20(3): 96–114.

———. 1993b. *Inventing America: Spanish Historiography and the Formation of
Eurocentrism.* Norman: University of Oklahoma Press.

———. 1992. "Historiografía colonial y la episteme occidental moderna. Aproximaciones a la etnografía franciscana, Oviedo y Las
Casas." In *Colección conmemorativa del Quinto Centenario del encuentro de
dos mundos.* 4 vols. Ed. Ysla Campbell. Ciudad Juarez, Chihuahua:
Universidad de Ciudad Juárez, 1992. 2: 105–39.

———. 1989a. "Columbus and the Scriptural Economy of the Renaissance." *Dispositio/n* 14: 271–301.

———. 1989b. "Utopian Ethnology in Las Casas's Apologética." In
Re/Discovering, ed. René Jara and Nicholas Spadaccini. Minneapolis:
Prisma Institute. 261–89.

Rabasa, José, Javier Sanjinés, and Robert Carr, eds. 1996. *Subaltern Studies
in the Americas.* Special issue of *Dispositio/n* 46.

Radding, Cynthia. 1997. *Wandering Peoples: Colonialism, Ethnic Spaces, and
Ecological Frontiers in Northwestern Mexico, 1700–1850.* Durham, NC: Duke
University Press.

Rael y Gálvez, Estevan. N.d. "Reading Mal-Criado Genizaros in and out
of Silence: American Indian Slaves (Dis)placed between Homelands
and Empires, 1680–1880." Unpublished ms.

Ramírez de Verger, Antonio. 1987. Introducción to *Historia del Nuevo
Mundo,* by Juan Ginés de Sepúlveda. Madrid: Alianza Editorial. 9–27.

Reff, Daniel T. 1996. "Text and Context: Cures, Miracles, and Fear in the
Relación of Alvar Núñez Cabeza de Vaca." *Journal of the Southwest* 28(2):
115–38.

———. 1995. "The 'Predicament of Culture' and Missionary Accounts
of the Tepehuan and Pueblo Revolts." *Ethnohistory* 42(1): 64–90.

———. 1991. "Anthropological Analysis of Exploration Texts: Cultural

Discourse and the Ethnological Import of Fray Marcos de Niza's Journey to Cibola." *American Anthropologist* 93: 636–55.

Relación postrera de Zívola: Esta es la relación postrera de Zívola, y de más de cuatrocientas leguas adelante. 1886. In *Coronado Expedition,* ed. George Parker Winship. Washington, DC: Government Printing Office. 566–71.

Remer, Gary. 1996. *Humanism and the Rhetoric of Toleration.* University Park: Pennsylvania State University Press.

Ribault, Jean. 1964 [1563]. *The Whole and True Discouerye of Terra Florida.* Facsimilar ed. by David Dowd. Gainesville: University of Florida Press.

Rivera, José Eustacio. 1974. *La vorágine.* Bogotá: Editotial Pax.

Robinson, Cecil. 1973. *With the Ears of Strangers: The Mexican in American Literature.* Tucson: University of Arizona Press.

Rodríguez-Vecchini, Hugo. 1982. "*Don Quijote* y *La Florida del Inca.*" *Revista Iberoamericana* 48: 587–620.

Rojas, Rosa. 1995. *Chiapas: La paz violenta.* Mexico City: La Jornada Ediciones.

Rosaldo, Renato. 1989. "Imperialist Nostalgia." *Representations* 26: 107–22.

Roseberry, William. 1994. "Hegemony and the Language of Contention." In *Everyday Forms,* ed. Joseph Gilbert and Daniel Nugent. Durham, NC: Duke University Press. 355–66.

Ruidíaz y Caravia, Eugenio. 1989 [1893]. *La Florida su conquista y colonización por Pedro Menéndez de Avilés.* Ed. José M. Gómez-Tabanera. Madrid: Ediciones Istmo.

Sahagún, Bernardino de. 1979. *Historia general de las cosas de la Nueva España: Códice Florentino.* Facsimilar ed. México City: Secretaría de Gobernación.

———. 1956. *Historia general de las cosas de la Nueva España.* Ed. Angel María Garibay. Mexico City: Editorial Porrúa.

———. 1950–1982 [ca. 1579]. *Florentine Codex: General History of the Things of New Spain.* 13 vols. Trans. and ed. Arthur J. O. Anderson and Charles E. Dibble. Albuquerque: School of American Research and University of Utah.

Said, Edward. 1988. "Through Gringo Eyes: With Conrad in Latin America." *Harper's* 278: 70–72.

Salas, Alberto M. 1960. *Crónica florida del mestizaje delas Indias, siglo* XVI. Buenos Aires: Editorial Lozada.

Saldívar, José David. 1997. *Border Matters: Remapping American Cultural Studies.* Berkeley: University of California Press.

Sánchez, Joseph P. 1990. "The Spanish Black Legend: Origins of Anti-Hispanic Stereotypes"/"La Leyenda Negra Española: Orígenes de los estereotipos antihispanos." Albuquerque: Spanish Colonial Research Center Series No. 2.

San Miguel, Andrés de. 1902 [ca. 1620]. *Relación de los trabajos que la gente de una nao padeció.* In *Dos antiguas relaciones de la Florida,* ed. Genaro García. Mexico City: J. Aguilar Vera.

Sayer, Derek. 1994. "Everyday Forms of State Formation: Some Dissident Remarks on 'Hegemony.'" In *Everyday Forms,* ed. Joseph M. Gilbert and Daniel Nugent. Durham, NC: Duke University Press. 367–77.

Scarry, Elaine. 1985. *The Body in Pain: The Making and Unmaking of the World.* New York: Oxford University Press.

Schwarz, Henry. 1997. "Laissez-Faire Linguistics: Grammar and the Codes of Empire." *Critical Inquiry* 23(3): 509–35.

Scott, James C. 1990. *Domination and the Arts of Resistance: Hidden Transcripts.* New Haven: Yale University Press.

Searle, John R. 1995. *The Construction of Social Reality.* New York: The Free Press.

Seed, Patricia. 1995. *Ceremonies of Possession in Europe's Conquest of the New World, 1492–1640.* New York: Cambridge University Press.

———. 1993. "'Are They Not Also Men?': The Indians' Humanity and Capacity for Spanish Civilization." *Journal of Latin American Studies* 25: 629–52.

———. 1992. "Taking Possession and Reading Texts: Establishing the Authority of Overseas Empires." *The William and Mary Quarterly* (s3) 49: 183–209.

———. 1991. "Colonial and Postcolonial Discourse." *Latin American Research Review* 26(3): 181–200.

Sepúlveda, Juan Ginés de. 1987 [ca. 1562]. *Historia del Nuevo Mundo.* Trans. Antonio Ramírez de Verger. Madrid: Alianza Editorial.

———. 1976 [1562]. *Hechos de los españoles en el Nuevo Mundo y México.* Ed. Demetrio Ramos and Lucio Mijares. Valladolid: Seminario Americanistas de la Universidad de Valladolid.

———. 1941 [1547]. *Democrates Alter/Tratado sobre las causas justas de la guerra contra los indios.* Latin/Spanish ed. Trans. Marcelino Menéndez y Pelayo. Mexico City: Fondo de Cultura Económica.

Sepúlveda, Juan Ginés de, and Bartolomé de las Casas. 1975 [ca. 1550–1551]. *Apología.* Trans. Angel Losada. Madrid: Editorial Nacional.

Serrano y Sanz, Manuel, ed. 1906. *Colección de libros y documentos referentes a la historia de América.* Vols. 5–6. Madrid: Librería General de Victoriano Suárez.

Serres, Michel. 1995. *The Natural Contract.* Trans. Elizabeth MacArthur and William Paulson. Ann Arbor: University of Michigan Press.

Shell, Marc. 1991. "Marranos (Pigs), or From Coexistence to Toleration." *Cultural Inquiry* 17(2): 306–35.

Sheridan, Guillermo. 1994. *Cabeza de Vaca.* Inspirada libremente en el libro *Naufragios,* de Alvar Núñez Cabeza de Vaca. Prologue by Alvaro Mutis. Introduction by Nicolás Echeverría. Mexico City: Ediciones El Milagro.

Simmons, Marc. 1991. *The Last Conquistador: Juan de Oñate and the Settling of the Far Southwest.* Norman: University of Oklahoma Press.

Smith, Buckingham, ed. 1857. *Colección de varios documentos para la historia de la Florida y tierras adyacentes.* 2 vols. London: Casa de Trübner.

Solís de Merás, Gonzalo. 1989 [ca. 1574]. *Memorial que hizo el Dr. Gonzalo Solís de Merás, de todas las jornadas y sucesos del adelantado Pedro Menéndez de Avilés, su cuñado, y de la conquista de la Florida, y justicia que hizo en Juan Ribao y otros franceses.* In *La Florida,* by Eugenio Ruidíaz. Ed. José M. Gómez-Tabanera. Madrid: Ediciones Istmo. 105–257.

Sommer, Doris. 1996. "At Home Abroad: El Inca Shuttles with Hebreo." *Poetics Today* 17(3): 385–415.

Spinosa, Charles, and Hubert Dreyfus. 1996. "Two Kinds of Antiessentialism and Their Consequences." *Critical Inquiry* 22(4): 735–63.

Spitta, Silvia. 1995. "Shamanism and Christianity: The Transcultural Semiotics of Cabeza de Vaca's *Naufragios.*" In *Between Two Waters: Narratives of Transculturation in Latin America.* Houston: Rice University Press.

Spivak, Gayatri Chakravorty. 1993. "The Politics of Translation." In *Outside the Teaching Machine.* New York: Routledge.

———. 1988. "Can the Subaltern Speak?" In *Marxism and the Interpretation of Culture,* ed. Cary Nelson and Lawrence Grossberg. Urbana: University of Illinois Press.

Stavenhagen, Rodolfo. 1988. *Derechos indígenas y derechos humanos en América Latina.* Mexico City: El Colegio de México and Instituto Interamericano de Derechos Humanos.

———. 1963. "Clases, Colonialismo y Aculturación." *América Latina* 6(4): 63–104.

Stoll, David. 1999. *Rigoberta Menchú and the Story of All Poor Guatemalans.* Boulder, CO: Westview Press.

Stone, Cynthia Leigh. 1996. "The Filming of Colonial Spanish America." *Colonial Latin American Review* 5(2): 315–20.

Street, Brian. 1984. *Literacy in Theory and Practice.* Cambridge, England: Cambridge University Press.

Swanton, John R. 1952. *The Indian Tribes of North America.* Washington, DC: Smithsonian Institution, U.S. Bureau of American Ethnology, Bulletin 145.

————, ed. 1939. *Final Report of the United States de Soto Expedition Commission*. Washington, DC: U.S. House of Representatives Document 71, 76th Congress, 1st Session.

Taussig, Michael. 1992. "Homesickness and Dada." In *The Nervous System*. New York: Routledge. 149–82.

————. 1989. "Terror as Usual: Walter Benjamin's Theory of History as a State of Siege." *Social Text* 14: 3–20.

————. 1987. *Shamanism, Colonialism, and the Wild Man: A Study in Terror and Healing*. Chicago: University of Chicago Press.

Taylor, E. G. R. 1967 [1935]. *The Original Writings and Correspondence of the Two Richard Hakluyts*. Originally printed as vols. 76–77 of The Hakluyt Society. Nedeln/Liechtenstein: Kraus Reprint.

Taylor, Patrick. 1989. *The Narrative of Liberation: Perspectives on Afro-Caribbean Literature, Popular Culture, and Politics*. Ithaca, NY: Cornell University Press.

Tedlock, Dennis, ed. and trans. 1985. *Popol Vuh: The Definitive Edition of the Mayan Book of the Dawn of Life and the Glories of Gods and Kings*. New York: Touchstone Book.

Todorov, Tzvetan. 1984. *The Conquest of America: The Question of the Other*. Trans. Richard Howard. New York: Harper Torchbooks.

————. 1977. *Théories du symbole*. Paris: Editions du Seuil.

Turner, Frederick Jackson. 1983 [1893]. "The Significance of the Frontier in American History." In *The Eloquence of Frederick Jackson Turner*, by Ronald H. Carpenter. San Marino, CA: The Huntington Library.

Tyler, Steven A. 1986. "Post-Modern Ethnography: From Document of the Occult to Occult Document." In *Writing Culture: The Poetics and Politics of Ethnography*, ed. James Clifford and George E. Marcus. Berkeley: University of California Press. 122–40.

Valdez, Luis, and Stan Steiner, eds. 1972. *Aztlan: An Anthology of Mexican American Literature*. New York: Vintage.

Varner, John Grier. 1968. *El Inca: The Life and Times of Garcilaso de la Vega*. Austin: University of Texas Press.

Verdesio, Gustavo. 1997. "*Cabeza de Vaca:* Una visión paródica de la épica colonial." *Nuevo Texto Crítico* 10 (19/20): 195–204.

Verstegan, Richard. 1995 [1587]. *Le théâtre des cruautés des hérétiques de notre temps*. Ed. Frank Lestringant. Paris: Editions Chandeigne.

Vidal, Hernán. 1993. "The Concept of Colonial and Postcolonial Discourse: A Perspective from Literary Criticism." *Latin American Research Review* 28(3): 113–19.

Villagrá, Gaspar de. 1992 [1610]. *Historia de la Nueva México*. Spanish/English ed. Ed. Miguel Encinias, Alfred Rodríguez, and Joseph

Sánchez. Trans. Fayette S. Curtis Jr. Albuquerque: University of
New México Press.
————. 1900. *Historia de la Nueva México.* Ed. Luis González Obregón.
México: Imprenta del Museo Nacional.
————. 1989. *Historia de la Nueva México.* Ed. Mercedes Junquera.
Madrid: Historia 16.
Wachtel, Nathan. 1971. *La vision des vaincus: Les indiens du Pérou devant la
conquête espagnole.* Paris: Gallimard.
Wagner, Henry Raup, and Helen Rand Parish. 1967. *The Life and Writings
of Bartolomé de las Casas.* Albuquerque: University of New Mexico Press.
Walker, Cheryl. 1990. "Feminist Literary Criticism and the Author."
Critical Inquiry 16(3): 551–71.
Watts, C. T., ed. 1969. *Joseph Conrad's Letters to Cunninghame Graham.*
Cambridge, England: Cambridge University Press.
Weber, David J. 1992. *The Spanish Frontier in North America.* New Haven:
Yale University Press.
————. 1982. *The Mexican Frontier, 1821–1846.* Albuquerque: University of
New Mexico Press.
————, ed. 1979. *New Spain's Far Northern Frontier: Essays on Spain in
the American West, 1540–1821.* Albuquerque: University of New Mexico
Press.
Weddle, Robert S. 1985. *Spanish Sea: The Gulf of Mexico in the North American Discovery 1500–1685.* College Station: Texas A&M University Press.
Wey-Gómez, Nicolás. 1991. "¿Dónde está Garcilaso?: La oscilación del
sujeto colonial en la formación de un discurso transcultural." *Revista de
Crítica Literaria Latinoamericana* 17(34): 7–31.
White, Hayden. 1987a. "The Question of Narrative in Contemporary
Historical Theory." In *The Content of Form: Narrative Discourse and Historical Representation.* Baltimore: Johns Hopkins University Press. 26–57.
————. 1987b. "The Value of Narrativity in the Representation of
Reality." In *The Content of Form.* Baltimore: Johns Hopkins University
Press. 1–25.
————. 1978. *Tropics of Discourse: Essays in Cultural Criticism.* Baltimore:
Johns Hopkins University Press.
————. 1973. *Metahistory: The Historical Imagination in Nineteenth-Century
Europe.* Baltimore: Johns Hopkins University Press.
Whitehead, Alfred North. 1969 [1929]. *Process and Reality.* New York: The
Free Press.
————. 1958 [1927]. *Symbolism: Its Meaning and Effect.* Cambridge, England: Cambridge University Press.
Wilford, John Noble. 1996. "A French Fort, Long Lost, Is Found in
South Carolina." *New York Times,* 6 June. A1.

Williams, William Carlos. 1956. *In the American Grain*. New York: New Directions.

Winship, George Parker, ed. 1896. *The Coronado Expedition, 1540–1542*. Extract from Fourteenth Annual Report of the U.S. Bureau of American Ethnology. Washington, DC: Government Printing Office.

Wyman, Walker D., and Clifton B. Kroeber, eds. 1957. *The Frontier in Perspective*. Madison: University of Wisconsin Press.

Young, Gloria A., and Michel P. Hoffman. 1993. *The Expedition of Hernando de Soto West of the Mississippi, 1541–1543*. Fayetteville: University of Arkansas Press.

Zaldívar, Vicente. 1599. "Relación de la xornada de las bacas de zívola que hizo el sargento mayor." Archivo General de Indias (Seville, Spain), Patronato, 22, ramo 15, fols. 1029r.–1032v.

Zamora, Margarita. 1988. *Language, Authority, and Indigenous History in the "Comentarios reales de los incas."* Cambridge, England: Cambridge University Press.

Zárate Salmerón, Gerónimo. 1856 [1629]. *Relaciones de todas las cosas que en el Nuevo-México se han visto y sabido, asi por mar como por tierra, desde el año de 1538 hasta el de 1626*. In *Documentos para la historia de México*, 3d series, vol. 1. Mexico City: Imprenta de Vicente García Torres.

Zavala, Silvio. 1977. "Aspectos formales de la controversia entre Sepúlveda y Las Casas en Valladolid, a mediados del siglo XVI." *Cuadernos Americanos* 212(3): 138–51.

———. 1973. "Instituciones indígenas en la Colonia." In *Métodos y resultados de la política indigenista en México*. Mexico City: Instituto Nacional Indigenista.

———. 1971 [1935]. *Las instituciones jurídicas en la conquista de América*. 2nd rev. ed. Mexico: Editorial Porrúa.

———. 1967. "The Doctrine of Just War." In *History*, ed. Lewis Hanke. Boston: Little, Brown. 1: 126–35.

Zea, Leopoldo. 1968. *El positivismo en México: Nacimiento, apogeo y decadencia*. Mexico City: Fondo de Cultura Económica.

Žižek, Slavoj. 1993. "Enjoy Your Nation as Yourself!" In *Tarrying with the Negative: Kant, Hegel and the Critique of Ideology*. Durham, NC: Duke University Press. 200–237.

Index

Garcilaso de la Vega, Inca, 13, 25–26, 199–225. See also *Comentarios reales de los Incas; La Florida del Inca; Limpieza de sangre*

Geertz, Clifford, 51–52

Glantz, Margo, 66, 78

González Arratia, Leticia: on hunters and gatherers, 294–95 n.12

González Echeverría, Roberto, 85–86

Gourgues, Dominique de, 222; *Histoire mémorable de la reprinse de l'isle de la Floride,* 232, 261–63

Guaraní women, abuse of, 73–79

Guerra a sangre y fuego (war of extermination), 109–111, 137, 306–307 n.10

Hakluyt, Richard, 222, 230–32, 270–72, 302 n.15

Hakluyt, Richard (elder), 230–31, 270–71

Hate speech, 6

Hegel, Georg Wilhelm Friedrich, 248, 281

Herrera y Tordecillas, Antonio de, 128, 249, 292 n.3

Historia de la Nueva México (Villagrá), 138–158, and Homer, 138–141; legitimization of massacre, 154; profanation of corpses, 155–158; and Rigoberta Menchú, 138–141; and trial of Acoma, 91, 137, 141, 149–150

Historia de las Indias (Las Casas): compared to *Brevíssima,* 86–87, 255, 298 n.21

Historia de Tlatelolco desde los tiempos más remotos, 1–6, 8–16, 287 n.1

Historia general y natural de las Indias (Oviedo): and atrocity, 170–71, 190–94; a comic portrait in, 194–95; exotic as dominat trope of, 168; functions of *cronista* and *historiador,* 167–68; and incompetence of de Soto, 195–96; and *Limpieza de sangre,* 210–11; moralistic terrorism in, 159–98; and Nuevas Leyes of 1542, 162, 184–190; and understanding of terror, 196–197

Historiography: a priori, 203; and authorial Indian, 216; and circularity, 213; colonial, 84–86, 95, 98, 220; and de Soto, 160, 170; medieval, 216; and moralizing, 205, 214; and the New World, 199–202, 205, 280; as production, 206; Protestant, 229, 247–48; and representation in history 278; sixteenth-century and twentieth-century, 279–280; Western,199, 225

Hodgen, Margaret, 204

Holinshed, Raphael (*Chronicle of England, Scotland and Ireland*), 146–48

Homer, 138–41

Horkheimer, Max and Theodor Adorno (*The Dialectic of Enlightenment*), 139

Iglesia, Cristina, 78

Imaginary places and cartography, 123–24

Indian guides: Jusepe, 130–31; Isopete, 126; El Turco, 126; Indigenous maps, 117–18, 129–30

Informe conjunto (joint report) (Oviedo), 48, 52, 165–66; and Rodrigo Ranjel, 165–68

Inimicus and *hostis:* difference between, 250–52, 260

International Congress of Americanists, 226–27

Menchú, Rigoberta, 138–141, 303 n.4, 304 n.8, 307 n.16
Menéndez de Avilés, Pedro, 222, 231, 253, 261, 263, 272
Mercator, Gerhard, 248–50
Merrim, Stephanie, 205
Miggrode, Jacques, 235, 262–63
Mixton War, 14, 27, 108–109
Monterrey, Count of, 107–108; *Discurso y proposición,* 114–19, 124–25, 143, 148, 302 n.16
Moral economy of violence, 242–54
Murrin, Michael, 305 n.10, 308 n.7

Narváez, Pánfilo, 38, 42, 44, 47–48, 63–64, 67, 72, 92, 94, 165–67, 185, 195–96, 205
Nietzsche, Frederich, 229, 250–51, 304 n.8
Niza, Marcos de, 122–24
Nuevas Leyes of 1542, 6–7, 88, 92–93, 162–63, 184–89, 255

Oñate, Juan: colonizing program of, 26; dossier on New Mexico, 107, 112–21; and rebellion of Acoma, 105–108
Ordenanzas of 1526: and Cabeza de Vaca, 5, 31; and *capitulaciones* (contracts), 38; and contract with de Soto, 186; and evaluation of *calidad* and *habilidad* of Indians, 41; and Las Casas, 70–71; and peaceful conquest, 67, 83; and *Requerimiento,* 40, 42, 46, 186–88; summary of, 39–41
Ordenanzas of 1573: and debates between Las Casas, Oviedo, and Sepúlveda, 88; and dossiers of Juan de Oñate and Pedro Ponce de León, 107–108; language of violence in, 89–92; and Las Casas, 6, 102; and mediation

of the law, 112–13; as model for writing, 92–93, 118; and *Requerimiento,* 89; similarities with Pedro de Castañeda's *relación,* 99–101; and wars of extermination (*guerra a sangre y fuego*), 109–111
Ovando, Juan, 97–98
Oviedo, Gonzalo Fernández de, 7, 47, 87–88, 94–95, 159–98; bio-bibliography of, 293–94 n.11; and biological differences, 168–171; change of heart of, 94–95, 161–62, 185; and *encomienda,* 186; and Garcilaso de la Vega, 214; and Las Casas, 87–88, 161; and rationalization of empire, 95, 186, 197

Peaceful conquest, 4–5, 67–72, 83–85, 281–82
Pittarello, Elide, 146
Pizarro, Francisco, 235
Plural-world dwelling, 283–84
Polo, Marco, 127–28, 131
Porque soy indio, 199, 203
Postcolonialism, 16–20, 290 n.13
Poststructuralist criticism, 200–201
Pratt, Mary Louise, 272
Protestant anti-Spanish pamphleteering, 226–74

Quevedo, Francisco (*España defendida y los tiempos de ahora*), 248–50
Quint, David, 145, 151, 215, 305 n.9
Quintillian, 50–51, 248, 236

Ranjel, Rodrigo, 161, 165–68, 172, 177, 188, 192, 194, 209
Reff, Daniel, 299 n.24
Relación: as legal and historiographic prototype, 86; and the production and evaluation of facts, 120–21

José Rabasa is Professor of Spanish and Portuguese at the University of California, Berkeley. He is the author of *Inventing America: Spanish Historiography and the Formation of Eurocentrism.*

Library of Congress Cataloging-in-Publication Data

Rabasa, José.
Writing violence on the northern frontier : the historiography of
sixteenth-century New Mexico and Florida and the legacy of conquest /
José Rabasa.
p.   cm. — (Latin America otherwise)
Includes bibliographical references (p.   ) and index.
ISBN 0-8223-2535-7 (cloth : alk. paper) — ISBN 0-8223-2567-5 (pbk. : alk. paper)
1. Southwest, New—Discovery and exploration—Spanish—Historiography.
2. New Mexico—Discovery and exploration—Spanish—Historiography.
3. Florida—Discovery and exploration—Spanish—Historiography.   4. New
Mexico—History—To 1848—Historiography.   5. Florida—History—1565–
1763—Historiography.   6. Violence—Southwest, New—History—16th
century—Historiography.   7. Violence—New Mexico—History—16th
century—Historiography.   8. Violence—Florida—History—16th century—
Historiography.   I. Title.   II. Series.
F799 .R23   2000
979'.007'2—dc21   00-029403